# SOCIAL WELFARE ALIVE!

An introduction to issues and policies
in health and welfare

**Stephen Moore**

St ) Ltd

First published in 1993 by:
Stanley Thornes (Publishers) Ltd
Ellenborough House
Wellington Street
CHELTENHAM GL50 1YD
UK

Reprinted 1994

A catalogue record for this book is available from the British Library.
ISBN 0 7487 1402 2

Typeset by GCS, Leighton Buzzard, Bedfordshire
Printed and bound in Great Britain by Scotprint Ltd, Musselburgh

# Acknowledgements

The author and publishers are grateful to the following for permission to reproduce material:

Central Statistical Office for HMSO material and all other government statistics quoted, all of which are Crown copyright; Claire Dyer for the extract from the *Guardian* on p. 255; The Guardian News Service Ltd; Macmillan Publishers Ltd for extracts from the *Health Service Journal*; Newspaper Publishing plc for extracts from the *Independent*; The New Statesman & Society; Northcote House Publishers Ltd; the *Nursing Times*; the *Observer*; Philip Allan Publishers Ltd for extracts from the *Social Studies Review* (now *Sociology Review*); Professor Colin Pritchard for the letter to the *Guardian* on p. 130; Radcliffe Medical Press; RNID; *Today*; Mrs Elaine Wheatley for the letter to the *Cambridge Evening News* on p. 197.

Every effort has been made to identify and contact copyright holders prior to publication and we apologise if anyone has been overlooked.

# Contents

# Preface

Four years ago I moved from teaching sociology in a college of further education to teaching social policy in higher education. My teaching consisted (and still consists) of a wide range of courses: from professional diplomas, short courses, vocational and non-vocational degrees in which students took a module in social policy to specialist social policy degree courses.

What I needed most was an interesting, accessible and up-to-date book which would provide me with a bank of information and activities for those students who had to study health and welfare issues, but who had no desire, or need, to go into great depth. To my great surprise no book was available which even remotely met my needs.

I began to phone my friends in FE and ask them if there was anything they could recommend.

'No,' they replied, 'if only there was something. We need a book like that too, as health and welfare is growing just as rapidly in schools and colleges. Why don't you have a go? After all, you've written a few books.'

Well, I thought, this is going to be a real doddle.

Here we are four years later, and I am certainly an older and possibly a wiser man. The task has been similar to that circus act – you know, the one where the man and his assistant (who I suspect of being both his daughter *and* the lovely Rosetta, tightrope walker 'all the way from Romania') make two hundred plates spin on top of canes. They have to keep sprinting around making sure the two hundred plates are all staying on, and of course there is always one that is about to wobble off.

Well, it is the same with the contents of this book. I race from computer file to computer file, desperately slipping new information into 'Community care' or 'Social security' to keep up to date and spinning away.

No one has yet written a book like this, because no one has yet kept two thousand plates spinning in the circus. Well, right now all my files are spinning merrily away and it is time to publish *Social Welfare Alive!* I hope you find it useful and interesting. If one or two 'plates' fall off while you are teaching, then write to me care of the publishers and for the next edition we will go for a new world record!

## Acknowledgements

I grew up in an extended family in Liverpool, with lots of love and not much money. Those who brought me up worked hard, and trusted in the Welfare State to look after them in their old age. Now they are in their old age, and I

## CHAPTER 1

# The Political and Administrative Context of Social Policy

## Introduction

Health and welfare in Britain are still largely provided by and within a framework devised and controlled by the State. It is the government that pays for social security benefits, the National Health Service and the personal social services. The government also provides the bulk of the funds for the voluntary organisations, and, through the local authorities, it sets down standards of care in the private sector (such as in elderly persons' homes).

When the government chooses new policies it has an impact on all our lives. The government may decide to provide more or fewer health services, higher or lower social security benefits or pensions. It may decide to raise taxes or lower them, and to do so in such a way that poorer or richer people benefit. Indeed it is impossible to separate politics and administration from the actual provision of health and welfare in Britain.

There are different levels or 'tiers' of government, three of which are of interest to us: the **European Community**, the **central government** and **local government**.

### The European Community

This is likely to become of increasing importance. The European Community has general powers which relate to issues such as equality of treatment of men and women and different ethnic groups, health and safety, the provision of employment and health and welfare benefits across national boundaries. The social chapter of the Maastricht agreement intends to extend the powers of the European Community in social affairs across Europe. The British government has so far refused to accept the social chapter, although it is likely that it will do so eventually.

### The central government

This is nationally elected, based in Westminster, and sets the laws of the country. It sets the levels of taxes and determines what is spent on health and welfare.

## Local government

This consists of the local counties or boroughs. They have powers given to them by central government and are responsible for the running of personal social services, amongst other things. The money they have to spend is determined by Westminster and, increasingly, they are told how they must spend this money.

This chapter will deal with the British administration at central and local levels. You will find a discussion on the European Community in chapter 10.

# Central government

## THE BRITISH GOVERNMENT AND ADMINISTRATION

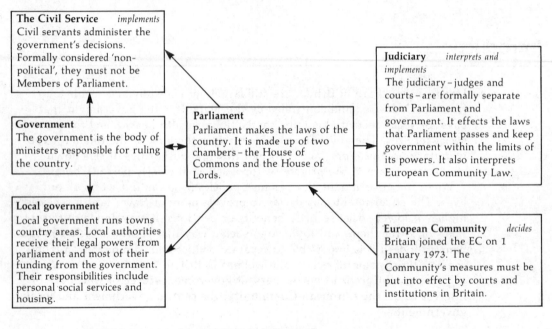

**The Civil Service** *implements*
Civil servants administer the government's decisions. Formally considered 'non-political', they must not be Members of Parliament.

**Government**
The government is the body of ministers responsible for ruling the country.

**Local government**
Local government runs towns country areas. Local authorities receive their legal powers from parliament and most of their funding from the government. Their responsibilities include personal social services and housing.

**Parliament**
Parliament makes the laws of the country. It is made up of two chambers – the House of Commons and the House of Lords.

**Judiciary** *interprets and implements*
The judiciary – judges and courts – are formally separate from Parliament and government. It effects the laws that Parliament passes and keep government within the limits of its powers. It also interprets European Community Law.

**European Community** *decides*
Britain joined the EC on 1 January 1973. The Community's measures must be put into effect by courts and institutions in Britain.

**1** Which two chambers are there in Parliament?
**2** Who makes the laws?
**3** Why is local government important to welfare?
**4** What is the role of the judiciary?
**5** Does any other political organisation have legal power to tell the British Parliament what to do?

## Central government departments affecting health and welfare

### The Department of Health

This department (the DoH) is responsible for all health matters. This involves making policy, and carrying out the administration of the health services and the personal social services. The actual provision of health services goes through regional health authorities and then district health authorities (these are discussed in chapter 5). The personal social services are run through the local authorities.

### The Department of Social Security

This is responsible for all welfare payments, including National Insurance and Income Support. Increasingly, it is being divided into 'agencies' which are relatively autonomous. It has regional and local offices through which policy is carried out. Between 1968 and 1988, the DSS was fused together with the Department of Health to form one large department which was known as the Department of Health and Social Security (the DHSS).

### The Department of Employment

This is responsible for the policies to maintain (as far as possible) full employment, including employment training. For those who are already employed, the department is responsible for good health and safety at work, and for enforcing the law regarding working conditions.

### The Department of the Environment

This has a wide range of functions concerning the environment, including regional and urban planning, and inner city policy. It is also responsible for the control of local government, and for housing matters.

### The Department for Education

This is responsible for primary and secondary education, and for the overview of higher education. Traditionally, education has been financed and controlled through local education authorities (LEAs), but there has been a considerable erosion of the powers and duties of the local authorities regarding education, with the shift of higher and further education to separate funding councils and the 'opting out' of many primary and secondary schools, which receive money directly from central government.

### The Home Office

This is responsible for law and order, covering such areas as the police, the judiciary, probation and prisons. It is also responsible for immigration issues, citizenship and race relations legislation. The Home Office also has responsibilities for some inner city programmes and for government co-ordination with the voluntary social services and private agencies.

## BRITISH GOVERNMENT DEPARTMENTS

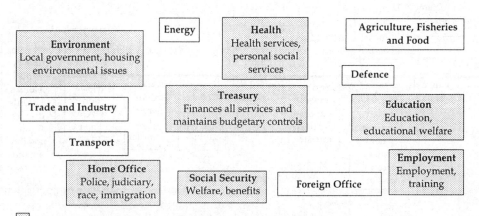

Departments most closely connected with areas of health and welfare

1 Which department is responsible for social work? Does it do this through any other agency or tier of government?
2 Which department is responsible for local government?
3 Which department gives out welfare benefits?
4 Which department determines the amount of money to be spent on health and welfare?
5 When the government introduced its National Health Service and Community Care Act in 1990 (see chapter 7), the aim was to provide a package of services for dependent people such as the infirm elderly, people with disabilities, people suffering from mental illness and those with learning disabilities. Which departments do you think were most closely involved?

### The Cabinet

The Cabinet consists of the ministers responsible for the departments shown in the diagram on page 3, plus a number of other senior political figures (approximately ten more). All these members of the Cabinet have a say in the decisions of the government in areas of health and welfare. Policies are not just the decisions of the ministers responsible for individual departments.

### The Treasury

In many ways this is the most important department of government, for here the amount of money that can be spent on health and welfare is decided. The Treasury is the department responsible for looking after the finances of the State.

The person most closely involved in controlling public spending on the health and welfare services is the Chief Secretary to the Treasury, who is responsible only to the Chancellor of the Exchequer.

Each year ministers meet the Chancellor and the Chief Secretary to make their bids for spending, and after considerable discussion (in what is known as the Public Expenditure Survey Committee) the government expenditure plans are announced. These give the budget within which each department must then carry out its programmes.

## THE LEGISLATIVE PROCESS

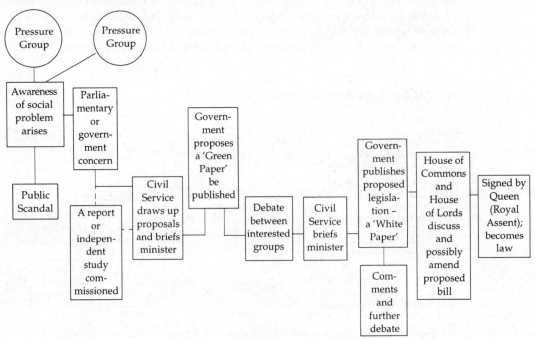

The diagram on page 4 gives all the stages that occur for an issue to develop into a government concern and finally to emerge as law. Choose one recent law and illustrate as many stages as you can of the process. An example recently used by my students was that of the Children Act 1989.

Your sources of information could include the following:

- your local authority department responsible for social services (in Essex, County Hall has an excellent information service/library where my students found the information);
- magazines such as **Community Care** and **Social Work Today**;
- your local library;
- your college library.

# Financing the social and health services

Approximately 50 per cent of all government expenditure is on health, social security and the personal social services. Together these form the single biggest item of expenditure for the government.

## GOVERNMENT EXPENDITURE

### General government expenditure[1]: by function

| United Kingdom | | | £ billion |
|---|---|---|---|
| | 1981 | 1986 | 1990 | 1991 |
| **Function** | | | | |
| Defence | 12.6 | 19.1 | 22.9 | 27.3 |
| Public order and safety | 4.3 | 6.8 | 10.9 | 12.8 |
| Education | 14.3 | 19.3 | 26.7 | 29.5 |
| Health | 13.4 | 19.2 | 27.7 | 30.9 |
| Social security | 31.1 | 49.9 | 62.9 | 73.9 |
| Housing and community amenities | 7.1 | 8.1 | 7.8 | 9.1 |
| Recreational and cultural affairs | 1.6 | 2.4 | 3.7 | 3.9 |
| Fuel and energy | 0.3 | -1.2 | -3.9 | -5.0 |
| Agriculture, forestry and fishing | 1.7 | 2.1 | 2.6 | 2.4 |
| Mining, mineral resources, manufacturing and construction | 3.6 | 1.9 | 1.2 | 1.7 |
| Transport and communication | 4.2 | 3.7 | 9.5 | 6.7 |
| General public services | 4.5 | 6.3 | 10.7 | 9.2 |
| Other economic affairs and services | 2.9 | 4.1 | 6.9 | 5.5 |
| Other expenditure | 15.4 | 20.7 | 25.2 | 19.7 |
| Total expenditure | 117.1 | 162.3 | 214.8 | 227.5 |

1 Includes privatisation proceeds.

**Source:** *Social Trends* (HMSO, 1993)

1 Which was the single biggest item of government expenditure between 1981 and 1991?

2 What was the second biggest in 1990 and 1991?

3 What is the total amount spent on health and welfare (excluding education) as a proportion of total government expenditure?

4 When people argue that health and welfare provision has little to do with politics and government – what reply do these figures suggest?

5 Can you suggest any reason why there have been such large increases in health and social security spending?

6 Overall welfare spending has risen by two-thirds since 1979. It now absorbs 12.3 per cent of total economic activity in the UK, and will rise by 3.3 per cent – more than the growth in the economy. Clearly this is unsustainable. What is your suggestion? Cut welfare? Cut other services? Which ones?

# Political parties

The political parties in Britain have noticeably different views on health and welfare. The various changes in policy made by them when they are in government very much reflect these different ideas on the best way to provide (or not!) programmes of health and welfare.

There are three major parties in British politics – the Conservative Party, the Labour Party and the Liberal Democrat Party.

## The Conservative Party

The Conservative Party is generally agreed to stand for free enterprise, that is the government should interfere as little as possible in the running of business and commerce. This idea of interfering as little as possible is also applied to the areas of health and welfare. The Conservative Party does support the Welfare State, but prefers the idea that people should look after themselves where possible, only falling back on the State when they, or their family, can no longer cope.

## The Labour Party

The Labour Party is much more closely associated with concern over health and welfare in the eyes of the public. It accepts the existence of free enterprise, although it argues for considerably more government intervention in the economic affairs of the nation than the Conservative Party. The Labour Party also argues for the State to use its power to bring about greater levels of equality, by redistributing wealth and income through taxation of the rich.

Regarding health and welfare, the Labour Party strongly supports the activities of the State in providing free health care, and wide-ranging social security payments.

## The Liberal Democrats

The Liberal Democrats are the smallest of the three major parties. The party was formed in 1991, when the Liberal Party and the Social Democrats merged to form a single party. The Liberal Party was last in government in 1915.

The Liberal Democrats also accept the importance of the State in controlling free enterprise, although they do not wish to have as great a level of interference as Labour does. They do not wish to move towards the same degree of equality for which Labour strives. They strongly support the existence of the NHS (the National Health Service), but support a narrower range of social security payments than Labour.

# Local government

An understanding of local government is important in the study of welfare provision. Social Services departments (which employ social workers) are run by local authorities; local authorities administer Housing Benefit; and they manage and provide housing.

The system in England and Wales is undergoing a review of how it is organised, but in 1993, it is divided into two levels: that of **county** and that of **district**. In general, districts are smaller areas with fewer people than the counties; they also have fewer powers.

## The structure of local government in England and Wales, 1993

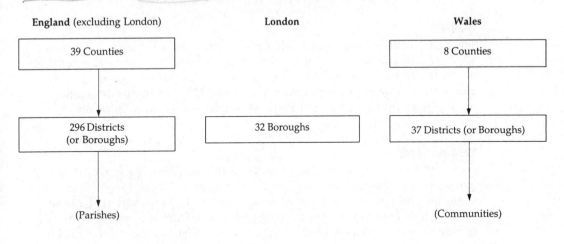

| England (excluding London) | London | Wales |
| --- | --- | --- |
| 39 Counties | | 8 Counties |
| 296 Districts (or Boroughs) | 32 Boroughs | 37 Districts (or Boroughs) |
| (Parishes) | | (Communities) |

## THE FUNCTIONS OF COUNTY AND DISTRICT COUNCILS

The diagram below shows the activities of the two levels or 'tiers' of local government.

| County councils | District councils | Metropolitan district councils |
| --- | --- | --- |
| Education[1] | Housing | District responsibilities, plus: |
| Personal social services | Environmental health | Education[1] |
| Libraries | Local planning | Libraries |
| Planning | Local parks | Personal social services |
| Highways, and traffic co-ordination | Refuse | |
| Police | | |
| Fire | | |

**Note:** [1]Government policies to give schools control over their own budgets (LMS) and the right to opt out of grant-maintained status means that local authorities' role in education is diminishing.

**1** Arrange a visit to your two tiers of local authorities. Before going, organise a list of questions to find out what services they are responsible for – focusing in particular on responsibilities for welfare services. The government is likely to bring in significant changes for local government in the future. Ask what these are and find out if the local authorities agree with them or not.

    If you cannot visit your district and/or county councils, then send off for an information pack to find the answers to your questions. Virtually all councils produce information packs.

**2** Have local authorities any responsibility for health?

**3** Find out how the finances of the local authorities are organised and how much they spend on the various services.

**4** Depending on where you live, you may have access to a number of different councils (or, of course, you could write to as many councils as you wish). Find out the different priorities in terms of spending and service provision – usually they vary considerably across councils. In my college, we invite local councillors from different political parties to address us on what they believe the local authorities should do – the resulting debates are always interesting.

**5** Draw a plan of the decision-making and executive structure of your local council. Do a particularly detailed section for the social services.

# Changes in local government

Local government has undergone massive changes in the last 25 years, and looks set for more changes again in the near future. These are likely to involve the counties losing powers to the districts.

Historically, local government was truly local with small towns and boroughs having a wide range of powers available to them.

### 1974-80

The main thrust of the changes that took place from 1974 until the early 1980s was of a gradual loss of powers by the lowest levels of local authorities (districts and parishes) and a shift in that power partially towards counties and partially towards central government. In 1972, five **county boroughs** were created in the larger conurbations to take power away from the districts.

### 1980 onwards

From the mid-1980s there was a change in this pattern. The five county boroughs mentioned above and the Greater London Council were all abolished and power was given back to the districts. However, at the same time, central government began *taking powers away* from all types of local government. An example of this is the way in which schools and colleges have been encouraged to opt out of local authority control and to receive funding directly from the Department for Education.

### The significance of these changes for health and welfare

It is interesting to note that it was largely the more enlightened local authorities which had created education, welfare and health services in the nineteenth and in the first part of the twentieth century. Parliament merely gave **permissive powers** to local authorities to introduce reforms. Today, local authorities have increasingly become the arm of the State, merely carrying out central government policies.

In your local library there is sure to be a book on the history of your area, and there is probably one on the history of the council (often the council itself will produce this). Find out the changes that have taken place over the last 100 years, and the changes in the services that the council has provided. (For example, did you know that until the 1940s most local authorities ran their own hospitals?)

# Central government control over local government

In the 1980s a number of 'left-wing' councils attempted to defy the central government by introducing local welfare initiatives that were contrary to government policy. These centred on issues of housing, anti-racism initiatives, employment patterns and improving and extending personal social services.

These policies led to a clash with central government, which eventually resulted in central government agents taking control of the local authority finances, personal surcharges (effectively fines) being imposed on local councillors and, finally, legislation.

The poor relationship between the central government and left-wing local authorities illustrates the tensions that exist between the different levels of democracy in Britain.

There are three main ways in which local government can be made to comply with the wishes of central government: **advice, finance** and **law.**

### Advice

Central government departments will send 'circulars' which advise the local authorities of what they should do. These do not carry the force of law, and so local authorities will interpret them according to the views of their councillors.

### Finance

This is the most commonly used power by central government. The government can send in auditors to see that the money is being spent according to the government's wishes, or they can actually control the amount of money borrowed by a local authority (as local authorities often need to borrow to finance particular projects, this is a powerful weapon).

The greatest power of all is the fact that about 60 per cent of local authority spending comes directly from the government in the form of a 'bloc grant', which is related to the amount of money that central government thinks a particular local authority needs (called the **standard spending assessment**). Local authorities are therefore very rightly controlled financially.

Local authorities also raise money through the council tax, which every household pays. Central government has the power to 'cap' this.

## A COUNTY COUNCIL BUDGET

**REVENUE EXPENDITURE £1,101 MILLION**

| Where it came from | £m |
|---|---|
| Collection Funds and Balances | 856 |
| Government Grants | 131 |
| Fees and Charges | 114 |
| TOTAL | 1,101 |

**What it provided**

Police £132m

Education £643m

Social Services £144m

Highways £ 91m

| Other services | £m |
|---|---|
| Fire and Public Protection | 38 |
| Library, Museum & Records | 19 |
| Environment | 18 |
| Other | 16 |

Total £1,101m

**CAPITAL EXPENDITURE £73 MILLION**

| How it was spent | £m |
|---|---|
| Building Works | 32 |
| Road Construction | 21 |
| Plant and Vehicles | 15 |
| Land Purchase | 5 |
| TOTAL | 73 |

**NET COST OF SERVICES PER HEAD OF POPULATION**

| | £ |
|---|---|
| Education | 308.09 |
| Social Services | 68.31 |
| Police | 72.55 |
| Highways | 32.68 |
| Fire & Rescue | 17.09 |
| Other Services | 30.68 |
| TOTAL | 529.40 |

**Source**: Essex County Council, 1992

The diagram on page 9 shows the 1991/92 budget of Essex County Council.

1 Where does a county council get its funds from?
2 In terms of expenditure, how high was social services in relation to other areas of provision in Essex in 1991/92?
3 How much did Essex spend per head of the population on social services?
4 Obtain figures for your own council. How does the spending compare? If it is very different, can you give some explanations? (Essex is a relatively large county in the south-east of England, with quite small towns and only a limited number of decaying urban areas, although it does have significant 'New Town' development.)

### Law

Central government can introduce laws which simply require a local authority to act in a particular way. An example of this was the introduction and subsequent withdrawal of the community charge or 'poll tax' in England and Wales in the early 1990s. Although many of the local authorities were unhappy about the tax, they were forced by law to collect it and administer it on behalf of the central government.

## The powers of local authorities

The table on page 7 shows the different functions of the local authorities. You can see they include a wide range of duties relevant to the area of health and welfare. The most obvious ones are the personal social services, housing and the police. However, certain local authorities may provide other services as well, for example leisure facilities, community centres, housing advice centres and transport services. Whether they provide these other services or not depends largely on the political views of the council and the financial ability to provide the services.

Local authorities therefore have two types of powers to get things done – **duty** and **permissive power.**

### Duty

This is a duty imposed on local authorities by law requiring them to provide particular services. For example, community care legislation in 1990 imposed the duty on local authorities to draw up plans and provide care in the community.

### Permissive power

The second sort of power is permissive, and this allows local authorities to initiate activities within certain areas. It is often the activities carried out under these powers that distinguish one authority from another.

One of the great debates in the 1980s concerned the extent to which local authorities should be involved in anti-racist activities, or anti-discriminatory activities in general (promoting equality of opportunity of women, the disabled and homosexuals). Some authorities used permissive powers to extend their activities into these areas.

# The policy-making process

Health and welfare programmes are determined by the government. However, in making their decisions and determining what policies to follow and how to spend their money, a process of policy making and implementation is followed. The most important element influencing the decisions of government is the activity of **pressure groups.**

## Pressure groups

The diagram on page 4 shows the importance of pressure groups in the political process in Britain. Pressure groups play the crucial role of bringing issues to the attention of the decision makers in society. The problems raised are then addressed throughout the normal political process, as illustrated in the diagram. But even when this process is in full flow, pressure groups maintain interest and try to ensure that their viewpoint becomes law.

### Types of pressure groups
There are two types of pressure groups:
- those which *defend* their own interests – known as **protective, defensive** or **self-regarding pressure groups**; and
- those which *promote* new initiatives which they claim will improve society, or at least will improve the conditions of a particularly vulnerable group – **promotional** or **pressure groups.**

In the field of health and welfare, the British Medical Association (BMA) is a good example of the first category, and the Child Poverty Action Group (CPAG) is an example of the second category.

**1** Find out what type of pressure groups the following organisations are: British Association of Social Workers; Howard League for Penal Reform; SHELTER; Royal College of Nursing; Community Health Councils; Royal College of Physicians; Mencap; Help the Aged.

**2** Find three pressure groups operating in the area of health and welfare. Write a brief outline of their aims and activities.

Pressure groups are not political parties, and usually represent only one particular group or cause. They try to persuade whoever is in power to introduce or amend legislation, and rarely seek power themselves.

### How do pressure groups influence decision makers?
There are a number of ways in which pressure groups try to influence those in power:
- **Lobbying in parliament**   This involves sending representatives to discuss issues with MPs to try to persuade them of the truth of their particular argument. There are professional lobbying organisations which, for a fee, represent particular companies and interests.

## LOBBYING REGISTER PLAN

Two Tory MPs have failed to stop a Commons committee from recommending yesterday the creation of a compulsory register of professional lobbyists working in Parliament.

The committee's report reveals that Peter Griffiths, MP for Portsmouth South and Sir Michael McNair Wilson, MP for Newbury, both members of the Select Committee on Members' Interests mounted a bitter rearguard action to amend the final report clause by clause, after attempts to block it failed....

The report, as predicted in the Guardian, proposes that Parliamentary lobbying companies should have to name clients and MPs acting on their behalf....

The proposed code of practice would make it an offence to give misleading information, lobby for conflicting interests, attempt to improperly influence government, legislators or lobby journalists. It would outlaw bribes to MPs or civil servants, and would also ban so-called success fees, when lobbyists receive bonus payments if they succeed in changing the law so that a client benefits.

*Third report of the Select Committee on Members' Interests, Parliamentary Lobbying, HMSO £11.85.*

**Source**: Adapted from the *Guardian*, 1 October 1991

**1** What would the new register for MPs do?
**2** Why do you think this is necessary?
**3** What activities are banned?
**4** Health and welfare issues concern the poor and the least powerful. Which groups in society do you think are the most likely to be able to lobby MPs?

- **Publicity**   If you examine a quality newspaper today, you are certain to find the influence of pressure groups. Many stories which appear in the newspapers and on the television reflect the views of pressure groups which hope to galvanise the public and the decision makers into awareness of a particular problem.

- **Protest**   Where groups have little power and influence they may turn to the last resort, which is public protest. Public marches and demonstrations attempt to attract the attention of the media. We have seen this in the area of health, when members of the health union, COHSE, which represents the lowest paid workers in the health service, as well as many nurses, has had to turn to public demonstrations outside hospitals. Their aim has been to draw attention to their opposition to alleged cuts in the health service budget over the last 15 years.

## PRESSURE GROUPS

A

**Britain vetoes drug ad curbs**
Attempts by European Community countries to impose stricter rules on advertising medicines after 1992 were fended off by the British government yesterday.

A meeting in Brussels of EC ministers agreed to a compromise which bans 'abusive, frightening, or misleading' advertisements for over-the-counter drugs.

This fell short of restrictions sought by France and other countries with much tighter regulations on the sale and marketing of medicines, which would have prohibited 'before and after' ads for drugs. These make graphic claims on the healing powers of medicines, and are more common in Britain than other EC countries.

The rules also ban advertising prescription medicines to the general public, and set minimum requirements on the amount of information to be contained in advertisements of prescription drugs to medical professionals.

**Source**: The *Guardian*, 23 July 1991

B

On the same day as the Government was condemned by the Royal College of Physicians for failing to prevent 'an avoidable annual holocaust' of 100 000 premature smoking deaths, the junior Minister of Health, Mr John Patten, met a delegation from the Freedom Organisation for the Right to Enjoy Smoking Tobacco (financed by the tobacco industry to the tune of £100 000 a year). This casts a revealing light on the Government's real attitude towards smoking and health.

Its complicity with the tobacco industry in perpetuating an epidemic that kills prematurely (many) young male smokers is rarely seen in its stark, true colours.

Another revealing chink of light came recently when the Health Education Council, which is funded by the Government to promote better health care, advertised for a new head of public affairs.

It soon became evident that one of the applicants, Mr Michael Daube, a senior lecturer in health education at Edinburgh University, was not only the best qualified but had majority support. At this point, however, the chairman said that Mr Daube was unacceptable to Ministers.

Why was Mike Daube blacked? Precise answers to such questions are difficult to establish, but it is easier to understand why Ministers were less than keen on Mr Daube. As a former very energetic director of the anti-smoking campaign, Action on Smoking and Health, he was no friend of the cigarette manufacturers. And there is considerable evidence to suggest that the tobacco industry lobbied hard within the department in a determined effort to block the appointment.

The Tobacco Advisory Council, the industry's lobbying arm, is a lavishly financed body whose writ runs much further than is generally realised. Two years ago it persuaded Mrs Thatcher to shift the then junior Minister of Health, Sir George Young, whose tough, anti-smoking campaigning policies had incurred its bitter hostility.

Sir George's removal to the Department of the Environment was secured through industry pressure exercised via the Tory Whip's office. Afterwards a senior civil servant in the Department of Health commented: 'I never knew the tobacco industry was so powerful.'

Source: *The Observer*, 4 December 1983

C

The Government's decision to scrap the Health Education Council, announced yesterday, will mean the end of the quango's political campaigns against tobacco and alcohol, senior council officials said yesterday.

Colleagues of the council's influential director, Dr David Player, fear there is unlikely to be a place for him in the new special health authority which will come under the direct control of the Social Services Secretary, Mr Norman Fowler.

Dr Player has been an effective critic of the Government's failure to curb alcoholism and its policy on the tobacco industry's sponsorship of sport.

It was under his direction that the council persuaded the BBC to clamp down on cigarette advertisements in televised snooker competitions, motor racing, and tennis...

He arrived four years ago from the Glasgow-based Scottish Health Education Group with a reputation as a 'tough cookie'. Ever since, he has been a thorn in the side of the tobacco and alcohol industries.

In September an HEC report showed that the BBC was broadcasting the equivalent of more than 500 cigarette advertisements a year.

Last month, Dr Player embarrassed ministers by publicly blaming pressure from the drink industry for the refusal of the DHSS to fund alcohol education programmes.

'The alcohol industry is even more powerful in its effect on government decisions than the tobacco industry', he said on the BBC 2 television programme, Brass Tacks.

Source: *The Guardian*, 22 November 1986

1 In extract B, why was the then junior minister moved?

2 In extract C, why was Dr Player unlikely to be appointed to head the Health Education Authority? What does this tell us about the influence of the tobacco and alcohol industries in government?

3 Extract A concerns pharmaceuticals. Why do you think the government could find these objectionable? (Incidentally, the British government has taken a similar position on tighter controls on cigarette sales in the EC.) Could you suggest reasons why they are so powerful?

4 Look through the 'quality' papers for this week, and pick out any articles or new items which you think reflect the power of pressure groups. Summarise what they are arguing for. What types of activities have they engaged in to attract attention? What explanations can you give for the different approaches to gain influence?

# Ideologies and social policy

If you present a group of people with a complex problem, of any kind, and ask them to solve it, almost always they will set about solving it in a variety of different ways. There is rarely any single 'correct' way of solving a problem. It is exactly the same when it comes to the issues concerning welfare and health provision; there is no agreement on one 'right' way of ensuring that people receive the best health and welfare services.

Different solutions to the social problems tackled by the health and welfare services have been suggested by the competing political parties, by various academics and by a range of practitioners and professionals. The result is that a series of different 'packages of ideas' have been put forward, which claim to *interpret the problems* and *provide answers* to them. These packages of ideas are known as **ideologies**.

Over time a number of ideological approaches to social policy have emerged. These include: the **New Right** approach, the **social democratic** approach, the **radical socialist** approach, the **feminist** approach and the **anti-racist** approach.

Ideologies can be described as 'packages of ideas'. What two elements do they all have?

Each of the approaches listed above claims that its analysis of society is more accurate than that of the others, and, furthermore, that putting into action the policies that it recommends will reduce or possibly eliminate social problems.

Before we move on to examine these approaches, we ought to be aware that there are others and, even more confusingly, different names for the same approaches! However, if you understand the five categories included here, you will be able to make sense of all the others you may encounter in your further reading.

## The New Right approach

This approach to social problems is also known as **market liberal, neo-conservative** or **anti-collectivist**.

The New Right approach believes that it is misguided for the government to step in to regulate peoples' lives. This causes more harm than good in the long run. Companies which provide high quality services at reasonable prices will do well, and those that fail are either inefficient or provide poor quality services. When governments try to provide services or to regulate them too closely, the result is almost always waste and inefficiency.

This approach says that competition between individuals and companies leads to higher standards of living overall, and the people who are successful should be allowed to spend their money as they wish without high levels of taxation; instead they should be left to choose which charities (if any) they wish to support.

People who are poor can be divided into two groups: those who are in a situation through no fault of their own (the deserving poor), such as those with disabilities; and those who have not really tried (the undeserving poor), such as those who opt out from finding work. The government should provide help only to the deserving poor.

Generally, therefore, this approach argues for the dismantling of the

Welfare State and the move towards individuals purchasing their own health and pension arrangements, which are subsidised by low taxation.

## The social democratic approach

Social democrats support the Welfare State wholeheartedly. They argue for greater State activity to iron out the extremes of poverty and affluence. Individuals should not be judged according to concepts such as deserving and undeserving, but according to their needs. Social democrats claim that the economic system of capitalism, while bringing many benefits, also harms large numbers of the more vulnerable of the population and it is the duty of the more affluent, through taxation, to support the less well off.

## The radical socialist approach

This approach is also known as **Marxist**, **Neo-Marxist** or **Post-Marxist**.

Radical socialists are very critical of the capitalist economic system in which a small proportion of the population is very rich. They argue that the political and economic system of capitalist societies like the UK are biased in favour of the rich, and only by very radical change can any fairness be introduced. They favour much greater state control of the economy, and the distribution of wealth from the rich to the majority of the population.

## Feminist approaches

These are very critical of the current society and the Welfare State. They point out that the majority of the poor are women, and also argue that the very structure of UK society is biased against women. This situation of **patriarchy** ensures that women are in a subservient position compared to men, and that their work in the home as housewives, in factories and offices as part-time employees, and in hospitals and caring situations as poorly paid employees effectively subsidises men.

## Anti-racist approaches

These place the situation of ethnic minorities in the focus of their analysis and claim that Blacks and Asians are those most likely to suffer from poor standards of living and to be engaged in the lowest paid jobs or to be unemployed.

They argue that there ought to be a clear analysis of the institutional racism which is built into British society, and that positive steps ought to be taken to break down the barriers which block off the benefits of society for these groups.

Like feminists, anti-racists believe that the role of the State is crucial in forcing through better, fairer conditions for ethnic minorities.

### TRAVELLERS AND THE WELFARE STATE

**Sickening service for scroungers**
I was dismayed to see the Department of Social Security squads setting up their trestle tables to pay benefit to the hordes of gipsies, hippies, addicts and drop-outs . . .

For all their sneering rejection of the state, these vagabonds have no hesitation in accepting hand-outs of £43.45 per week social security benefit and they expect medical treatment when they are ill.

**Approaches to social policy**

| Issues | Perspectives | | | | |
|---|---|---|---|---|---|
| | New Right | Social Democratic | Radical Socialist | Feminist | Anti-Racist |
| ECONOMICS | A free market unfettered by government interference. People should have very low taxes, and decide what to do with their money. | A free market, but with government control to even out the extremes of wealth and poverty. Relatively high levels of taxation. | State to own all business and commerce. Salaries and conditions related to government decisions. | A radical approach to what is considered work, therefore housework is of equal status to employment. Work should be made more flexible to respond to demands on women (such as family). | Employment practices should be radically examined. Positive action programme should be introduced to give Blacks and Asians preference in employment to compensate for past discrimination. |
| INEQUALITY between people | Good, necessary and a spur to make people work harder. People should be rewarded for their hard work and should not pay high rates of tax. | Acceptable and inevitable, but *extremes* cannot be allowed. So a Welfare State would provide for the less well-off and this will be paid for by heavy taxes on the rich. | Inequality is wrong and needs to be eliminated by State action. There should be, as far as possible, a classless society. No wealth and no poverty. | Inequality is wrong, women have always been discriminated against, and economic/social policies need to be introduced specifically to benefit women. | Inequality is wrong, Blacks and Asians have always been discriminated against and economic/social policies need to be introduced specifically to benefit ethnic groups. |
| WELFARE STATE | Bad, creates a **dependency culture**, where people rely on the government for help, instead of self-help or family. Welfare is enormously expensive, wasteful bureaucracy. | Good. Welfare State helps pull people together by providing sense of shared citizenship. Compensates those who 'lose out' in a market economy. | Majority and minority views which differ. *Majority* – Welfare State is good and should be improved. The result of working class pressure. *Minority* – bad, introduced to stop the people demanding a radical overhaul of the capitalist system. | Concept is good, but is based on exploitation of women, both as low paid carers/professionals and as unpaid carers in the home. Needs to be restructured taking into account the specific needs of women. | Concept good, but institutional racism exists. Needs to be more aware of, and responsive to, needs of Blacks and Asians. |
| HEALTH CARE | Should be private, insurance-based for the majority of people. For those with limited incomes there would be assistance with fees or a residual State health care sector. | National Health Service free and fully funded by the government. | National Health Service, but also a belief that much illness is a result of capitalism and therefore eliminating capitalism would reduce ill health. | Provided (cheaply) by women, both formally and informally. Women suffer worse health than men but some areas of women's lives have been 'medicalised', e.g. drugs for depression, childbirth. | Greater awareness of ethnic groups' needs by the NHS. Large numbers of poor paid Black workers in the NHS labour force. |

**Approaches to social policy** *continued*

| Issues | New Right | Social Democratic | Perspectives | | |
| --- | --- | --- | --- | --- | --- |
| | | | Radical Socialist | Feminist | Anti-Racist |
| SOCIAL SECURITY | Bad, undermining individual effort, creates dependency on the State. Has a distorting effect on wages, by forcing employers to pay higher rates – can lead to higher unemployment. If it has to be paid, then strict **means-testing** and targeting. | Important for social stability. Payments should be at a high level and be as widespread as possible. Certain benefits ought to be universal. | Payments are inadequate and, in the short-term, need increasing. In the long term, social security prevents radical social change by 'muting' opposition to capitalism. | Concern over a number of benefits and how they affect the lives of women, e.g. Income Support is inadequate for lone-parent families of which 9 out of 10 are headed by women. Also, pensions system discriminates against women. | Accusations made of racism in social security offices, e.g. Asians asked to show passports, etc. |
| PERSONAL SOCIAL SERVICES | In majority of cases self-help/family help is preferable. Should be left to agencies or, as in the provision of elderly persons' homes, to the private sector. | Predominantly by the State, but also a mixture of charity and voluntary encouraged. The private sector should be discouraged. | Many problems caused by capitalism – should this be replaced, then many problems would disappear. However, the only agency that should be allowed to provide personal social services is the State. | They rely totally on women as unpaid carers. Ninety per cent of people being cared for are outside the State sector, and 70% of these people are cared for by women. Greater State intervention is needed. | Services do not respond to specific needs of Blacks and Asians, where they differ from Whites, e.g. in elderly persons' homes. Personal social services need to recognise Britain as a multi-racial society. |
| POVERTY | Inevitable in any society – but the free market can generate enough wealth to minimise this. The Welfare State only increases poverty. Rejects idea of relative poverty. | A consequence of capitalism that can be eliminated through effective tax and social security systems. | Caused by capitalism. The only real way of combating it is through a radical, socialist, alternative structure. | Majority of people in poverty are women. Economic and welfare systems conspire to keep them there. Need to recognise this and alter the system to give women the chance to escape from poverty. | On every indicator of deprivation, Blacks and Asians score highly. This is the outcome of a racist society. Need to tackle racism through positive action policies. |
| LAW AND ORDER | Heavier sentences, larger police force and the development of protective schemes such as Neighbourhood Watch. Custodial (prison) sentences. | Good policing, but also an awareness of social causes of crime (deprivation, unemployment). Alternatives to prison. | Crime an outcome of greed and inequality of capitalism. Law enforced against ordinary people, not the rich. | Women are treated differently by police and the judiciary. Often they are likely to be treated as mentally disturbed as their behaviour is at odds with the female stereotype. | Racism by police and the judiciary lead to the harassment and imprisoning of young Blacks. At the same time, high levels of deprivation force Blacks towards crime. |

It's galling to witness such people, who have declared war on civilised society and have no respect for the property of others, taking advantage of the fruits of the labours of others, openly abusing common decency.

It's doubtful whether they will ever put anything back into the system they are milking. . . .

Source: Adapted from the *Southend Standard Recorder*, 6 August 1992

1 What viewpoint regarding the Welfare State does this letter reflect?
2 Should a Welfare State distinguish between those who are regarded as deserving and undeserving, or should it provide people solely on the basis of need?
3 If you think that the answer is 'only the deserving', then which groups would you stop from getting benefit?

## APPROACHES TO SOCIAL POLICY

Study the table, Approaches to social policy, on pages 16–17.

1 Which approach wants the least government interference in economics?
2 Which approaches say that we need positive action programmes?
3 What is meant by the term 'inequality'?
4 What do anti-racists say about inequality?
5 Do all radical socialists believe in the Welfare State? Explain your answer.
6 What do we mean by 'dependency culture'?
7 According to radical socialists, what causes bad health? Explain this as fully as you can.
8 According to feminists, who provides the bulk of health care? What do feminists mean by 'medicalised'? Give examples.
9 Which approach(es) fully support the NHS?
10 Why does the New Right criticise social security?
11 What are the advantages of the social security system, according to radical socialists, for today's capitalist society?
12 Why do the feminist and anti-racist approaches criticise the personal social services?
13 Which group comprise the majority of people in poverty?
14 How can poverty be eliminated, according to the social democratic approach?
15 Compare the views on law and order provided by the New Right, social democratic and anti-racist approaches. Are there any similarities?
16 Take each of the headings Economics/Inequality/Welfare State, etc., and, having read all the arguments of the various approaches, put in your own views. Which approach(es) do you find yourself most in favour of? Find another person in the class/group with a different view – see if you can change their mind.

### THE ROLE OF LOCAL GOVERNMENT IN WELFARE PROVISION

# Assignment

You are employed by a local authority Social Services department as an administrator. A group of dignitaries are visiting from a European country. You are asked by the Director of Social Services to explain how the department fits into the political and administrative structure of British government.

You are asked to develop a brief but accurate paper illustrating the system. Since the visitors' English is not particularly strong, you should, wherever possible, use clear diagrams, cartoons and illustrations.

# CHAPTER 2

# Social Security

## Introduction

This chapter deals with the face of the Welfare State that millions of people are familiar with, and which is generally seen as the main component of welfare in Britain. It provides benefits for an enormous section of the population who would be unable to cope financially without them.

The chapter begins with a look at the development of social security, and provides a detailed examination of the changes which were introduced from 1988 onwards and which form the basis of the current system for eligibility and receipt of State benefits.

We then move on to look at one of the key debates relating to social security, that of universal provision of benefits compared to targeted or means-tested benefits. One group of writers argues that welfare benefits should be much more widely provided, with no need for people to prove that they go beyond a certain threshold of need in order to be eligible for benefits. On the other side are those who believe that there should be controls on the level of income people already have before they can claim benefits from the State.

We then begin a long and detailed examination of the benefits available, and the problems or advantages of them. This includes issues such as the poverty trap, where, for example, those obtaining work can actually be worse off than they would be if they were unemployed and are thus discouraged from entering employment; and the role of social workers in regard to benefits such as the Social Fund, where there is a restricted amount of money available and where social workers have been asked to discriminate between those truly in need and those not so desperate.

## The introduction of social security

The system of social security was first introduced in 1946 as part of the Beveridge reforms which created the Welfare State. The Beveridge Report (1942) had argued that the aims of the Welfare State should be to eradicate the 'five giants' of **disease, ignorance, squalor, idleness** and **want.** Each of these giants was to be tackled through government action to ensure their elimination.

- **Disease** was to be tackled by the NHS.
- **Ignorance** was to be tackled by the Butler Education Act 1944 which created an educational system guaranteeing secondary education for all.

- **Squalor** referred to poor housing and was to be tackled by a massive expansion of local authority building programmes.
- **Idleness** meant unemployment, and was to be tackled by the government committing itself to managing the economy in such a way that there would be jobs for all.
- **Want** (or **poverty**) was to be tackled by the system of social security payments.

Throughout British history, attempts had been made to eradicate poverty – always without success. However, Beveridge believed that he had located the causes of poverty in the issues of unemployment, old age and ill health. If provision could be made to ensure that people in these situations had adequate help, then poverty would be eliminated once and for all.

### Unemployment

Unemployment caused poverty because if there was no wage coming in, not only the unemployed person, but the entire family, was affected. Beveridge therefore decided that some form of unemployment benefit had to be paid, which would allow a man to support his family and keep them above subsistence level. (Please note, it was Beveridge's assumption, not mine, that the *man* was the supporter of the family!)

### Old age

Old age caused poverty because people were unable to save enough during their working lives to provide for themselves adequately in their retirement. A system of compulsory saving was required, in which the State would add extra funds.

### Ill health

Ill health caused poverty as it prevented individuals from earning a wage, or at least an adequate wage. Ill health included people who were injured at work or who became chronically (long term) sick, as well as people with disabilities. Beveridge therefore proposed a system of insurance for those with employment, in case they should fall ill. This was to be tied into the same scheme as the insurance taken out against unemployment (see below). For those who were unable to work for health or other reasons, he proposed a 'safety net' system of benefits which would cover everybody who was unable to work but who for some reason was not covered by insurance.

The safety net element of National Assistance has today become Income Support. Beveridge also set up various specific, means-tested benefits for those with disabilities.

The insurance element of his plan became National Insurance, which insures people against unemployment and medical treatment. It also forms part of the State pension scheme.

## The 1908 and 1911 reforms

There had been an insurance system for unemployment, sickness and pensions since as early as 1908. This had been set up as a result of Acts passed by the Liberal government in 1908 and 1911. These benefits, however, covered too few people and the benefits paid out were too low for people to have a decent standard of living.

# The original social security system, 1946–1948

## National Insurance

Compulsory National Insurance is the system whereby people pay into a common fund, as do the government and employers. In the event of unemployment or illness, and in the period of retirement, every person has a right to claim through the National Insurance system for the relevant benefits: free health care, State payments when unable to find work, or a pension in retirement provided until death by the State.

National Insurance was based on a number of 'principles', as Beveridge called them. These included the following.

### Comprehensiveness

The scheme was to cover as many people in society as possible, and as many risks as possible. However, Beveridge realised that a scheme which required contributions over a long period of time would not be appropriate for certain groups in the population, for example the long-term disabled, who could never work enough to contribute to an insurance scheme. Therefore National Assistance was developed (see below).

### Flat-rate benefits and contributions

The contributions were to be paid at the same rate, regardless of earnings. Similarly, the benefits were to be paid at a flat rate.

### Adequate benefits

The State benefits should be of a decent minimum standard, which would allow a reasonable standard of living. Beveridge believed that the level of payments would be high enough to enable people to live free from poverty. There would be no need for any other form of supplementary payments.

## National Assistance

This was to replace any vestiges of the Poor Law. The underlying idea, as explained earlier, was that it was to be a 'safety net' for all those who could not be included in the National Insurance scheme, for whatever reason. Unlike National Insurance, which was a contractual right between employees who paid and the government who received, National Assistance was seen as part of the benefits of being a British citizen. Beveridge believed that payments under this scheme would be small, and would be received by a decreasing number of people. For example, according to Beveridge, at the beginning the elderly would not qualify for State pensions because they had not had enough time to build up adequate contributions. At first, therefore, they would receive National Assistance. Over time, this would be phased out as the 'newer generations' of workers came to pensionable age. Eventually this entire group would not need National Assistance. As for the sick, it was genuinely believed that the NHS would eradicate virtually all ill health in Britain and so, over time, there would be little need for National Assistance for the ill.

The benefits paid from National Assistance were to be based on an assessment of the needs and the means of each claimant, in other words, they were **means-tested** benefits.

## Related welfare provision

It is important to remember that National Insurance and National Assistance were not introduced in isolation, but were closely linked to other benefits.

### Family allowances
Closely related to the system of National Insurance was the introduction of family allowances, payable for each child, after the first child, as long as they remained in full-time education.

### Full employment
It was assumed that the government would be able to maintain full employment in the future, unlike the dreadful times of high unemployment experienced in Britain in the 1920s and 1930s. This assumption was based on the belief in new economic theories developed by an economist called Maynard Keynes, who argued that by increasing government spending in times of rising unemployment, the government could actually limit the amount of unemployment. This is contrary to the economic thinking of the 1930s, which argued for decreasing government spending in order to solve economic depressions.

### Health services
One of the main causes of poverty before the Second World War (1939–45) had been the illness of the main wage earner (usually the man) in a family. No work meant no income. By introducing a health service that would eliminate most illness, there would be fewer people unable to work, and hence less poverty. Of course, it also meant that there would be lower demands on the social security system.

### Education
An educated workforce would be more likely to bring general prosperity to the country and limit the extent of unemployment.

# Important legislation and administrative changes in social security

- **National Insurance Acts 1944** and **1946**: introduced National Insurance and created the Ministry of National Insurance.
- **Family Allowances Act 1945**
- **National Assistance Act 1948**: created the National Assistance Board.
- **National Insurance Act 1959**: introduced graduated pensions.
- **National Insurance Act 1966**: introduced earnings-related benefits, which were withdrawn in 1982.
- **1966**: Ministry of Social Security was created to take over the job of the National Assistance Board. Included in this was the Supplementary Benefits Commission which replaced the National Assistance Board.
- **1968**: Ministry of Social Security was renamed Department of Health and Social Security.
- **Family Income Supplement Act 1970**: the forerunner of Family Credit
- **Child Benefit Act 1975**: Child Benefit replaced Family Allowance and Income Tax Relief for children. Payable for all children, including the first.

- **1978**: State Earnings Related Pension Scheme was introduced to give higher levels of pensions in the future.
- **Social Security Acts 1980**: introduced a range of cut-backs in social security, and a considerable 'tightening up' of the rules on discretionary benefits. Abolition of most earnings-related supplements for benefits.
- **Social Security and Housing Act 1982**: shifted responsibility for payment of Housing Benefit to local authorities.
- **Social Security Act 1986:** introduced the first major changes in social security since 1948. The changes included introduction of Income Support, Family Credit and the Social Fund. Changes in pensions to come into effect as a result of the 1978 legislation were severely 'watered down'.
- **1988**: Department of Health and Social Security split into two – the Department of Health (DoH) and the Department of Social Security (DSS).
- **Child Support Act 1991**: came into effect in 1993. The Act required absent parents (usually fathers) to contribute to the maintenance of their children.

# Social security between 1948 and 1979

The administrative structure of the social security system saw no profound change over this period, but a gradual change took place in the nature of the benefits. Most significantly, the levels of payment from National Insurance were never high enough to provide people with adequate standards of living, and so increasingly people had to turn to supplementary benefits. (National Assistance was later renamed Supplementary Benefit, and is now known as Income Support.)

Sexism was a problem of the social security system, in that the benefits were based on the idea of a 'normal' family, with the male breadwinner as the head of the household. As a result of this, women were excluded from benefits or received reduced rates.

The changing nature of the family also meant that there was an enormous growth in the number of lone-parent families. The woman (most lone-parent families are headed by a woman) and her children were forced into poverty, as the system required them to live off supplementary, means-tested benefits and effectively prevented the women from working.

There was always an overlap between low paid employment and social security levels. Therefore, in 1970, the government introduced Family Income Supplement in which a payment was made by the State to make up a low wage to the level of pay that was thought to be necessary for a family. This was a major change away from Beveridge, because it moved the idea of social security from insurance against unforeseen mishaps, such as illness and unemployment, into a form of subsidy for low paying employers.

By the end of the 1970s, the social security system had failed to keep up with the changing nature of society, in that the insurance element had become far less important than the safety net of Supplementary Benefit. The system was altered over time in a piecemeal fashion in order to cope with some of the changes in society, and the result was a mass of complex benefits which few people understood. This lack of understanding led to a large number of errors, which in turn led to both under- and over-payments. The benefits available were inadequate for the people they were supposed to help – the poorest; and they were not reaching certain groups – particularly low income families and lone-parent families.

# Social security from 1979 onwards

In 1979, a Conservative government was elected with very clear views about the future of social security. The system had drifted away from its original aim of providing help for those who were unable to find work or who were unable to perform work because of ill health or disability. Instead the system, according to their view, had become a wasteful bureaucratic structure that actually encouraged people not to work.

## ATTITUDES TO STATE BENEFITS

*The table on page 25 shows the results of a national survey carried out in 1988.*

*1 Look through the table. Overall, would you say there is a substantial measure of agreement or disagreement by respondents? If you had to summarise the information in one sentence, what would you say?*
*2 When it comes to the questions on false claims and 'fiddling', do any differences emerge by (a) social class and (b) voting?*
*3 Some differences emerge on issues along age divisions. Which issues are these and what are the differences?*
*4 Is there any relationship between voting intention and attitudes to social security? (Look particularly at 'benefits for the unemployed'.)*
*5 Are there any differences by income and if so what are they? Do they surprise you? (Look at the 'fiddling' question.)*
*6 As a group, using some of the questions from the table above, design and carry out a simplified questionnaire. You need only ask ten people, but try to ask a range of ages and types of person. Compare the answers. Do any obvious patterns emerge?*

The aims of the government in 1979 included ensuring that:
- money was well spent;
- the state bureaucracy was weakened;
- the most needy should be targeted;
- a new enterprise and self-help culture would be created to replace what they believed was the 'dependency culture';
- private business, such as private insurance companies, could do a better job of providing pensions and certain other welfare benefits than the State.

These ideas were put into effect by means of small alterations to the benefits system in the early 1980s. For example, the government broke the link between increases in earnings and increases in benefits, and instead linked benefits to increases in prices which are usually lower.

## DEPENDENCY

Universal welfare provision works its damaging effects on everyone, not just the poorest. The expectations that society, the State, the government, 'they', will look after our problems tricks us into abdicating from self-reliance and social responsibility. This is a major cause of escalating crime, the collapse of the family, inadequate schools, and health care, and economic decline. Despite what universal welfare provision pretends, it is down to each of us, individually and in voluntary co-operation.

We should encourage those at the bottom of the pile to aspire and struggle to improve their lives. Universal welfare provision instead locks them tight into under-caste dependency. For example, it offers incentives for staying unemployed, or under-employed, though work is the major source of independent dignity....

**Attitudes towards State benefits by social class, party identification, age and annual household income**

| | Total | Social class | | | | Party identification | | | | Age | | | Household income | | | |
|---|---|---|---|---|---|---|---|---|---|---|---|---|---|---|---|---|
| | | I/II | III non-manual | III manual | IV/V | Cons. | SLD/ SDP[3] | Labour | Non-aligned | 18—34 | 35—54 | 55+ | Less than £6000 | £6000 — £11999 | £12000 — £19999 | £20000 + |
| **Many people falsely claim benefits** | % | % | % | % | % | % | % | % | % | % | % | % | % | % | % | % |
| Agree strongly/slightly | 65 | 59 | 70 | 70 | 66 | 73 | 58 | 59 | 70 | 66 | 66 | 65 | 63 | 70 | 67 | 61 |
| Disagree strongly/slightly | 26 | 32 | 23 | 22 | 26 | 19 | 31 | 33 | 19 | 29 | 27 | 23 | 25 | 24 | 26 | 32 |
| Don't know/not answered | 8 | 9 | 7 | 8 | 8 | 8 | 10 | 8 | 12 | 5 | 8 | 12 | 12 | 6 | 7 | 7 |
| **Many people fail to claim benefits[1]** | | | | | | | | | | | | | | | | |
| Agree strongly/slightly | 84 | 84 | 83 | 84 | 85 | 81 | 84 | 86 | 84 | 86 | 88 | 77 | 79 | 84 | 87 | 87 |
| Disagree strongly/slightly | 10 | 9 | 10 | 9 | 10 | 13 | 8 | 8 | 5 | 11 | 7 | 11 | 10 | 9 | 10 | 8 |
| Don't know/not answered | 7 | 7 | 7 | 7 | 6 | 6 | 8 | 6 | 11 | 4 | 5 | 11 | 10 | 7 | 3 | 5 |
| **Benefits for the unemployed are:[1]** | | | | | | | | | | | | | | | | |
| Too low and cause hardship | 52 | 48 | 46 | 52 | 61 | 33 | 55 | 71 | 47 | 60 | 52 | 44 | 56 | 54 | 51 | 50 |
| Too high and discourage job finding | 27 | 29 | 32 | 26 | 21 | 40 | 21 | 14 | 30 | 21 | 28 | 31 | 24 | 28 | 30 | 26 |
| **Many people who get social security don't deserve help[2]** | | | | | | | | | | | | | | | | |
| Agree strongly/agree | 28 | 25 | 27 | 32 | 29 | 35 | 22 | 20 | 28 | 19 | 28 | 36 | 32 | 28 | 29 | 21 |
| Neither agree nor disagree | 27 | 26 | 28 | 29 | 25 | 32 | 27 | 20 | 30 | 26 | 25 | 29 | 24 | 28 | 25 | 27 |
| Disagree strongly/disagree | 45 | 48 | 45 | 37 | 45 | 32 | 50 | 58 | 43 | 53 | 46 | 34 | 42 | 43 | 46 | 52 |
| **Most people on the dole are fiddling[2]** | | | | | | | | | | | | | | | | |
| Agree strongly/agree | 31 | 24 | 29 | 36 | 38 | 36 | 25 | 28 | 35 | 31 | 29 | 34 | 35 | 32 | 34 | 24 |
| Neither agree nor disagree | 31 | 30 | 35 | 33 | 26 | 35 | 30 | 25 | 34 | 29 | 29 | 34 | 31 | 31 | 28 | 32 |
| Disagree strongly/disagree | 37 | 45 | 35 | 30 | 34 | 28 | 43 | 46 | 31 | 39 | 40 | 31 | 33 | 36 | 37 | 44 |
| Weighted | 2930 | 734 | 695 | 637 | 689 | 1157 | 330 | 982 | 208 | 931 | 1050 | 942 | 671 | 645 | 676 | 563 |
| Unweighted | 3029 | 764 | 725 | 659 | 702 | 1198 | 335 | 1017 | 215 | 933 | 1098 | 988 | 733 | 657 | 680 | 574 |
| Weighted | 2529 | 654 | 607 | 551 | 574 | 1033 | 292 | 830 | 169 | 817 | 915 | 791 | 556 | 570 | 606 | 506 |
| Unweighted | 2604 | 676 | 633 | 567 | 584 | 1069 | 302 | 848 | 176 | 813 | 956 | 826 | 606 | 578 | 608 | 517 |

**Notes:**
[1]Base: all respondents
[2]Base: self-completion
[3]SLD/SDP now merged to form the Liberal Democratic Party

**Source:** British Social Attitudes (HMSO, 1988)

By ridiculing competition and excellence, it deprives the children of the welfare-dependent under-class of self-improvement through education – in the past the salvation of even the most disadvantaged ...

Source: Adapted from D. Marsland, 'Face to Face', *Social Studies Review*, November 1989

1 What ideological viewpoint does Marsland support? (see pages 16–17.)
2 What does he mean when he refers to 'universal welfare provision'?
3 From whom to whom does the culture of dependency shift responsibility?
4 When Marsland refers to each of us individually and in voluntary co-operation, what does he mean?
5 What ought people in the culture of dependency to be doing?
6 Is there any relationship between this idea and the culture of poverty? (See pages 62–3.)
7 What can Marsland mean when he says that there are incentives for staying unemployed or under-employed?
8 Do you agree or disagree with Marsland's analysis? Give reasons for your answer.

## Pensions

In 1978, an all-party agreement brought about a change in the pension scheme, to a system called SERPS (State Earnings Related Pension Scheme). In the future, State pensions would be paid at different levels according to how much people had paid into the system over the years (those on higher salaries were to pay in more than those on lower salaries).

The Conservative government in the 1980s was very concerned that the increase in the number of pensioners would make the scheme impossible to finance, as population projections showed that there was likely to be a threefold increase in pensioners in the following 40 years. As a result, the earnings related pension levels were substantially reduced and employees were encouraged to take out private pensions. (See chapter 11 for a full discussion of welfare and the elderly.)

## Child Benefit

This was not directly affected by the 1986–8 changes, but Child Benefit was frozen during the mid-1980s in order to save money. The intention was to phase it out altogether. In the 1990s, Child Benefit remains one of the major debates between those who believe in selectivity or targeting and those who believe in universal benefits.

## Housing Benefit

This remained a part of social security but continued to be handled by local authorities. The levels of benefit actually declined, as new restrictions and methods of working out entitlement were introduced.

Look at the table opposite.

1 What is the benefit with the largest number of recipients?
2 What was government policy towards this during the mid-1980s?
3 What is the most costly benefit?
4 What is likely to happen to the cost of this in the future? Why?
5 What was the government response?
6 How much is spent on healthy people of working age without employment?
7 Is social security an expensive system to administer, do you think?

**ESTIMATED DISTRIBUTIONS OF SOCIAL SECURITY EXPENDITURE, 1988-9**

| Benefit | Amount (£ million) | Percentage of total benefit costs | Recipients (thousands) |
|---|---|---|---|
| Retirement Pension | 19 390 | 41 | 9 735 |
| Invalidity Pension | 3 410 | 7 | 1 040 |
| Unemployment Benefit | 1 143 | 2 | 755 |
| Widows Benefit | 908 | 2 | 395 |
| All other insurance benefits | 749 | 2 | |
| **Total insurance benefits** | 25 600 | 54 | |
| Income Support | 7 650 | 16 | 4 925 |
| Family Credit | 422 | 1 | 470 |
| Housing Benefit | 3 817 | 8 | 4 465 |
| Social Fund | 164 | 0 | |
| **Total means-tested benefits** | 12 053 | 25 | |
| Child Benefit | 4 532 | 10 | 12 015 |
| Attendance Allowance and Invalid Care Allowance | 1 202 | 3 | 7 704 |
| Mobility Allowance | 655 | 1 | 540 |
| Other contingent benefits | 1 132 | 2 | |
| **Total 'contingent' benefits** | 7 521 | 16 | |
| Administration, etc. | 2 414 | 5 | |
| **Total** | 47 588 | 100 | |

# The 1986 legislation

The most significant changes since the introduction of social security in 1948 occurred with the legislation of 1986. Three of the main changes in the social security system concerned Income Support, Family Credit and the Social Fund, summarised below.

## Income Support

Supplementary benefits, which were the means-tested payments, were replaced by Income Support. This aimed to withdraw money from those who did not need it (such as young, single people) and to give it to those in greatest need (such as lone parents and the disabled). This concept of targeting the benefits available to the groups regarded as most deserving of assistance was supposed to increase the real value of benefits to those truly in the greatest need and, at the same time, to strike a blow against the **dependency culture** (see page 60).

### Gainers or losers?
Did the change to Income Support achieve this targeting of the most needy? According to the government, there were 3.8 million losers and 2.16 million gainers. However, other estimates are more critical, and claim that anything from 43 per cent to 60 per cent were worse off. One particularly critical report by the Benefits Research Unit suggested that 81 per cent of couples and 74 per cent of lone parents would lose out.

## YOUNG PEOPLE

In a civilised country with an advanced economy no one should be denied the means of staying alive. That should be a basic objective of policy. But for some people aged 16 and 17, the safety net has been taken away.

The Department of Social Security sees itself as a honey pot surrounded by benefit-seeking wasps who must be kept out. When the Government decided that teenagers must be prevented from leaving home in order to live on benefit, it concluded that those aged 16 and 17 should be denied the option of benefit and made to choose between education, work or the "guarantee" of a Youth Training place. This system was put in place by the Social Security Act, 1988.

A fall-back scheme of Severe Hardship Payments was introduced in the same Act but it has widely been regarded as unsatisfactory. It has now been investigated in a report by Mori which discloses a disturbing state of affairs.

Among those who have to claim Severe Hardship Payments are teenagers waiting to take up Youth Training places, pregnant women, and young people who have become estranged from their parents or who have been in care.

In Mori's sample of 551, 21 per cent admitted they had supported themselves by theft, 6 per cent by begging, and 2 per cent by selling drugs.

Five per cent had been living off their social workers (not the most affluent section of our community) and 46 per cent had slept rough. In the event, 75 per cent were successful in applying for Severe Hardship Payments, but there was no visible correlation between the extent of hardship and the success of the application...

Youth Training is provided by firms with the freedom to refuse to take on an employee.

In the Mori sample, 6 per cent of those refused Youth Training places had been turned down because of their appearance. Satisfactory appearance has not hitherto been a condition for the right to eat.

The Government does not admit to any failure of the guarantee, and it is only by reading between the lines of a parallel report issued by the Department of Employment on 17 July that it is possible to deduce that the guarantee failed for 9.25 per cent of Mori's sample.

Others, who are offered places, may have no means of support until they begin. A Citizens Advice Bureau in Hampshire found a 17-year-old who was homeless and had not eaten for several days. He was due to start a Youth Training placement six days later, and was denied benefit until then.

Many placements are short—only 16 per cent last longer than six months. Those who have completed a placement and not found a job have a bridging allowance of £15 a week for eight weeks, and are told they are expected to live on it.

Pregnant women are denied Income Support until the last 11 weeks, yet are often refused Youth Training because they will be unable to complete it. They too often have nothing to live on, and are less successful than the average in applying for Severe Hardship Payments.

Those estranged from their parents—many of whom have been forcibly thrown out—are also less successful than average in obtaining payments.

Those who have been in care, and those too near their 18th birthdays to complete Youth Training courses, are also often left with no means of support.

Source: Adapted from the *Independent*, 24 July 1991

1 What are Youth Training places?
2 What happened to the provision of benefits for those under 18?
3 What are Severe Hardship Payments?
4 How had the young people in the study supported themselves?
5 What does this suggest about the relationship between poverty and crime?
6 What are the major flaws in Youth Training, and its relationship to Income Support?
7 What is the particular problem faced by young pregnant women?

### Simplifying the system

As supplementary benefits had developed piecemeal over the previous 40 years, by the mid-1980s there was considerable complexity in the number and amounts of benefits. Income Support proposed basic benefits plus categories of extra payments ('premiums') for certain groups, such as lone parents, children and the disabled.

### Targeting

Certain categories of persons were excluded from payments, particularly the young, and those who become voluntarily unemployed. This brings back the idea of deserving and undeserving poor, which was the basis of charity in Britain before the introduction of the Welfare State.

## Family Credit

This replaced a benefit called Family Income Supplement, and is a similar attempt to provide extra income for those in low paid jobs. The search was continuing for a way of encouraging people to take low paid jobs where a person who did a full week's work would effectively bring home no more than if she/he were on Income Support. Family Credit is a system of government support for employers who pay low wages. The main issues, apart from the morality of subsidising low paying employers, centre on **means testing**, the **poverty trap**, and **take-up rates**, all of which will be discussed in the following section on debates in the provision of social security.

## The Social Fund

One of the main features of the previous supplementary benefit system was the number of payments for exceptional needs – for example, clothing. These payments had become a central feature of supplementary benefit. The 1986 Act abolished most of these payments and instead introduced the Social Fund.

The Social Fund has two elements to it. The first is a system of **grants**, for those who have exceptional needs. The second is a system of **loans**, for those people who, in the eyes of the DSS official, are not in exceptional need. Research by the Citizens Advice Bureaux showed that in the first year of the new system (1988), 68 per cent of applications for grants were rejected, as were 64 per cent of applications for loans.

# Debates in the provision of social security

There are a number of key themes which reappear in debates on social security provision. These are **targeting** (or selectivity) versus **universalism**, the **poverty trap** and **take-up levels**.

## Targeting and means testing

'Targeting' is the term used to describe a system of welfare provision that aims benefits at particular groups in the population – those who are identified as most in need. The very concept of 'most in need' usually has a moral element in it that says these people are the most deserving, as opposed to others who, if forced to, could escape from their poverty. The best known example of targeting is the exclusion of young people under 18 from Income Support. The arguments underlying this are that it is up to the parents of the young people to support them, and that they ought to be on a work experience programme. As the newspaper extract on page 28 shows, this has led to cases of significant hardship.

Targeting is closely linked to the idea of **means testing**. By this we mean that individuals are eligible to certain benefits not just because they fall into a certain category, such as pensioners, the disabled, etc., but because they fall into this category *and* are poor. The idea of means testing has a long history in the provision of social benefits, from outdoor to indoor 'relief' (under the Poor Law of nineteenth-century Britain), through to today's Income Support.

Means testing is a system of awarding benefits on the basis of comparing the actual income of a person or famiy against what the State thinks they need in order to have an adequate standard of living. The person or family have then to prove that their income is so low that they cannot manage, and then the State makes up the difference between the actual income, and the State's level.

This system is the way in which most social security benefits are provided.

### The advantages of means testing

- It targets help to the most needy, and does not give money or services to those who could afford to pay and who would otherwise be subsidised by the rest of the population. Some of these people may actually be worse off than those receiving benefits. For example, free travel is given by some local authorities to pensioners, yet many of these pensioners may, in fact, be well off, whilst other people, paying the full fares, could be earning lower wages.
- Providing help to targeted groups should cost less to the State, as fewer people should receive benefits.
- The savings made could be spent on providing better services for the recipients, or it could be used by the government to lower taxes.

### The disadvantages of means testing

- Means testing is complex and creates a large bureaucracy to administer it. Large bureaucracies cost a large amount of money. Much of the 'savings' would not return to the government but would be used up in higher administration charges. This is precisely what happened when the community charge (now replaced by the council tax) was introduced in 1991.
- As targeting is complex, it means that quite often mistakes are made by those giving out the benefits.
- People are often confused as to what they are entitled to have, as the complexity of the system acts as an obstacle to claimants.
- It is claimed that people often fail to take up the benefits because they feel embarrassed to ask (they feel 'stigmatised') or because they are ignorant of what they might claim.
- As income rises, so State benefits decline, and this can lead to what is called the poverty trap, whereby people actually lose more in State benefit than they gain from the increase in income they receive when they get a job.

## Universalism

The alternative to targeting through means testing is to give benefits to everybody who falls into a particular category. Unemployment Benefit, for example, is not means tested. Everyone who becomes unemployed, and has paid adequate contributions to National Insurance, receives Unemployment Benefit – even though some people may not need it. Similarly, everyone who has a child receives Child Benefit.

When everyone in a particular category receives benefits, then it is known as universalism. Those who argue for universalism claim they are defending the Welfare State, yet very few benefits available since the Welfare State began are truly universal. The overwhelming majority of State benefits are means tested, as we shall see later on pages 34–41.

### Advantages of universalism

Supporters of universalism argue:

- that it eradicates the poverty trap;
- that it ensures that everyone who is in need obtains the benefits, and no one

is omitted through their ignorance of benefits available or through fear of stigma;
- that it is cheap to operate because there is no expensive bureaucracy working out entitlement through means testing.

### Disadvantages of universalism

Critics of universalism dismiss these points, claiming that it is highly expensive because so many people receive benefits unnecessarily. Money is wasted, which could go to other more needy groups. Critics also argue that giving people benefits which are not really needed encourages them to rely on the State rather than on their own resources.

### AN ARGUMENT AGAINST UNIVERSALISM

Universalism has many harmful consequences. By multiplying public expenditure, it distracts finances from productive investment which would raise the general standard of living. By creating huge centralised bureaucracies, it weakens the vitality of the family, the local community and voluntary associations, which are the natural arenas of genuine mutual help. It fails to get help to those who most need it. The disadvantaged lose out to more sophisticated, better organised fellow citizens. It gradually reduces the capacity of the population for personal autonomy by schooling them to welfare dependency.

**Source:** D. Marsland, 'Face to Face', *Social Studies Review*, November 1989

### THE CASE FOR THE PRINCIPLE OF UNIVERSALISM

The alternative to universal provision for education, health and social security is not independence but selective provision. If these things are left to markets and families, then a substantial minority will not be able to afford them. This means a choice between leaving them to die, and providing selective 'targeted' services for those who can prove they are in serious need of state provision.

Selective 'targeted' services really do create a kind of one-way dependence, ...excluding [people] from the opportunities and incentives enjoyed by their fellow citizens. For example, if a person who is unemployed can get free education, free health care and means-tested benefits, while a person in paid work must pay for schools and [medical] treatment, and food out of [their] wages, then many unskilled and partially disabled people will not be able to afford to work. If people with low wages get benefits and services which they lose as their earnings rise, they have no incentives to improve skills and increase earnings. And if savings disqualify people from getting benefits and services, poor people won't try to save.

**Source:** B. Jordan, 'Face to Face – The Case Against', *Social Studies Review*, November 1989

Throughout its [the social security system's] history, its primary role has been to uphold the operation of a capitalist labour market, with its social and sexual divisions of labour, and to control and contain the inequalities and poverty that result.

**Source:** Novak, 1988, quoted in M. Hill, *Social Security Policy in Britain* (E. Elgar Publishing, 1992)

1 Marsland rejects universalism and puts forward four objections to it. Explain what he means by 'distracting finances from productive investment which would raise the general standard of living'.
2 In what way do you think bureaucracies weaken the family, the local community, etc.?
3 Explain clearly what is meant by 'the most needy losing out to the better organised'.

**4** Explain the concept of 'welfare dependency'.

**5** Jordan defends the principle of universalism. What does he mean by 'selective provision'? Why is selective targeting bad?

**6** What positive arguments does he make for universalism?

**7** Explain the point that Jordan is making about poor people and saving.

**8** Novak, in the third extract, takes a completely different viewpoint. What is this argument? Which ideological approach does this reflect? Why would he reject both universal and targeted benefits?

**9** Which argument of the three do you find most persuasive?

## The poverty trap

This is the situation where people on means-tested benefits such as Family Credit can actually lose more money by working hard and increasing their income than they can by remaining solely on State benefits. The situation arises with virtually all means-tested benefits because as people increase their income through hard work, or through a wage rise from their employer, the State withdraws benefits for every extra pound earned over a certain 'threshold'. Usually, the threshold is so low and the decline in State support (usually known as a 'taper') so great, that it is possible for poorer people to be less well off working than accepting State benefits.

### The poverty trap: an example

A person on Income Support can early up to £5 before the income is deducted in full; a couple may earn £10, a single parent £15.

A person claiming benefits while working stands to gain very little through an increase in earnings. The calculation is very complicated, because Housing Benefit and Family Credit are worked out only after tax and National Insurance have been deducted, but it works out eventually like this: for each £1 earned, a claimant might lose from April 1988 (when the 1986 Act came into force):

27p in tax
9p in National Insurance
16p in Housing Benefit
44p in Family Credit

-----

96p total

-----

A family earning between £40 and £140 may be little or no better off for an increase in wages.

**Source:** P. Spicker, *Social Housing and the Social Services* (Longman, 1989)

## Take-up rates

A considerable number of benefits have low take-up rates, by which we mean that people who are entitled to the benefits simply do not apply for them. For example, in 1992, of those eligible, 24 per cent failed to take up Income Support, 46 per cent failed to take up Family Credit and 23 per cent failed to take up Housing Benefit.

### The reasons for low take-up rates

- **Language** – there may be a language barrier which prevents the person claiming, although the main benefits are explained in Bengali, Chinese, Gujarati, Hindi, Punjabi, Turkish and Urdu, as well as English.

- **Lack of knowledge** – there may be ignorance of the benefits available, as most people do not have an awareness of the entire range of benefits available.
- **Complexity** – the forms may be so complex that they discourage potential claimants from completing them. For example the form FC1 (1991) to claim Family Credit is 12 pages long!
- **Too little benefit** – the complexity of the form, the amount of time spent finding out about the appropriate benefits, the time spent waiting in Social Security or Housing Benefit departments all adds up to too great a commitment to be seen as worthwhile. This is particularly true if the person imagines that the situation of need will be short-lived.
- **Stigma and embarrassment** – many people find it embarrassing for others to know that they are claiming benefits. This is particularly true for Family Credit and Housing Benefit. Older people feel that there is a stigma attached to asking for help from the State.
- **Consequences** – the consequences of claiming some benefits, particularly Housing Benefit, may dissuade people from putting in the claim in the first place. Landlords may not want their rent known to the tax authorities, for example.

## FAMILY INCOME SUPPLEMENT

**Family Income Supplement: expenditure and caseload estimates, 1985-1986**

| | |
|---|---|
| Expenditure based take-up | 54% |
| **Value of benefit** | |
| – claimed | £105 million per annum |
| – unclaimed | £90 million per annum |
| **Average** | |
| – award | £11.70 per week |
| – unclaimed amount | £8.90 per week |
| **Caseload based take-up** | |
| **Number of** | |
| – recipients | 180 thousand |
| – eligible non-recipients | 190 thousand |

**Source**: *Family Expenditure Survey 1985 and 1986* and administrative data (HMSO)

1 Family Income Supplement is the forerunner to Family Credit. In terms of the total value of of the benefit, what were the amounts (a) claimed and (b) unclaimed?
2 In terms of the average amounts of money these figures represent, (a) how much was the average award paid out? (b) how much would have been the average award that was not claimed?
3 Of those who were eligible, did more people claim than not claim? Illustrate your answer with figures.

# Social security today

The social security system is in a mess. The system is incomprehensible to many claimants; its own administrators often do not know the rules. The benefits fail to reach many of the people who are entitled to them, and it is widely believed (though disputable) that many of the people who do get benefits shouldn't.

**Source:** P. Spicker, *Social Housing and the Social Services* (Longman, 1989)

The social security system is made up of the following main types of benefits:

- contributory benefits;
- means-tested benefits;
- non-contributory benefits.

Social security is the responsibility of the Department of Social Security. It has two semi-autonomous 'agencies' – one for the collection of National Insurance and one for the payment of benefits.

# Contributory benefits

Contributory benefits are the ones we pay for through our National Insurance payments, which are automatically deducted from pay packets in much the same way as income tax. It is the State's way of making us pay for insurance against redundancy and assurance against our old age.

Our rights to payments under the National Insurance scheme are related to the amount of time we have paid into the scheme. An important feature is that, like private insurance (and assurance) schemes, the person receives the money no matter how much income he/she has from another source. For instance, if a person becomes unemployed and has paid enough contributions, then he/she receives unemployment benefit even if he/she is receiving a large income from investments.

The main contributory benefits are described below.

### Unemployment Benefit

This lasts for one year from the date of unemployment. It is a flat-rate benefit (it is not raised or lowered according to the previous income of the unemployed person), which is paid no matter how much income the person has from other sources, or even if the partner of the unemployed person is working and earning a full salary. After one year, the person goes on to Income Support. Unemployment Benefit is, however, taxable.

Unemployment Benefit only supports about 30 per cent of the unemployed. Because of the requirement to have paid into National Insurance for a long period of time, most young people and many women are not eligible to claim.

### Retirement Pension

This is paid to men and women aged over 65, who have paid National Insurance contributions in full. Retirement pensions have declined as a proportion of average income, and stand at about 17 per cent of average male salaries.

---

### THE VALUE OF BENEFITS

*During the 1980s, the Conservative government, in an effort to lower the costs of pensions and Child Benefit, stopped relating them approximately to increases in earnings. Instead they related them to rises in inflation. The result has been a lowering of the value of pensions. For similar reasons, changes were made in other benefits.*

Pensions and child benefit are to rise by only 4.1 per cent next April, as a result of yesterday's inflation figure—but a much bigger jump of 7.2 per cent is due on means-tested benefits such as income support.

Falling mortgage rates have helped push the headline figure on which pensions and child benefit are adjusted down to 4.1 per cent. For 10 million pensioners, that will produce increases next April of £2.15 and £3.40, giving single people £54.15 a week and couples £86.65, if the usual rounding conventions are used. Child benefit will rise by 40p to £9.65 for the first child and 30p to £7.80 for subsequent children.

However, inflation minus housing costs— the figure used to adjust income support, family credit, housing and community charge benefit—has remained at 7.2 per cent. The least well-off are due larger cash increases than basic state pensioners—on past form, the adult income support rate will rise by £2.85 to £42.50 a week, and by £4.50 to £66.75 for a couple.

That puts fresh pressure in the public spending round on the social security bill. Unemployment alone adds £275m for every extra 100,000 jobless. The 7.2 per cent rise also compounds the argument over whether to scrap the 20 per cent contribution to the poll tax made even by the least well-off.

**Source**: The *Independent*, 12 October 1991

**1** By how much were pensions and child benefits uprated?

**2** What was the basis of the uprating?

**3** By how much were Income Support, Family Credit, etc., upgraded?

**4** Which group therefore lost out?

**5** When a government says that benefits are uprated in line with prices, what does this mean in practice?

**6** How much is the pension according to the article?

**7** Using this figure (from question 6) as your base, explore the needs and spending patterns of a small group of local pensioners – does the State pension provide adequate finance for a 'decent' standard of living? (You may need to check the current pension level.)

### Statutory Sick Pay and Statutory Sickness Benefit

Statutory Sick Pay is for most employed people who are sick or disabled and unable to work. It is paid by the employer for the first 28 weeks and is earnings related (that is the more you earn, the more you receive). Statutory Sickness Benefit is a similar benefit for those who are self-employed or become unemployed. It is flat-rate payment.

### Invalidity Benefit

This is a long-term replacement for Statutory Sick Pay/Sickness Benefit which comes into force after 28 weeks. It is a flat-rate payment. There is also an invalidity allowance available for certain groups of people, which is paid in addition. The number of people receiving Invalidity Benefit tripled in the 1980s.

### Maternity benefits

As a result of the European Pregnancy Directive, from 1994 working women receive 14 weeks' maternity leave and payment at the level of Statutory Sick Pay. Women do not have to be in full-time employment and there is no qualifying period for which they have to have been working.

### Widow's benefits

There are three widow's benefits:

- **widow's bereavement payment** for those paying, or with husbands paying, National Insurance. This is a one-off payment (1991 = £1,000);

- **widowed mother's allowance** for widows with dependent children. This is related to the number of children. Widows may also receive husband's earnings' related pension;
- **widow's pensons** available for those aged 45–65. Widows may receive husband's earnings related pension.

## Means-tested benefits

You need not have paid National Insurance contributions to obtain means-tested benefits, but the State only pays them if the person falls below a certain level of income. In other words, there is a test of your means (income) before you can receive them. No matter what their income, however, certain groups are not eligible for means-tested benefits, in particular students and (in all but exceptional circumstances) 16–18-year-olds.

### WOMEN AND THE SOCIAL SECURITY SYSTEM

'Feminist analysis is most obviously about putting women in where they have been left out, about keeping women on the stage rather than relegating them to the wings.'

**Source:** G. Pascall, *Social Policy – A Feminist Analysis* (Tavistock, 1986)

**Income Support: Recipients of regular weekly payments in a week: one-parent families (thousands)**

| Year | Total one-parent families | Families headed by a man | Situation of man | | | | |
|------|------|------|--------|---------|----------|----------------------|-----------|
| | | | Single | Widowed | Divorced | Prisoner's partner | Separated |
| 1988 | 727 | 32 | 3 | 5 | 13 | — | 12 |
| 1989 | 771 | 34 | 5 | 5 | 13 | — | 11 |

| Year | Families headed by a woman | Situation of woman | | | |
|------|------|--------|---------|----------|---------------------|-----------|
| | | Single | Widowed | Divorced | Prisoner's partner | Separated |
| 1988 | 694 | 288 | 13 | 194 | 5 | 194 |
| 1989 | 737 | 322 | 12 | 201 | 4 | 199 |

**Source:** *Annual Statistical Enquiry* (HMSO, 1991)

**1** Why is the quotation relevant to lone-parent families, the poverty trap and 'old age' pensions?
**2** What is the relevance of the tables below the quotation?

The main means-tested benefits are described below.

### Income Support

This is the major form of benefit in Britain today, with approximately 5 million people receiving it. It exists to ensure that nobody falls below an income which the government thinks is reasonable to obtain a person's 'requirements' (a government term for 'necessities'– see pages 43–4 for discussions on absolute and relative poverty). It is primarily a benefit for those people who are unemployed and not entitled to unemployment benefit, but also provides income for the sick, lone parents and some of those aged over 60.

Income Support carries with it the 'passport' to other State benefits such as free prescriptions, help with housing costs, and possibly 'help' from the Social Fund.

The basic level of Income Support, known as the **personal allowance**, varies according to the category of person (for example, child, adult, etc.). These personal allowances are then increased in certain circumstances by **premiums**, which are paid out to people who, for example, are carers, lone parents, have children (more for a disabled child), are severely disabled, or are pensioners.

When income from other sources plus given levels of savings (which in 1991 varied from £3000 to £8000) reach certain levels, then Income Support decreases accordingly. (See the discussion on the poverty trap on pages 64–5.)

### Family Credit

This benefit was designed to help families on low incomes (but, see again page 64–5 on the poverty trap). The benefit is paid to people in employment working for more than 16 hours each week, and who have at least one child. Adults and children are allocated 'credits' worth a certain amount of money. These are paid in full if the income is at or below Income Support levels. The greater the income, the more the payments are decreased, or 'tapered'.

### Disability Working Allowance

This is a tax-free, but income-related benefit for those with disabilities which put them at a disadvantage in their job.

### The Social Fund

This is a system whereby people on low incomes, almost always on Income Support, can apply for either grants or loans. The grants are severely restricted, and so usually the payment takes the form of an interest-free loan, which is then directly subtracted from Income Support at source (that is before it is handed over to the individual). The entire Social Fund for each DSS office has a fixed budget, which the official responsible (the 'Social Fund Officer') cannot exceed.

There are seven categories under which loans or grants can be made:
- funeral payments;
- maternity payments;
- crisis loans – to help pay for something needed urgently;
- budgeting loans – to help spread the cost of buying more expensive items;
- community care grants – to help those coming out of institutions;
- cold weather payments;
- Settlement or Resettlement Loans for people settling or returning to Britain as a result of a war elsewhere.

### THE ROLE OF SOCIAL WORKERS AND THE SOCIAL FUND

Before 1988 (when the 1986 Act came into effect), social workers would advise their clients on social security matters and do their best to obtain many of the one-off payments for clothing, furniture, etc., that were available under the supplementary benefit scheme. If the person had a need that fell into the categories of one-off payments, then they received the money.

With the introduction of the Social Fund, however, the government said that there was to be a fixed budget for spending by each DSS office, and when this was spent there would be no more cash. This meant that not everyone's request for a grant or a loan could be accommodated. The result was that the government expected social workers to *prioritise* their clients according to how needy they were. Those in greatest need would then receive priority for a grant. The role of the social worker was to be changed, then, from that of *adviser* to that of *judge* of need. Many social workers feel unhappy with this new role.

---

Social workers have adopted a policy of ... determined advocacy ... which means in practice that social workers will give every help to clients applying to the Social Fund for a grant or a loan. They will, however, restrict themselves to the facts of the case: they will resist pressure to provide judgements and they will not co-operate with Social Fund officers' attempts to set priorities. Social Fund officers will not be invited to participate in case conferences and there will be no joint visiting of clients by social workers and Social Fund officers.

**Source**: Johnson, *Reconstructing the Welfare State*

---

**1** Do you agree with this approach on the part of social workers?
**2** You are a social worker with two clients who have approached you for assistance in making their claims for the Social Fund. You know that the budget from your local DSS office is almost finished as the Social Fund Officer has 'tipped you off' informally. One client you regard as in desperate need, while the other you feel less sympathy for, as you know some personal details about how they have wasted money on a number of occasions.

Of course you know the policy of BASW (the social workers' organisation) of not prioritising or assisting the Social Fund Officer. But what do you do? Do you wash your hands of it, under the cloak of not being 'judgemental' (this is social work terminology for not letting your personal feelings interfere in the practice of social work), and assist each claimant equally? Do you help one more than the other? Do you informally tell the Social Fund Officer of your feelings and leave the final judgement to him/her?

---

Social Work departments have a limited budget for providing cash aid. This budget is referred to as Section 1 or Section 12 monies. Below are some true examples, where the social worker has chosen to give assistance from these funds. (Incidentally, it is important to remember that no loan under £30 can be made by the Social Fund.)

---

*Wandsworth. Third case review snapshot.* The case concerned an under eighteen Afro-Caribbean lone parent living on Income Support in her parental home. No application to the Social Fund had yet been made. The social worker wrote:

"16 yr old woman, had a baby on XX/XX/89. Made claim for IS but as yet no money from DHSS. Arranged interview for client with DHSS in 4 days time. No money for food and immediate necessities".

The social worker gave £15 from the Section 1 budget.

*Grampian Region. Fourth case review snapshot.* This case concerned a lone parent living on Family Credit. She had made an application for both a Budgeting Loan and, later, a Crisis Loan, both of which had been refused. Her social worker wrote:

"Attempting to budget whilst also paying outstanding debts. DSS loan refused on basis of inability to repay. Financial situation has knock-on effect on lone mother's ability to cope with her child acting-out destructive behaviour knowing damage cannot be repaired if no money available."

She was given £10 from the Section 12 budget.

*Kensington and Chelsea. Fifth case review snapshot.* The case concerned a couple with children living on Income Support and Child Benefit. Their application for a Community Care Grant had been refused.

"Family with 6 children, burnt out of home 3 weeks ago. All possessions lost. Budgeting Loan given then of £300 to replace essential clothing. CCG now refused – family told 'not eligible'. Review of decision being heard X/X/89. Having no 'start-up' grant, family have been very stressed by not knowing where to get furniture. Flat being offered by council but nothing to go in it. Added extreme stress to an already devastating situation. This in my opinion was a clear case of eligibility of CCG being payable on grounds of 'home became uninhabitable'. Council confirmed it was not fit to live in . . . Mr H. also long-term sick with arthritis of the spine".

The SSD made a payment of £702.88 from their Section 1 budget and referred the family to a charity.

*Leicestershire. Sixth referral snapshot.* The case concerned a young lone parent. She was living with her mother and brothers. She had not made an application to the Social Fund as yet. The social worker who saw her outlined the nature of her case:

". . . Had to give up work to look after sick 3 month old baby who was recently admitted and discharged from hospital, she made application for IS but DSS mislaid papers . . ."

The social worker gave £10 from the Section 1 budget and advised her to apply for a Crisis Loan – which was against departmental policy.

**Source:** S. Becker and R. Silburn, *The New Poor Clients* (Community Care, 1990)

## SUCCESSFUL SOCIAL FUND CLAIMS

**Expenditure by client group, 1988-1990**

|  | 1988/89 | | | 1989/90 | | |
|---|---|---|---|---|---|---|
|  | CCG | BL | CL | CCG | BL | CL |
|  | % | % | % | % | % | % |
| Pensioners | 17 | 4 | 1 | 21 | 4 | 1 |
| Disabled | 14 | 8 | 3 | 16 | 6 | 2 |
| Unemployed/family premium | 8 | 20 | 18 | 7 | 18 | 20 |
| Unemployed/no family premium | 15 | 18 | 37 | 12 | 17 | 34 |
| Lone parent | 36 | 45 | 19 | 35 | 51 | 22 |
| Others/family premium | 2 | 1 | 1 | 2 | 1 | 1 |
| Others | 8 | 4 | 21 | 8 | 3 | 20 |

**Source**: DSS, 1989, 1990.
**Notes**: CCG – Community Care Grants
      BL    – Budgeting Loans
      CL    – Crisis Loans
All percentages rounded.

**Source**: HMSO, 1991

1 Explain the difference between community care grants, budgeting loans and crisis loans.
2 Which group was most likely to receive 'help' under all three categories according to the table?
3 Does this tell us anything about the financial status of this client group, or not?
4 Pensioners are generally accepted to be amongst the poorest of the population, yet their claims

are relatively low (or at least their successful claims, which this chart demonstrates). Could you suggest any explanation for this?

**5** How would you go about making a Social Fund claim?

### Government sponsored charitable foundations

These have been set up by the government to provide similar sorts of loans as the Social Fund to people with disabilities. The foundations are funded by the government, but are independent and left alone to make decisions on individual cases.

### Housing Benefit

This is a payment, made through the local authority housing departments, to cover the costs of rents and local government tax. It is available to those on Income Support, and to other low income individuals or families. The calculations for Housing Benefit are extremely complicated, and it is claimed that even the officials who calculate the amounts have trouble understanding it. However, the principle of working it out is similar to that used in Income Support and Family Credit. The various 'needs' of an individual or family are worked out according to government guidelines and the total cost is called the 'applicable amount'. The income of the individual or family is then totalled and if this falls below the applicable amount, payments are made. The higher the income, the smaller the payment. Students do not qualify for Housing Benefit.

Mortgage payments support is available through a different system paid through social security offices.

## Non-contributory benefits

These are benefits from the State, for which individuals do not have to have paid National Insurance contributions. They are generally targeted at those who have very clear physical needs, such as the disabled or young children. These are not means tested (that is income is not taken into account when giving these), what is more important is whether the person falls into the appropriate category of disablement or disadvantage.

### Attendance Allowance

This is for people aged 65 or more who are severely disabled (mentally or physically) and who need supervision. There are two levels of payment – a lower rate for those who need help all day *or* all night and a higher rate for those who need help all day *and* all night. It can be paid on top of other social security benefits and is tax free. It is normally only available for those who have needed personal care for six months.

### Disability Living Allowance

DLA is for those under 65 who need help with personal care in such things as washing, dressing or using the toilet, either because they are ill or because they are disabled. If the person is over 16, they may claim DLA if they need help to prepare a cooked meal. This benefit is also available for people aged 5–65 who have difficulty walking. DLA can be paid to people who do not actually have anyone looking after them. There are special arrangements for the terminally ill.

There are two components of Disability Living Allowance – a **care component** and a **mobility component**. They are assessed separately, and paid at different rates.

[Poverty] is defined by reference to the actual needs of the poor and not by reference to the expenditure of those who are not poor. A family is poor if it cannot afford to eat.... A person who enjoys a standard of living equal to that of a medieval baron cannot be described as poor for the sole reason that he has chanced to be born into a society where the great majority can live like medieval kings.

The picture which emerges is one of constant restriction in almost every aspect of people's activities... The lives of these families... are marked by the unrelieved struggle to manage, with dreary diets and drab clothing. They also suffer from what amounts to cultural imprisonment in their home in our society in which getting out with money to spend on recreation and leisure is normal at every other income level....

**Source:** All extracts quoted in R. Lister, *The Exclusive Society*, (CPAG, 1990)

It is not just money that decides how people live – it is access to resources that makes the difference between drowning in poverty and managing just to keep your head above water. To measure poverty only by income is inaccurate – what facilities people have and what social activities they are able to engage in, are the real indicators of poverty.

**1** The quotations above reflect different approaches to defining poverty. Indicate which of the three approaches (absolute, relative and consensual) you think underlies each one.
**2** Which of the quotations do you feel is (are) the most accurate?
**3** Look back to page 42, where you discussed three definitions of poverty given to interviewees in a research project. Can you see any link between the quotations above and the definitions of poverty given in the research?

The following article in the *Independent* followed a speech by an ex-Conservative Minister for Social Security, who stated that the least well-off were actually more affluent in real (absolute) terms than they had ever been before.

Welfare groups and Labour politicians yesterday continued their attack on John Moore's speech "The End of the Line for Poverty" as researchers said that however poverty was defined it was clear that those on benefits were falling behind those in work...

As one Tory backbencher, Simon Burns, MP for Chelmsford, tabled a Commons motion congratulating Mr Moore, another, Sir Anthony Meyer, MP for Clwyd North West, said that while it was true the poor were better off today than in Victorian times, "we have also to compare the plight of today's poor with the affluence of the rich who have benefited so greatly from the Chancellor's tax cuts..."

Andrew Dilnot of the Institute of Fiscal Studies, said Mr Moore's claim that all groups were better off was broadly true.

But this week the institute published figures showing that the single unemployed are worse off in absolute terms than in 1979.

And while each 10 per cent of the population has gained after tax and benefit changes over the past decade, he said, within that 22 per cent of the poorest 10 per cent and 26 per cent of the next poorest 10 per cent were worse off in real terms.

With benefits rising only in line

| Average gain in income 1979–1989 by tenths of the population. Effect after tax, social security changes. | | |
|---|---|---|
| Gain £0        £10        £20        £30 | Losers | Gainers |
| Poorest tenth | 22% | 59% |
| 2nd tenth | 26% | 56% |
| 3rd tenth | 32% | 53% |
| 4th tenth | 32% | 53% |
| 5th tenth | 22% | 60% |
| 6th tenth | 18% | 69% |
| 7th tenth | 14% | 73% |
| 8th tenth | 15% | 73% |
| 9th tenth | 10% | 80% |
| Richest tenth | 12% | 78% |
| Source: IFS                              Overall | 20% | 65% |

with prices, not earnings, "one has to say that people who are unemployed are doing relatively less well, and there are more of them than in 1979.

"Living standards of those on social security, although they are much higher than in 1948, are becoming progressively further and further behind those of the population in work.

"Mr Moore is right to say that compared to 100 years ago all those on benefit are not in the sort of grinding poverty seen then, but within that there is a subset of benefit recipients, including the homeless, who are poor to the point where it's affecting their health, and another group who are better off but nonetheless seriously excluded from things they should not be excluded from. Whether you want to call that poverty or not, most people would call it unacceptable."

If benefits had risen only in line with prices—the broad thrust of current government policy—the single person's pension of 1948 would last year have been worth only £17.37, instead of £41.40.

"That shows what can happen if over the years you link benefits only to prices not earnings," Mr Dilnot said.

Mr Moore's speech, accompanied by a clutch of tables one of which shows that the poorest 10 per cent have seen a 6 per cent rise in their living standards between 1979 and 1985, against 9 per cent for the whole community, came as Department of Social Security figures also show a drop in the value of several key benefits over the past two years as a percentage of average earnings . . .

**Source:** Adapted from the *Independent*, 13 May 1989

1 Do you agree with the comment made by the Conservative MP, Sir Anthony Meyer (since retired)? After all, why is the extent of wealth relevant to a discussion of poverty?

2 According to Dilnot, which groups in particular were less well off in real terms in 1989 than they were in 1979?

3 What is important about the linking of State benefits to rises in prices as opposed to rises in general living standards?

3 What is the difference between a pension that would have been uprated according to prices only and the actual level of the pension in 1989?

5 What type of poverty definition is Dilnot using when he talks about 'another group who are better off but nonetheless seriously excluded from things they should not be excluded from'?

6 What is the increase in income for the poorest 10 per cent between 1979 and 1989?

7 What is the increase for the richest 10 per cent between 1979 and 1989?

# The extent of poverty

The number of people living in poverty depends on how poverty is defined. If we take the absolute definition, then there are very few poor (destitute) people in Britain. Taking Mack and Lansley's index of deprivation, as many as 12 million people can be considered poor (deprived of one or more of the most commonly agreed necessities).

The figures below are increasingly being used by researchers. They are based on a relative definition of poverty as less than 50 per cent of average income. This is similar to the measure used by the European Commission in its studies of poverty across Europe.

| Categories in poverty | Numbers in poverty |
|---|---|
| The unemployed | 3 000 000 |
| The low paid | 2 700 000 |
| The sick and disabled | 500 000 |
| The elderly | 2 200 000 |
| Single-parent families (not working full time) | 1 150 000 |
| Unavailable for work, such as carers | 900 000 |
| Total number of people living in poverty | 10 500 000 (approx.) |

## CHILDREN IN POVERTY

Proportion of children and population living in poverty between 1979 and 1987 (living below 50 per cent of average income after housing costs)

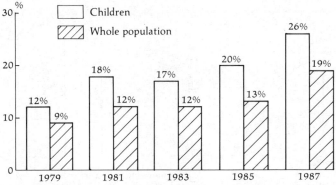

**1** What proportion of children were in poverty in 1987?
**2** What proportion of adults were in poverty in 1979?
**3** How has the situation changed since 1979?

**Note**: In 1987 there were 3,090,000 children living in poverty. This compares with 1,620,000 in 1979.

**Source**: Redrawn from R Lister, *The Exclusive Society* (CPAG, 1990)

The categories of people living in poverty only tell part of the story, however, as certain groups of people are likely to be in all or at least most of the categories listed in the table on page 48. Women, for example, form the majority of the elderly, the disabled, single parents and the low paid. Very often too, as single parents, women are unable to work because although they would like to have employment, their family responsibilities prevent it. Similarly, we know that Afro-Caribbeans and certain groups of Asians are more likely than average to be in more than one of these categories. Thus they are disproportionately represented amongst the poor. (Later, on pages 66–7, we discuss both these groups in more detail.)

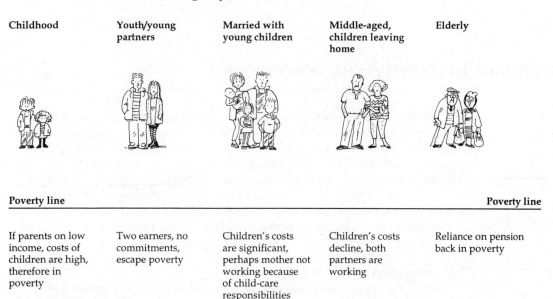

| Childhood | Youth/young partners | Married with young children | Middle-aged, children leaving home | Elderly |
|---|---|---|---|---|
| **Poverty line** | | | | **Poverty line** |
| If parents on low income, costs of children are high, therefore in poverty | Two earners, no commitments, escape poverty | Children's costs are significant, perhaps mother not working because of child-care responsibilities | Children's costs decline, both partners are working | Reliance on pension back in poverty |

**The life cycle and poverty**

## THE RISK OF POVERTY

A

The risk of poverty by economic status in 1987

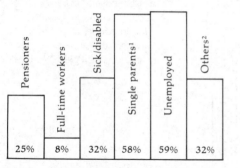

25%   8%   32%   58%   59%   32%

Proportion living in poverty
(below 50 per cent average income after housing costs)

**Notes**: [1]Single parents who are not in full-time work.
[2]Men aged 60–64, widows, students, people
temporarily away from work, carers, people who
are unemployed but not available for work.

B

The risk of poverty by family status in 1987

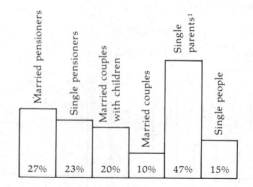

27%   23%   20%   10%   47%   15%

Proportion living in poverty
(below 50 per cent average income after housing costs)

**Note**: [1]All single parents

**Source**: Redrawn from C. Oppenheim, *Poverty: The Facts* (CPAG, 1990)

Look at diagram A.
**1** Which two groups of people had the highest proportions of their members in poverty?
**2** What percentage of pensioners were in poverty?
**3** How can any full-time employees be in poverty?
**4** There is a category headed 'others'. What groups do you think this includes? Suggest an
explanation why each of these groups might be in poverty.
Look at diagram B.
**5** What does this diagram illustrate?
**6** Which type of family has the highest proportion of its members in poverty?

# Groups in poverty: the unemployed

The number of people who are out of work changes with the overall
situation of the economy. However, there have been very significant changes
in the British economy over the last 15 years, and these seem likely to
maintain a permanently high level of unemployment. The main changes
include increasing automation in industry and related increasing productivity,
so that fewer workers are required, and the general decline of British
manufacturing because of foreign competition.

Certain groups in the population, however, are more likely than others to
be made unemployed. These include the following.

### The least skilled

These people have been replaced by automated machinery. Unemployment
levels for unskilled manual workers can be as high as six times that of
professional workers.

### Those living away from the south and south-east of England

The south-east of England has a number of advantages for employers, including a skilled workforce, proximity to Europe and a large, affluent population to purchase goods or products.

### Ethnic minorities

Partly as a result of racism, and partly because skill levels tend to be lower overall amongst Afro-Caribbeans and some of the Asian communities, there are significantly higher levels of unemployment amongst the ethnic minorities. It is estimated that twice as many Blacks and Asians are unemployed as are Whites.

## Long- and short-term unemployment

However, a distinction must be made between long- and short-term unemployment, as those who are unemployed for a long time face much greater problems than those out of work for a limited period. These problems include a lower level of income, as a result of the way benefits are worked out (this is explained later), exhaustion of savings, and a gradual running down in the condition of clothing, furniture and general possessions. Also, the psychological effects of lack of confidence, stress and depression are more acute for the long-term unemployed.

1 Which groups are the most likely to become unemployed?
2 Why are unemployment levels higher amongst some of the ethnic minorities?
3 Why is there greater concern over those unemployed for a long time?
4 From your library, obtain copies of the most up-to-date editions of **Social Trends** or **Economic Trends**. Find the extent of unemployment and the different levels of unemployment by category.
5 If possible use a copy of **Regional Trends** (if not available at your college, then certainly to be found in your central library) to find the unemployment statistics for your area. You should be able to obtain the statistics if necessary from the local Department of Employment office.

## State benefits for the unemployed

There are two major benefits for the unemployed – **Unemployment Benefit** and **Income Support**. (For a detailed description of these benefits, please turn back to chapter 2, pages 34 and 37).

### Unemployment Benefit

In 1990/91, less than 30 per cent of the unemployed were receiving Unemployment Benefit. Unemployment Benefit is very low, in fact it is now worth only 13 per cent of average male earnings, yet 20 years ago it was worth 17.5 per cent.

If a person is 'voluntarily unemployed' – meaning that they have left a job as a result of their own choice – or if a person has been sacked rather than made redundant, then he/she is not eligible for Unemployment Benefit; for six months, furthermore, the person also has Income Support cut by at least 20 per cent.

### Income Support

This is the major source of income for 70 per cent of the unemployed. Income Support is means tested, which means that other family income is taken into account. If a woman is unemployed, and her husband is working, then his income will generally mean that she is not eligible for Income Support.

Income Support for young, single people is particularly low, as there is a special lower rate for 18–24-year-olds. Those aged 16–17 years are not eligible for benefits at all, unless they are engaged on a job training scheme (see the extract on page 28).

A woman, Mrs A., is unemployed because the company for which she worked has gone bankrupt. She has been paying her National Insurance contributions for the last three years. Her husband is in full-time employment. What benefit can she claim?

Her friend Ms B., is in exactly the same situation except that she left the company two weeks before it closed as she said she could no longer stand the rudeness of her boss. What is she entitled to?

A third woman, Ms. C., who is now unemployed as a result of the company going bankrupt only started working nine months ago, after she left college. What is she entitled to?

## The effects of unemployment

### Families

A government study in 1990 found that, after three months of unemployment, the average disposable income of a family dropped by 59 per cent.

If a man becomes unemployed, it is likely that his wife will have to give up work as well, because the benefit system works in such a way that what she earns he loses from Income Support. By the time travel, etc., is taken into account the family becomes worse off if the wife continues to work. As a result, the two-earner family rapidly becomes the no-earner family.

### Individuals

Unemployment has powerful effects on an individual's mental state too, which can help trap him/her in poverty. When people are made unemployed, they lose their self-esteem, and of course this affects their ability and will to seek a job. The stress resulting from lack of employment affects people's health, and standards of health amongst the unemployed are significantly lower than the population in general. This also means they are less able to take on employment. And so a cycle begins, preventing the person getting employment and thereby escaping from poverty.

### Communities

As we have seen, unemployment is more likely to occur amongst certain groups and in certain areas than others. When this occurs, then a gradual run-down of an entire area can begin. Without adequate income, people cannot afford to maintain their accommodation, they cannot afford to shop or to purchase decent leisure services. The result is a lack of shops and leisure amenities, high crime levels and a general dowdiness in the area, which, in turn, puts off employers and new businesses. Thus a cycle begins, leading to yet more poverty and further decline in the area.

# Groups in poverty: the low paid

Although wage levels have increased over the last 15 years, there has been a widening of the gap between the bulk of those in secure, higher-skilled and professional employment and those who are in jobs requiring little skill or who have skills that are no longer in demand. Although both males and females are affected by this, there is a greater proportion of women in the workforce in low paid jobs. This may have been acceptable when female labour was regarded as a second income, but with the increase in female headed families, and the increase in the numbers of men unemployed, the issue of low pay for women has become prominent.

## The extent of low pay

The **Low Pay Unit** estimates that 45 per cent of British workers are on low pay. (Low pay is defined as less than two-thirds of the male median hourly wage.) This figure is composed of 78 per cent of part-time workers (four million people, mainly women) and 29 per cent of full-time, adult workers. As many as 71 per cent of women in all forms of employment were on low pay.

Low paid workers are particularly often caught in the poverty trap, whereby an increase in earnings means the loss of means-tested benefits. In 1990, over 400 000 people in Britain were caught in this 'poverty trap'.

## The low paid with children

Over half of all those living in poverty comprise the low paid and their children. In recent years there has been a relative increase in the standards of living of many elderly people who have traditionally formed the bulk of the poor. However, with the growth of low paid and part-time employment since the early 1980s, for many lower skilled workers, or for families headed by women, the income earned from employment is inadequate to pay for the very significant extra costs of having children. Although benefits are available for children, these are inadequate to pay for additional food, housing, clothing and leisure costs.

## Reasons for the increase in the numbers of the low paid

### Legislation
There has been a significant amount of government legislation concerning employment since the 1980s. Most of these changes have weakened workers' rights, and have even excluded part-time employers from having many effective rights at all. Examples include the fact that a person now has to have been employed for more than two years to make an appeal against 'unfair dismissal', and minimum wages for young people have been abolished.

### Working conditions and employment patterns
A second important factor has been the changing nature of employment in Britain. There has been a growth in the number of part-time workers: between 1984 and 1994 the increase in the number of part-timers is estimated to be nearly 20 per cent while the comparative figure for the increase in the number of full-time employees is about 8 per cent.

Likewise, there has been an increase in the number of temporary employees: between the early 1980s and the early 1990s, the number of temporary employees grew by 12 per cent. Women make up 90 per cent of this temporary workforce.

### Unemployment
As we saw in the previous section, there have been changes in the levels of unemployment. This affects the low paid in the sense that when unemployment is high, employers are able to offer lower wages.

# The minimum wage

The Labour Party is committed to introducing a minimum wage into Britain. By doing so, it hopes to eliminate low pay as one of the causes of poverty. The Conservative Party has steadfastly opposed this, arguing that it would raise costs and would result in fewer jobs. Instead of low paid workers, there would be unemployed people receiving State benefits. (Interestingly, a similar type of argument was put forward to oppose the abolition of slavery, as it was argued that paying the workers wages would lead to economic disaster.)

In most of the European Community countries minimum wages exist (see the diagram below).

## MINIMUM WAGE RATES IN EUROPE (1991/92)

The graph below shows what you are able to purchase in different countries in the European Community for the lowest official wage rates. It therefore shows us the reality of life for the lowest paid in these countries. The term used for this comparison is 'purchasing power parity'.

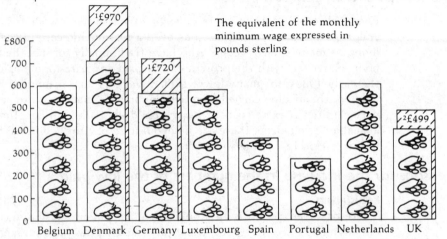

The equivalent of the monthly minimum wage expressed in pounds sterling

**Notes**: [1]Minimum wage rates vary between the two amounts shown depending on the particular industry.

[2]Different recommended minimum wage rates exist only in certain sectors. There will still be people earning less than these amounts.

**Source**: Redrawn from material supplied by the Low Pay Unit

1 Which country has the highest minimum wage rates in Europe? How much is it in terms of purchasing power parity?
2 Which countries have the three lowest minimum wage rates? What are they?
3 When there are debates about Britain 'joining Europe', does this suggest that Britain will be held back or advanced by the EC in terms of social policies? Explain your answer.

## Groups who would benefit from a minimum wage

The introduction of a minimum wage would benefit **young people**, **women** and **manual workers** – all groups who traditionally receive low wages.

Women are traditionally the lowest paid workers – six million women earn less than two-thirds of the average (median) male wage.

The poorest paid male manual workers today earn relatively less compared with average wages than they did 100 years ago.

## WHO GAINS?

**Average annual gain per household from a minimum wage of £3.50 per hour**

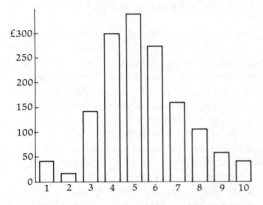

Households are grouped according to income. Each block represents 10 per cent of the total from the poorest to the richest. Middle-income families gain most from the minimum wage.

**Source**: Redrawn from the *Guardian*, 1 October 1991

1 Which is the single largest group which would benefit from a minimum wage?
2 Why do some groups hardly gain at all?

### Groups who do not benefit from a minimum wage

Certain groups of poor people would not benefit from the introduction of a minimum wage – pensioners, the unemployed and the disabled.

Pensioners would gain nothing at all, at least in the short term. If it is true that a minimum wage would push prices up, then pensioners would actually lose out from the higher costs of goods and services.

Likewise, the unemployed would be unaffected; indeed it could be argued that a minimum wage would make it more difficult for them to get jobs.

Those with disabilities would be helped by a minimum wage only if they are employed.

### THE MINIMUM WAGE DEBATE

Read the following text. Then, bearing in mind what you read earlier, summarise the arguments for and against a minimum wage.

The Conservative Government strongly opposes the introduction of legislation on minimum wages. The government argues that having a minimum hourly rate of pay adds additional costs to employers' wage bills, so that they are less likely to employ people – indeed they may actually get rid of staff. The result of minimum wage is therefore an increase in unemployment.

The government estimates that if the Labour Party proposal for a minimum wage of two-thirds of the average male pay was ever to be introduced, it would lead to an increase over the present unemployment figures of 2 million more unemployed. Not only would the minimum wage increase unemployment, it would raise the cost of living. If firms were forced to raise their minimum wage rates, then they would pass the additional costs on to consumers in higher prices.

The British Government claims that this would result in £40 billion increase in wage bills, a consequent increase in inflation, and a decline in the country's economic growth.

The Low Pay Unit, which is a pressure group supporting a minimum wage, argues that the true increase in the wage bill would be more like £4.5 billion. The Unit points out that higher wages will be offset by the increase in tax revenue for the government and by the fact that fewer people will claim state benefits such as housing benefit or Family Credit.

One commonly argued point is that increases in the wages of the lower paid will encourage the better-off skilled workers to seek to maintain the difference in pay between them and the less skilled workers who are traditionally paid less. The Low Pay Unit argues that this is not necessarily the case, as a large increase for a very low paid worker still leaves them a long way behind the better-off. For example, a 60 per cent increase in the wage of a shopworker may only mean 60 pence increase an hour.

Supporters of minimum wages also point to the fact that higher wages mean people have more to spend and can actually help to create prosperity....

The argument concerning minimum wages is not just an economic debate, but a moral one as well. Supporters of a legal minimum wage say that it is wrong that firms who treat their workers badly and pay them an exploitive wage should be allowed to gain an advantage over those companies who seek to pay a fair wage.... Most countries in Europe have a minimum wage level, including such prosperous countries as Germany.

# Groups in poverty: single-parent families

Poverty is not something that occurs to particular individuals, but rather to individuals in particular situations. Therefore, someone who is low paid but who manages to live adequately, or who has been married and is then abandoned by her partner, can be pushed into poverty by, for example, the extra burden of children.

One of the more common causes of poverty derives from the high costs of having children, and the low income that can be earned because of limited earning opportunities. If we look at the lowest earning quarter of the population, those without children earned significantly higher amounts of money than those with children. An example might make this clear: in 1990, a couple in the lowest earning group without children earned £50 per week more than a similar couple with two children. Single parents with one child earned only half the average income of single people in the lowest quarter of earners.

Single parents are likely to be the poorest of the poor. Of the 1.3 million lone parents in Britain, just under a million are on Income Support.

## Reasons for the increase in single-parent families

Since the 1970s, there has been a rapid increase in the number of single-parent families in Britain. Today, more than one in every six families is headed by a single mother. This is caused mainly by the growth in the divorce rate and by the increase in single parenthood (that is women having and raising children on their own).

## LONE PARENTS

A **Proportion of all families with dependent children headed by lone mothers: by marital status**

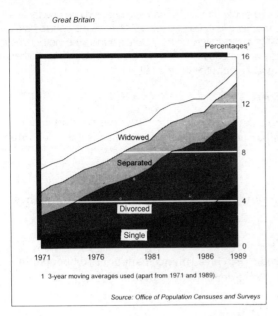

Great Britain

Percentages¹

Widowed

Separated

Divorced

Single

16

12

8

4

0

1971    1976    1981    1986  1989

1  3-year moving averages used (apart from 1971 and 1989).

Source: *Office of Population Censuses and Surveys*

Never-married lone mothers now represent 6.4 per cent of all family heads, compared to 1.2 per cent in 1971 and 3.2 per cent in 1986.

**Source:** *Social Trends* (HMSO, 1993)

B **Live births outside marriage as a percentage of all births: by registration**

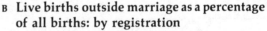

England & Wales

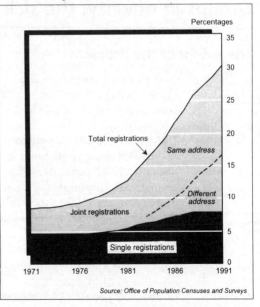

Percentages

Total registrations

Same address

Different address

Joint registrations

Single registrations

35

30

25

20

15

10

5

0

1971    1976    1981    1986    1991

Source: *Office of Population Censuses and Surveys*

**Source**: Both charts: *Social Trends* (HMSO, 1993)

The diagrams above show us the different groups of lone mothers with dependent children and the increase in the numbers of births outside marriage.

**1** Overall, what is happening to the numbers of lone mothers in Britain?

**2** What was the main cause of lone parenthood in 1989? Give the percentage figure.

**3** How has this changed from the situation in 1971?

**4** What is happening regarding births outside marriage?

**5** Diagram B refers to joint registrations (of a child's birth). What does this mean? What implications about a couple's relationship might this have?

**6** In April 1993, the government required single mothers (who were not divorced or widowed) to name the father of their child. If the mother fails to do this, the DSS reserves the right to hold back 20 per cent of her Income Support. What is your view on this? Does it punish the mother unfairly, or is it right that she should have to name the father? (Fewer than one in four lone mothers on Income Support receive any maintenance from the absent father.)

## State support for families with children

For the families of single parents and the low paid, the government has a number of policies to help combat poverty. These were discussed in chapter 2, but are listed again here.

### Child Benefit

This is a flat-rate payment for all families with children – its real value has declined over the last 30 years.

### Family Credit

Introduced in 1986, Family Credit provides financial support for people in low paid employment and who have dependent children.

### Income Support premiums

People with families can obtain additional income under the Income Support scheme in the form of Income Support premiums.

# Groups in poverty: the sick and disabled

## The extent of the problem

According to government statistics, there are 6.2 million adults (14 per cent of all adults) and 360 000 children (3 per cent of all children), who suffer from one or more disability.

### The incomes of the disabled

For people under pensionable age, the average income for an adult with a disability is 72 per cent of the average income for non-disabled people. Of all people with disabilities, 34 per cent are living in poverty. Many people with disabilities are unable to work, or are limited to particular kinds of employment, usually that which is low paid.

### The expenses of the disabled

A person with a disability not only has problems obtaining employment, but also has greater outgoings than a fully able person. Approximately 8 per cent of disabled people's incomes goes on expenses related to their disability.

### Increases in the numbers of those with disabilities

There have been significant increases in the number of people with disabilities. This is mainly as a result of people living longer and therefore being more prone to disabilities in old age, and also because improvements in medicine have led to higher rates of survival of younger people and infants with disabilities.

## Government support for people with disabilities

There are a number of government funded benefits and schemes for people with disabilities. These are listed below (please see also chapters 2 and 14).

### Income Support premiums
The Income Support scheme offers additional payments for those with disabilities – the extra amount depends on the severity of the disability.

### Independent Living Trust
Those with severe disabilities can apply to the Independent Living Trust, which is a government funded charity.

### Attendance Allowance
This is the benefit paid to those who can prove that they need to be looked after.

### Invalidity Benefit
This is tax free and consists of three components – invalidity pension, invalidity allowance and additional pension.

### Severe Disablement Allowance
Those who cannot claim Invalidity Benefit can apply for Severe Disablement Allowance.

### Disability Living Allowance
This is for those under 65 with very significant disabilities.

### Disability Working Allowance
This is for those of working age in employment who can use this benefit to top up their wage.

### Invalid Care Allowance
This is available for carers rather than for the person with disability.

# Groups in poverty: the elderly

## The extent of the problem

Approximately 18 per cent of the population is over retirement age, numbering approximately 11 million people. Women form over 65 per cent of the elderly. With the gradual raising of life expectancy, the numbers of elderly people in the population are likely to continue increasing until the end of the first decade of the twenty-first century.

### Incomes
The elderly are dependent on pensions for their income. State pensions are

pitched so low that anyone living only on them will automatically be in poverty. The State pension in 1990 was about 16.5 per cent of the average male weekly earnings. This means that elderly people are forced to live off their savings or apply for State assistance if they do not have an employment-based pension.

Poverty in old age is not something that happens to all pensioners – rather, the poverty reflects the divisions in employment, income and fringe benefits that exist throughout a person's employment. Those who are poor in old age are most likely to be the ones who have earned least in their lifetime. Therefore, the groups we looked at before – the low paid, the single-parent families, the disabled and the unemployed – are all likely to be poor in their old age.

## Government benefits for the elderly

The two main government funded benefits for the elderly are listed below.

### State Pensions

These have declined in real terms over the last 20 years. Before 1980, they were index-linked to rises in wages, but they are now linked to rises in the cost of living. As wages generally have risen faster than the cost of living, this is a commitment to stabilise pensions at a low level. (See the debate on relative and absolute poverty on pages 43–5).

### Tax concessions for private pension schemes

The Conservative government in 1986 introduced incentives for people to enter private pension schemes. Contributions to such schemes are deducted from a person's income before tax is assessed, so that less income tax is paid.

# Explaining the causes of poverty

There are two different types of explanation for the causes of poverty. The first group of explanations stresses the process of **dependency**, and the second type tends to stress the process of **exclusion**. We shall look at each in turn.

## The dependency approach

Explanations which centre on the concept of dependency stress that people who are poor are in that state because of some deficiency either in themselves or which is passed on in the group to which they belong in society. Such people have become dependent on the State, and have no desire to work or to cope with the problems of budgeting, as the bulk of the population has to do. This idea has considerable similarity to nineteenth-century views on poverty.

Within this overall approach to explaining the causes of poverty, we can distinguish three categories: the individual, the underclass and the culture of poverty.

### The individual

Here the stress is placed on the failure of the individual to achieve through his/her own efforts. People who are poor are lazy and should try harder.

The £58bn spent annually by the Department of Social Security to relieve or prevent poverty is being poured into a black hole and neither the Government nor the poverty lobby care how families spend the money, according to a report published today.

Dr Digby Anderson, director of the Social Affairs Unit, a right-wing research organisation, says that the efficient use of benefit to relieve poverty depends on how families spend the money.

In *The Unmentionable Face of Poverty in the Nineties—Domestic incompetence, improvidence and male irresponsibility in low income families*, Dr Anderson suggests that "domestic incompetent economy" has as much to do with hardship as low income.

He says the biggest weekly outlay is on food, accounting for a third of families' budgets. "However, there is little sign that most take much time and trouble to shop well or to cook well, although clearly they are not short of time.

"They buy expensive convenience foods, designed for people who do not have time; tinned pies, tinned hamburgers, tinned carrots, packets of shepherd's pie, ready prepared stuffing, soups, sauces, fish fingers . . .

"They do not buy breasts of lamb (75p each at the time of the study and yielding 1lb of lean meat) and bone, stuff and roll them or mince them."

Dr Anderson says poverty is prolonged or made worse by inadequate budgeting, inefficient spending on food, patterns of borrowing and the allocation of money between husband and wife.

**Source**: The *Independent*, 5 August 1991

**1** According to the author of this article, is social security money being spent sensibly? Why not?
**2** Whose fault is poverty?
**3** What form of policy do you think Dr Anderson would support to eradicate poverty?

. . . poverty is not a problem of the poor – a sad but inevitable consequence of misfortune, inadequacy or fecklessness. On the contrary, poverty can only be understood as a feature of society as a whole, disfiguring and diminishing the lives of some as a result of the way we organise our collective way of life . . .

The institutional injuries inflicted by punitive social security regulations, racist and sexist welfare legislation, or increasingly differentiated educational provision, deny large numbers of people their full social rights. . . . There are major costs imposed by the requirements made by a society increasingly organised around consumption and market values. . . .

Poverty does not make people a group apart from society so much as victims of the injustice and incivilities of the social order of which they are very much a part. . . .

**Source:** R. Lister, *The Exclusive Society* (CPAG, 1990)

**1** Which perspective(s) on poverty does this extract support?
**2** What implications for social policy would emerge if we accepted this argument?

### The underclass

This is a development of the explanation concerning the individual, but is more 'sociological' in orientation. The argument, which was first developed by an American writer, Charles Murray, centres on the existence of an 'underclass' of people are who lazy and who make no effort to work or look after themselves. They prefer to live off the State.

It is important to remember that the underclass refers only to those poor people who make no effort to help themselves. Murray accepts that there are poor people who are in this state through no 'fault' of their own. Nevertheless, the bulk of poverty is caused by those who do not make the effort to earn a living, and/or squander what they do have.

The underclass spawns illegitimate children without a care for tomorrow... Its able-bodied youths see no point in working and feel no compulsion either. They reject society while feeding off it, giving the cycle of deprivation a new spin.... No amount of income redistribution or social engineering can solve their problem.

**Source:** Editorial in *The Sunday Times*, 26 November 1989

For increasingly, low incomes are associated with behaviour such as irresponsible sexual habits and unstable family formation, lack of commitment to work... and failure to save or spend prudently.

**Source:** D. Anderson, *The Sunday Times*, 29 July 1990

## A CRITICISM OF THE IDEA OF THE UNDERCLASS

The existence, even the creation, of a group identified as the poor serves to set them apart from the rest of the population. The result is not just . . . that the working class is divided and thereby weakened. Rather, the use of the poor as a reference group persuades those sections of society (which are neither wealthy nor poor) that their lot in terms of status, resources and power is acceptable. Consequently, the possibility that they will strive to change the position of the elite is reduced. Further, they (the poor) act as a warning. They demonstrate the fate of those who do not conform to prevailing work and social standards. Their plight is needed to reinforce the will of others to work for low returns in unpleasant and even degrading conditions from which the economic output gives a disproprotionate financial reward to a minority of existing resource holders. Not least, those in poverty act as scapegoats, a vulnerable group on whom the blame for social problems can be placed, so diverting attention away from that minority which has some control over social affairs.

**Source:** R. Holman, 'Another model of poverty' in E. Butterworth and R. Holman, *Social Welfare in Modern Britain*, 1975, p. 411

**1** What purposes does poverty serve? Who benefits from this? Is it the fault of the poor?
**2** Which approach to the cause of poverty does this represent?
**3** What would be the solution to poverty according to this approach?

### The culture of poverty

This approach stresses that the way people act is the result of how they are brought up by their family. It differs from the underclass explanation because it does not see poverty as a fault of the person, rather individuals are brought up in such a way that they never have a chance to escape the poverty of their parents.

Cultures develop to give people a guide as to how they should behave. In different societies people behave differently because they learn from different cultures. Usually a particular culture develops because it enables people to cope with their surroundings. Cultures are always changing, but the broad outlines are passed on from one generation to another by parents and those who influence people when they are young.

The culture of poverty argument was first developed by Oscar Lewis when he studied very poor people in Central America. The values and behaviour (in other words, the culture) of these poor people was significantly different from the majority of the population. Lewis argued that this was because these particular values enabled the very poor to cope with circumstances which would otherwise lead to despair and hopelessness.

A development from the culture of poverty argument is the claim that a **cycle of poverty**, or a cycle of transmitted deprivation, exists. This idea was developed by a former Secretary of State for Health and Social Services, Sir Keith Joseph. His view of transmission, however, ignored the way in which the culture of poverty was supposedly a response to intense deprivation and a certainty that the person had no future. Instead it concentrated on the way in which some poor people failed to help and support their children.

## A CULTURE OF HOPELESSNESS AND DESPAIR

The culture of poverty is both an adaptation and a reaction of the poor to their marginal position in a class-stratified society. It represents an effort to cope with feelings of hopelessness and despair which develop from the realisation of the improbability of achieving success in terms of the values and goals of the larger society....

On the level of the individual, the major characteristics are a strong feeling of marginality, of helplessness, of dependency and of inferiority.... Other traits include a high incidence of maternal deprivation, of orality, of weak ego structure, confusion of sexual identification, a lack of impulse control, a strong present-time orientation with relatively little ability to defer gratification and to plan for the future, a sense of resignation and fatalism, a widespread belief in male superiority, and a high tolerance for psychological pathology of all sorts.

**Source:** O. Lewis, *La Vida* (Random House, New York, 1969)

## A CYCLE OF POVERTY?

The Economic and Social Research Council commissioned a review of evidence about transmission of deprivation. Cycles of Deprivation – the review by Rutter and Madge – concentrates upon longitudinal studies like the National Child Development Study, which follow the progress of a cohort of individuals, gathering information about them and their circumstances at regular intervals.... 'With respect to intelligence, educational achievement, occupational status, crime, psychiatric disorder and problem family status there are moderate continuities over two generations'... yet 'Over half of all forms of disadvantage arise anew each generation'.

... At least half of the children born into a disadvantaged home do not repeat the pattern of disadvantage in the next generation....

**Source**: M. Banton, 'The Culture of Poverty', *The Social Studies Review*, January 1990

Look at the first extract.
1 In what circumstances does the culture of poverty arise?
2 Go through each of the traits of the culture of poverty. Explain each term.
3 The culture of poverty, or variations of it, has been very influential in social policy, especially in the USA. Do you find these traits convincing? Would you argue, however, that people who are poor (some/all/a majority?) hold different values from the rest of society?
Look at the second extract.
4 Does this support or undermine the culture of poverty thesis?

# The exclusion approach

The second set of explanations for poverty are based on the idea of exclusion – meaning that the poor are in that situation because they are squeezed out of a decent standard of living by the actions of others. Another term for this process is a process of **marginalisation**.

This approach stresses differences in power between the various groups in society. Those who lose out – the disabled, the elderly, women, the ethnic minorities and, of course, children – have significantly higher chances of living in poverty.

Within this explanation we can distinguish two approaches: the **dyswelfare** view and the **economic system** approach.

### The dyswelfare view

Dyswelfare refers to the process in which some people lose out in complex industrial societies through no fault of their own. They are the casualties of industrial and social change. The 'victims' of dyswelfare include the physically and mentally disabled, single parents, and so on. The points to emphasise here are that their poverty is blameless and is the result of changes in the nature of society. Secondly, a society does not deliberately discriminate against any group (compare this view with the following **power** approach), but it is inevitable that some people will lose out in any form of society.

It was this explanation for poverty that largely underlay the foundation of the Welfare State.

### The economic system approach

The final and most radical explanation for the continuation of poverty comes from those who argue that society is a competition between various groups. Some groups have considerably more power than others and are able to impose their will on the rest of society. Power and wealth generally go together, as do poverty and powerlessness. The groups in poverty are largely formed from the powerless, in particular women, children and the ethnic minorities. Low pay and poor State benefits result from the view that to pay more would be harmful to the interests of those who are more affluent.

This approach contrasts with the dyswelfare explanation, because it says that poverty is the direct result of the intended development of modern Western society.

## The poverty trap

The poverty trap occurs in situations such as the following. A person (or family) receives a number of means-tested benefits from the State when they are unable to obtain work. If the person then finds employment, the gains in income from that employment may well be lost, because the Department of Social Security withdraws some or all of the means-tested benefits. The person (or family) is no better off in employment, and may even be poorer than when they were living only on State benefits.

**The poverty trap**

# Poverty: the centre of a web of deprivation

**Deprivation**
Living in poverty means going without necessities. Those in poverty spend half the national average on food, and 75 per cent lack two or more necessary items of clothing. More than 50 per cent have less heating than they want.

**Lack of leisure**
There is no money for leisure or social activities – 85 per cent of free time is spent inside the home, as 'normal' social activities are too expensive.

**Negative effects on children**
Children brought up in poor homes are less likely to go out, to have presents and 'treats', or to have holidays. They are more likely to lack clothes.

**Stigma and lack of status**
Being poor usually means having little or no status in society, and having the stigma of taking 'handouts' from the State.

**Stress**
The constant struggle to make ends meet leads to disputes between family members and can affect health. Women in particular are stressed through having to cope with the budgeting.

**POVERTY**

**Poor housing conditions**
Those in poverty are likely to fall behind with rent or mortgage payments. They are likely to live in the worst housing conditions in damp, overcrowded, insanitary buildings. In the extreme, they are likely to become homeless, and have to be accommodated in bed and breakfast.

**Debt**
This is an increasing problem in the UK. The government itself helps create a problem of debt through its policy of the Social Fund. In 1990, there were almost 400 000 people repaying Social Fund loans.
If people are unable to cope with the ordinary budgeting on their incomes, then they are forced into debt, which magnifies the problem. In 1990, over 20 000 households had their electricity disconnected.
One in seven single parents are in 'severe' debt.

**Extra costs**
Supermarkets which offer the best choice/cheapest prices are increasingly moving to out-of-town locations, which require cars to shop there. Small corner-shops tend to have higher prices. Also, bulk purchase is considerably cheaper, but the initial costs are too great for the poor and the quantities too great for pensioners.

**Neighbourhood**
The poorest groups live in the most deprived areas with fewer GPs per 1000 people than most areas, the worst schools, problems of crime, etc. However, we should remember that it is not just inner cities that have high levels of poverty, some of the worst poverty is in the countryside.

**Ill health**
There is a direct relationship between deprivation and ill health. This is caused by inadequate nutrition, poor housing conditions and lack of warmth, plus the effects of stress.

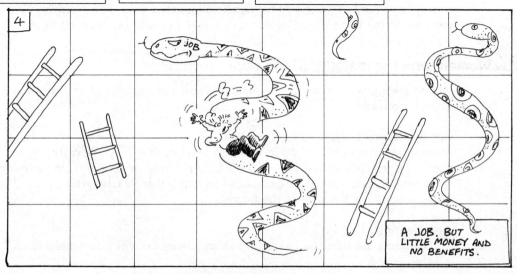

A JOB, BUT LITTLE MONEY AND NO BENEFITS.

# Race and poverty

Afro-Caribbeans and Asians have substantially higher rates of unemployment – almost twice that of White people. This holds true even if a Black or Asian person has the same educational qualifications as a White person.

Afro-Caribbeans and Asians are more likely to earn lower wages than White people, and to be employed in the lower paying sectors of the economy (although Afro-Caribbean women earn more on average than White women).

There is evidence of discriminatory practice in the provision of welfare benefits. For example, it is becoming normal practice to request passports from Black and Asian claimants.

Every indicator of poverty shows that black people and other ethnic minority groups are more at risk of high unemployment, low pay, shift work, and poor social security rights. Their poverty is caused by immigration policies which have often excluded people from abroad from access to welfare, employment patterns which have marginalised black people and other ethnic minority groups into low-paid manual work, direct and indirect discrimination in social security and the broader experience of racism in society as a whole.

**Source**: R. Skellington and P. Morris, *Race in Britain Today* (Sage, 1992)

# Women and poverty

The majority of the poor in Britain are women. In fact there are approximately 4.5 million women in poverty today. Earlier we categorised the poor in Britain into the following groups: the unemployed, the low paid (71 per cent), single parents (96 per cent), the sick and disabled and the elderly. Each one of these groups is dominated by women, except perhaps the unemployed (and there is a fierce debate about that too!). For example, 71 per cent of the low paid are women, as are 90 per cent of single parents.

## Why women form the majority of the poor

The following reasons as to why women form the majority of the poor have been suggested.

### Family responsibilities

Women are more likely to be in low paid jobs because they are restricted by family responsibilities (whether married, co-habiting or single) from pursuing a career. It is generally regarded as the woman's role to take primary responsibility for the care of the family.

### Childbearing

Childbearing disrupts the continuity of employment, which is necessary to gain promotion.

### Ineligibility for non-means-tested benefits

The disruption of a woman's working life caused by childbearing and family responsibility also prevents her from building up enough contributions for non-means-tested benefits. This means that when she needs State assistance she almost always has to turn to Income Support. In 1990, 96 per cent of single parents on Income Support were women, and over three times as many women over pensionable age were receiving Income Support compared to men.

### Caring

Women are expected to care not only for their children, but also for the elderly and for disabled partners or relatives. There are almost 4 million women 'carers' in Britain today, of whom about half spend more than 50 hours a week in unpaid caring.

Within the two-parent family, it is usually the woman who goes without if there is any shortage. So although the family may not be poor, the woman often is.

# Assignment

You are employed as researchers by a county council. The council wish to find out the extent of poverty in the county, but are unsure how to go about the task. As a starting point, there appears to be considerable disagreement over the definition of poverty. You must draft a short briefing paper to be presented to the relevant council sub-committee, explaining the best way of defining and measuring poverty in the area. Secondly, you must outline the possible actions the council could realistically take to combat poverty in their area.

### FINDINGS FROM THE SOCIAL SURVEY ON BRITISH ATTITUDES (PAGE 42)

The following figures represent the percentage of people who responded positively to each statement as their preferred definition of poverty.

| Statement 1 | 95% |
|---|---|
| Statement 2 | 55% |
| Statement 3 | 25% |

### RESULTS OF MACK AND LANSLEY'S RESEARCH (PAGE 46)

| Standard-of-living items in rank order | % classing items as necessity | Standard-of-living items in rank order | % classing items as necessity |
|---|---|---|---|
| 1. Heating to warm living areas of the home if it's cold | 97 | 18. New, not second-hand clothes | 64 |
| | | 19. A hobby or leisure activity | 64 |
| 2. Indoor toilet (not shared with another household) | 96 | 20. Two hot meals a day (for adults) | 64 |
| 3. Damp-free home | 96 | 21. Meat or fish every other day | 63 |
| 4. Bath (not shared with another) household) | 94 | 22. Presents for friends or family once a year | 63 |
| 5. Beds for everyone in the household | 94 | 23. A holiday away from home for one week a year, not with relatives | 63 |
| 6. Public transport for one's needs | 88 | 24. Leisure equipment for children e.g. sports equipment or a bicycle[a] | 57 |
| 7. A warm water-proof coat | 87 | 25. A garden | 55 |
| 8. Three meals a day for children[a] | 82 | 26. A television | 51 |
| 9. Self-contained accommodation | 79 | 27. A 'best outfit' for special occasions | 48 |
| 10. Two pairs of all-weather shoes | 78 | 28. A telephone | 43 |
| 11. Enough bedrooms for every child over 10 of different sex to have his/her own[a] | 77 | 29. An outing for children once a week[a] | 40 |
| | | 30. A dressing gown | 38 |
| 12. Refrigerator | 77 | 31. Children's friends round for tea/a snack once a fortnight[a] | 37 |
| 13. Toys for children[a] | 71 | 32. A night out once a fortnight (adults) | 36 |
| 14. Carpets in living rooms and bedrooms | 70 | 33. Friends/family round for a meal once a month | 32 |
| 15. Celebrations on special occasions such as Christmas | 69 | 32. A car | 22 |
| 16. A roast meat joint or its equivalent once a week | 67 | 35. A packet of cigarettes every other day | 14 |
| 17. A washing-machine | 67 | | |

Average of all 35 items = 64.1
[a]For families with children only

**Source**: J. Mack and S. Lansley, *Poor Britain* (Allen & Unwin, 1985)

# CHAPTER 4

# Housing

## Introduction

Housing was one of the central elements in the original idea of the Welfare State when it was first envisaged by Beveridge. The provision of good quality, low rent, local government accommodation was certainly as important as a National Health Service in the original plans for a Welfare State. This chapter explores housing as a social issue, illustrating its relationship to the health and welfare services.

We begin the chapter by focusing on changes in housing policy, first looking briefly at the historical background and then examining in more detail the policy changes since 1979. The date 1979 is significant as it is the year of the election of the Conservative Party into government. The policies which the Conservative government has introduced since 1979 are in striking contrast to those of the period immediately after the introduction of the Welfare State. Probably the most important changes during the period since 1979 have been the decline in local authority housing and its partial replacement by housing associations and, secondly, the growth of home ownership.

Recognising that housing is a key element of the Welfare State, the next section of the chapter looks at the importance of housing to people, and at the relationship of housing to other social issues, such as poverty and ill health.

The greatest contemporary problem regarding housing is the fact that there is not enough of it available at prices which the lower paid sections of the population can afford – either to buy or to rent. So, in the next part of the chapter, we move on to look at homelessness, analysing its causes, measuring the numbers of people without adequate housing, and discussing the government's response to this problem.

Although local authorities have lost much of their powers to provide, maintain and administer housing, they are still legally obliged to find housing for certain priority groups, and they are still the main agencies running housing estates. We therefore have a look at the role and activities of local authorities in housing.

After a brief look at the State benefits available to those renting property, and the more generous benefits for people purchasing their own homes, the chapter ends with an examination of the issues surrounding gender and race in the context of housing.

# Historical background

In the nineteenth century, inadequate housing and town planning had been clearly linked on the one hand to poverty and, on the other, to such things as poor health and other social problems. So, from about 1840 onwards, numerous charitable organisations began to set up housing schemes to try to provide better housing conditions for the working class. Schemes such as those known as 'philanthropy at 5 per cent' (referring to the rate of interest investors would receive for lending money to the charitable housing associations) had some success.

However, without government involvement, there was little possibility of seriously tackling the problems of homelessness, overcrowding and sub-standard housing, which were rife. Although an Act in 1866 allowed charities to borrow money cheaply from the government for the construction of new houses for the poor, it was not until the early part of the twentieth century that local government became involved in a serious way in providing houses for the poor. By the 1930s, an average of 50 000 homes were built each year for local authorities to rent out.

After the Beveridge Report (1942) and the end of the Second World War, there was general agreement that everyone had a right to a home, as well as to free health care and decent employment. Both Conservative and Labour governments supported large programmes of local authority rented housing, while also encouraging home ownership through the use of tax relief on mortgages.

By the 1960s, however, local authorities were recognising that they were unable to keep up with the demand for housing and were looking at cheaper ways of providing accommodation for those with lower incomes. The result was the developments of high-rise flats in all the major British cities, even though it emerged later that these flats could actually cost up to 70 per cent more than the low-rise buildings!

By the end of the 1970s, with the British economy entering a period of stagnation, it became apparent that the traditional mix of public and private housing was not going to satisfy the demand for housing, and more radical approaches were needed.

# Housing policy since 1979

## Legislation

- **Housing Act 1980**: introduced the right for council house tenants to buy their own homes. The Act took away some rights of tenants renting from private landlords
- **Social Security and Housing Benefit Act 1982**: introduced Housing Benefit payable by the local authority rather than by social security
- **Housing and Planning Act 1986**: made the purchase of council property easier
- **Housing Act 1988**: ended the control of the privately rented sector with a resulting loss of security for tenants and increases in rents. Possibility of transfer of entire council estates to private interests or to housing associations. Creation of Housing Action Trusts (HATs) to take over and improve run-down council estates

- **Local Government and Housing Act 1990**: prevents local authorities from subsidising the rents of their tenants. Controls placed on the income from sales of council housing under the **'right to buy' scheme**.

## An overview

Since the 1930s, there had been a broad agreement between all political parties on the importance of maintaining a balance between local authority housing programmes and private house building. This was broken in 1979 when the Conservative government decided that local authority provision of housing was wrong. The emphasis shifted to encourage the growth of housing association rented accommodation for those who could not afford to buy, while for the majority of the population the chance to own a home was, and still is, strongly encouraged.

Home ownership has now increased to about 65 per cent of the population, through a combination of subsidised sales of council properties to tenants and the encouragement of the private sector to build new houses for sale. With the rapid increase in prices up until the end of the 1980s, the real cost of mortgage interest rate relief (MIRAS) increased too. Government policy now makes local authority tenants pay for the full amount of the costs of housing in their rents, yet central government subsidises house buyers through MIRAS. It is quite possible for council house tenants to be subsidising owner occupiers through taxation. The role of the local authorities is undermined as the government prefers to encourage voluntary **housing associations** to provide cheaper accommodation for rent and for the various groups with special needs.

## Local authority housing

In the period since 1979, there has been a great decline in council properties, both in the numbers being constructed and in the numbers available for rent. The government's dislike of local authority housing led them to introduce the 'right to buy' scheme in 1980, which allowed tenants living in a property for three years or more the right to buy that property at discounts on the market value of between 30 and 50 per cent. During the 1980s over 1.1 million flats and houses were bought under this scheme. Most of the properties bought were the better quality ones, meaning that increasingly council stocks are of poorer quality. It also means that the supply of council housing available for rent has effectively disappeared.

### Why the government objected to local authority provision of housing

- Firstly, because of an ideological 'belief in the market': the Conservative government of the 1980s believed that housing was best left to 'the market', in other words to a system known as *laissez-faire*. Under this principle, the best way of rationing things is to see how much people are prepared to pay. The government believes that local authorities drive out private landlords, and dissuade people from saving their money and eventually buying their own house.
- Secondly, the government believes that people should look after themselves, 'stand on their own two feet', and not rely on the State to provide things.
- Thirdly, the government argued that bureaucracies are unresponsive to the real needs of people. Rather than serving people, they are intent on looking after themselves. Local authority housing departments are good examples of bureaucracies, according to some Conservatives.

## SALES OF LOCAL AUTHORITY DWELLINGS

### Sales of dwellings owned by local authorities and new towns[1]

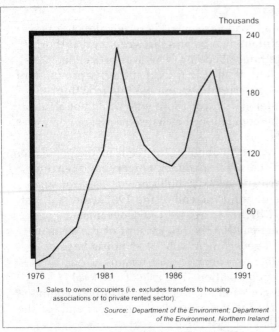

1. Sales to owner occupiers (i.e. excludes transfers to housing associations or to private rented sector).

*Source: Department of the Environment; Department of the Environment, Northern Ireland*

**Source:** *Social Trends* (HMSO, 1993)

Look at the graph.

1 Why did people start to buy their own council housing after 1979?

2 Why was there a peak in 1982/3, and another in 1988?

3 What total of council house sales has taken place?

4 What has happened since 1989?

## Housing associations

In order to limit the role of local authorities in providing and running housing, the government increasingly switched its funding to housing associations, which are voluntary organisations set up for the purpose of providing cheap housing for rent. There are about 2600 housing associations in England and Wales, with a stock of over 600 000 houses and flats, representing about 3 per cent of all dwellings. In 1989, the government invested about £1 million in housing associations through the funding body **The Housing Corporation** – more than was given to local authorities.

The government only funds 75 per cent of housing association projects, which means that significant amounts of money must be obtained commercially, and this in turn is reflected in relatively high rents. This is a major problem, particularly as a survey of housing association tenants showed that 98 per cent have lower than average incomes, and 66 per cent receive State benefits.

## Housing Action Trusts

In 1988, Housing Action Trusts, or HATs, were introduced. These were housing estates (nine in all) designated by the government as having special problems. They were to vote on 'opting out' of council control and having significant amounts of money spent on improving them. At the time of writing, only one ballot resulted in a HAT being formed.

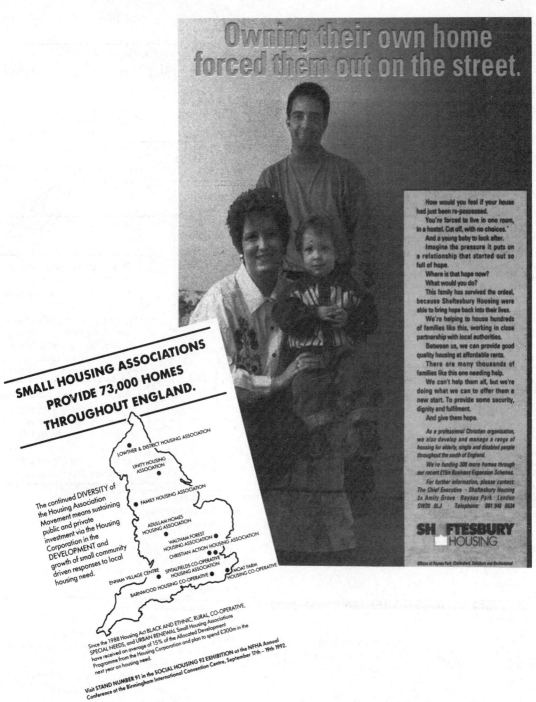

Source: National Federation of Housing Associations

1 For whom do housing associations provide accommodation?
2 In what ways are they different from local authority housing departments?
3 Find the reference to the 'Housing Corporation'. What is this and what role does it play in housing?

# Tenure

'Tenure' is the term used to describe the relationship between a person living in a property and the ownership of the property.

## Types of tenure

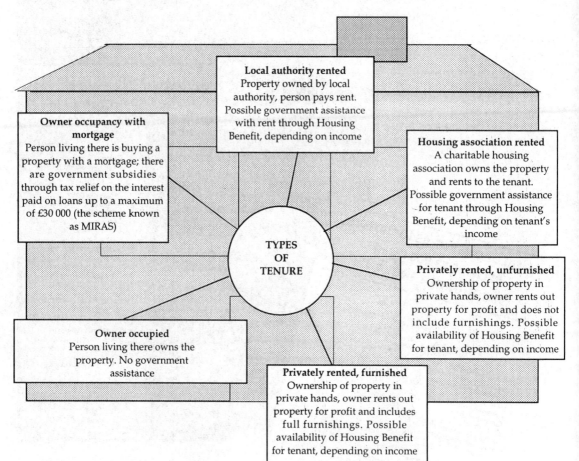

**Local authority rented**
Property owned by local authority, person pays rent. Possible government assistance with rent through Housing Benefit, depending on income

**Owner occupancy with mortgage**
Person living there is buying a property with a mortgage; there are government subsidies through tax relief on the interest paid on loans up to a maximum of £30 000 (the scheme known as MIRAS)

**Housing association rented**
A charitable housing association owns the property and rents to the tenant. Possible government assistance for tenant through Housing Benefit, depending on tenant's income

**TYPES OF TENURE**

**Privately rented, unfurnished**
Ownership of property in private hands, owner rents out property for profit and does not include furnishings. Possible availability of Housing Benefit for tenant, depending on income

**Owner occupied**
Person living there owns the property. No government assistance

**Privately rented, furnished**
Ownership of property in private hands, owner rents out property for profit and includes full furnishings. Possible availability of Housing Benefit for tenant, depending on income

## CHANGES IN HOUSING TENURE, 1900–2000

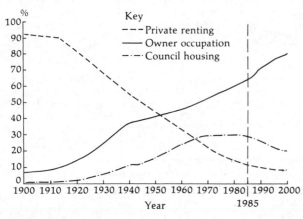

Key
--- Private renting
— Owner occupation
—·— Council housing

1 Summarise the changes in forms of tenure over the period shown in the graph.
2 At what date did private renting fall below owner occupation?
3 At what date did private renting fall below council housing?
4 What percentage of households were in owner occupation in 1900?
5 How does this compare with 1990?

**TENURE BY SOCIAL GROUP**

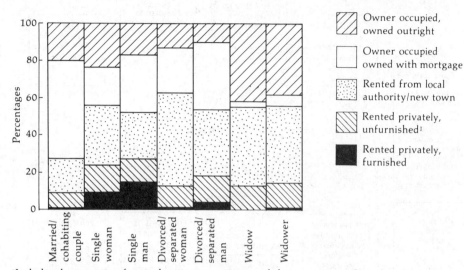

Tenure: by marital status and sex of head of household, 1987, Great Britain

*Owner occupied, owned outright*

*Owner occupied owned with mortgage*

*Rented from local authority/new town*

*Rented privately, unfurnished¹*

*Rented privately, furnished*

¹Includes those renting from a housing association and those renting with a job or business

**Source**: Redrawn from *Social Trends* (HMSO, 1993)

1 What types of tenure does this graph distinguish? Which one is missing?
2 Which social group has the highest levels of owner occupancy? Why do you think this is?
3 Is there any difference in the tenure patterns of divorced men and divorced women?
4 Which is the least common form of tenure? Which groups are most likely to be in it? Can you suggest any reasons why?
5 This final type of tenure has been in decline. What implications, if any, might this have (a) for homelessness and (b) for the types of people who might end up homeless?

# Housing as a social issue

Housing is a critical source of material and emotional comfort, protection and health. Both the quality and quantity of life are connected with accommodation (see below).

Where somebody lives also plays a major role in determining access to a wide range of other goods and services – such as health care, education, transport, leisure facilities and retail outlets.

Furthermore, the home and its immediate environment are very widely regarded as a source of personal identity, of self-expression and social status. This is reflected in high levels of expenditure on items such as furnishings, fittings, decor, gardening and the like.

For the young, acquiring a home of one's own is an important step in attaining adult status; for the old, losing it is often experienced as a painful erosion of social standing and independence.

The home both reflects and shapes gender divisions. It has also been argued that political support is influenced by housing. Thus a property-owning democracy is sometimes said to be more likely to vote for political parties of the right (such as the Conservatives).

For most people, housing represents the single most expensive thing purchased over a lifetime. For some, this means that housing becomes a valuable asset . . . for others it represents a major drain on their financial resources.

Location in the housing market is closely connected with location on the labour market.

**Source**: Adapted from N. Jewson, 'No place like home', *Social Studies Review*, March 1989

## The importance of housing

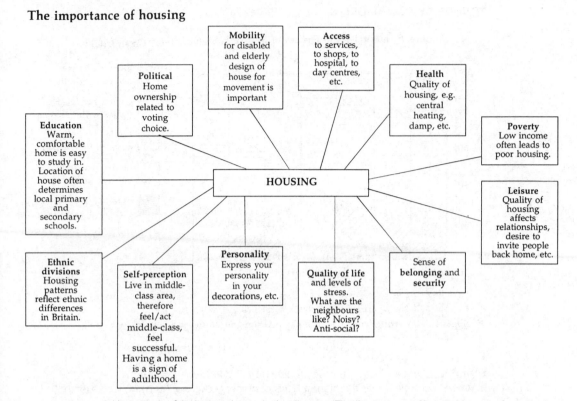

Political
Home ownership related to voting choice.

Mobility
for disabled and elderly design of house for movement is important

Access
to services, to shops, to hospital, to day centres, etc.

Health
Quality of housing, e.g. central heating, damp, etc.

Education
Warm, comfortable home is easy to study in. Location of house often determines local primary and secondary schools.

Poverty
Low income often leads to poor housing.

HOUSING

Leisure
Quality of housing affects relationships, desire to invite people back home, etc.

Ethnic divisions
Housing patterns reflect ethnic differences in Britain.

Self-perception
Live in middle-class area, therefore feel/act middle-class, feel successful. Having a home is a sign of adulthood.

Personality
Express your personality in your decorations, etc.

Quality of life
and levels of stress. What are the neighbours like? Noisy? Anti-social?

Sense of belonging and security

1  How many of the points shown in the diagram 'The importance of housing' can be found in the extract on page 75?

2  Are there any other points you can find showing why housing is so important as a social issue?

3  What does the author of the extract mean when he says that the home 'reflects and shapes gender divisions'?

4  Explain why certain groups in society find housing a 'major drain on their financial resources'. If this is the case, what possible consequences can come from this?

5  The Conservative Party has followed a policy of encouraging people to buy homes, rather than rent them; it has also prevented local authorities providing council accommodation. Explain what political benefits emerge from this.

## Housing, health and poverty

Numerous studies have indicated the close link between poor housing conditions and premature death or chronic illness. Damp, infested homes cause ill health and, of course, as it is usually the poor who live in bad housing, they are already disadvantaged by inadequate heating, poor diets and general deprivation.

### HEALTH AND HOUSING

#### A bad start in life

Eighteen-month-old Michelle lives with her parents in a late Victorian brick-built terraced house.

She was a healthy baby despite the privately-rented house being very damp and in chronic disrepair.

But a year ago the ancient coal-fired heating system broke down and began leaking dangerous fumes. Despite repeated attempts, the parents could not persuade the landlord to repair it.

They were left with a choice – suffer the poisonous fumes or turn the heating off completely in the middle of winter. They decided to turn the heating off but by that time Michelle had developed severe respiratory problems and she has little chance of making a full recovery while living in such a cold, damp environment.

### Mental health

The mental health of children and their parents is so often closely intertwined.

Children are sensitive to the moods of their carers and a child exposed to a parent depressed about their living conditions will undoubtedly be affected.

A depressed mother who is breast feeding may find her milk dries up; a parent out of work because of their problematic housing situation may become frustrated and take his or her aggression out on the children; a whole family living in one room are likely to affect each other's mental state, with no privacy, constant noise and no space for the children to play.

Respiratory infections are the most common cause of death in children between the ages of one and 14 years.

For many years, health professionals have argued whether damp really causes respiratory problems. It is generally accepted that asthma is often exacerbated by poor housing conditions. As with so many other illnesses, asthma may also be aggravated by the effects of stress caused by living in these same conditions.

Recent research from Edinburgh University, however, appears to confirm that children living in damp conditions are more likely to suffer respiratory problems such as persistent coughs, wheezes, runny noses and are more susceptible to infections causing fevers, sore throats and headaches. The housing studied had poor ventilation and heating, contributing to mould and damp.

This study is perhaps one of the most important in relating poor health to poor housing as, unlike many others, it has taken into account most other variables such as low income, overcrowding and smoking. However, it does support the findings of earlier research. Strachman found an association between respiratory problems reported by parents and damp, mouldy housing…

Other studies make similar findings as well as showing the effects of living in certain urban environments. Freeman demonstrated links between living in highrise flats or on run-down estates with some psychiatric conditions. A North Manchester Health Authority report supports these findings showing that the mental health of adults improves when they move out of tower blocks.

More recent research from Edinburgh University shows that children living in environments internally polluted by damp and mould are more likely to experience poor educational and intellectual performance as well as suffering more emotional distress.

**Source** (both extracts): Adapted from Annette Furley, *A Bad Start in Life – Children, Health and Housing* (Shelter, 1989)

1 What are the most common causes of death for children up to 14 years of age?
2 In what way(s) can this be linked to housing?
3 According to the extract 'Mental health', however, is poor housing the **root cause** of the illness mentioned? Explain your answer.
4 Explain the relationship between mental health and housing.

# Homelessness

## What is homelessness?

1 Would you consider a person homeless if their present accommodation had any of the following characteristics?
- overcrowded – for example a married couple living with one of the partner's parents;
- dangerous – a house in such poor condition that an accident may occur;

- damp – for example with mould growing on the walls;
- lacking basic amenities – for example, sharing a kitchen or bathroom with other families;
- insecure – a person is unsure how long he/she may stay in the accommodation, for example a squat or an 'informal' tenancy (such as renting a room from someone who is trying to pay their mortgage off).

2 If you had to make a list of priority for housing from the people below, in what order would you place them? Rank them individually first, then bring your ranking to the group you are working with and try to arrive at a consensus of opinion.

- An elderly single person
- A pregnant woman
- A 19-year-old male with a criminal record
- A young couple with young children who have had an argument with the husband's parents with whom they have been living
- A young couple with children who live in a damp, vermin-infested house
- A mentally ill middle-aged man who prefers 'sleeping rough'
- A married woman who has left her husband and children
- A married man who has left his wife and children
- A disabled woman of 25, on Income Support, who no longer wishes to live with her parents, although they are quite happy for her to remain
- A family newly arrived from Sri Lanka who are seeking a better life away from violence there
- A Bangladeshi family who have lived in Britain for 12 years, but are being harassed by neighbours in a block of flats
- A student who claims to have been sexually assaulted by her landlord on frequent occasions (but has no proof)

## Homelessness – a definition

Until 1977, the definition of homelessness used by the government was of families that had been placed in temporary accommodation by the 'welfare authorities'. The local authorities were not obliged to place people in temporary accommodation, and more people were turned away than accepted. In 1966, 2518 families had been provided with such accommodation by local authorities.

In 1977, following immense pressure, the Housing (Homeless Persons) Act was passed. This provided a wider definition of homelessness and imposed on local authorities the legal obligation to provide accommodation for certain 'priority' groups and to provide 'advice and assistance' for other groups.

A person is homeless if they have no legal right to housing, or if threats of violence prevent them from exercising that right. Accommodation may be unfit for human habitation, or severely overcrowded, even dangerous to health, but these are not grounds for homelessness. So, quality of housing is irrelevant.

Those in 'priority need', for whom councils must provide accommodation, include people with families; single, pregnant women; the disabled; and the elderly. One important point is that a person's homelessness must not be intentional. It must occur through *no intentional action* of a person. If the homelessness is intentional, then the local authority has no legal duty to rehouse that person.

In 1991, 162 000 'households' were homeless (according to the official definition), involving about 480 000 people. However, by using an alternative definition, which includes all the characteristics we considered at the beginning of this section, plus young people who have left home for a vast variety of personal reasons, Shelter (a housing pressure group) estimated that the real extent of homelessness in Britain is over three million people.

The gap between the official statistics and the number of people who believe they are homeless is shown in the diagrams below. You can see that of the total of 344 000 enquiries in England and Wales in 1991, 160 000 were found to be 'in priority need'. Clearly there is a distinction between those who believe they are homeless and the official definition of homelessness.

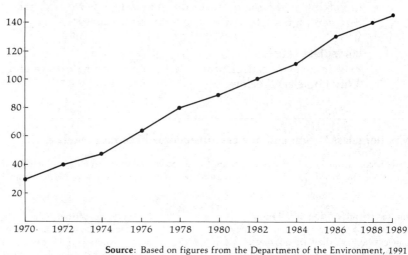

**Households accepted as homeless by local authorities, Britain 1970–89**

Source: Based on figures from the Department of the Environment, 1991

**1** Has homelessness decreased or increased since 1970?

**2** What happened in 1977 to change the way in which homelessness was defined and counted (see page 78)?

**3** Approximately, what was the number of (officially) homeless households in 1989?

## Local authority enquiries under the homelessness legislation: by outcome

| Great Britain | | | Thousands |
|---|---|---|---|
| | 1986 | 1990 | 1991 |
| **Households applying as homeless** | | | |
| Accepted | | | |
| - in priority need | 109 | 151 | 160 |
| - not in priority need | 10 | 14 | 9 |
| Intentionally homeless | 3 | 5 | 6 |
| Given advice and assistance only | 59 | 86 | 81 |
| Found not to be homeless | 68 | 83 | 88 |
| Total enquiries | 249 | 339 | 344 |

## Homeless households in temporary accommodation[1,2]: by type of accommodation

| Great Britain | | | Thousands |
|---|---|---|---|
| | 1986 | 1990 | 1991 |
| Bed and breakfast | 9 | 12 | 13 |
| Hostels, including women's refuges | 5 | 10 | 12 |
| Short life tenancies and and other accommodation | 8 | 27 | 40 |
| Total in temporary accommodation | 23 | 48 | 64 |

1 At end of year.
2 Includes households awaiting outcome of homelessness enquiries.

Source: Department of the Environment; Welsh Office; The Scottish Office

**Source** (both tables): *Social Trends* (HMSO, 1993)

**1** Were all the people who claimed to be homeless ('enquiries') accepted?

**2** What is the difference between those accepted and those claiming to be homeless?

**3** Why are some groups given 'advice and assistance only' and other groups accepted even though they are 'not in priority need'?

**4** Why are people, do you think, put into temporary accommodation, and why is the figure increasing each year?

**5** If you cannot answer questions 3 and 4, then call or telephone your local authority Housing department and ask them!

### Young single people

Although not regarded officially as a priority, one of the biggest problems of homelessness today faces young single people. It is estimated that there are 150 000 homeless young people in Britain today.

## Causes of homelessness

In looking at the main causes of homelessness, we can make a distinction between **immediate** causes and **structural** causes.

### Immediate causes

Four immediate causes of people becoming homeless are shown in the chart 'Why homeless?' below.

---

**Why homeless?   Some of the reasons people become homeless**

People become homeless because they cannot find accommodation which is suitable for them, and which they can afford. There are many reasons which explain how people become homeless.

**Families/friends falling out: 43%**
Many young people in particular become homeless because they are no longer able or willing to live with their parents. Some people have to leave their homes because they find they are unable to share accommodation with friends.

**Partners separating: 17%**
The second most common cause of homelessness is the break down of marriages or relationships. When a couple splits up, one or both partners are often left with no home.

**Landlord problems: 12%**
About one in eight people who become homeless do so because they are forced to leave their privately rented homes. Landlords have the power to evict tenants after their agreed tenancy period has finished.

**Cannot pay mortgage: 6%**
The fastest-growing group of homeless people comprises those who have lost homes which they owned themselves. Owner-occupiers are vulnerable because of high interest rates, which have pushed up their mortgage repayments. In 1991 more than 75 000 properties were repossessed because their owners fell behind with their mortgages.

**Source**: Redrawn from the *Guardian*, 1990

---

### Structural causes

The immediate causes we looked at above are the ones you will find in most publications. However, they focus on the specific problems of the individuals and seem to suggest that it is the fault of the individual or their family or landlord that has led to the situation of homelessness.

An alternative way of explaining homelessness is to put the immediate causes within a wider context. For example, why is it that people cannot afford to repay their mortgage? One explanation is that they must have made a miscalculation over how much they could afford, and now have to suffer the consequences. An alternative explanation is that it has been government policy since 1979 to encourage as many people as possible to buy their own homes, including those on low incomes. It was also government policy in the early 1990s to raise interest rates. Those who had bought under government encouragement were then trapped with much higher repayments.

## A STRUCTURAL EXPLANATION

But Professor John Greve, a specialist in housing policy at York University, says the rise in the numbers of homeless people, especially among under-25s, is largely a *result* of the Government's housing policies.

Professor Greve says: "The Government took the view that housing could be left to the open market and encouraged people to buy their own homes. More than one million council homes have been sold since 1981—which has left far fewer cheap homes for people on low incomes to rent."

Last November the Government an-nounced it was spending an extra £1bn on housing over two years. Most of that money will go to housing associations—bodies run as charities or voluntary organisations which provide cheap homes to rent. About £250 million will be spent in London, to help people who sleep rough on the streets.

But, at the same time, spending on building council houses has been sharply cut. Government spending on all public housing has fallen by almost three-quarters since 1979.

**Source**: The *Guardian*, 1990

## CHANGES IN HOMELESSNESS OVER TIME

### Homeless households[1] found accommodation by local authorities: by reason[2] for homelessness, 1981 and 1991

*Great Britain*

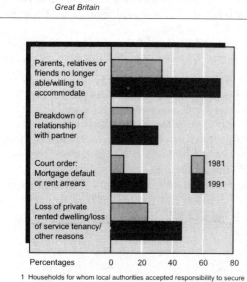

Parents, relatives or friends no longer able/willing to accommodate

Breakdown of relationship with partner

Court order: Mortgage default or rent arrears — 1981 / 1991

Loss of private rented dwelling/loss of service tenancy/ other reasons

Percentages  0  20  40  60  80

1 Households for whom local authorities accepted responsibility to secure permanent accommodation under the *Housing (Homeless Persons) Act 1977* and the *Housing Act 1985*, which defines 'priority need'.
2 Categories in Wales differ slightly from those in England so cases have been allocated to the closest English category. Data for Wales include cases given advice and assistance.

*Source: Department of the Environment; Welsh Office; Scottish Office*

**Source**: *Social Trends* (HMSO, 1993)

1 Look back at the chart 'Why homeless?' Rank the reasons for homelessness by importance, according to this diagram.
2 In the text we have distinguished between immediate causes and structural ones. Using the chart 'Why homeless?' and the extract 'A structural explanation', explain why they are examples of this distinction.
3 The graph 'Changes in homelessness over time' illustrates the changes between 1981 and 1991 in the causes of homelessness. Which ones have increased the most? Could you suggest any reasons for this?
4 Below is one explanation which comes from the article that the material above was taken from.

The government says that the number of young homeless people is rising because teenagers are leaving their parents' home at an earlier age than before. The government has cut State benefits for people under 25 and tied Income Support for 16–17-year-olds to YTS. It says this will encourage young people to return to their parents.

(Incidentally, over one-third of the young homeless come from local authority care, and have not been living at home at all).

Do you think the government's action will limit the numbers of young homeless?

If someone takes out a mortgage on a house and then, as a result of interest rate changes, can no longer afford to pay the mortgage, whose fault is it?
What, if anything, should be done?

Below are some of the **structural causes** of homelessness that have been suggested.

- **Number of houses built** – government spending on public housing has been cut by 75 per cent since 1979. There has been a clear decline in the numbers of new houses built in the public sector. In the 1970s, New Towns and local authorities built 161 000 homes per year on average, but by the end of 1990 the figure had fallen to less than 20 000. Houses built in the private sector are often too expensive for the lower paid.

- **Council house sales** – government policy in the 1980s and early 1990s was to sell off as many council homes as possible. In all, over 1.1 million homes were sold. These, traditionally, are the ones which are available for rent to the lower paid sections of the community.

- **Social security benefit changes** – the government has lowered State benefits for those under 25 and tied benefits for the under 18s to attendance on Youth Training Schemes. Linked to these changes is the assumption that young people ought to be living at home, supported by their parents. Only in exceptional circumstances will they be awarded Housing Benefit to enable them to live away from home.

- **Decline of the private rented sector** – the government has altered the law twice to increase the financial return for private landlords, and at the same time has given landlords much greater power over tenants. The result has been a greater number of evictions, while at the same time rents have risen too fast for the low paid to be able to afford them. The private rented sector has therefore continued to shrink since 1979. Today only about 8 per cent of homes are privately rented. Traditionally, apart from council housing, private landlords provided the accommodation for the lowest paid. This is not the case today.

- **Poverty** – perhaps surprisingly, there is no housing shortage; there is enough accommodation for those who want it. The real problem lies in the fact that up to three million people in Britain simply cannot afford to pay the rents or to purchase a home. The issue could therefore be regarded as one of poverty, not of homelessness.

- **Employment patterns** – house prices and rents are lowest in the north of England and Scotland. This is precisely where unemployment rates are at their highest. In order to find work, people are forced to move to the south-east, where rents and house prices are at their highest.

- **Changing nature of the family** – the rise in divorce rates cuts across all social classes and reflects a changing set of attitudes in British culture towards relationships. Those who are made homeless through divorce are reflecting a significant change in the culture, they have not 'failed' in marriage.

## Temporary accommodation

One of the responses of local authorities to the housing crisis has been to house people in 'temporary accommodation'. Often the conditions are reminiscent of the nineteenth century. The accommodation includes Bed and Breakfast, hostels, shelters, refuges and short-life tenancies.

### Bed and Breakfast accommodation

With the decline in council housing availability, local councils have increasingly turned to placing the homeless in 'Bed and Breakfast' accommodation. Today, this form of accommodation provides for about half those accepted as homeless and placed in temporary accommodation. The next largest provision is in the form of 'short-life tenancies' (see below).

Usually Bed and Breakfast accommodation is in run-down hotels which no longer attract tourists or, increasingly, in private hotels (invariably of a poor standard) run especially to take in the homeless. In 1990, there were over 12 000 people in Bed and Breakfast accommodation.

The quality of the accommodation is extremely poor. Yet, in London, some local councils have been charged as much as £250 per week for single rooms. In 1990, local councils paid out approximately £100 million on Bed and Breakfast. Apart from the obvious point that this money could be better spent *building* properties for these people, the actual conditions in Bed and Breakfast accommodation are so bad that, according to a British Medical Association and Health Visitors' Association study in 1989, this form of accommodation formed a serious risk to health.

---

## LIFE IN BED AND BREAKFAST

Over 11,000 households are living in temporary accommodation and the detrimental effects on health of living in bed and breakfast hotels have been well documented. One particularly alarming report shows that pregnant women who are homeless are three times more likely to be admitted to hospital and more likely to have underweight and premature babies.

Generally, conditions in hotel accommodation for homeless people are appalling and totally unsuitable for family life.

Privacy is virtually non-existent; marital disputes can increase, children have nowhere to do their homework and high levels of stress often lead to increased incidence of non-accidental injury.

Lack of space and reduced motivation can severely delay children's development. Walking and speech problems are particularly common.

Children living in hotels are also more likely to have behavioural and emotional problems.

It may be difficult for them to get into regular patterns of sleep with the whole family living in one room and often having to share beds.

Children are more likely to suffer accidents in this environment.

Standards of hygiene are difficult to maintain when nappies have to be washed in the same sink as hands or food because of lack of facilities. It is no surprise that infectious diseases spread so rapidly. One research project in progress in hotels and the casualty department within Parkside Health Authority is showing that children living in hotels are three times more likely than other children to get gastroenteritis.

Nutritional standards are also difficult to maintain. Hotels offer inadequate cooking facilities and storage space so that families are often forced to rely on takeaways which are expensive and not always nutritionally sound. Hotel living can be generally very expensive and families are known to go short of food.

In addition, families whose diets are governed by their religion can have major problems because of lack of proper facilities and the provision of traditional English breakfasts by hotels.

Depressed mothers may find that it is difficult to breast feed. Lack of facilities to sterilise bottles lead to an increased risk of gastric infections.

**Source**: Adapted from Annette Furley, *A Bad Start in Life* (Shelter, 1989)

1 Read the extract and then make a list of the problems faced by people in Bed and Breakfast accommodation.

2 If you live in a moderate to large-sized town, there are certain to be people living in Bed and Breakfast accommodation. Through your local council or housing charity/action group, arrange

to meet representatives. Invite them to come to your college for a question and answer session. (Don't forget to offer crèche facilities.)

---

### Hostels
These are run either by local authorities or by voluntary orgnisations. Generally, they differ from shelters (see below) in that they provide rather longer-term accommodation.

### Shelters
These are increasingly being provided and run by charitable organisations such as St Mungo's, Centrepoint and the Salvation Army. Shelters provide a place to sleep overnight, somewhere to wash, and sometimes food. They could not be described as 'home', or even a substitute for home. More and more, they are being used by the 150 000 young homeless as their last place of refuge. Since 1989, the social security rules have been changed so that people staying in shelters receive less money. Young people sleeping in shelters are often not considered to be officially homeless. Even after all the initiatives, on one night in April 1991, 2700 people were found sleeping on the streets of London.

### Women's refuges
These are provided for women who are the victims of male violence. They are generally local authority aided, but are run as independent charities. Women staying in these refuges are not necessarily accepted as being officially homeless – it depends on the policy of the council.

### Short-life tenancies
Where properties are about to be demolished, or their condition is so poor that most people will not accept living there, local authorities use them on a temporary basis for those accepted as homeless. They are the second most common form of accommodation offered to those accepted as homeless by local authorities.

## Access to housing and housing quality

When people discuss homelessness, they tend to view it only in terms of individuals lacking a roof above their heads. However, this is too simple. It is more a question of access to housing and quality of housing.

### Access to housing
There are 24 million 'dwellings' in the UK. These would provide enough places for all the homeless. However, there is no simple fit of numbers of people and amount of accommodation, because some people own second homes, some people live in homes which are too large for them, homes are located in one part of the country and the demand is in another, or people cannot afford to rent or buy properties.

### Quality of housing
A second issue concerning homelessness is that of the quality of housing. Is a person homeless who has a roof over their heads, but the conditions in which they live are considered unsatisfactory?

The government's survey of England's housing conditions reveals that over 900 000 homes are 'unfit for human habitation'. Nearly three million dwellings are in poor condition. 900 000 people are living in extreme overcrowding. Forty-two per cent of dwellings in the private rented sector are in poor condition, as are thirteen per cent of owner-occupied and seven per cent of council properties.

**Source**: A. Booth, *Raising the Roof on Housing Myths* (Shelter, 1989)

# Local authority Housing departments

The local councils are responsible for housing, through the local authority Housing departments. There are two separate strands to their role.
- They are responsible for the assessment and payment of Housing Benefit.
- They are responsible for building, maintaining and running local authority housing.

Today, local-authority housing departments have many complex statutory obligations to both private and council tenants alike. These include demolition of condemned property, the provision of new houses, the monitoring of building standards, and the granting of subsidies to individuals or voluntary organisations for the restoration of ageing property. In addition, housing departments advise on people's rights to housing benefit and adjudicate on the assessment of fair rents for private tenants. They also have a responsibility towards vulnerable people within the community – the disabled, the elderly, and the homeless – and since 1980 they have been directed to actively involve the public more closely in decision-making processes. The Chronically Sick and Disabled Persons Act 1970 empowered local authorities to require all new public buildings to be accessible to disabled people and to provide separate facilities for their use.

**Source**: D. Tossell and R. Webb, *Inside the Caring Services* (Edward Arnold, 1986)

Make a list of the responsibilities of your local council regarding housing.

## The waiting list

One of the most important jobs performed by the Housing department is to prioritise applicants on the housing waiting list. This is based on a **points system**. In order to place people in the correct position in the queue the following measures are used. The applicant is given 'points' and the more points he/she has, the higher up the list he/she is placed.

Despite the concerns and publicity about homelessness, in 1990 over 60 per cent of those moving into council accommodation did so through the ordinary waiting list system, compared with 25 per cent who were rehoused because they were homeless.

### The points system
Points are awarded according to the following criteria.

**Level of amenities** – e.g. sharing bathrooms and kitchens
**Multi-occupancy** – a house which is occupied by a number of households
**Overcrowding** – based on the number of people and the number of rooms at time of first application
**Age** – as elderly people are more likely to have problems, extra points are awarded
**Medical condition** – if present housing causes 'unacceptable hardship' to someone with a medical condition
**Children at height** – it is desirable that young children live at ground level

**Property condition** – state of repair. If a house is classified as 'unfit for human habitation' then maximum points are awarded
**Time on waiting list** – if a person is not high on the housing list, then over the years people may come above them and they will never progress. Points are awarded for every year spent on the list
**Insecurity** – people who are about to be made homeless, for example having been served with a court order to quit their rented home.

## Running council estates

The Housing department runs and maintains the council housing in the area. This can be a huge operation, for example in Birmingham in the mid-1980s there were almost a million people living in local authority housing. State spending on all forms of housing was over £4 billion in 1990, with approximately £1 billion of that given by the central government to local government for housing. Clearly the financial responsibilities of local government Housing departments are huge.

It should be remembered, however, that from 1979 onward, the Conservative government chose to channel most of its funding into housing associations.

## Advice

Housing departments are required by law to give advice to certain categories of persons without homes. This varies considerably, from handing out lists of Bed and Breakfast accommodation in the town, to running advice shops in town centres, where people can 'drop in' to discuss their housing difficulties and find out about their rights.

# State benefits and financial support

## Housing Benefit

Housing Benefit is paid to people who are on low incomes or who receive Income Support. If the person is already a council tenant, then their rent is automatically reduced by the appropriate amount. If the person pays rent to a private landlord, then the Housing Benefit can either go directly to the tenant or to the landlord.

As we have seen, Housing Benefit is means tested (see also chapter 2), so that anyone with, for example, savings over a certain level (currently £3000) has to have them taken into account. Basically, you are more likely to receive Housing Benefit the lower your income and the greater your family responsibilities, although factors such as disability and age are also taken into account.

One of the problems with means-tested benefits such as Housing Benefit, is persuading those who are entitled to them to apply. The graph on page 87 shows the take-up levels of some selected State benefits in 1985.

## TAKE-UP OF BENEFITS

**Take-up of selected social security benefits, 1985, UK**

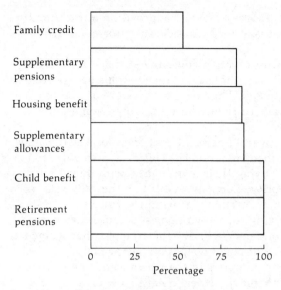

Percentage

*Source of figures*: Department of Social Security

**Source**: Redrawn from *Social Trends* (HMSO, 1990)

**1** What proportion of people entitled to Housing Benefit actually take it up?

**2** Why do the rest not apply? What can be done to improve take-up? (Look at a copy of the Housing Benefit handbook, which you can get from your local Housing department.)

### Those with a mortgage, who are in difficulties

There is no State provision to help employed people in difficulty with mortgages, although building societies claim to be sympathetic if a person falls behind on payments.

If a person becomes unemployed, however, then, according to financial circumstances, the Department of Social Security will assist with the interest element of mortgage payments, through Income Support.

After the changes in State benefits in 1988, the numbers of people in arrears with their mortgages rose within six months by 37.5 per cent.

## Subsidies for home owners

Those who buy their own homes with the help of a mortgage automatically receive financial support from the government in the form of mortgage interest rate reliefs or MIRAS.

### MORTGAGE RELIEF

Mortgage interest tax relief was equivalent in the late 1980s to a subsidy of £4.75 billion, while rather less than £1 billion was allocated in government and local authority subsidies to council housing. Means-tested subsidies to those in greatest need have been cut, yet mortgage subsidies to households on higher incomes have gone unchecked. Over £1 billion a year has gone to households with incomes in excess of £20 000 a year.

Who benefited more from financial help with housing in the 1980s?

# Housing and gender

In recent years concern has been expressed over the provision of housing for women. The Housing Act 1988, it is argued, considerably worsened the situation for women.

As we have seen, since 1979, Conservative governments have shifted the emphasis and financial support away from local authority housing towards property ownership (with a mortgage). The benefits therefore accrue to higher income families who can afford to purchase their own homes, and receive tax relief.

Of female-headed households, over 42 per cent rent from local authorities and only 11 per cent are buying their own homes. This compares with 43 per cent of male-headed households buying their own homes, with only 25 per cent renting from the local authority. The gap revealed by these figures between men and women will amost certainly grow in the future.

Women are less likely to be buying their own homes, because they earn relatively low wages compared to men. We know, for example, that women earn a little more than 70 per cent of males' wages on average.

When women do become owner-occupiers in their own right, the statistics show us that they are likely to inhabit the older, cheaper properties in less desirable positions with few amenities. More than one third of women buy property built before 1919, compared to less than a quarter of men.

Women tend to concentrate in council property; indeed, over half of all divorced, separated and widowed women turn to the local authority for housing.

The control by men of the income coming into a house, and therefore the payment of the rent or mortgage, has far-reaching repercussions for women (and children). According to Jenny Morris, commenting on a study carried out in the late 1970s, women accepted violence by their partners for an average of seven years without leaving, mainly because they had nowhere else to go.

The 1988 Act limits the right of succession for local authority and private tenants. In other words, the automatic right to take over the tenancy from the parent is denied. One in five women over the age of 40 are caring for a sick, disabled or elderly person. When that person dies, then the carer is faced with a new tenancy agreement (or none at all), which will probably have a significantly increased rent.

# Housing and race

Blacks and Asians have quite different tenure patterns from each other and from Whites. At its simplest, those of Afro-Carribean origin are more likely than other groups to be in council housing, whilst Asians have the highest levels of owner occupation of all three groups.

However, when it comes to quality of housing measured by amenities or overcrowding, it seems that Whites emerge well ahead. The explanations for these patterns are not difficult to find.

## Quality of housing

Housing reflects the divisions in society in general, as we saw with the situation of women and housing. Asians and Blacks are less likely than Whites to be in well paid employment. They are therefore less likely to have housing of as good a quality. The reasons for Blacks and Asians earning less than Whites is partially due to discrimination, a fact of life that affects all areas of their lives, not just housing tenure. (Chapter 13 discusses the issue of discrimination in more detail.)

## Owner occupation

The high levels of owner occupation amongst Asians represents a reflection of their culture, and a response to racism.

### Reflection of culture

Amongst many of the Asian communities in Britain, there is a belief in the value of owning property, and family groups will club together to purchase housing. The reason for the higher density of people living in Asian households is a reflection of the strength of the extended family, and of this mutual aid to buy property. Living together gives them the economic power to purchase property.

### Response to racism

When Black and Asian immigrants first came to the UK in large numbers in the 1950s, they were excluded from most forms of housing. Their housing conditions were appalling. Asians responded by purchasing property through extended family networks. Blacks did not have this family network, and were anyway less culturally interested in the purchase of property. As a result they suffered for many years from some of the worst housing conditions. They began to enter local authority housing because their accommodation was so poor, gaining points on the housing lists for this reason.

It is interesting to note that Blacks and Asians who have council accommodation are heavily over-represented in the worst council properties.

## Racial harassment

One of the major problems faced by Asians, and to a lesser extent Blacks, is that of racial harassment. (Please see chapter 13 for more discussion of this issue.)

## RACE AND TENURE

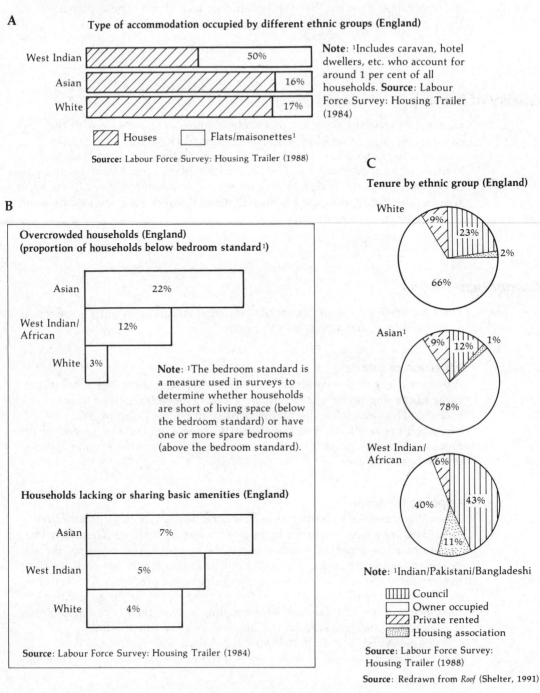

**A**

**Type of accommodation occupied by different ethnic groups (England)**

West Indian — 50%
Asian — 16%
White — 17%

Houses  Flats/maisonettes[1]

**Source:** Labour Force Survey: Housing Trailer (1988)

**Note:** [1]Includes caravan, hotel dwellers, etc. who account for around 1 per cent of all households. **Source:** Labour Force Survey: Housing Trailer (1984)

**B**

**Overcrowded households (England)**
**(proportion of households below bedroom standard[1])**

Asian — 22%
West Indian/African — 12%
White — 3%

**Note:** [1]The bedroom standard is a measure used in surveys to determine whether households are short of living space (below the bedroom standard) or have one or more spare bedrooms (above the bedroom standard).

**Households lacking or sharing basic amenities (England)**

Asian — 7%
West Indian — 5%
White — 4%

**Source:** Labour Force Survey: Housing Trailer (1984)

**C**

**Tenure by ethnic group (England)**

White
9% / 23% / 2% / 66%

Asian[1]
9% / 12% / 1% / 78%

West Indian/African
6% / 43% / 11% / 40%

**Note:** [1]Indian/Pakistani/Bangladeshi

Council
Owner occupied
Private rented
Housing association

**Source:** Labour Force Survey: Housing Trailer (1988)

**Source:** Redrawn from *Roof* (Shelter, 1991)

Diagram A.
**1** Which ethnic group is most likely to live in houses? What is the percentage?
**2** Which ethnic group is least likely to live in houses? What is the percentage?
Diagram B.
**3** Which group has the highest percentage of those lacking basic amenities? What is the figure?
**4** Which group has the most overcrowded households? Give the figure.

Diagram C.

**5** The tenure patterns of West Indians, Asians and Whites are significantly different. Rank the groups in order of their percentage tenure:
- Owner occupiers
- Council
- Private rented
- Housing Association

All diagrams.

**6** Combining the information you have extracted from the diagrams, what statement can you make about Asian households in Britain?

**7** What statement can you make about 'West Indian' households?

**8** How would you compare both Asian and West Indian households to White housing patterns?

# Assignment

You have recently obtained a job with a research agency holding a contract from the European Community, which is gathering information about housing conditions in selected parts of the Community. Your local area has been chosen as representative of a typical British rural/urban/suburban community in Britain.

The research agency needs to find out:
- the extent of official homelessness in your local area;
- the policy of the local authority to combat homelessness;
- the numbers of people the local authority turn away as a proportion of all enquiries;
- the main reasons given for homelessness.

They also wish to have a breakdown of the categories of those who approach the agencies as homeless (e.g. single, with children, etc); and to find out if there is any voluntary or charitable organisation in your town attempting to combat homelessness.

The agency also needs interviews with five homeless families/individuals explaining how they became homeless, and what they hope and expect will happen.

This information should be collated in terms of a report for the EC, and it should include demographic information about the town.

# CHAPTER 5

# The Health Service

## Introduction

The National Health Service (NHS) is the largest employer in Western Europe. It forms, in most people's eyes, the most important service of all those provided by the government. The ideal of a 'free' health service providing high standards of care to all people as a right still commands almost universal respect and admiration. Yet the complexity of financing and providing adequate health care is quite staggering.

Since the mid-1980s, the government has moved towards giving hospitals and GPs much greater freedom to spend as they wish. For many commentators, this is the only way forward; for others the granting of greater freedom to the hospitals is a move towards 'privatisation' of the NHS and away from the principle of equal treatment for all. This chapter tackles these issues, describing the changes that have taken place and assessing their impact.

The chapter opens with a look back at the history of health provision and how the NHS developed, following the changing structure of the NHS since its inception in 1948. One of the major issues has always been how to balance the demands for health care, which seem inexhaustible, and the funds available from government, which are limited. The chapter takes a look at the issue of finance and of rationing of health services, and how the government achieves a reasonable spread of finance across the country.

We then move on to examine the re-structuring of the Health Service, with the move away from central control to self-governing trusts and budget-holding GPs. The arguments for and against the reforms are considered.

Finally, we look at the users of health care services and the way in which different groups of the population have different standards of health and make different demands on the NHS. We also briefly look at the explanations for these differences in health.

## Health provision before the NHS

In the nineteenth century, hospitals were used only by poor people, as they were dangerous places where it was far more likely that the patient would end up dying rather than being healed. This is because there was little awareness of hygiene, and the standards of care were very low.

The affluent paid for a doctor to visit them at home, and had a noticeably higher chance of survival. At the time this was regarded as the result of the work of doctors, though now the higher survival rates are understood to be as a result of better diet, housing and work conditions.

## Friendly Societies

Insurance companies, or Friendly Societies, developed amongst the regularly employed working class, often organised by trade unions. They paid doctors a fixed amount per subscriber to provide health care. By 1900, over half the working class were covered by such insurance.

## State intervention

During the Boer War (1899–1902), a third of all recruits were judged to be physically unfit to serve because of illness (which was generally caused by malnutrition). In a time of empire and imperial armies, this caused serious concern to the government. Social reformers used the information as evidence of the need for the government to provide better health and welfare services than those that existed at the time.

The government was also concerned about the possibility of serious social unrest, and were looking at ways of undermining support for the radical elements in the Labour movement. A limited amount of health reform would help do this. An example of how limited State provision served to dampen tension was provided by Germany. Its Chancellor, Bismarck, had introduced a social insurance system which covered a range of issues including accidents at work, disability and old age pensions.

## Health insurance

This was introduced by the government in 1911 and covered workers between the ages of 16 and 65, who earned a range of incomes. (Agricultural workers were omitted because they earned too little to afford to pay the contributions!) This provided access to doctors at home and cash benefits for sickness, accidents at work and for disability. The scheme did not cover any hospital treatment. The group of doctors who provided the medical treatment were paid a fixed amount by the agencies running the scheme, and they were generally referred to as 'the panel'.

All the dependants of workers were excluded. As most workers were male, this meant that the majority of women and children received no automatic right to medical care.

The reasoning behind this was simple: the wage earner was the male in the majority of households and therefore if he could not work the family would fall into poverty. By keeping the male well, or by tiding the family over in the short periods in which he was ill and unable to provide (as employers did not give sick pay), the family would not become poor. The worker would therefore be able to afford to pay for health care for the rest of his family.

By the beginning of the Second World War, in 1939, over 40 per cent of the working population had coverage giving them access to a GP (or 'family doctor').

# The introduction of the NHS

In 1939, the outbreak of the Second World War forced the government to intervene in the provision of medical services, as it had to organise health care for the armed forces and the civilian casualties. The Emergency Medical Service (EMS) was established, which consisted of hospital bed provision, a national blood transfusion service and an ambulance service.

As we saw in chapter 2, the Beveridge Report (1942) isolated five 'giants' which blemished the lives of ordinary people – disease, ignorance, squalor, idleness and want. The report argued that the government after the war would have to tackle these problems, and so 'disease' was placed on the political agenda.

A third factor leading to the introduction of the NHS was the desire of the government to maintain the morale of the population during the war, and to provide them with a vision of a bright future, including free health care for all, if Britain won the war.

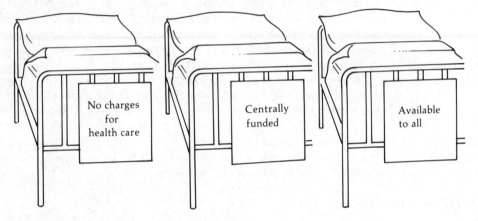

**The founding principles of the NHS**

# The changing structure of the NHS

The National Health Service (NHS) was formally inaugurated in 1948. However, the route to the establishment of the NHS was not an easy one, as GPs and consultants demanded high incomes and limited government control. Indeed, it was the opposition of doctors to the National Health Service that delayed its introduction by almost three years. When the NHS was finally started, the doctors gained considerable advantages from it.

- GPs remained independent practitioners.
- Consultants could work part-time for the NHS and part-time in private practice.
- Consultants were offered special 'merit' awards, which were extra payments for selected consultants.
- Private patients (of consultants) could use NHS facilities.
- Doctors were to have considerable power in the running of the NHS at all levels.

Local authorities, which had previously run hospitals, were given only a minor role in running the NHS. The structure of the NHS has changed gradually since then. Overall, the move has been to simplify the structure and to place greater power in the hands of managers, with doctors and other health care professionals gradually losing power.

# The NHS today

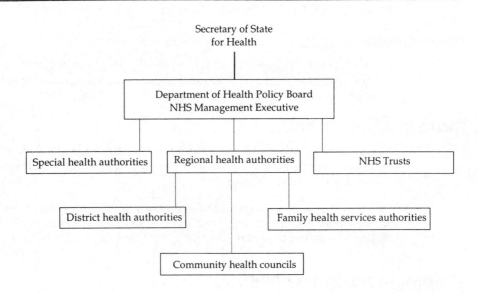

## Regional health authorities

There are 14 regional health authorities in England, and one each in Scotland, Wales and Northern Ireland.

The regional health authorities are responsible for:
- planning the development of services within the context of national guidelines;
- allocating resources to district health authorities, family health services authorities, GP fundholders and hospital Trusts;
- monitoring the performance of district health authorities and family health services authorities.

## District health authorities

There are 189 district health authorities. They may or may not have hospitals or community units which they manage directly. This depends on the decision of the local hospital to opt out or not.

The district health authorities are responsible for:
- purchasing services for the local population;
- managing the hospitals and community care services under their control;
- assessing the health needs of the local population;
- public health.

## Family health services authorities

The family health services authorities (FHSAs) have taken over from the family practitioner committees (FPCs).

The FHSAs are responsible for:
- assessing the population's need for health care;

- planning the services to meet those needs;
- ensuring the services are provided efficiently and cost-effectively;
- managing GPs' and dentists' contracts.

## Hospital Trusts

Hospital Trusts are hospitals that have chosen to opt out of district control and to bid for contracts to provide care in a similar way to a private hospital. Legally, they are still NHS hospitals.

## Special health authorities

Special health authorities are a mixture of organisations, including the London postgraduate teaching hospitals and the Health Education Authority.
See also the chart on page 110.

Find out where your local regional and district health authorities are and obtain the address of the local FHSA. Ask them to send you information about their activities and/or ask for a representative to visit you to talk about the work of the FHSA. Prepare questions in advance!

# Employment in the NHS

**STAFF EMPLOYED DIRECTLY BY THE NHS, 1988**

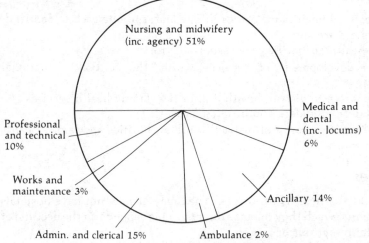

Staff salaries and wages are the biggest single item of expenditure for the NHS, comprising 70 per cent of the total. As well as the directly-employed staff 25 300 GPs, 15 100 dentists and 11 500 opticians are employed as independent contractors. There are also 10 100 retail pharmacists.

Pie chart labels:
- Nursing and midwifery (inc. agency) 51%
- Medical and dental (inc. locums) 6%
- Ancillary 14%
- Ambulance 2%
- Admin. and clerical 15%
- Works and maintenance 3%
- Professional and technical 10%

**Source**: C. Ham, *Managing Health Services* (Radcliffe Medical Press, 1991)

1 What proportion of staff employed by the NHS are nursing and midwifery?
2 What proportion are medical?
3 What does 'ancillary' workers mean?
4 When critics of the NHS say it is too expensive and that economies should be made, what would appear to be the major savings that could be made? What would the results of this be?
5 Critics also argue that there are too many clerical staff. What is their proportion to the entire workforce? Compare that to the organisation you are working or studying in. Do you think the figures are unreasonable?
6 It has been suggested that the National Health Service is one of the most sexist organisations in Britain, and that it routinely oppresses women both in its treatment and in its organisation. Can you make any comment on this, from the information provided above?

# The cost of the NHS

The assumption underlying the introduction of the NHS in 1948 was that there was a large number of ill people who needed to be cured, but that once this had been achieved the role of the NHS would consist mainly of keeping people in good health and dealing with emergencies. This view was based on two ideas:

1 that there was an objective, fixed standard distinguishing good health from poor health; and
2 that the entire range of welfare initiatives, including council housing, social security payments and full employment, would ensure that the diseases caused by poverty would never return.

In both these assumptions, planners were proved to be wrong.

## EXPENDITURE

A

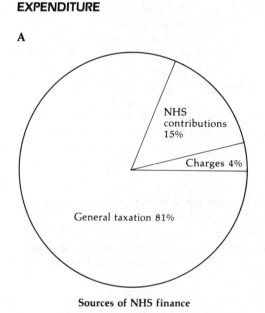

**Sources of NHS finance**

The NHS is often claimed to be free. It is not. We do not pay directly for services when we receive them, except for those in employment who pay for prescriptions. But we do pay indirectly. Health services consume about 13.5 per cent of total public expenditure. Diagram A shows where funding for the NHS comes from.

B

**Expenditure in £s per head on hospital and community health services by age group, 1986–87 (England)**

| | |
|---|---|
| Total (all ages) | 215 |
| All births | 1185 |
| 0–4 | 195 |
| 5–15 | 95 |
| 16–64 | 110 |
| 65–74 | 415 |
| 75–84 | 927 |
| 85+ | 1452 |

**Source**: HM Treasury (1989) and Department of Health

C

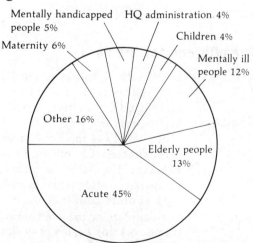

**Health authority expenditure by patient group, 1988–9**

**Source**: C. Ham, *The New National Health Service* (Radcliffe Medical Press, 1991)

1 What proportion of all public expenditure goes on health care?
2 Where does this money overwhelmingly come from?
3 Voters in Britain have consistently stated that they are prepared to pay extra for a good health service, but have consistently voted for a political party which promised low taxes. Given the information from diagram A, what implications does this have for long-term quality of care in the NHS?
4 Table B presents the spending per age group in the NHS. Which group costs the most per head?
5 What is the total amount of money spent on the elderly (those aged 65 and over)?
6 How do you explain the apparent discrepancy between the last two answers?
7 Which age group has the lowest expenditure per head?
8 Which group of people had the lowest expenditure on them, apart from children?
9 Look now at diagram C. What is the single biggest cost of the NHS?
10 How much is spent on administration?

## Standards of health

Health is not a fixed, objective thing but, in a similar way to poverty, it varies depending on the expectations of the population of a society. Therefore, illness and disease that would have been accepted as normal or at least bearable for one generation come to be regarded as insupportable by another. Once free health care became available, people wanted to use it, and expectations of health rose. The healthier people became, the more aware they were of symptoms that previously they had accepted as natural or unchangeable.

Therefore, contrary to what the planners had expected, usage of the NHS increased through the 1950s and afterwards, and did not decrease as they had thought.

## Technology

Linked to the changing views on health standards was the introduction of new technology. Previously, people had accepted that there was nothing to be done about certain diseases, but the rapid increases in technology – both in machines and in drugs – have revolutionised the capabilities of medicine. The problem is that these new developments are highly expensive, and add to the costs of health care.

## The efficiency of the NHS

In 1953, the Ministry of Health was so concerned that it ordered an inquiry into health care costs – but the committee that reported on this (the Guillebaud Committee) actually recommended an *increase* in funding for the health service.

In 1949, £444 million was spent on the NHS; in 1990, the figure was approximately £30 billion. In real terms, this is a 400 per cent increase. However, the NHS is an efficient, cheap means of providing health care compared to alternative models used by other countries.

Most other countries use an insurance-based model run by the State (as in Germany) or by private companies with the State merely regulating the framework for health provision and providing a safety-net health system for those who cannot afford insurance (as in the USA).

The debate between insurance-based systems, where an individual or company pays into an insurance scheme and then receives benefits as a subscriber, and the British welfare state model, in which everyone has a right to health care as a citizen of the country, has been the basis for a bitter dispute.

**1** What two factors have contributed to the enormous increase in health costs since the beginning of the NHS?
**2** If the government was to increase its spending on the NHS, do you think this would lead to a decline in waiting lists and people feeling healthier? Explain your answers fully.

Critics of the National Health Service argue that it is inefficient, unaccountable, and that because there are no limits to treatment people make demands which they would not do if they had to pay for them. In reply, supporters of the NHS argue that free health care is a human right, and that it is wrong for anyone to suffer simply because they cannot afford to pay.

Nevertheless, the result of free treatment is that the demand always outstrips the supply, and so in place of charges as a way of rationing the available health care, the NHS has waiting lists. (We discuss waiting lists below on pages 106–7.)

The amount of money spent on the NHS each year is not a reflection of the demand of people for treatment, but is determined by negotiations between the Treasury and the Department of Health. Each year, a Public Expenditure White Paper is published which says how much the government intends to spend on all its services. Currently, the NHS accounts for between 13 and 14 per cent of all government expenditure. Within the NHS, about 70 per cent is spent on hospital and community services, and 25 per cent on family health services. The most expensive items are drugs, followed by GPs, dentists and opticians.

## FREE HEALTH CARE FOR ALL?

Private medical insurers find that their premiums are rising at a rate which deters many individuals from renewing their subscriptions. They are trying to hold back the rate of rise by restricting the cover available to policyholders . . . the NHS may need to take a leaf out of the private insurers' book, and limit the cover to which its subscribers – and their families – are entitled.

Instead of facing a virtually open-ended commitment, NHS purchasing managers need to know much more clearly which services they should contract to provide, and which claims they can reject. This would allow their inevitably limited funds to be targeted more precisely on patients most in need and most likely to benefit . . .

The range of possibilities [of treatment] is very wide and expanding with advances in medical science and in response to political pressure. Since April, GPs can now prescribe visits to alternative practitioners for some complementary therapies, despite a complete lack of scientific evidence for their efficacy.

This situation cannot go on. Limited resources available to health authorities will force them into making choices – and inevitably, certain exclusions from complete coverage by our national health insurance scheme will be agreed. As part of the *Patient's Charter* we need a policy document describing our entitlements and making the exclusions clear, even in small print. Here are some possibilities.

Many operations now conducted frequently on the NHS apparently have little scientific evidence of clinical benefit. Extraction of wisdom teeth, insertion of grommets for glue ear, removal of tonsils, many hysterectomies, even coronary artery bypass surgery can be considered of doubtful benefit. Considerable spending covers procedures conducted on otherwise healthy individuals. Family planning, sterilisation and termination of pregnancy are provided to a differing extent from district to district already. Cosmetic surgery is another example.

Health authorities could choose to be more stringent in buying these services of doubtful medical value, and do so only if there is a clear health need....

The use of novel techniques or of new drugs will not be acceptable without strong evidence of a clinical benefit which is superior to existing, less expensive procedures.

It is also worth looking at ailments which are clearly self-inflicted. Tobacco and alcohol-related conditions account for a high proportion of total health service spending. After many years of publicity, few smokers and drinkers can be unaware of the risks they run to their health. Yet, damage to a minority of self-indulgent individuals is being repaired at a considerable cost to the majority. The £500m of

our NHS insurance subscriptions spent on treatment of smoking-related disorders could be better used in additional hip replacement operations, more intensive care facilities and more incubators for sick children. Perhaps the treatment cost of self-inflicted conditions should be met instead from a specific tax on cigarettes, beer or spirits.

Similarly, treatment of sports injuries should not be a burden on the taxpayer. Instead, all sports clubs should be required to carry private insurance to cover the risks of their members' sporting activities.... in placing these sensible restrictions on the cover provided through our state health insurance system, the government would still guarantee that patients with clinically significant conditions will receive their approved treatment without charge and without undue delay.

**Source**: Anthony Byrne, *Health Service Journal*, 9 July 1992

**1** What is the difference at present between the provision of health care by the private sector and by the NHS?

**2** Why should the NHS begin to copy some of the approaches of the private sector?

**3** Find out and explain the meaning of the 'Patient's Charter'. Contact your local GP or your hospital for further information, or ask your community health council (CHC) for a pamphlet.

**4** What sort of activities would the author of the above article like to see curtailed by the NHS? Do you agree?

**5** In the state of Oregon in the USA, legislators have decided that the only way to reflect public opinion in the rationing of health care is to present people with a list of 500 ailments and ask them to rate them. Those that come highest get more money and those that come lowest get the least. In Britain, at least one health authority has conducted research on similar lines, in order to try to reflect the public's opinion on health matters. Do you think this would be the way to solve the problems of finance in the NHS?

**6** Conduct a small survey. Below is a list of well-known medical conditions/situations. (Add some more or alter them if you wish.) Ask a small sample of people to rate these in order of importance (i.e. the most important should have the most money spent on it, and so on). It would be helpful to ask people to explain to you very briefly their reasons. You could then summarise these at the end of your research.

- Improvement in abortion services
- More equipment to help premature babies survive
- More equipment for the treatment of cancer
- Better facilities for AIDS patients
- Nursing homes for the elderly
- Hip replacements

- Dialysis machines
- Hospital accident and emergency units
- Better facilities for the mentally ill
- Heart transplants
- Improving treatment for serious burns
- Speech therapy

Are there any conclusions you can draw about the priorities people have for medical care? Do you think this would be a good/equitable method of deciding on priorities? If you do not think so, then how would you decide on the priority of spending for health?

# Co-ordination with the personal social services

A constant difficulty for the NHS has been the need to co-ordinate its response to caring and health care with the personal social services of local authorities.

The original idea of the NHS was to provide health services for the general population, but as the numbers of the elderly, the chronically sick and the disabled has increased (partially due to the work of the NHS), a demand has risen for a *caring* as opposed to a *curing* role. But who should pay? And who should provide for the care of elderly and disabled people who, though unable to look after themselves, are not curable? The local authorities have said it should be the NHS, and the NHS has argued that it is the responsibility of the local authorities. As a result, little progress has been made.

## Reasons for lack of progress

There are two principle reasons why there has been so little progress.

The first is financial, in that neither the local authorities nor the NHS want to spend more money on these groups.

The second is professional rivalry. Both the health professionals and the social services professionals are very wary of each other. Each group has a very different approach to care – for social workers the stress has always been on social and often political issues, while for health professionals the stress is placed on medical models of comfort and well-being. Even today there are great differences between the two groups of professionals.

Attempts were made throughout the 1950s and 1980s to overcome these barriers, with a strong stress being placed on **joint decision making** by NHS districts and local authorities, and the introduction of **co-terminous boundaries.**

### Co-terminous boundaries

These represent the attempt to align local authority Social Services divisions with the administrative divisions of the NHS. The idea was that by having Social Services departments of local authorities and NHS districts with the same geographical boundaries, then the care could be organised. This would also mean that only one set of representatives from Social Services and the NHS would have to negotiate. However, there were few successes, as the problems of finance and professional rivalry managed to ambush the majority of initiatives.

Write to or telephone your local authority Social Services department, and ask if you could interview a senior social worker.

Write to or telephone your local community care unit of the NHS. Ask if you can interview a community nurse manager.

Construct a simple, clear questionnaire about the basic needs of clients/patients. Include questions about what best could be done to improve patient/client care of the disabled and elderly, and questions on who they think should be in charge of the care of these groups.

If you know an elderly infirm person, or you know (or are) a disabled person, ask them about what services they think are or would be most useful to them.

Draw the information together in a group. What similarities, differences and issues emerge?

# Regional differences in health care provision

As we saw earlier, the demand for health care has always been greater than the government was prepared to spend on provision. This has led to the necessity of rationing, but it has also forced the government to have to choose between the competing claims for money from the different health service regions.

If there is a fixed amount of money to be divided amongst the regions and districts in Britain, then if one region gets more, another must get less. Historically, the teaching hospitals were in London and their influence and prestige meant that they swallowed up a disproportionate amount of money.

Secondly, as the government had no real method of working out how much was a fair (or equitable) amount for each region and district, the approach taken was one known as **incrementalism**. This meant that each year an allowance was made for increases or decreases in government spending, plus the funding to compensate for the degree of inflation, and then this was added to the previous year's spending of a particular region or district.

## The Resource Allocation Working Party (RAWP)

In 1975, a body known as the Resource Allocation Working Party (or RAWP) was set up to try to make some sense of how funding for the NHS was distributed.

The basis on which the funding was to be allocated was intended to reflect the differing health needs of the various regions. The complexity of working out differences in health and illness levels was too great for any simple formula to be constructed, so the working party suggested a simple guide. This would be the number and age of the population (the elderly and the very young cost more); the mortality ratio (number of deaths per 1000 of the population) and the birth rate (number of births per 1000 of the population).

This formula produced evidence that some areas were over-resourced compared to others, and the government set out to draw the areas nearer their target levels over the succeeding 11 years.

However, even the RAWP system had flaws, for it allowed unfair distribution *within* areas (until 1982 when the area health authorities were abolished) and then within districts. Thus, London, which had a concentration of large teaching hospitals, used to have much of its funding sucked into supporting these to the detriment of other health services and hospitals. This has come to be particularly apparent with the shift to the **internal market** (which is discussed below under 'The 1990 Reforms').

## MORTALITY RATIOS

"The decline in mortality during the century can be attributed to environmental, social and economic factors as well as to improving health care. It is always difficult to know how much is due to which factor."

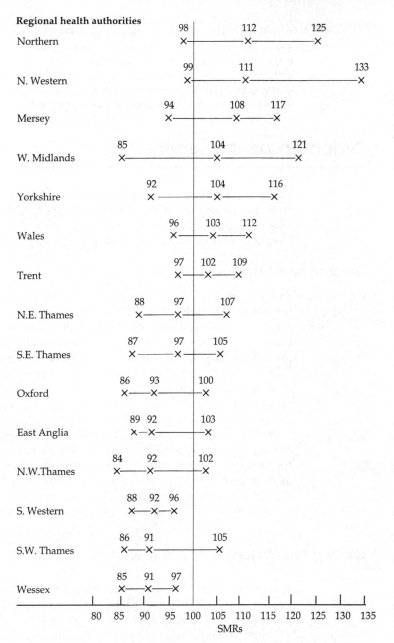

Regional health authorities

Northern — 98, 112, 125

N. Western — 99, 111, 133

Mersey — 94, 108, 117

W. Midlands — 85, 104, 121

Yorkshire — 92, 104, 116

Wales — 96, 103, 112

Trent — 97, 102, 109

N.E. Thames — 88, 97, 107

S.E. Thames — 87, 97, 105

Oxford — 86, 93, 100

East Anglia — 89, 92, 103

N.W. Thames — 84, 92, 102

S. Western — 88, 92, 96

S.W. Thames — 86, 91, 105

Wessex — 85, 91, 97

SMRs: 80  85  90  95  100  105  110  115  120  125  130  135

**Source**: E. Beck, S. Lonsdale, S. Newman and D. Patterson, *In the Best of Health* (Chapman and Hall, 1992)

By taking an average across the whole country, we know the number of people who are likely to die before they reach retirement age. This is known as the standardised mortality ratio (SMR). We also know the different mortality ratios for each region of the country, and we can compare these against the national average to get a picture about which regions have particularly high or particularly low levels of mortality before retirement age.

In the diagram above, to make things simple, the figure 100 represents the national average. The lower the figures are, the lesser the chance of people in that region dying before retirement age, and the higher the figures, the greater the chance.

There are three figures given. These represent the districts in the various regions with the highest SMR, the lowest SMR and the average. For example: the Northern Region has an average SMR of 112, which means that there is an above average chance of death before retirement age. Within the Northern Region the worst district has an SMR of 125 (meaning that there is a 25 per cent greater chance than average of premature death) and the best district has an SMR of 98 (meaning that there is a slightly below average chance of premature death).

1 Which region has the highest average SMR?
2 Which region had the highest individual district SMR?
3 Which region had the lowest individual district SMR?
4 Which region had the lowest overall SMR?
5 Which is your region? How high do you score on average?
6 Find out the SMR for your district. Ask your community health council (CHC).
7 What does the SMR tell us about the health care in your region/district?

# Rationing health services

Rationing health services to the population is a major issue facing the NHS. How do you ensure that people receive the health services they demand, when there is inadequate finance to cater for these demands? The answer is to ration the delivery of services in some way.

## The process of rationing

There is usually greater demand for health and welfare services than there is the supply available. In most commercial situations this would not be a problem, as the suppliers of the services would simply raise their prices until there was a balance between the numbers of people able and willing to pay the price asked, and the amount of services available.

In the health and welfare services, however, the services provided are usually because people are in need. The services are not commercial. This means that generally other means of rationing services have developed. These are shown in the diagram below.

One basic division needs to be made: that between **formal rationing** where the agency involved (such as the NHS) sets out to use a particular technique, for example, waiting lists, and **informal rationing**, where the individual or agency uses techniques which are not formally acknowledged, such as the activities of the receptionist in a social services agency who decides which callers to send to the intake team, and which to keep waiting.

## Waiting lists: rationing in practice

If someone is involved in an accident, then they can expect to be treated immediately in a British hospital, and about half the people who are admitted to hospital do not have to go on a waiting list.

However, those who require treatment, but who are not in desperate urgency, are put on to a waiting list. The length of time people have to wait is often the subject of great controversy. In 1990, there were 720 000 people on the waiting lists of hospitals. Twenty years earlier, there were around 600 000 people waiting at any one time. Although waiting lists are longer now than in the past, it is important to note that the numbers of people being treated have actually increased.

The Patient's Charter, which was introduced in 1992, promised that in non-urgent cases patients would have a maximum waiting time of 18 months. There is considerable debate over whether this has been achieved.

Waiting lists today are longer than they were 25 years ago, yet more people are being treated. Can you explain this apparent contradiction?

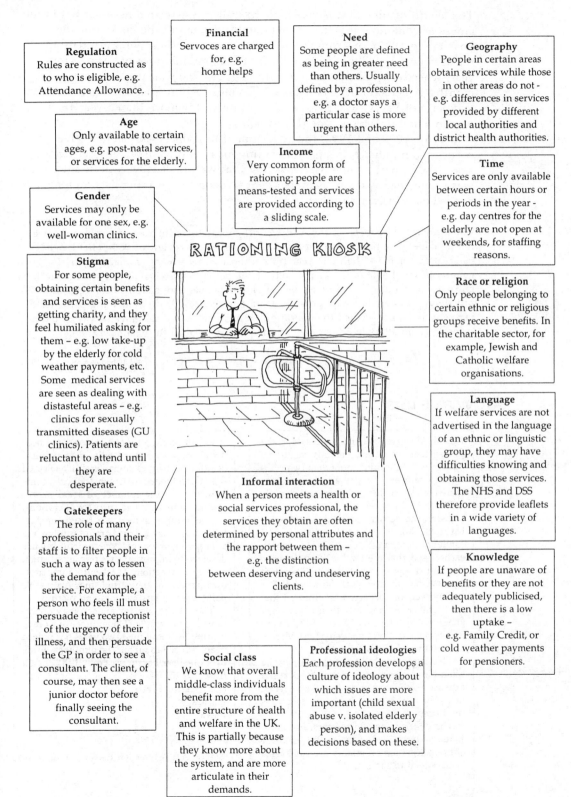

**Regulation**
Rules are constructed as to who is eligible, e.g. Attendance Allowance.

**Financial**
Servoces are charged for, e.g. home helps

**Need**
Some people are defined as being in greater need than others. Usually defined by a professional, e.g. a doctor says a particular case is more urgent than others.

**Geography**
People in certain areas obtain services while those in other areas do not - e.g. differences in services provided by different local authorities and district health authorities.

**Age**
Only available to certain ages, e.g. post-natal services, or services for the elderly.

**Income**
Very common form of rationing: people are means-tested and services are provided according to a sliding scale.

**Time**
Services are only available between certain hours or periods in the year - e.g. day centres for the elderly are not open at weekends, for staffing reasons.

**Gender**
Services may only be available for one sex, e.g. well-woman clinics.

**Stigma**
For some people, obtaining certain benefits and services is seen as getting charity, and they feel humiliated asking for them – e.g. low take-up by the elderly for cold weather payments, etc. Some medical services are seen as dealing with distasteful areas – e.g. clinics for sexually transmitted diseases (GU clinics). Patients are reluctant to attend until they are desperate.

**Race or religion**
Only people belonging to certain ethnic or religious groups receive benefits. In the charitable sector, for example, Jewish and Catholic welfare organisations.

**Language**
If welfare services are not advertised in the language of an ethnic or linguistic group, they may have difficulties knowing and obtaining those services. The NHS and DSS therefore provide leaflets in a wide variety of languages.

**Gatekeepers**
The role of many professionals and their staff is to filter people in such a way as to lessen the demand for the service. For example, a person who feels ill must persuade the receptionist of the urgency of their illness, and then persuade the GP in order to see a consultant. The client, of course, may then see a junior doctor before finally seeing the consultant.

**Informal interaction**
When a person meets a health or social services professional, the services they obtain are often determined by personal attributes and the rapport between them – e.g. the distinction between deserving and undeserving clients.

**Knowledge**
If people are unaware of benefits or they are not adequately publicised, then there is a low uptake – e.g. Family Credit, or cold weather payments for pensioners.

**Social class**
We know that overall middle-class individuals benefit more from the entire structure of health and welfare in the UK. This is partially because they know more about the system, and are more articulate in their demands.

**Professional ideologies**
Each profession develops a culture of ideology about which issues are more important (child sexual abuse v. isolated elderly person), and makes decisions based on these.

RATIONING KIOSK

**Types of rationing**

The length of time that people have to wait is not related necessarily to their illness or condition, it is just as likely to be related to the district or the hospital. In 1990, for example, over 60 per cent of those who wanted hip replacements in Hillingdon, a suburb of London, had to wait for over one year, whereas in the adjoining health districts, the wait was only a few months. A person in the North-east Thames Region (east and north London and parts of Essex) was twice as likely to wait for more than a year than a person living on Merseyside (Liverpool).

In 1987, 1990 and 1992, the government introduced special incentives to reduce the number of people on waiting lists, who were waiting for over one year. The initiatives involved ensuring that waiting lists were accurage – and it was found that as many as 60 per cent of people on waiting lists no longer needed or wanted treatment.

The numbers [of people on the waiting list] appear to be inflated by people who are not genuine patients waiting for hospital admission. A review of 950 patients who had waited for more than one year for orthopaedic treatment at a large district general hospital eliminated 20 per cent of the patients who had already had operations but had not been removed from the list. These people may have had the operation privately or under the NHS, possibly as an emergency. Of the remaining patients, 17 per cent no longer wished the operation, 33 per cent had died, moved away or did not respond.... In all, only 38 per cent of the patients wished to remain on the list.

Source: E. Beck *et al.*, *In the Best of Health* (Chapman and Hall, 1992)

## WAITING LISTS

Mr Waldegrave claimed success for the pledge that by the end of this month no patient will be waiting more than two years for an operation. In January, he said, the two-year waiting list had been cut by nearly 9,000 or 30.3 per cent.

Later, the department said the two-year list total stood at 20,494 at the end of January, compared to 29,385 a month earlier, and that the total waiting between one and two years had fallen by 7 per cent over the month from 100,398 to 93,419.

However, the department admitted that the number waiting less than a year had gone up in January from 813,824 to 817,441, a rise of 0.4 per cent. Last March, the total was 778,400.

This lends weight to critics who say the scramble to clear the two-year list is at the expense of those waiting less than a year, many of whom may have more serious conditions.

The department said the total list fell in January, by 1.3 per cent to 931,354, but critics allege some patients are no longer being added to the list.

Source: The *Guardian*, 6 March 1992

It was interesting to see a recent announcement by our supposedly non-political health authority of some carefully selected statistics intended to demonstrate a welcome reduction in the number of local people waiting more than two years for operations.

The figures quoted are based on performance over the last six months following a large injection of government finance designed to improve the waiting list situation before the election. The health authority's own figures for the period since April 1990 paint a much less encouraging picture.

The waiting list for gynaecology operations is an example. The number of women waiting for more than two years has indeed been reduced to nil but the number waiting over one year has increased by 148 per cent from 197 to 488!

(Dr) **Shaun Firth**,
Harlow,
Essex.

Source: Adapted from the *Guardian*, 21 March 1992

1 Are waiting list statistics a reliable indication of the numbers of people actually waiting for an operation? Explain your answer clearly.

2 Can you explain clearly, using examples from the extracts above, the relationship between the two-year and one-year waiting lists?

3 Find out what the respective waiting lists are at your local hospital, for two specialities. You should be able to obtain the information by telephone (if they cannot tell you, then ask why not, as there is no medical reason).

# The 1990 reforms

By the late 1980s, the NHS was suffering from a severe lack of resources. This was the result of three factors:

- the policies of the government, which was cutting back on public expenditure;
- the increasing numbers of elderly with their demands on the health services;
- the increasing demands for higher standards of health.

The situation was so bad that districts were not paying their bills, and operations were being cancelled. Waiting lists were increasing rapidly. As a result, a review of the NHS was announced.

The Government Review produced a list of the strengths and weaknesses of the NHS, and suggested that one of the main problems lay in the *lack of incentives* for employees of the NHS to make savings and be more efficient. The government was strongly influenced by an economist, Enthoven, who argued that by introducing an **internal market** to the NHS, managers would be encouraged to become more efficient and, without extra spending, many of the NHS problems could be solved.

What Enthoven meant by the internal market, was that each hospital or community care unit would compete against others to win contracts to care for specified numbers of patients. This is similar to the situation faced by companies in the private sector of the economy, which compete against each other to win commercial contracts.

This idea of competition between hospitals and community care units was the basis for the NHS and Community Care Act 1990.

## The National Health Service and Community Care Act 1990

This Act contains three main elements of relevance to the provision of health care: the **internal market**, **National Health Service Trusts**, and **budget-holding GPs**.

### The internal market

The roles of the *provider* of health care and the *purchaser* of health care were separated. District health authorities are now funded according to a type of RAWP formula (see page 102) to purchase services for their population from any provider (hospital) they regard as the best. As suggested by Endhoven, the hospitals now compete with each other to offer the best terms to the districts (that is the lowest prices, combined with the best quality possible) for contracts to provide health care for the people living in a district health authority. It is perfectly possible for a hospital to fail to win enough contracts to keep all its staff employed. In 1992, a hospital in east London found itself in just this situation, when the local district decided to give contracts to other hospitals.

### NHS Trusts

Hospitals and community care units were encouraged to become independent 'trusts' within the NHS. This new status allowed the managers great freedom to organise and manage their hospitals, so that they could compete in the most efficient way for the new contracts. In all normal respects, the hospitals are 'private', but they are still owned officially by the State.

Hospitals have to provide a range of core accident and emergency services, but can choose which other services to concentrate on, and can determine their own prices for their services, which they charge to districts and budget-holding GPs (see below).

Trusts started to come into effect in April 1991.

### Budget-holding GPs

The concept of a 'market' was extended to include GPs, in that larger practices could gain a degree of freedom to choose the hospital they wanted. In many ways they could become mini-districts, negotiating with hospitals to get 'the best deals' for their patients. Because these GPs were allowed to control their own budgets instead of having to obtain hospital services for

---

## THE FUTURE FOR GPs – FROM DOCTORS TO BUSINESSMEN?

Here is an example of an entrepreneurial budget-holding GP. It is a good example of the different attitude to health care provision that the government has sought to introduce.

List the services available. Check with your non-fundholding GP. Are these services available through his/her practice?

their patients through the districts, the term 'GP fundholders' is used to describe them.

The 1990 contract brought about other significant changes in the funding of GPs. General practitioners are independent professionals who are under contract with the National Health Service, but are not employed by it. The organisation which funds and co-ordinates the activities of GPs is the family health service authority (FHSA). When the contract came up for renewal in 1990, the government proposed sweeping changes to the role and payment of GPs.

- GPs could choose to hold their own budget, if they had more than 9000 patients. (This figure was later reduced to 7000.)
- A higher proportion of GPs' income would come from the number of patients they have (the capitation allowance).
- Targets were set for health screening of the elderly, and payment depended on reaching the target.
- Immunisation and vaccination targets were set for the patients according to the socio-economic status of the GPs' practice, and payment was made only on achieving the set percentage of immunisations and vaccinations.
- GPs were to take a more active role in preventive medicine and were to be paid for running health promotion workshops.

# The internal market for health care

### Advantages of the internal market
Supporters claim that the internal market:
- makes hospitals more efficient, because competition forces hospitals to seek to lower their costs;
- forces hospitals to work out the true costs of medical care (before the 1990 Act, few hospitals knew how much operations actually cost!);
- transfers the power away from the vested interests of consultants to managers. It gives greater choice to the districts and the budget-holding GPs on behalf of their 'clients';
- will provide higher standards of care by attaching money to particular patients, such that hospitals realise that patients are clients who are paying, and not simply patients, without rights, who are there to be treated.

The internal control given to managers of hospitals and community units with Trust status also allows them to pay staff differently, and hire and fire in such a way as to make the hospitals and quality of services more efficient.

### Disadvantages of the internal market
According to critics of the 1990 arrangements:
- there will be a gradual shift towards a semi-private system of health care, as Trust hospitals gain increasing levels of independence. Gradually, the NHS and all it stands for would be abolished;
- there has been a move towards a two-tier system of health care. A two-tier system means better quality Trust hospitals, which can pick and choose the sorts of services they offer, and the remaining fully integrated NHS hospitals, which would have to treat all the rest of the population for the illnesses and operations that are expensive and time-consuming;
- care for the elderly and chronically ill will decline, as the hospitals and community units find they are too expensive to care for;

## The NHS after the 1990 Act

**Parliament** As a public service, the NHS is responsibile to Parliament

**Department of Health Policy Board**
Headed by the Secretary of State for Health, the DoH Policy Board has the responsibility for running the NHS in England. It divides money between different regions and services.
In Scotland, Wales and Northern Ireland, responsibility falls with their respective Secretaries of State.

**NHS Management Executive**
Board of directors of the NHS led by chief executive. In charge of the day-to-day management of the service.

**Regional Health Authorities**
Fourteen in England (Scotland, Wales and Northern Ireland do not have this tier of health authority). They plan services in each region and award money to DHAs, Family Health Services Authorities, and GPs who manage their own budgets.

**Family Health Services Authority**
These manage the services provided by GPs, NHS dentists, pharmacists' shops and opticians.

**NHS Trusts**
Hospitals or services that have 'opted out' of health-authority control (see below).

**District Health Authority**
189 DHAs in England, 9 Health Authorities in Wales, 15 Health Boards in Scotland and 4 Health Boards in N. Ireland. Each is usually responsible for 1 large district hospital and 2–3 smaller hospitals, plus clinics.

£

**Budget-holding GP**
Funded from the Regional Health Authority.
Can send patients to all three types of hospital, depending on which will provide (in the GP's opinion) the best treatment for the lowest price (except for emergency, maternity or community service patients).
Cost of treatment is paid for by the GP unless over £5,000, when the DHA pays.

**Three types of hospital**
1. Directly-managed: Managed by the District Health Authority, but they have to win contracts to treat patients from health authorities or budget-holding GPs.

2. NHS Trust ('opted-out'): They obtain their money by competing with other hospitals to treat patients.

3. Private: Fee-paying hospitals. Individuals can pay to go here, or budget-holding GPs can decide to send their patients here. District Health Authorities can buy services from private hospitals.

£

**Non-budget-holding GP**
Funded from the District Health Authority. Can send patients to a hospital with which their health authority has a contract, or to other hospitals, if the services needed cannot be obtained locally and the local DHA is willing to pay.

**Mrs Mehta needs hospital treatment for a damaged hip. What sort of GP she visits may determine what hospital she will attend.**

**Source:** Redrawn from *The Guardian*, 25 June 1991

- the clinical judgement of consultants and doctors concerning what is best for patients would be overruled by managers in the interests of 'efficiency'.

## A MEDICAL MARKET PLACE

Answer these questions using information from the text and from the diagram on page 110.

1 What two types of GP are there? Explain the differences between them.
2 What types of hospital are there? What are the differences?
3 Explain how hospitals were funded until 1991.
4 What criticisms were made of the pre-1991 system?
5 What was the Act that introduced the changes?
6 How are hospitals funded today?
7 What criticisms have been made of the new funding system?
8 Arrange an interview with a representative of your local Trust hospital (there is likely to be a public liaison officer) and ask him/her to explain the new system. If possible, arrange for a hospital doctor or a GP to attend your meeting. If that is not possible, arrange to talk to a doctor before you meet the hospital representative, so that you can ask informed questions.

### St. Thomas's to close in London health shake-up

One of London's great teaching hospitals, St. Thomas's, faces closure under a policy plan drawn up by South East Thames Regional Health Authority....

There are three large hospitals close to each other in south-east London – Guy's, St. Thomas's and King's College and the rationale behind closing one is to avoid duplication. Guy's is London's flagship trust hospital; St. Thomas's is marked for trust status in April.... 'Forty per cent of our patients come from outside our region. But no notice is taken of what people want and they identify with particular hospitals.'

St. Thomas's has 800 beds and more than 3,500 staff, including 500 doctors and nearly 900 nurses. It has treated 31,500 in-patients and 71,500 casualties over the past 12 months. It is a centre of excellence for skin disorders (housing St. John's Dermatology Centre), eye treatment and cancer. The accident and emergency department is about to be expanded to take over casualties from Westminster Hospital, which is due to shut.

'St. Thomas's is vulnerable', said Geoff Martin, director of London Health Emergency, a pressure group monitoring hospital closures, 'and it's being squeezed out of business by market forces. But it's not like closing down a school. It provides essential services for many deprived inner city areas.'

The concentration of acute hospitals, medical schools and research centres in the capital has created an expensive pattern of care that leaves London short on primary and community care....

All London hospitals are losing income because routine in-patient referrals are dwindling, and it is cheaper to treat patients closer to home in district general hospitals.

Health care in London costs one-fifth more than elsewhere, according to a report on the future of the capital's health care by the King's Fund, an independent health think-tank, which recommended closing 15 hospitals.

The money, it argued, should go to family doctors and community care.

**Source**: The *Observer*, 2 August 1992

1 The article mentions the South East Thames Regional Health Authority. What is a regional health authority? Why should it be able to close down a hospital?
2 What is your regional health authority? What is the difference in function between a region and a district? What is your district health authority?
3 The article refers to a Trust hospital. What does this mean? Is your local hospital a Trust? Find out where your nearest one is. Are your community health services provided by a Trust?
4 It is argued by opponents of the new 1990 reforms that hospitals which specialise in certain medical areas, and therefore take a significant number of patients from outside their region/district, are losing out in the new model. The extract explains why this may be the case – can you find the explanation?
5 The hospital, it is claimed, 'provides essential services for many deprived inner city areas'. Do you think that there is evidence in the extract either way to support or contradict this?

# Performance indicators and QUALYs

Traditionally, there has been little attempt in the NHS to measure how effective health care is. The assumption has always been that the experts know best and if they say a medical activity is worth undertaking, or that surgery would be of little use, then these judgements have been accepted by the 'customers'. Outside health, people are far more critical of the services and goods they obtain (from shops and banks, for example), and it is only recently, with the writings of people such as Ivan Illich, that the need to assess the impact of medical services on patients has been judged necessary.

Most of the skyrocketing medical expenditures are destined for diagnosis and treatment of no or of doubtful effectiveness.... Doctors have affected such patterns [of disease] no more than priests did in earlier times.

**Source**: Ivan Illich, *Medical Nemesis* (Calder and Boyars, 1975)

## Measurements of health care effectiveness

In 1983, a set of performance indicators were first introduced into the NHS to see just how effective different districts are in their provision of health care. Because of problems in comparing different people by illness, the measurements of effectiveness were done in terms of comparing mortality.

The first measurements based on mortality said very little about the general effectiveness of the NHS in dealing with illness, and therefore measurements of health status were later derived, which would allow the comparison of different medical procedures or hospitals.

### Comparing outcomes of medical intervention

A large number of measurements of health status were developed, all of which constructed a score of how positive the outcome of the medical process had been. People would be graded on a before-and-after basis on the following criteria:
- physical function;
- social function;
- emotional well-being;
- pain;
- energy;
- cognitive functions (e.g. how alert they were).

### Cost-benefit analysis: measuring the worth of medical intervention and establishing priorities

In the 1980s, the use of measurements in health was taken further with the introduction of QUALYs, or 'Quality of Life Years'. This is a way of measuring the costs of different forms of health and medical intervention for the positive benefits obtained, measured in terms of length of life and quality of that life. The point of this is to pinpoint those operations that may be performed at great cost to the NHS, using up resources which could be better utilised in some other treatment, and then producing an outcome of only limited benefit. From this, priorities on the most efficient ways of spending limited resources can be established.

QUALYs allow you to make choices in situations where you have to choose because of lack of resources. What would you do in the following situation?

Two patients have a desperate need for a renal dialysis machine. One is 16 years old, blind and physically disabled. The other is 70, but has no other obvious health problems, apart from the need for dialysis. Which do you choose for treatment?

Construct your own version of QUALY to arrive at your decision.

# Private-sector health care

The NHS is a State-funded health service in which every British (and EC) person has the right to appropriate health treatment, free of charge. However, people can choose to have private health care. There are various reasons as to why a person may opt for private health care. These include:

- choice of consultant and hospital;
- belief that a better standard of medical and nursing care is given in the private sector;
- desire to avoid waiting lists;
- wish to have better control over treatment and to be consulted;
- desire for private room;
- company offers private medicine as a 'perk' of the person's employment.

Before the NHS, health care was based on voluntary and private provision. With the introduction of the NHS in 1948, the private health care market collapsed, as people realised that they could obtain high standards of care without payment. Only 230 small, poorly equipped hospitals remained outside the NHS. In the 1950s, most commentators on the NHS argued that private medicine would disappear. However, private medicine remained and even managed to grow slowly. In the late 1970s, there was a faster rate of growth in the numbers of people using private medical services, and this increased rapidly in the 1980s. The majority of the provision was through medical insurance companies such as BUPA (British United Provident Association) and PPP (Private Patients' Plan).

Between 1979 and 1992, there was a 60 per cent increase in the number of private hospital beds available, and a 40 per cent increase in the number of private hospitals. In 1991, there were approximately 2.3 million people with private health insurance.

## The growth in private health care

The growth in private medicine was influenced by a number of factors. These are listed below.

- The Conservative governments encouraged the development of private health care, and 'placed it on the agenda'. Tax relief was given for elderly people who wished to take out private health insurance.
- There was a change in people's attitudes in the 1980s, in that it became acceptable to pay for health care; whereas in the 1950s and 1970s there was a common view that it was somehow immoral to 'jump queues' for health care by paying.
- Employers began to provide employee purchase schemes for private health cover as a part of the normal employment package, along with company cars and sometimes assistance with school fees. In fact the growth in private health was mainly through these schemes, rather than through individual subscribers.

- Public debate about the state of the NHS and the problems that were beginning to emerge, of underfunding and long waiting lists, began to worry people. Because of the growth in prosperity of the 1980s, many more people and companies were prepared and able to pay into private insurance schemes. The private health care companies were able to play on people's fears.
- A further development, that was both a result and a cause of the growth of private health care, was the rapid growth in small, local private hospitals. This meant that people could have private treatment without having to travel to London or another big city.

The growth in private health care has not been just in hospital beds (the acute sector), but also in private residential care homes and in private nursing homes. The residential homes have increased their bed numbers by 400 per cent since 1979, and the private nursing homes by 250 per cent.

It has often been argued that private treatment takes the heat off the NHS by treating large numbers of patients who would otherwise increase the length of the NHS waiting lists. In 1990, over half a million operations were carried out privately, representing an increase of almost 50 per cent over five years. However, research by Nicholl suggests that those who opted out of the NHS, choosing private treatment, did not necessarily shorten waiting lists, as the response of the government to shorter waiting lists has been to hold back government money. The more affluent simply bought themselves health care and, in doing so, left the less well off in the same situation as before.

The private sector also takes staff who have been trained in the NHS at public expense. Furthermore, tax relief for the over 60s helps to reduce government resources and therefore takes possible funds away from the NHS.

---

...the work carried out by the private sector, has redistribute[d] access to resources and manpower in favour of better-off patients of working age who live in London and the south-east of England. The more privileged sick (in terms of income, class and power) have been substituted for the less fortunate sick who remain on the NHS lists.

**Source**: E. Beck *et al*, *In the Best of Health* (Chapman and Hall, 1992)

Explain the above extract.

---

My mother has been in severe pain for the past several years with a form of arthritis and can now walk only with considerable difficulty. It is very distressing to see her in this state every day. She has now been told that her condition can be considerably alleviated by a hip replacement operation. She recently went to see the consultant surgeon in the NHS hospital in Newcastle who told her that this is correct. He then told her that she can either remain in pain and semi-crippled for the next 12 to 18 months or she can pay more than £5,000 and he will do the operation straight away.

Some people might call this choice but from my mother's position it feels very like blackmail. She is in pain. The pain can be relieved, but only if you have a lot of money. This is a condition which primarily affects the oldest and weakest members of society. Is it right that they be offered the "choice" of 12 months pain or parting with their savings? She is very brave but the pain often reduces her to tears.

**David Brazier,**
Jesmond,
Newcastle upon Tyne.

1 Some people have argued that private health care should be banned and that treatment should only be available on the basis of 'need'. Do you agree with this?

2 Do you think this would have any effect on the possibility of the lady in the above extract getting a hip operation more quickly?

# Primary health care

By 'primary health care' we mean the services dealing with people in the community. Such community-based services consist of GPs, practice nurses, district nurses, health visitors, community midwives and physiotherapists, occupational and speech therapists and chiropodists.

Find out about, and briefly describe, the role of the following primary care staff and services. If necessary, contact your local family health service authority or community health executive.

- Community psychiatric nurse
- Community mental handicap nurse
- Chiropodist
- Health visitor
- Practice nurse

- District nurse
- Occupational therapist
- Well-woman clinic
- Genito-urinary clinic
- Family planning clinic

In any one day in Britain, approximately 650 000 people are seen by GPs, and 100 000 are seen by nurses or other community health professionals. Although the GP is generally the hub of primary health services, the provision of care in the community is the responsibility of a **primary health care team**. These teams were instituted as a result of the Harding Report (1981), and in 1986 the Cumberlege Report argued for the setting up of groups of nurses and other health professionals to cover a geographical 'patch'. The groups were to be based in health centres, or GP surgeries, but were employed by the health service rather than the GP. This system has been successful, but with the growth in budget-holding GPs, there has been a great increase in health professionals actually employed by the GPs to undertake work delegated by them. These employees are usually 'practice nurses', who undertake the role of the district nurse but are answerable directly to the GP, their employer. District nurses are professionals in their own right; they are independent of GPs and can use their own judgement independently.

# Health promotion

The improvement in the nation's health at the beginning of the twentieth century resulted less from medical care than from better nutrition, housing and immunisation. In the second half of the century, while medical knowledge and services have developed substantially, the diseases most responsible for premature mortality – coronary heart disease, cancer and stroke – are similarly more likely to be controlled by prevention than by treatment. So it is a paradox that far less emphasis is given to prevention than is given to treatment, both in medical practice and in health service provision.

## Preventive health

Traditionally, the NHS has stressed the importance of *curing* people rather than *preventing* them becoming ill in the first place. Yet it is known that by reducing smoking it is possible to limit the number of people dying from heart disease and lung cancer. By reducing excess consumption of alcohol, it is possible to prevent cirrhosis of the liver and motor-related deaths. Safe sexual practices help to limit HIV infection and other sexually transmitted diseases. By putting fluoride in drinking water, the amount of tooth decay can be radically reduced.

Preventive health measures can be divided into three approaches: primary, secondary and tertiary.

- **Primary**   is the prevention of disease in the first place through actions such as immunisation.
- **Secondary**   is the early detection of disease by activities such as screening, and then intervening if possible.
- **Tertiary**   is to minimise the disability and handicap resulting from a disease that cannot be cured or which leaves the individual with some loss of function.

Preventive health can be defined as medical action to maintain or bring about good health in the population. Health promotion, however, goes beyond this and recognises that illness and disease do not simply hit people at random, but are the result of particular ways of living or particular experiences of life. Health promotion therefore aims to draw the government in to influence people's lifestyles. The extent to which the government should do this, though, has been an issue of great debate.

[Illness is...] related less to man's outside environment than to his own personal behaviour, what might be termed our lifestyle.... [Consequently,]...much of the responsibility for ensuring his own good health lies with the individual.... [The responsibility of governments and health professionals] is limited to ensuring that the public have access to such knowledge as is available about the importance of personal habits to health and, at the very least, no obstacles are placed in the way of those who decide to act on that knowledge....

McKinlay (1974) studied the significance of the social and political environment in his analysis of the political economy of health. According to McKinlay, the efforts of the health care system can be called 'downstream activities' devoted as they are to the rescue of the sick. However, this type of activity cannot influence the level of health of a population when various interest groups and large-scale profit oriented corporations are operating 'upstream', constantly adding to the pool of those in need of rescue. Problems such as lung cancer, heart disease, obesity, alcohol abuse and road traffic accidents can be linked to organizations such as the food and tobacco industries, who spend billions of dollars promoting unhealthy lifestyles.

**Source**: D. Locker, 'Prevention and Health Promotion' in G. Scambler (ed.), *Sociology as Applied to Medicine* (Ballière Tindall, 1991)

## The Health Education Authority

The approach of the British government is that people ought to be provided with information on the potential dangers to health posed by certain activities and then they ought to be left to themselves to decide to heed the warning. Therefore, it uses the Health Education Authority as its agency to inform people of the dangers of certain sorts of lifestyles and the benefits of healthy activities.

Critics of this approach point out that there are many factors influencing people's choices of lifestyles and many of these are outside the control of the individual. Obvious examples include pollution, stress at work, poverty, poor housing, etc. Government critics argue that it is therefore essential for governments to tackle the causes of ill health and not simply to advise people of the potential dangers.

### 'MARLBORO MAN'

Wayne McLaren, who portrayed the rugged "Marlboro Man" in cigarette ads but became an anti-smoking crusader after developing lung cancer, has died, aged 51.

Mr McLaren, who was diagnosed with the disease about two years ago, died on Wednesday at Hoag Hospital in Newport Beach, California. His mother said: "Some of his last words were 'Take care of the children. Tobacco will kill you, and I am living proof of it'."

Last spring, he appeared before a meeting of shareholders of Phillip Morris Inc., maker of Marlboro, and asked them to curb their advertising. He made other public appearances to warn about smoking.

Mr McLaren, a rodeo rider, actor and Hollywood stuntman, was one of several dozen models hired in 1975 to appear in Marlboro magazine and billboard ads, evoking a tough and handsome smoker's image for the brand.

He once said he was a pack-and-a-half-a-day smoker for about 25 years.

In an interview last week, Mr McLaren said his habit had "caught up with me. I've spent the last month of my life in an incubator and I'm telling you, it's just not worth it." – AP.

**Source**: Adapted from the *Guardian*, 25 July 1992

**1** How many people in the class/group smoke?

**2** What reasons do they have for smoking?

**3** What is their response to this extract?

**4** As a group carry out a simple survey. Ask a sample of people:
  a) if they smoke;
  b) if they could list the disadvantages/advantages of smoking;
  c) which they think outweigh the other;
  d) if they do smoke, what they think of the extract;
  e) if, having read the extract, it would stop them smoking.

**5** What does your research tell you about health education programmes which seek to show people the dangers of particular activities?

**6** What approach would you take to curbing smoking?

**7** Do you think this has any relevance to preventing the spread of AIDS?

### FACTORS AFFECTING HEALTH

Write a paragraph on each of the factors in the diagram on page 118, explaining its importance and suggesting what could be done to improve an individual's standard of health.

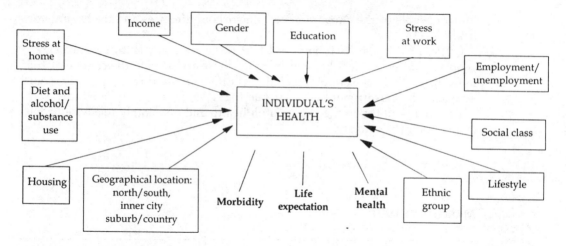

# Inequalities in health

Most people believe that health and illness are natural states, that is a person is unlucky or genetically predisposed when they fall ill. However, research indicates that health and illness are not random: certain groups in the population are far more likely than others to be ill and to die at a younger age than normal. The main differences in health are related to social class, gender, ethnic group and geographical location. But there are other factors that also affect an individual's health: see the chart above.

### HEALTH CARE USAGE

The conclusion is that the better off appear to receive more health care under the NHS relative to need than the less well off.

There are several reasons why the costs of using a free service will be greater for potential working class users from the lower . . . social classes. . . .

Time spent travelling will be greater because they are more reliant on public transport. . . . Also they are likely to have further to travel, for the areas in which they live are poorly endowed with medical facilities. The costs of waiting are higher since they cannot so easily make appointments by telephone.

Not only may the lower groups lose more time using the NHS than the higher ones but the cost of each hour thus lost may be greater, particularly for those in work. Many professionals and managers are paid an annual salary and hence are unlikely to lose income for time spent visiting the doctor during working hours, whereas workers in manual occupations paid by the day or the hour may have to forgo their pay for any time thus taken off.

Not only costs but perceptions of the benefits from health care may differ. . . . This may be because the health knowledge of the lower groups is poorer in some respects . . . Individuals from lower social groups can find the Health Service – staffed as it is with largely middle-class personnel – at best unhelpful and at worst actively hostile to their interests. Immigrant groups in particular may encounter actual discrimination.

There is much evidence . . . the better off will always be able to make more effective use of even a freely provided service than the less well off.

**Source**: J. Le Grand, *The Strategy of Equality* (1982)

**1** List the reasons why the poorer groups may use the health services less often than the middle class.

**2** In what ways, if any, can the NHS combat this different use of health services?

**3** If it is true that the free health service is used more often by the middle class, is it right that there should be no charges at all to these middle-class people?

**4** In the letter written to the Guardian newspaper (see page 114), do you think that the author is working class? What evidence could you put forward to support your answer?

## Social class and health

Evidence from the Black Report (1980) and the Whitehead Report indicate quite clearly that the lower a person's social class, the greater the possibility of ill health and of relatively early death. For example, the Black Report, which was based on statistics from the 1970s, calculated that for the two-year period it was studying, if one assumed that working class people (social classes IV and V) had the same expectation of life as the professional and managerial classes (social class I), then 75 000 working-class people would not have died. This figure includes 10 000 infant and child deaths. However, the statistics on which the Black Report was based are now outdated, and it would be reasonable to argue that changes in society have lessened the differences between the middle and working classes. Unfortunately, a study by Marmot and McDowell in 1986 showed that the differences may well have widened since the 1970s. Over the last 20 years, although there has been a decline in the number of early deaths (that is deaths before pensionable age) for working-class people, the fall has been greater for middle-class people.

When it comes to illness (or **morbidity**), we know that working-class manual workers are far more likely to suffer from long-standing chronic illness than non-manual, professional people. Once again, when looking at changes over time, it seems that the middle class have improved their health faster than the working class.

### Explanations for social class inequalities in health

Four types of explanation have been suggested for the apparent gap in the morbidity and mortality levels of the various social classes.

- **Artefact**   This approach suggests that the statistical evidence is giving a misleading picture. In the last 20 years a great change has taken place in Britain in terms of employment. Whereas 30 years ago, nearly two-thirds of the population were in manual jobs, today the figure is almost reversed. The majority of employees are in white collar jobs. When, therefore, statistics show an improvement in the health and mortality levels of the middle class they refer to the bulk of the population including many people (or their children) who were in the manual working class in the past. In short, the actual number of people who are working in manual jobs and have poor health is declining all the time. Therefore, the growth in the gap between the middle and working class is a sign of overall improvement. This is not to say that people are unconcerned about the poor health levels of those remaining in manual jobs, simply that the numbers in poor health are small and getting smaller.

  *Policy implications*

  The policy implications of this explanation are that inequality will decline without interference, but a limited amount should be spent on screening and health education.

## MORTALITY BY SOCIAL CLASS AND REGION

| Standard region/country | Men | | | Women | | |
|---|---|---|---|---|---|---|
| | I & II | IV & V | IV & V as % of I & II | I & II | IV & V | IV & V as % of I & II |
| North | 81 | 152 | 188 | 80 | 136 | 170 |
| Wales | 79 | 144 | 182 | 79 | 125 | 158 |
| Scotland | 87 | 157 | 180 | 91 | 141 | 155 |
| North-West | 83 | 146 | 176 | 86 | 135 | 157 |
| Yorkshire & Humberside | 79 | 134 | 170 | 78 | 120 | 154 |
| West Midlands | 75 | 127 | 169 | 77 | 113 | 147 |
| South-East | 67 | 112 | 167 | 71 | 100 | 141 |
| East Midlands | 74 | 122 | 165 | 73 | 110 | 151 |
| South-West | 69 | 108 | 156 | 70 | 96 | 137 |
| East Anglia | 65 | 93 | 143 | 69 | 81 | 117 |
| Great Britain | 74 | 129 | 174 | 76 | 116 | 153 |

Infants (less than 1 year), 1984     Men aged 20–64, 1979–83     Women aged 20–59, 1979–83

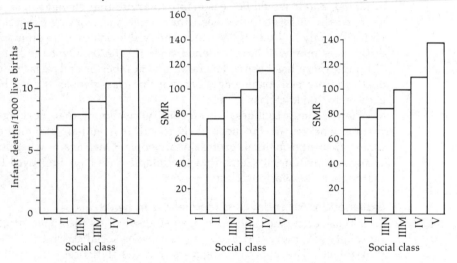

**Source**: P. Townsend, *Inequalities in Health* (Penguin, 1982)

In the diagrams and the table, social class is measured using the Registrar General's classification in which I and II are managerial and professional, IIIN are white-collar workers, IIIM are skilled manual workers and IV and V are less skilled manual workers.

SMR is a way of measuring whether groups of people have above or below average chances of dying for a given age range, in this case 20–64 for males, or 20–59 for women.

**1** What is the relationship between social class and infant mortality?

**2** What differences are there in adult mortality levels, by social class?

**3** Summarise the information provided on the chances of premature death by social class and region.

● **Natural or social selection**   This explanation suggests that it is not social class and employment which causes poor health, but poor health which causes the level of unemployment. Therefore, it is statistically true that those in worse jobs are likely to die earlier and have higher levels of illness. However, the poor job is a reflection of this poor health.

*Policy implications*

There are no policy implications except to say that it is unnecessary to target the working class for health education, as these people are unlikely to be able to alter their health status.

- **Behavioural and cultural explanations** Both these approaches stress the importance of lifestyle. What we eat, smoke and drink and the amount of exercise and stress we encounter all have a bearing on our health. However, the behavioural approach stresses individual choice and activity, while the cultural approach places much greater emphasis on the wider influences that create those choices of activities. Therefore, the argument here is that working-class people are more likely to engage in activities which are bad for their health, for example, smoking or eating fatty foods. One group of academics (behavioural explanation) argue that this is their individual choice and another group (cultural explanation) argue that this must be understood in terms of advertising, or by pressure of other people around an individual.

*Policy implications*

The policy implication of the cultural explanation is to change the way people view unhealthy activities, possibly by banning advertising for such things as smoking or even banning smoking itself. The policy implication of the individual or behavioural explanation is to persuade people to make healthier choices in their lifestyles.

- **Materialist explanations** This approach is the most radical one of all, and suggests that the conditions in which people work and live, and the differences in income and wealth, are the real causes of ill health and premature death. Supporters of this explanation argue that stress, poor diet, long hours of work, exposure to pollution at work and outside are far more important than individual actions.

*Policy implications*

The policy implication here is a radical appraisal of wealth distribution and conditions of work and housing.

## Research on health inequalities

Recent research by Fox on the differences in health levels between civil servants came out with some interesting information which relates particularly to the artefact and the natural or social selection models.

Fox found very different levels of mortality between civil servants of different grades. Those in the lowest civil service grade were three times more likely to die before pensionable age than those in the highest grades. All the civil servants are in white collar employment.

All civil servants in the study were given a thorough medical examination at the beginning of the study and, in the group which had apparent good health, there were very clear-cut differences in mortality by the different grades of civil servant over the following years. This strongly suggests that good health is not what determines employment levels in the first place.

Townsend studied 678 electoral wards in the north-east of England and a further smaller sample of wards in inner London. He found that there was a quite conclusive relationship between material deprivation, such as high unemployment levels, low car ownership levels, low owner occupancy rates (indicating people who are too poor to buy) and high levels of overcrowding, and standards of health such as sickness, premature death, levels of disability and low birth weight.

A Californian study tried to separate the effects of poverty from those of 13 'risk factors' including smoking, alcohol consumption and exercise. The researchers concluded that if a poor person and a rich person engaged in exactly the same sort of behaviour, the poor person would be one-and-a-half times more likely to die.

*What do the pieces of research stated above tell us about the various explanations for differences in health?*

## Women and health

Women have greater life expectancy than men, with a life expectancy of 76 years at birth compared to a man's 70 years. Seventy per cent of those alive over the age of 75 are women. Interestingly, in Third World countries it is men who live longer. When it comes to illness, it is women who report higher levels of acute (short-term) and chronic (long-term) illness. More than two-thirds of disabled people in Britain are women – though this may be to do with the fact that they live longer and are therefore more likely to have disabilities. Nevertheless, when planning health care, it is necessary to remember the gender imbalance in the population, and decide what special facilities may be appropriate for women.

One area where women are over-represented is that of mental illness. Women are particularly likely to be suffering from depression. Explanations for women's physical and mental health centre on the stress that women are placed under in the dual roles of housewife and worker, and from the fact that women are noticeably poorer than men.

Firstly, the biological facts of women's greater longevity and their role in human reproduction go some way to explaining the higher rates of morbidity (illness) amongst women and their greater use of services. . . . Because of the greater time that women spend in the home, housing conditions have been found to be a more important influence on women's than on men's health.

Overcrowding, dampness and high-rise housing have all been linked to health problems in women and the children they care for. Research has also noted women's vulnerability to poverty. Women are over-represented and men are under-represented in many of the groups in poverty in Britain.

**Source**: H. Graham, 'Women, Health and Illness', *Social Studies Review*, September, 1987

*List the reasons given for women's ill health.*

## Ethnic minorities and health

Ethnic minorities in the UK have significantly lower levels of health and shorter expectation of life than the majority of the White population. The main explanation is that of material deprivation. The suggestion is that as they have significantly lower standards of living than the general population, they are more likely to suffer from diseases in just the same way that deprived White people are particularly susceptible to illness.

### A questionnaire for your local hospital and community health unit

Most hospitals claim they are doing all they can to make their institutions acceptable and accessible to ethnic minorities. The questionnaire below was designed by experts in the field and published in a specialist journal for health service managers.

*Arrange an interview with a member of the management of a local hospital or community health unit or Trust. To what extent do they provide the services or fulfil the criteria?*

## CHECKLIST OF PROVISION FOR ETHNIC MINORITIES

**Access to Services**
Advocacy and interpreting
- Is there provision for patients to communicate with health workers in the language in which they feel most comfortable through trained advocates or interpreters?
Using untrained members of staff or family members to translate is not appropriate. An interpreter's role is to find out from the patient the answers to the staff's questions and to relay to the patient the staff's wishes or directives. An advocate's role is the exact opposite: to find out from the staff answers to the patient's questions and communicate their wishes.

Information
- Are your hospital and health clinic signposts translated into languages relevant to your local community?
- Is your information for patients available to local community languages?
- Is your interpreting or advocacy service publicised in the letter of admission?
- Do you have an arrangement to correspond with or send communications to patients in languages of their choice?
- Is information about complaints procedures available in languages relevant to your local communities?
- Is your information available in other forms, such as audiovisual or pictorial?

Physical access
- Is the service conveniently located?
- Are clinic times convenient and in the evening as well as day time?

**Acceptability of Services**
- Do you have an equal opportunities policy which encourages the recruitment and career development of staff from minority communities?
- Do women patients have the option of consulting women doctors, professionals allied to medicine, and so on?
- Does your hospital provide meals that meet the religious and cultural dietary requirements of your patients?
- Is there provision for inpatients to have a place of worship?
- Have your staff and managers undergone training about cultural traditions relevant to the local population, such as traditions of death and bereavement, and hygiene and grooming? Does this training include acknowledgement of diversity within communities?
- Is there provision for your staff to have racism awareness training?
- Is there a mechanism whereby patients from ethnic minority groups are consulted about the acceptability of the service and can participate in the needs assessment and service specification process?

Appropriateness of services
- Do you provide appropriate dietary advice, for example, to diabetics?
- Do you ensure that health education is adapted to make it relevant to your patients' cultural backgrounds?
- Is there a mechanism for monitoring the types of treatment given to black and ethnic clients?

*Source: Health Service Journal, 5 March 1992*

*The above is a checklist of ethnic awareness activities suggested for hospitals. Does your local hospital do these things? Do you think it important that hospitals do the activities in the checklist?*

# Assignment

It is generally accepted that smoking and excessive consumption of alcohol carries serious health risks, that the use of most drugs such as cocaine and heroin are extremely harmful and that unprotected sex can lead a person to contract AIDS or a sexually transmitted disease.

You are advising the Department of Health on the best and most effective way of running government health promotion campaigns regarding two of these issues. Choose your two issues.

How would you advise the DoH to go about its task? You should consider some of the following points:

You should consider some of the following points:

- target groups
- forms of access to these groups
- aims of programme?
- the role of punishment and coercion
- the role of manufacturers or providers of drugs
- the best/most effective/most cost-efficient means of getting the message across

You might include sample material concerning your programme, by making a video, posters etc.

What underlying message should you give? (Sex is potentially dangerous, sexual activity outside marriage is wrong, enjoy alternative means of sexual activity, etc.).

You should also be able to prove your assertions that drugs/unprotected sex/excess alcohol is dangerous. Therefore, you should research the relationship of harm and the activity you wish to stop.

For each activity you suggest, please also advise the government on the benefits and any possible risks/costs to the Treasury, as well as likely opposition from vested interests.

Finally, where possible, relate these arguments to the explanations of health inequalities presented here.

# CHAPTER 6

# The Personal Social Services and the Practice of Social Work

## Introduction

In this chapter we will explore the personal social services and the activities of social workers employed by them and by voluntary organisations. The chapter begins with an overview of the development of personal social services and a description of the current structure and nature of Social Service departments. We then look briefly at how these are financed, before examining the different types of social workers and the sorts of tasks they undertake.

Social work is a general name given to the role of a wide variety of professionals who have very different views on how they may best achieve the aims of improving the quality of their clients' lives. We spend some time in the chapter examining these different approaches, which vary from the belief that social workers ought to counsel clients to help themselves, to those who believe in quite radical community and even political action.

The chapter then moves on to look at a much neglected group of social workers, those who are employed in residential settings.

Finally, there is a section on one of the key skills needed by those who work in welfare and care settings – effective communication.

## The personal social services

The personal social services are those services, generally staffed by social workers, which look after the needs of groups such as physically or sexually abused children, elderly people, the mentally ill, those with learning disabilities and the physically disabled. The services are run by the local authorities or by voluntary organisations of various kinds.

The settings in which these groups are cared for are primarily in the community (that is in their own homes), where the 'clients' are visited and given the assistance regarded as necessary. In extreme cases, people are cared for in residential settings (hospitals, hostels, elderly persons' homes).

# The origins of social work

Social work developed as a response to poverty and unemployment. In the nineteenth century, conditions in the large industrialised towns had become appalling for enormous numbers of people, and their plight was painfully obvious to the more affluent living in those towns. Various initiatives developed to combat poverty and the problems associated with it. On the one hand, the workers themselves combined together in friendly societies and later trade unions to try to improve working conditions and provide themselves with some basic forms of health and welfare benefits. On the other hand, the more affluent began to develop charitable organisations which, in their eyes at least, would alleviate some of the greatest problems of the poor. By the middle of the nineteenth century, a large number of such organisations existed, offering limited assistance.

One of the best organised and successful of these was the Charity Organisation Society (today it still exists as the Family Welfare Association). This organisation set out to distinguish between people who were poor or needy through no fault of their own, and the rest of the poor. The society then undertook to work with individual families to improve their situation.

In London, Octavia Hill, a housing reformer, organised the purchase and building of blocks of flats for the poor, where they were encouraged to follow particular patterns of behaviour which she believed would help alleviate their poverty.

These were the beginnings of social work as we would define it today – that is a consistent, organised approach to the social problems of individuals, which focuses on enabling them to change their situation and to help themselves.

The first **probation officers** also emerged at this time, when magistrates began to 'bind people over', instead of sending them to prison. The person had to report to a clergyman or someone appointed by the court, who would ensure that the person behaved in a lawful way.

Finally, hospitals began to appoint **almoners** or **medical social workers**, whose job developed into assisting patients and their families.

Throughout the early part of the twentieth century, the belief grew that there ought to be some form of State provision of social work for certain needy groups – ideally to be provided through the local authorities. An example of this is the establishment in the 1920s of services for the physically and mentally 'disabled' by local authorities with grants from central government.

However, these beginnings have only limited links with modern social and probation work, as the real beginnings of the modern form of social work can be traced back to the period after the Beveridge reforms.

# Social Services from 1948 onward

By 1948, three different sets of personal social services had developed.

### Children's departments

In 1946, the Curtis Report recommended the setting up of departments of local authorities which were responsible for fostering and adoption, child care, family casework and children's homes. Gradually the powers of the Children's departments were extended, so that by 1952 they were given the power to investigate cases of abuse and, in 1963, they were given powers to undertake preventive action.

### Health services

Various health services which were related to existing or possible social problems were also provided by local authorities under the power of the Medical Officer of Health. These services included health visiting, occupational therapy, mental welfare officers, hospital social workers and day nurseries.

### Welfare departments

Welfare departments of local authorities covered a wide range of responsibilities and activities that the other two omitted. These included residential care for the elderly, assistance for homeless families and services for the disabled. In 1962, they had their powers extended to provide meals, a range of social services (such as day centres) and recreational facilities.

## The Seebohm Committee

This was set up in 1965, and reported in 1968. The result was the structure of the Social Services which exists today – and is only now being broken up under the influence of the Community Care legislation of 1990.

Seebohm recommended that the various different elements of personal social services should be unified into one organisation, which would be run by local authorities. In 1970, as a result of the Local Authority Social Services Act, the new local authority Social Services departments were set up. The Health departments were broken up, with some of the responsibilities handed over to the NHS, including health visiting and much of the occupational therapy work.

The Welfare departments and Children's departments formed the basis of the new Personal Social Services departments. Medical social workers joined later in 1974. The importance of the Social Services departments also increased at this time with the passing of two Acts which placed greater responsibilities on the shoulders of the local authorities regarding children and the long-term sick and disabled. (The two Acts were the Children Act 1969 and the Chronically Sick and Disabled Persons Act 1970.)

As a result of the changes, the new social workers were to be 'generically trained', by which it was meant that they would not have a narrow specialism, but would be able to deal with the problems of a range of different groups. It was argued that, in the past, social workers could only deal with a very narrow range of problems, and that when the problems went wider than this, more social workers would have to be brought in. This wasted time and energy and often led to poor co-ordination and duplication of effort.

Social Services are generally run through area officers rather than through a central headquarters.

## The Barclay Report

In 1980, the Barclay Report argued for a radical rethink of social work, and in particular pushed for the **community approach**. Peer Barclay, the author of the approach, argued that the bulk of assistance was provided by family, friends and neighbours, rather than the statutory (i.e. government) or voluntary organisations. Therefore, he argued, the task of social workers should be to try to build up this community, so that it could care for its own. In order to do this, the report recommended that small groups of social workers should be attached to a neighbourhood or 'patch', to foster good community relations and to help weld the community together.

Explain the following ways of organising social services. If you were a new head of a Social Work department and were asked to consider the best way to organise the provision of social services, which model would you choose and why?
● generic social work
● specialist social work
● patch based social work
Now, find out how your local Social Services department is organised.

## Recent changes

The reorganisation of social work training with the Qualifying Diploma in Social Work, which was gradually introduced in the early 1990s, and the requirements of the introduction of the Community Care legislation at about the same time, has meant a shift for social workers back towards specialisation. The two-year qualification provides a year of generic study and a year of specialisation.

The 1990 legislation (the National Health Service and Community Care Act) has had a significant influence on the role of the Social Services departments – such that they will decreasingly be seen as the provider of all services to clients, particularly in the field of community care, but more of a purchaser of those services. This is discussed in greater detail in chapter 7, 'Community Care'.

### The changing role of Social Services departments

In future, Social Services departments will have to have a strategic view of all the sources of care available in their area. Direct provision of care by the local authorities will only be one of a variety of forms of provision – charity, private and State. In fact the most important role of the social services is no longer the provision of care but (a) ensuring that their clients receive decent standards of care and (b) supporting the efforts of the community itself to provide care.

The chart on page 129 shows the traditional structure of a local authority Social Services department. The NHS and Community Care Act 1990 has, however, brought about many changes. Read pages 153–9 and then ask your local social services what changes have taken place in the department, and why.

# Paying for social services

In the 1990s, there has been a gradual introduction of charges for various welfare activities. The most noticeable has been the charging for home help services. Charging has become a topical issue and closely relates to the debate on universal and targeted services, which are fully discussed on pages 29–31.

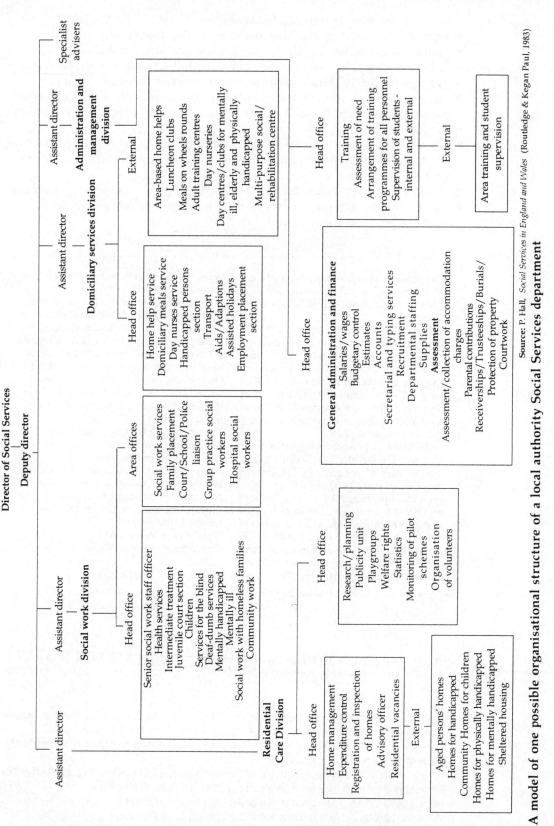

**A model of one possible organisational structure of a local authority Social Services department**

**Source:** P. Hall, *Social Services in England and Wales* (Routledge & Kegan Paul, 1983)

Five reasons have been given for charging:
- to reduce to the taxpayers the cost of providing free services;
- by implementing small charges, the demand for services declines – as people have to make a choice about what they do with their money, when services are not free they may choose other activities to spend their money on;
- placing a charge on one activity and providing another free indicates where the priorities of the Social Services are (for example, preventing child abuse versus home helps);
- when provision is free, people tend to use it without thinking of its real cost (to the taxpayer) – a small charge brings the issue of cost into the mind of the client;
- charges act as 'symbols' which reflect the ideology of Conservative thinking.

Critics of charges say they simply punish the poor, who are the main consumers of welfare services.

---

The personal agony, and the "special local circumstances" of Colin Smart, led to a shabbily distorted analysis of British social services.

Since the Williams Report 1965, the shortcomings of the residential sector has been known. But who is to blame, that residential staff have not been supported by adequate training, status and salary? Why people like Mr Smart, who rather than blow-the-whistle, compromised, and complied with central and local government's chronic 20-year neglect.

His belief that resources are not an issue is naive. During the 70s, social services received only 0.9 per cent of GDP, ie, nine pence out of every £100 of GDP – the high point of 1.1 per cent in 1987/8, was reduced by 1990 to 0.9 per cent. Yet Britain's total government expenditure, as a proportion of our GDP, has been one of the lowest in Western Europe for more than a decade and our welfare and community services, including social services, was the second lowest in the EC – Britain leading only on police and defence!

His callous disregard for the commitment of the vast majority of field social workers is despicable. In 1973 Britain had one of the highest levels of cruelty to children, seen in the bad and infant homicide rates; but we have had the biggest reduction in such fatalities in the whole developed world. Indeed, in 1990 we had our lowest ever level, an indicator of very successful protection of children.

There is evidence that social services have done more with proportionately less, and staff deserve commendation, not further attacks on their morale. Social work, like kidney dialyses, can achieve much, only the political and economic will are lacking to provide the support that vulnerable and troubled citizens need.

(Prof) **Colin Pritchard**
Department of Social Work
  Studies,
University of Southampton.

**Source**: The *Guardian*, 8 September 1992

GDP stands for Gross Domestic product, which means the total value of goods and services in any one year in a country. In effect, it is a measure of a country's economic wealth.

The above is a letter published in a national newspaper, replying to a criticism of social workers.
1 For how long have the 'shortcomings' of the residential sector been known?
2 How has the government's spending on social services changed according to Dr Pritchard? According to him, is this adequate?
3 Where does Britain come for spending on social services out of the 12 EC states? What did Britain spend more money on proportionately than any other EC member state?
4 What changes have occurred in the treatment of children in Britain?
5 What would improve British social services according to Dr Pritchard?

# Types of social workers

## A SOCIAL WORKER'S VIEW

Serge Paul is district manager for Sandwell Social Services in the West Midlands....

Social workers, explains Mr Paul, deal with the people who do not have the opportunities offered to most. He says: 'We work with the poor, children in difficulties, black people in deprived areas, carers, elderly people who are dependent, people recovering from illness, people with learning difficulties. I am talking about the people who do not always have the opportunities that others have in the new Europe.'

As with all social work, Mr Paul's job is to put his clients in touch with the people who can help. He says 'Social work is the interface between agencies. It's about enabling. The task is to help people help themselves.'

There is a continuous balancing act in social work, with social control versus social change and personal versus societal responsibility the constant dilemmas.

A good example is the thorny issue of child abuse. Clearly, Mr Paul accepts without question that children have to be protected and this must be the first and foremost duty of the social worker involved in child abuse case work.

However, he also believes that it is a cyclical phenomenon – that people who were abused as children grow up to become abusers themselves. Mr Paul's gut feeling about child abusers is that they should be 'put away for ever'; his rational and professional judgement is that punishment is not appropriate. But the attempt to remove child abuse from the crime and punishment arena seems to run contrary to society's needs to control abuse. 'There are continual conflicts and contradictions,' he says.

Mr Paul adds: 'Like everybody else we are seeking to find the balance between personal responsibility and societal responsibility. If society expects children to be protected, and quite rightly so, it has to do a number of things for children and also for some adults.

'The danger at the moment is that the government will play very heavily on family and personal responsibility, because that's a rationalisation of why money should not be spent on care in the community.' This applies to housing, poverty, care of the elderly – you name it. Yes, he says, families have a duty to care for their own, but they can do that only if there is sufficient public investment in support systems.

*Source*: D. Carlisle, 'Working at the Margins', *Nursing Times*, 11 July 1991, Vol. 88, No. 28.

1 Which groups do social workers deal with?
2 Explain in your own words the task of social work, as described by Mr Paul.
3 Mr Paul describes a balancing act – can you explain this in your own words?
4 One of the elements of social work is to be non-judgemental – that is not to allow your personal feelings to intrude into your work with clients. What example of this is there in the extract?
5 According to Mr Paul, where does the blame lie for social problems such as child abuse?
6 Look at the different approaches to social work (see pages 137–40). Which one(s) do you think Mr Paul's views relate to?

There are two main types of social worker, **field social workers** and **residential social workers**.

## Field social workers

These are social workers generally based in social work offices in the community, and who deal with the problems of individuals and families. Their work involves liaison with other government and voluntary agencies to provide a service to keep individuals and families playing as normal a role as possible within society. Their work will often involve visiting individuals in their homes.

## Residential social workers

These tend to have a much lower profile than field social workers. They work in residential institutions ensuring that clients who are unable or unwilling to live in the community, or who are prevented from lack of resources from living in the community, can lead as positive a life as possible. Although the work of residential social workers requires a high level of skills and abilities, this branch of social work tends to have lower status than field work.

### STRESS IN RESIDENTIAL WORK

Trevor Ackerman has spent six years working in residential units....

Residential work is often thought to have the highest stress level. Workers often have "sleep-in" shifts, but are on call throughout the night. Anyone living in and entitled to time off may have difficulty persuading clients to recognise the fact. Low staffing levels also bring stress. Trevor Ackerman remembers with a shudder the time when, aged 22, he had sole responsibility, throughout each shift, for seven unhappy children aged between eight and 18. One of them had a two hour temper tantrum every evening and had to be physically restrained. During this time,

there was no one to supervise the others, who would gather round and taunt. As Trevor points out, "A lot of people put in that situation early on leave straight away."

Anyone who survives such challenges can feel legitimate satisfaction. But the achievements and expertise of residential social workers have long been underestimated. Trevor thinks they're just starting to be recognised. "We've been bottom of the pile and disregarded for a long time. If one of us was at a case conference with eleven others, often what we said would be brushed aside while the psychiatrists and educationists carried on."

**Source**: Jane Hodgkin, 'Who helps the Carers?', *New Society*, 1 May 1987

1 Which group of social workers according to the extract has the lower status?
2 Which form of social work 'is often thought to have' the highest stress levels?
3 Visit a residential institution. Talk to the staff about their job. Show them this extract. Why do they think that residential social work is understaffed, as stated in the extract?

# The activities of field social workers

Social workers are frequently called upon when people are in crisis, whether environmental or personal. The task is to reduce difficulties to more tolerable proportions.
**Source**: J. Cooper, 'The Future of Social Work: A Pragmatic View' in M. Loney (ed), *The State or the Market* (Sage, 1987)

When clients come to see social workers, or are referred to them by other agencies, the role of the social worker is to assess the problem and sort it out in the most effective manner that is acceptable to the client and which falls within their (relatively limited) power. The aim, apart from sorting out particular problems, is also to ensure that the client does not have to face these problems again.

There are a considerable number of activities which social workers may perform on, or on behalf of, their clients. These could include the following.

### Activities to alter personal behaviour patterns

Individuals who have particular anti-social behaviour can work through their problems with a social worker – for example, violent husbands/fathers.

### Activities to alter the relationships between family/group members

There may be tension and misunderstandings between couples or between parents and children. Often social workers can help small groups to explore their relationships and feelings.

### Counselling and advice

Many clients simply do not have the knowledge of where to turn for help for their specific problems – problems with debts, for example.

### Advocacy

Here the social worker's role is to act on behalf of a client to ensure that their view is put forward. Individuals may be unable to express themselves for a variety of reasons.

### Education (personal or group)

Often clients do not have the knowledge or skills to cope with situations. When this is allied to other difficulties, it can lead to social problems. An example would be mothers and fathers who lack parenting skills and who are suspected of poor standards of child care or even violence.

### Welfare rights

This is where specialist social workers may spend their time trying to change or clarify the interpretation of welfare benefits so that they give higher payments or include greater numbers of people than the way the benefits are currently being interpreted. Often this involves going to DSS tribunals and using the case of one client to benefit a whole category of clients.

### Ensuring provision of resources or advice

It is within the power of social workers to give certain resources. Perhaps the easiest is advice. Social workers can, for example, provide small loans to help individuals in crisis situations.

### Contract work

Here a social worker draws up a 'contract' with an individual or family to ensure compliance with a particularly important pattern of behaviour. It is a way of coercing positive forms of behaviour out of certain individuals. In return, the social worker will give something to the client. An example of this could be that a parent agrees not to drink alcohol as part of a package to try to keep a family together.

### Legal enforcement for the protection of individuals

In certain situations regarding children and mental illness, social workers share with other professionals some legal powers to ensure the protection of these groups. Social workers have legal powers in relation to the mentally ill when the clients are likely to be a danger to themselves or others. With the agreement of a community psychiatrist, they may be forced to 'section' a person, which involves a compulsory period of residential medical treatment.

## A DAY IN THE LIFE OF A FIELD SOCIAL WORKER

London wakes up to a thick blanket of snow and a blizzard is raging over the city. There are two of us on today, both with years of social work experience behind us. When we arrive at 9.30 a.m. muffled in our coats and scarves, the waiting room is already full and the duty desk has disappeared beneath a heap of casefiles, post and urgent messages. An urgent message reads: "Police phoned, Mr A at station needs mental health assessment after smashing up flat last night."

As we decide who should tackle this the receptionist comes over with a bundle of new messages: "Ring probation urgently, a mother is in prison as from today with no one to care for her children; Ms X has rung to say that her gas has been cut off, you know she has four young children; a 15-year-old in council care has been at the police station all night and needs to talk to you." We thank the receptionist who has held the public at bay for the half hour before we arrived....

Jill takes a glance at the people waiting while I begin negotiating with the local hospital who now have the mentally ill young man with them. They say he is well drugged and that they have already organised the requisite medical recommendations. What, I ask myself wryly, happened to the Mental Health Act of 1983?

This case has gone on for days. Neighbours had already alerted us to his deteriorating mental state. We have not had the resources to make an immediate assessment. Now he has become so disturbed that the police have been called in. This crisis should have been averted....

Meanwhile Jill deals with the problem of the imprisoned woman. Our own employers have put her there for non-payment of bills. Jill speaks with barely concealed anger to the relevant council department and tries to point out that paying this debt would be cheaper than taking her three children into care. But to no avail. Eventually she locates the woman's partner who offers to see us today and discuss caring for the children. There is a worrying history of non-accidental injury which was eventually resolved. We have to trust he will cope – there are no placements for the children....

The receptionist calls me over. The woman with no heating has now arrived ...

Ms X tells me she needs £550 to reconnect the gas. Our budget won't stretch to that. A hasty phone call to the gas board informs me that they won't negotiate. Finally we decide on an electric heater from a local store and we assure her we will try and raise charity money to pay off her gas bill. I watch her leave for a cold walk to the shop. I want to know why her bill has been unpaid for so long and what is happening in her household....

As I begin talking about my concern to Jill both phones on the desk jangle simultaneously. A woman speaking no English has asked a friend to ring us. She is to be evicted by the council next week....

On the other line the daughter of a 99-year-old gasps that her mother has just tried to gas herself. I ring the woman in question who says that she is "about to do it". I glance at the map and grab my coat and a few minutes later arrive out of breath at her flat. To my relief she answers the door and I try to summon up an air of calm for some counselling.

As is so often the case, this elderly woman is desperately lonely. She has had 12 children and a busy life. Now she is alone and has been ill. I ring the GP from her home....He will call later. I think she feels better for having talked....

I rush off now to the psychiatric ward. It is lunchtime, ... As Jill heads to the door she notices an elderly woman with crutches sitting crying quietly. She recognises her as the mother of the man I am out sectioning. She takes the woman into a mercifully vacant interview room and counsels her about the admission of her son. A profoundly sad interview....

I return to the office with sandwiches and we eat them at the desk. I tell her about the man in hospital who had been fairly abusive and who had accused me of "grimacing" at him. I had felt quite frightened and had insisted a staff nurse stood between us.

We sit down for a few quiet moments, gazing at the pile of paperwork. We still haven't solved the problem of the woman in prison and there is a new message about a recently housed refugee family with no money for food or heating.

A colleague arrives and offers to visit the family. He returns to report that there is no bedding, clothes or cooker. The task is immense and he spends the rest of the day mobilising supplies. There are no special resources for refugees.

In comes the partner of the imprisoned woman. I speak with him and give him some money with which to care for the children. Many phone calls later I find a way of paying the fine. The prison assures me the woman will be released immediately if the fine is paid. I give assurances that it will be paid but this is not enough. We have not got the cash in this office and a cheque takes 10 days to raise. I think of raiding my own bank account. Eventually I'm able to arrange collecting the cash in the morning. I worry about her spending the night in prison and the fact that her children are so young.

Jill emerges again from an interview. She looks troubled. "This woman is in bed and breakfast because of marital violence. She has just had her handbag stolen. Their eight-year-old child looks so forlorn. I gave her money but she needs much more help than that."

She had barely sat down when reception rang with details of new cases.

A young man has no money. DSS have moved to Glasgow and the emergency office is closed. He has no children so we can only give £2 for food.

A young single parent says her boyfriend has gone off with their baby. She has a custody hearing in two days. We promise to write a special report supporting her and to liaise with her solicitor.

Jill talks to a woman who alleges that her childminder ties their two year old in his buggy all day. We promise to investigate.

I see a woman whose car is threatened to be seized tomorrow by the court bailiffs. She hasn't paid a parking fine. She desperately needs her car to visit her child who has just had a transplant in Cambridge. It's a lot of mony but we pay it. Later, we will try and recoup it from charities.

Back at the desk I take a phone call. It is the secretary of a councillor asking me to do some shopping for an elderly client. Have councillors any idea of how stretched we are? . . .

Five o'clock and the day is nearly over. . . . It could have been worse. At least there were no child protection cases or children sleeping rough.

**Source**: L. Davies and J. Goldson, 'Snowed Under', *Social Work Today*, 1 August 1991

## THE PROBLEMS SOCIAL WORKERS DEAL WITH

1. List all the problems mentioned in the article. Look at the diagram – how many of these problems occur? Are there any missing?
2. In the extract, the social worker mentions the Mental Health Act 1983. Why does she mention it do you think? Look up page 301 for further information.
3. What does 'non-accidental injury' mean?
4. A household can have an adequate income coming in, but not have enough money to pay for bills. This is discussed on page 241. Suggest possible reasons.

**5** There is a comment in the extract about a woman phoning for help concerning eviction. Find the sentence. What is the underlying issue? This raises some very important issues which are discussed on page 263. What actions could you suggest to improve the social services for people such as this woman?
**6** There is a threat of an attempted suicide – the social worker contacts a GP. What other services would be useful?
**7** The importance of charity in social work is quite noticeable. List and explain all the examples given of charity.
**8** It is very unlikely that you will be allowed to spend a day with an intake team, because of issues of confidentiality. However, try asking your local Social Services to request a social worker to keep a diary of one day of her/his work and then to come to meet you and to discuss this.

## THE TASKS OF A PERSONAL SOCIAL SERVICES DEPARTMENT

| Objectives | Examples of specific aims | Activities |
|---|---|---|
| Support the family | To relieve the situation of families in stress; to keep children with their parents when it is in the interests of the child; to prevent loss of home | Personal help and information; cash or material aid; domestic help (e.g. home help); removal of family member for day or short breaks |
| Support those with disabilities | To help people manage their disabilities; to organise occupational and recreational activities for those excluded from 'normal' activities; to enable people to live in the community wherever possible | Personal help, advice and information; aids and adaptations in the home; mobility training for the blind; occupational day centres, social day centres, lunch clubs, holiday entertainment; personal help, advice and information; domestic help; meals; aids and adaptations to housing |
| Provide care for those dependents without family, or with family unwilling to help | To help provide a home; to provide substitute for family relationships; to enable people to live in the community | Residential care; adoption and fostering; boarding out; personal help, advice and information |
| Protect the vulnerable | To prevent and deal with child abuse; to purchase and ensure quality of standards in the private sector | Personal help to families; investigation of children at risk; removal of child to substitute home; registration, inspection and supervision of child minders, private nurseries and playgroups; inspection and supervision of private nursing homes, etc.; protection of private foster children |
| Provide assistance in the treatment of deviant behaviour | To devise and implement therapeutic programmes for 'disturbed' or 'deviant' children and adults | Personal help, advice and information; intermediate treatment; rehabilitation for adults; residential work |
| Strengthening the community | To help promote activities and action benefiting the community as a whole | Community work, e.g. encouragement of tenants' associations; holiday projects; playgroups |

**Source**: Adapted from C. McCreadie, *The Personal Social Services* (Policy Studies Institute, 1977)

The table above summarises many of the tasks of the Personal Social Services departments of local authorities.

Using it as a guide, find out how many of these activities are actually performed, and which other ones there are that are not in this list. (I have deliberately omitted information about the new Community Care activities as this should be easy to find out about – each authority is required to publish plans about them.)

For example, near where I live in Southend, Essex, there is a Family Finders shop, where those interested in short-term fostering or in adoption can drop in and chat. Which of the above activities does this relate to? How does your area provide this service?

### Referral to expert agencies

Often the social worker cannot solve a problem, but does know exactly who to turn to for help for their client – it may be another part of the Social Services, a government agency or even a charity. For example, an elderly person needing assessment for households aid and adaptations will see a social worker, who may then arrange for an occupational therapist to view the person and his/her situation.

### Purchaser of services

Since the introduction of the Community Care Act in 1990, and the bringing into effect of the relevant sections of the Act in 1993, social workers are empowered to act as a 'care manager' for the purchase of services for the elderly or those with disabilities who need care in the community. (This will be covered in more detail in the next chapter.)

# Approaches to social work

There is no one correct way of going about the process of social work, and there is great debate amongst social workers as to exactly how they should carry out their tasks. Theories of psychology, sociology and even politics have been adopted and adapted to provide often conflicting guidelines on how social workers should undertake their activities. Very broadly, we can group the approaches under the following headings:

- individual;
- relationships;
- community work;
- radical social work;
- welfare rights.

Sometimes social workers may be influenced by a mixture of approaches, while other social workers may be persuaded by the merits of one particular approach.

## Individual

This is the idea that most of the problems of an individual or family are related to the personalities of the particular people involved. By changing the behaviour of an individual person, the social worker hopes to prevent the problems. In this approach the dominant method used by the social worker is some form of counselling or psychological-based intervention. This approach is often linked to the term **casework**.

## Relationships

This is based on the idea that the relationships between people are strained, and that the resulting misunderstandings can be sorted out by discussion and interpersonal activities. In this approach the main aim is to persuade the members involved in the particular problems to explore their feelings and attitudes to each other, and through this to bring about some solution, if it is possible. This approach is also heavily influenced by psychological ideas about roles and relationships. The approach is often known as **groupwork**.

# Community work

This is based more on the belief that it is better for communities to be encouraged and supported in attempts to improve their own situation. A community can be a geographical area, for example a housing estate or even a block of flats, or a group which shares some distinguishing characteristics, such as an ethnic group. There are three main forms of community work.

## Community action

Here the social worker supports the attempts of the local community to voice its views and possible grievances on issues of concern.

## Community development

Here the community does not fully have an identity. The role of the social worker is therefore to develop a sense of community integration as a prerequisite for community action.

## Community education

In this situation, a community exists and has grievances but lacks the skills and knowledge to put its case forward.

### A COMMUNITY APPROACH TO SOCIAL WORK

Last weekend, a grandmother, plagued by break-ins in her tenement flat, complained that she could not afford an alarm; a pregnant woman was looking for a second-hand pram; a single mother pointed to her son's leaking shoes. Not everyone on low incomes reaches these straits but those who lack supportive kin, or who move frequently, or are overwhelmed by debt, can become literally penniless . . . .

Taking income support level as the poverty line, in 1987 some 6,240,000 families were poor. Poverty entails material hardship. It is associated with reception of children into care, ill-health and earlier death. Not least, it can mean deep un-happiness. I once sat with a debt-ridden, unemployed man who could not afford Easter eggs for his children – and this macho guy wept as he declared himself a failure.

What can we, who witness the effects of poverty, do about it? Local authority social workers frequently see poor people. Gibbons and her colleagues discovered that "material problems were the commonest reasons for contact with social services".

Social workers, however, may be uneasy about the poor who knock on their door. Becker and Silburn suggest that social workers see them for only "short periods of time" and "there are lingering doubts about the quality of service that a poor client may expect".

While some social workers do develop welfare rights expertise, it is clear that others see their "real" job as dealing with personal relationships. But social workers should accept practical aid as a legitimate and major social work role.

Practical aid may help to counter the dislike and fear which some poor people now express towards them. In one area of Glasgow, a community newspaper describes social workers as "the happy band of child snatchers and social controllers'. . . . Social workers, who in the more radical 1970s were often regarded as the allies of the poor, are now frequently seen as an outside force which controls them. . . .

Practical services are also of value to families with child care difficulties. Gibbons and her colleagues found not just that such help improved the material lot of clients but also contributed to a "significant positive association with improvement in parenting problems". The practical services included welfare rights advice, small grants and, in particular, linking families with voluntary groups which provided day care and other support. Interestingly, while numbers of social work staff continued to insist that counselling was their main input, their clients appreciated the practical help.

I am not proposing that social work neglects child protection nor that it becomes an income maintenance agency. I am reasoning that poverty now causes such massive harm to families that social workers should accept its modification as a priority. Just as resources are found for child abuse training and services so they should be sought to equip social workers with the skills, knowledge and materials which are so useful to families whose difficulties spring from or are intensified by poverty.

Local authorities possess powers to run family centres and to fund voluntary ones. These centres may be of the client-focused or the neighbourhood type.

The former category concentrate on a few families selected mainly because of possible child abuse. Client-focused centres offer skilled, intensive help but can stigmatise the families and be isolated from their communities. Neighbourhood centres, however, provide a wide range of activities for and draw many volunteers from their neighbour-

hood. But the drawback is they can be expensive.

Family centres are relevant to poverty in that they tend to be located in areas of high social need. An investigation of several neighbourhood type centres showed they "were reaching a large proportion of the families with the greatest needs"; yet the users did not feel stigmatised because the centres also served many other families in the community.

Poverty can undermine self confidence and has its greatest impact on families who lack informal support systems. Significantly, therefore, this research recorded that the families benefited by taking on new responsibilities, by gaining in confidence, by forging new friendships and by strengthening their personal support systems.

**Source**: R. Holman, 'Going for Broke', *Social Work Today*, 5 September 1991

1 Look at the section 'Approaches to Social Work'. What approach(es) do you think underlies the argument in this extract?

2 What are the most common reasons for contact with the Social Services?

3 What does the phrase 'welfare rights expertise' mean?

4 The author refers to some social workers who see their main job as 'dealing with personal relationships'. What approach does this reflect?

5 What does the author mean by the description of social workers as 'a happy band of child snatchers and social controllers'?

6 What other agencies, apart from government ones, does the author see as playing a particularly important role? Given the author's approach to social work, does this seem surprising to you?

7 The author refers to families feeling 'stigmatised'. Explain this and why it is an important concept in social services work. (You may need to look at page 291.)

8 What is the author's preferred solution to social problems? Do you agree? Do you think they are possible?

# Radical social work

This approach stresses that the people who are suffering from social problems are the victims of a political and social system that harms them in order to benefit others. They point out that poverty is one of the main causes of social problems and that if this could be eliminated then many of the social problems of society would not exist. Here the role of the social worker is to help challenge the unfairness of society, often through political and **pressure group** action. Pressure groups are groups of people who form an association to press for change in laws or regulations which they regard as unfair. Radical social workers are also enthusiastic supporters of community action and welfare rights approaches.

# Welfare rights

This approach is one which stresses the fact that individuals have rights as citizens of the country and that the law should reflect their needs and demands just as much as those of the more articulate. In practice, welfare rights stresses the constant demand for the rights of the social work clients in relation to such things as social security, health and housing, and the support for legal and administrative changes which would benefit the clients of social workers.

## SOCIAL WORKERS: CARERS OR CONTROLLERS?

Social workers have been described as a means by which the rest of society could control a troublesome minority – the policing or control function – and also as a caring profession which really does help the poor and the downtrodden. Which of these descriptions do you think is correct? Give the reasons for your answers.

# Residential social work

Residential social work takes place in a variety of settings, and with a range of groups. Therefore the skills required of residential social workers very much depend on which particular client group they are working with, and the aims of the residential programme. Residential social work settings include the following.

## Children's homes

There is a considerable variety of these, but generally if a child goes into care it is the 'last resort', as wherever possible children are looked after by foster parents (officially a child is a person 16 years of age or less). Children in these homes usually display forms of behaviour which are very difficult for foster parents to cope with. Working in children's homes, residential social workers must walk a very narrow line between providing warm and reassuring relationships for the children, and yet dealing firmly with those in their charge.

## Elderly persons' homes

Usually only the senior staff are qualified social workers. The aim of these homes is to ensure that elderly people are able to live with as much comfort and dignity as possible. Only those persons with the most severe forms of problems associated with ageing, such as dementia, are now accepted into the remaining State-funded elderly persons' homes. The majority of EPHs are now run by private or charitable organisations, in line with the government's Community Care Act of 1990.

## Institutions for those with severe physical disabilities

Where possible, those with severe physical disabilities are looked after in their own home, especially since the move towards community care. However, there are still those whose needs are so great that they need constant attention in special institutions.

## Institutions for those with learning disabilities

Homes and hostels for those with learning disabilities (often combined with some physical disabilities) are more common than those for people with only physical disabilities. Social workers here will often spend part of their time living in with their clients, and their main aim is to create as normal a living pattern, and as wide a range of choices and activities, as is possible.

## Institutions for those with mental illness

There is a move towards providing shared flats and houses, rather than larger institutions. Usually, social workers are attached to a number of these. They spend their days (and often nights) helping the mentally ill to cope with a normal pattern of life. Very often, these shared houses and hostels are regarded as 'half-way-houses' in that they take people who have been undergoing therapy in a hospital and who are considered to be ready to begin the process of adjustment to living independently again.

## Day-care institutions

These are institutions which cater for any of the above groups, plus the elderly, for one or two days a week. The clients live at home and are brought to the day-care centre for social and therapeutic activities. Other medical and personal services are usually provided.

## Probation hostels

These are for people who have not been placed in custody by judges or magistrates, but instead are required to be supervised by a probation officer and for whom a 'condition of residence' order has been made. The senior warden will most likely be a qualified social worker and will have the responsibility of ensuring that the legal requirements of the court are met, whilst at the same time attempting to develop the life skills and employment skills of the people in her or his charge.

## A checklist of good practice in residential social work and caring

- **High standards of physical needs**   There should be good food, a pleasant environment and comfortable rooms.
- **Independence**   Clients should be encouraged to do as much for themselves as possible.
- **Choice**   There should be genuine choices between alternatives.
- **Self-esteem**   Individuals should be encouraged to value themselves and to view their achievements positively, however 'small' these may appear to an outsider.

- **Privacy**   Each person has the right to a degree of private space and, should they wish to be alone, this too is their right. This is of particular importance in view of the way in which many residents are forced to share a room.
- **Confidentiality**   Each person has the right to keep personal information private, or at least limited to those who must know.
- **Individuality**   Every person must be encouraged to express themselves, as long as they do not harm others in the process.

# Communication skills

Whatever role you have in the health or welfare services, one of the most important skills is that of effective communication. In normal life people express their views and desires either openly or in some slightly more subtle way where they hope that the listener will pick up the clues they are giving. Think of your own ways of getting what you want.

Communication is also a way in which we can pass the time, gain information and inject controversy, humour or emotions into our life. Perhaps most important of all good communications with others allows a person to feel important and valued.

Many social work clients feel unimportant, that they have nothing to give, and marginalised from normal life. They are very often isolated and feel lonely.

The social worker or carer who can effectively communicate helps to break down many of these negative feelings, and can also understand the needs and wishes of the clients better than those who think they know what is best for the client.

The term **phatic communication** has been used to describe a situation where two people are supposedly having a conversation, but in fact it is entirely one way as the listener is not really interested in the views of the speaker and merely makes token gestures to indicate that he/she is listening. The conversations between parents and children are often like this, when young children attempt to engage in conversation with their parent who only half listens while concentrating on something else. The parent merely agrees and nods in response to the child's speech. In what other situations does phatic communication occur? What relevance does the term have to social work?

## Blocks to effective communication

Here are three typical examples of blocks to effective communication.
- The social worker both initiates and terminates the conversation. (For example, 'How are you today?'... 'Well, got to go now. Bye!')
- The questions used by the social worker are closed, that is the answer can only be 'yes' or 'no'. This prevents any real discussion. (For example, 'Do you want this or not?')
- The social worker lacks cultural understanding, and is unaware, for example, of the degree of modesty required by Asian men and women.

1 In the first example, how could the social worker have ended the conversation?
2 In the second example, what sort of questions would lead to effective communication between social worker and client?
3 How could social workers cope with lack of cultural awareness?

## Essential skills

### Empathy
It is important to show people that you truly understand and can sympathise with their views or situation.

### Body language
Show interest by the position of your body. When someone is interested in another they lean forward and stare at the person talking. You should aim to keep eye contact and not look over someone's shoulder or let your eyes glaze over.

### Height and seating position
It is normal to try to stay at the same height as a person with whom you are having a conversation. Also, try not to place a table or other object to form a barrier between you.

### Silence
There is no need to talk or to make the client anxious to talk. Sometimes a pause in the conversation is natural and allows time to reflect. It is also not necessary to respond fully to what people say, they may just want an interested listener. The social worker can simply indicate that she is listening.

### Open-ended questions
Questions should usually be open-ended, which means that respondents can organise their thoughts and respond in the way they think best. Clients very often try to please their carers and will try to give the answers they think are wanted. Try not to give away your own views.

### Responding
Give honest, accurate responses to questions put by clients, within the limits of confidentiality.

# Assignment

You work for a large county council, in the central policy unit. A group of German visitors is coming to make a detailed comparison between the structure and provision of social services in the UK and in the FDR. They have been funded by the European Commission to do this, and the long-term aim is to foster co-operation.

You have been given the task of preparing a detailed report on the administrative structure and financing of your Personal Social Services department. To give them a flavour of the work of the social services, it has been decided to include in the briefing a case study of one residential institution run by the county, or of the work of a day centre. This would show the roles of the staff and the aims of the particular institution.

The report should be illustrated and the diagrams should clearly demonstrate the main points.

# CHAPTER 7

# Community Care

## Introduction

This chapter discusses the main issues concerning the provision of care to people in Britain who are in some way prevented from caring for themselves to a standard that most of us would consider acceptable. These people include many of the elderly who are housebound and other people with mental or physical disabilities.

Community care is one of the most talked-about issues in social welfare, with everyone agreeing it is a good thing, but for very different reasons. Social workers believe it is better for most clients to continue to live in their own homes. Governments believe it is cheaper for people to be helped at home rather than be maintained in a State institution. Families who care for the disabled would like some extra help, but do not want their disabled relatives to be placed in institutions.

In this chapter we will examine the extent of the need for community care, and discuss the different meanings that community care has. We will look at the main factors behind the development of the recent community care legislation, the nature of the legislation that now governs the provision of community care in Britain and its implementation. The later parts of the chapter discuss the implications of community care for the professionals involved, for the clients and for the carers. Finally, we look at the criticisms made against community care.

## Community and residential care: an overview

According to the British Association of Social Workers, there are ten million people who need someone to help them to look after themselves. The overwhelming majority of these people receive adequate levels of help by members of their own family. However, there are many who have greater needs which cannot be looked after by family members, or who have no family to look after them.

There are about 8.5 million people in Britain over the age of 65, of whom about one million are receiving care. A further half a million under 65 have a physical disability or a learning disability. Over 600 000 people are referred to psychiatric services each year.

For these people the State intervenes to provide care. State intervention takes many forms, but they all fall between the two 'extremes' of **residential care** and **community care**. For example, of these groups, about 300 000 are in publicly funded residential care (in hospitals, nursing homes, elderly persons' homes, etc.). A further one million are receiving day care or domiciliary services (home visits from such people as home helps).

## Residential care

By residential care, we generally mean care in institutions such as large mental hospitals, children's homes or elderly persons' homes. The individuals being cared for in these institutions live there permanently – eating, sleeping and having their leisure there.

Many residential institutions are characterised by the following.

- They are usually run by the State, by charities, or by profit-making companies.
- Individuals live in the institution, receive their services within it and rarely have to leave the buildings.
- Individuals living there have limited privacy.
- The staff are often trained, and almost always paid a salary.
- There are usually clear-cut rules of behaviour and formal routines for activities such as eating.
- Because of organisational needs, the institutions generally limit individual choice and freedom.

## Community care

Community care is the approach which provides care in the person's home, if possible. There are considerable variations within this definition, however, as individuals may be living in a group 'home', where three or four people share accommodation (often used when shifting mentally ill people out of long-stay hospitals), or it may be that the person lives in accommodation which is 'watched over' by a warden (such as sheltered housing). Ideally, community care has the following characteristics.

- The person is living at home and has privacy.
- There are no staff living in.
- Normal living routine is determined by the individual.
- The individual receives services from outside.

## The continuum of care

The table on page 146 illustrates the *continuum* of care provided by the health and social services. It shows the relationship between the two types of care, residential (or 'domiciliary') and community. There are overlaps, and really it is unclear at what point residential care turns into community care. The following distinctions may help.

### Care in a home

This is the care that takes place within an institution whether isolated in the countryside, as most of the original mental institutions were, or located in the heart of the suburbs or town centres, as most elderly persons' homes are today.

### Care from home

This refers to the caring services which are based in institutions (such as hospitals), but are available to people who live at home. The people are generally taken there by bus for the particular services they need and then taken home afterwards. Examples of these include day centres for the elderly and the mentally ill.

### Care at home

This refers to people who receive their services at home, either informally from friends and family or formally by Social Services.

## A RANGE OF CARE SETTINGS

| Types of care setting | Institutions | Institutional care in 'the community' | 'Community care' in the institution | Domiciliary care by statutory and voluntary organisations | Domiciliary care by friends, neighbours and kin |
|---|---|---|---|---|---|
| | Care *in a* Home | | Care *from* Home | | Care *at* Home |
| Examples | Hospitals Clinics 'Asylums' | Hospital hostels Hostels Rest Homes Nursing Homes Children's homes <br><br> Bed and Breakfast accommodation Sheltered housing | Respite care Day care Day hospitals Luncheon Clubs Travelling day hospitals Occupational therapy Industrial therapy Physiotherapy Out-patient treatment | Health visitors Community psychiatric nurses GPs Home helps Social Workers Care attendants Meals on wheels Sitting services 'Tucking-in' services | Many forms of care including: bathing toileting feeding cooking leisure shopping dressing |
| Types of solution | Residential and caring (with services) | Residential and usually caring, with services | Caring, with services, but not usually residential | Caring, with services, but not residential | Caring and not residential |
| Length of stay | Often short-term and temporary | Often long-term and permanent Some short-stay | Often long-term and regular but part-time | Often long-term and regular but part-time | Long-term regular and often full-time |
| Volume of care to dependant groups | Approx. 3.5% of total | | Approx 15% | | Approx. 80% |

1 Give two examples of 'institutions'.
2 What is the difference between 'institutional care in the community' and 'community care in the institution'?
3 Give four examples of domiciliary services provided by professionals.
4 Who does the bulk of the caring? It is worth turning to pages 161–5 for more information on this.
5 When the government says it wishes to see more caring in the community – is it clear what this means?
6 Commentators (and textbooks) often make clear distinctions between residential or institutional care and community care. What comment can you make as a result of the above table?

# Community care services

## Care in the community and care by the community

One more distinction needs to be made, before we can be clear about the meaning of community care. When people use the term 'community care', they usually have some vague idea of a local community to which people belong and which provides a network of support. Yet research has shown

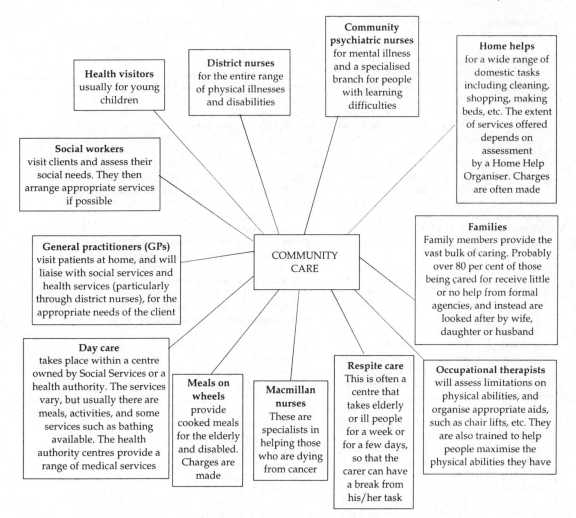

Health visitors
usually for young children

District nurses
for the entire range of physical illnesses and disabilities

Community psychiatric nurses
for mental illness and a specialised branch for people with learning difficulties

Home helps
for a wide range of domestic tasks including cleaning, shopping, making beds, etc. The extent of services offered depends on assessment by a Home Help Organiser. Charges are often made

Social workers
visit clients and assess their social needs. They then arrange appropriate services if possible

General practitioners (GPs)
visit patients at home, and will liaise with social services and health services (particularly through district nurses), for the appropriate needs of the client

COMMUNITY CARE

Families
Family members provide the vast bulk of caring. Probably over 80 per cent of those being cared for receive little or no help from formal agencies, and instead are looked after by wife, daughter or husband

Day care
takes place within a centre owned by Social Services or a health authority. The services vary, but usually there are meals, activities, and some services such as bathing available. The health authority centres provide a range of medical services

Meals on wheels
provide cooked meals for the elderly and disabled. Charges are made

Macmillan nurses
These are specialists in helping those who are dying from cancer

Respite care
This is often a centre that takes elderly or ill people for a week or for a few days, so that the carer can have a break from his/her task

Occupational therapists
will assess limitations on physical abilities, and organise appropriate aids, such as chair lifts, etc. They are also trained to help people maximise the physical abilities they have

that this idea of community is a myth. The vast bulk of caring is by the family (see pages 161–3).

This has led some commentators to make a distinction between all the forms of care except for that provided by family and friends and to call that **care *in* the community**, while that given by family and friends is known as **care *by* the community**.

The assumption behind community care is that something called a community exists. This conjures up a vision of neighbours interested in each others' welfare and passing the time of day when they meet in the street. However, many writers have questioned whether communities can honestly be said to exist nowadays. This situation is particularly significant in the debate about community care.

## AN UNCARING COMMUNITY

Three adults—two women and a man—have been forced out of their home in a quiet cul-de-sac in the market town of Alton, Hampshire. They have not been thrown on the streets for non-payment of rent. They have had no dispute with their landlord. The closure of the house, and its sale, was forced on the owners by local residents because the three people living there were mentally handicapped.

They moved into the house two years ago, as part of the district health authority's policy of introducing community care for mentally handicapped and mentally ill people in its charge. . . .

The three mentally handicapped residents all came from the town, although none had any close relatives. They were carefully chosen for a group home; none was disruptive. Indeed, the eldest—a woman of about 40—is a deaf mute. After many years in institutions, they would spend much of their time sitting quietly and watching television. With care staff on duty at all times, it was not thought that even the most excitable resident would disturb or alarm her new neighbours.

Although the three were all severely handicapped, they quickly justified the health authority's faith in the policy of community care. Soon after moving into the house, they made striking progress. They learned an independence and self-sufficiency that had proved impossible in the institutional environment from which they came.

The actual conversion of the house to a group home had occurred with little fuss and minimum publicity. The health authority had used a deliberately low-key approach in the interests of the three mentally handicapped residents and the care staff.

But, two years later, the home has closed after a campaign conducted by several residents in the road and, in particular, the next-door neighbour, Mr C.

Mr C. and his wife explain their objections with the conviction of ordinary people who have been wronged by a huge, anonymous organisation. They were not prejudiced against the mentally handicapped, or anyone else, said Mrs C. But "the patients" next door ruined their health, because of the stress they caused . . .

"If these people were looked after by their own families," Mr. C. added, "there would be no need for the health authority to look after them and house them next door to people like us."

It is an argument used by others in similar situations. But it ignores the fact that most of the mentally handicapped living in the community have no immediate family. This situation is growing more widespread as elderly parents, caring for a mentally handicapped son or daughter, become unable to cope, or die.

Mr C., however, is unmoved. "I've nothing against the mentally handicapped," he said during his campaign, "but this house is in completely the wrong position. Those people were just moved in and devalued our house without the health authority even consulting us. If we did get a buyer, we wouldn't get the full market price."

The house bought by the health authority, they argued, was too close to others in the road. Its tiny garden offered no "protection" to local children who might—and did— encounter the mentally handicapped residents. (According to the DHA, it was this very closeness which made the house so suitable as there was—or should have been—daily contact with neighbours.)

Property values are at the heart of arguments put forward by many opponents of similar schemes, although estate agents in Alton are divided as to whether such a group home does affect property prices.

Any hopes that local residents might become reconciled to their mentally handicapped neighbours died as accusations and counter-accusations flew. Mr C. maintained that the mentally handicapped were noisy and disturbed his family. He cited one incident when, he said, a "patient made threatening gestures and noises" at him while he was trying to paint the outside of his home.

"The noises have been appalling," Mr C. said. "When my elderly mother-in-law has been ill in bed, we've found her clutching the bed clothes to her mouth, terrified by the horrific sounds coming from the next door house."

Even those who were initially indifferent—it would be impossible to describe anyone as an active supporter—became hostile after isolated incidents. One young mother said her three year old son was too frightened to play in the front garden because one of the mentally handicapped people "waved her arms and shrieked" at him. Care staff suggested that the woman recognised the little boy and was trying to persuade him to play. But the mother, discouraged by her son's tears, put her name to a petition signed by most people in the road, saying it was not the right place to house mentally handicapped people . . . Eventually DHA members voted to close the home and move the residents to another area. . . .

As one doctor, who works with the mentally handicapped in Hampshire, observed: "The whole policy of community care assumes that there is a community and that it does care. But is that really the case?"

**Source**: J. Mills, 'An Uncaring Community', *New Society*, 12 February 1988

**1** What was 'different' about these three adults?

**2** Were they disruptive? How would you describe their behaviour?

**3** Were they left unsupervised?

**4** What were Mr C's complaints?

**5** How would you define 'prejudiced'?

**6** Sociologists often argue that once people are labelled in a particular way then people interpret their behaviour in a stereotyped way. Are there any examples of this here?

**7** Placed in the same situation as Mr C, what would your view be? Please be honest!

**8** Is it right to place 'mentally handicapped' people in houses in 'the community'? Conduct a simple test of opinion in your college, by asking ten people their opinion. Pool the results.

**9** If you were the health or social work professional responsible for the setting up of such a household in a suburb, how would you go about tackling the possible problems? Devise a strategy.

# Legislation leading to community care

- **Mental Health Act 1959** set out to establish a community care service for the mentally ill, not requiring hospital treatment
- **1963 White Paper on Development of Community Care**, but no Act followed
- **1969 Report of Ely Hospital scandal** where the treatment of the mentally ill in Ely Hospital was severely criticised
- **1974 Joint Planning** introduced. In section 10 of the NHS Reorganisation Act, a statutory (legally binding) responsibility was laid down for local authorities and health services to co-ordinate their activities
- **1975 White Paper on Better Services for the Mentally Ill**. This planned for the growth of local authority Social Services departments to deal with the mentally ill in the community, and for the medical treatment to be provided by psychiatric units of local hospitals
- **1977 Joint Finance** introduced. Health authorities were required to earmark funding for joint services with local authorities
- **1983 Care in the Community Initiative**: £15 million was made available for a programme to explore the best ways to move people from institutions into the community
- **1986 Audit Commission Report** – very influential official government study of costs of institutions, and the inadequate provision of community care. Urged a radical rethink
- **1988 Wagner Report** – detailed study of residential care which recommended a fundamental shift in attitudes towards residential care, with the new emphasis on flexibility and variety of institutional care, which could dovetail into community care
- **1988 Griffiths Report** – the most influential report on community care, which decided that the role of local authorities must change. They should take on the role of purchaser of care for those in need of community based assistance, instead of the traditional role of provider of care
- **National Health Service and Community Care Act 1990** passed. This was largely based on the Griffiths Report, and shifted the emphasis on care for the elderly, the mentally ill and those with learning difficulties away from institutional provision to community care provision. It also provided funds to local authorities to undertake the bulk of the caring work for those without medical needs.

# The background to community care

The modern concept of providing care in the community can best be traced back to the early 1960s with the publication of the White Paper *Health and Welfare: the Development of Community Care*. In this, the government proposed the setting up of district general hospitals to replace the large variety of smaller hospitals then existing. These new DGHs were to focus on acute (immediate and short-term) illnesses. The chronic illnesses, the problems of the elderly, the mentally ill and those with learning difficulties would all be dealt with in the community.

The part of the plan concerning the creation of district general hospitals was carried out, but no moves were made to introduce community care. Indeed, even though other reports and White Papers (such as *Better Services for Mentally Handicapped People*, 1971, and *Better Services for the Mentally Ill*, 1975), continued to call for the run-down of residential institutions, it was not until the Audit Commission Report of 1985, that the truth emerged. (Audit Commissions are investigations by government-appointed accountants and experts who see if the government is getting value for money in its services.) There had been no move forward in the provision of community care for those in need, rather things had taken the worst possible turn for some groups. For example, there were 37 000 fewer mentally ill and 'mentally handicapped' patients in hospitals in 1985 compared to 1975, yet there had been no corresponding build up in community care provision. Even worse, there was no knowledge of what had happened to these 37 000 people.

Moves towards community care were slow for various reasons.

- There was a lack of funds available to local authorities from local government, which they could use for community care.
- The National Health Service was not willing to hand money over to local Social Services to provide community care for some of its patients.
- There was a 'perverse incentive', as the Audit Commission called it, for local Social Services to place people in institutions rather than look after them at home. If the Social Services provided community care, then they had to pay for that out of their income. However, if they placed people in institutions, then social security paid the cost. This meant that it was cheaper to put people in institutions than care for them in the community.

The year 1985 then marked the beginning of a definite government commitment to move towards community care.

# The main factors leading towards community care

There were three main factors causing the government to take the issue of community care seriously: cost, demographic changes and ideological beliefs.

## Cost

By 1986, the government was spending approximately £6 million in the area of community care. By the late 1980s, the cost of social security benefits for people in residential accommodation was £1 billion, and this was continuing to rise sharply. Today, the DSS pays out over £1.6 billion.

# Demographic changes

It was estimated that by the year 2001, there would be at least 1.25 million people over the age of 85, compared to 700 000 in 1986. This figure is important, because it is around this age that elderly people need substantial assistance from the State.

However, not only was there likely to be a growth in the dependent elderly, there was also a similar growth in the numbers of severely disabled. In 1986, it was estimated that there were approximately one million severely disabled people living in Britain (although remember the numbers of the elderly and the disabled overlap considerably).

## THE ELDERLY POPULATION

Expectation of life at birth has increased by more than twenty years during this century. A new born boy can today look forward to an average 72 years, while a girl might expect over 77 years. Many people are living very much longer, as the numbers aged 85+ testify.

Trends in the ageing of the population are shown in the Table. Between 1901 and 1981 the numbers of people in Great Britain aged at least 65 rose from 1.7 million to almost 8 millions. Increasing as a proportion of the total population from less than 5% to 15%. The rate of growth has now slowed. Between 1981 and 2001 it is expected that the total elderly population will grow by just under one million persons—an increase of around 12.5%. By comparison, the previous twenty year period 1961–1981 had witnessed an increase almost twice as great, with a growth of nearly one third.

The changing balance of the elderly population is, however, becoming increasingly important, and a concentration on overall numbers can obscure the growth of the very elderly.

- In the twenty years from 1981 to 2001 the population aged 85+ is expected to more than double—from 552,000 to 1,144,000.
- By 2001 almost half (48%) of the total elderly population will be aged at least 75. In 1961 this was true of just over one third.
- One person in every 50 will be aged at least 85 by 2001, while 1 in 6 will be 65+.
- A hundred years earlier only 1 in 20 people were aged 65+, and 1 in nearly 700, 85 or older.

### The elderly population: past, present and future, thousands and per cent total population

| | 65+ | % | 75+ | % | 85+ | % |
|---|---|---|---|---|---|---|
| **Historical trends 1901 to 1981** | | | | | | |
| 1901 | 1734 | 4.7 | 507 | 1.4 | 57 | 0.15 |
| 1931 | 3316 | 7.4 | 920 | 2.1 | 108 | 0.24 |
| 1951 | 5332 | 10.9 | 1731 | 3.5 | 218 | 0.45 |
| 1961 | 6046 | 11.8 | 2167 | 4.2 | 329 | 0.64 |
| 1971 | 7140 | 13.2 | 2536 | 4.7 | 462 | 0.86 |
| 1981 | 7985 | 15.0 | 3053 | 5.7 | 552 | 1.03 |
| **Projections (1987 based)** | | | | | | |
| 1987 | 8624 | 15.6 | 3699 | 6.7 | 746 | 1.3 |
| 1991 | 8838 | 15.8 | 3925 | 7.0 | 875 | 1.6 |
| 2001 | 8984 | 15.6 | 4309 | 7.5 | 1144 | 2.0 |
| 2011 | 9425 | 16.1 | 4372 | 7.5 | 1291 | 2.2 |
| 2021 | 10642 | 18.0 | 4699 | 7.9 | 1287 | 2.2 |
| 2027 | 11472 | 19.2 | 5308 | 8.9 | 1326 | 2.2 |

**Sources**: 1901–1981 Census data OPCS. *Population projections by the Government Actuary 1987–2027* PP2 No. 16

1 What proportion of the population were over (a) 65, (b) 75 and (c) 85 in 1901?
2 What proportion were over (a) 65, (b) 75 and (c) 85 in 1991?
3 By 2027, what is the expected proportion of the population over (a) 65, (b) 75 and (c) 85?
4 Which group is likely to put the greatest strains on community care?
5 Within the elderly population, what is happening to the various age groups?
6 By 2001, what will the balance of ages be within the elderly population?
7 There are implications and issues of stereotyping about the health and the abilities of the elderly hidden in this debate (it is sometimes called 'ageism'). What are these implications and stereotypes? Why is this relevant to community care?

## Ideological beliefs

The Conservative government of the mid-1980s was dominated by the ideas of the so-called New Right, whose members believed strongly in 'traditional' values, such as self-reliance, independence and the family. In particular, the government asked why it was that the State was having to care (in institutions) for people who could (and the implication was *should*) have been looked after by family members. A strong belief of the New Right is that the family has a duty to look after its members, and that wherever possible the State should encourage people to do so.

A further consideration was that there were already six million people (generally women) caring for others in the community, and of these up to 1.5 million were acting as unpaid carers for more than 20 hours a week. These people were doing exactly what the New Right believed in and so it was argued that the government had a duty to provide some support.

### THE FAMILY

I shall begin by considering three well-known myths which, despite the efforts of social scientists and others over several decades, still appears to exercise a strong influence over popular political discussion and probably over policy making as well. It runs something like this: in the past, families had a stronger sense of obligation to care for their own sick, elderly and handicapped members. They are less inclined to do so now because family ties generally have weakened, and also because women who have traditionally provided this care are likely to be out at work. A variation on this theme is that women's role as carers in the family has been undermined by feminism.

Translated into social policy terms, this produces a commitment to 'support the family' to enable it to care for its members better, a commitment characteristic of all recent governments of whatever political party. It has found its most obvious expression in the development of policies for the so-called community care of various groups, which actually means that female relatives carry the major burden, with limited support – if any – from outside the family.

**Source**: Janet Fitch, 'Family Ties', *New Society*, 20 March 1987

1 According to the author of this extract, what are the key issues concerning the policy makers' view of the family?
2 Does the author agree?
3 Is this approach linked to one particular political party?
4 What do we really mean when we talk about 'the family' caring, according to Janet Finch?

# The Griffiths Report and the 1990 Act

In 1988, the Griffiths Report was published. It recommended sweeping changes to the system of community and residential care, and as a result the Conservative government introduced legislation in 1990 (the National Health Service and Community Care Act 1990). This amounted to an enormous 'shake-up' in the provision and arrangement of community care, as the text below illustrates.

## FUNDING THE COST OF CARE

There has been a massive shake-up in the provision of services to the elderly and disabled. Local authorities have been given the main role in arranging care services for elderly and disabled people. The aims are to enable more people to live at home, and to limit the ever increasing growth in the cost of social security payments for residential and nursing homes. In 1992, the bill for these totalled £2.5 billion.

The Minister of Health announced that there would be a phased transfer of social security money to local authorities starting in 1993. In the first year there would be a shift of £399 million in England alone from the social security budget to local authorities, and there would also be an additional £140 million 'new' money. This gives a total budget of £539 million in 1993–4.

In 1993, this money would only be allowed to be spent on community care, and in 1994–5 £650 million would be ring-fenced but this ring-fencing would be gradually withdrawn over future years, with £520 million earmarked in 1996–7, a small amount of 1998 and nothing thereafter....

75 per cent of the 1993–4 budget, which is equivalent to all the transferred monies would have to be spent on care in the independent sector, and only the remaining 25 per cent could be spent on local authority homes or services....

The point of this structure of funding was to 'give further impetus to the development of a mixed economy of care', the minister announced.

The funding is to be for 110,000 elderly and disabled people in need of care in 1993–4.... 50 per cent of the transferred Social Security money is being distributed to local authorities on the basis of the numbers of people in the local population, and 50 per cent according to the numbers in care homes. The idea underlying this is to prevent the clustering of care homes in certain traditional retirement areas.

Local authorities will have to honour peoples' choices of homes, and will not be allowed to give priority to its own homes.

A spokesman for the Confederation of Health Service Employees, Bob Abberley said, 'We are horrified that the Secretary of State appears to have effectively instructed local authorities to spend 75 per cent of the provision on private facilities.... Simply decanting thousands of older people into poorly regulated private homes is not care in the community, it is straightforward privatisation.'

1 What is the point of the 'shake-up'? What Act is the 'shake-up' the result of?
2 How much was spent in 1992 on social security payments for residential and nursing home care?
3 How much was to be spent on community care by local authorities?
4 What does 'ring-fencing' mean?
5 The article refers to transferred social security funds having to be spent in the independent sector. What does this mean? What are the implications for local authority run homes? If you do not know the answer to this, contact your local authority and find out.
6 Explain the meaning of the term 'mixed economy of care' (see also pages 195–8).
7 Which groups were to receive community care in 1993/4?
8 The allocation of funds to councils is based on the ratio of 50 per cent according to the population and 50 per cent according to the number of care homes. This is an important decision because of

the fact that at the moment there are certain towns (principally along the coast in the south of England) with a large number of private homes, and yet other towns have very few private homes. What is the thinking behind the decision to split the funding along the lines indicated?

**9** What criticism is made of the new system? What does Mr Abberley mean when he talks about 'privatisation'?

---

The Government's £539 million community care shake-up next April will be £200 million short of the money needed to make it work, local authority leaders claimed yesterday after the funding arrangements were announced.

The Labour-controlled Association of Metropolitan Authorities said the shortfall meant 12,000 elderly and disabled people would be at risk of not getting the care services they required.

Virginia Bottomley, Health Secretary, dismissed the complaint as "technical".

She said the total £539 million she announced for 1993/94 was only £11 million less than the authorities had estimated was needed, on the assumptions being used by Whitehall.

**Source**: The *Guardian*, 3 October 1992

**1** What criticism is made of the government's plans?

**2** Enquire about the situation in your local authority. (Remember the local authority is under an obligation to produce plans, and to make them available to the public.)

---

## Principle elements of the new system

### 'One door'

In the past, community care had been provided by a number of different agencies, with the main two being the Health Service and the local authority Social Services. With the implementation of the 1990 Act, however, the *local authority* would have the major responsibility for social care of the elderly, those with physical disabilities and people with learning disabilities. The role of the Health Service was to become far less important. The idea here was that people would know exactly where to go for their requests for help in caring for relatives, friends or for themselves. This signalled a major change in the role of social workers and community nurses.

### Distinction between health and social needs

A clear distinction was made between the health needs of a person and his/her social needs. So, where a person's needs were concerned with their health, they would be provided for by the GP (or hospital). It was decided that people with **mental illness** clearly fell into the category of having health needs, and so, for these people, the health authority was the 'one door'.

This has led to some confusion over the exact dividing line between health and social needs. Who is responsible for the services of elderly people who are at home and who have both social needs, such as isolation, and also physical/mental health problems?

### Planning

One of the major flaws of traditional approaches to community care had been the failure to transfer good intentions into practice. As a result of this, the government placed a duty on local authorities to produce and publish clear plans for community care in their areas.

Originally, the entire community care programme was to be introduced in April 1991, but the Conservative government was concerned about the electoral consequences of introducing a very expensive community care programme which was bound to raise local authority taxes considerably. They therefore suggested a timetable, with full implementation of the community care programme complete by April 1993. The major advantage of the delay was to allow good planning.

### From category to individual

Under traditional systems of care, the client was regarded as a member of a category, such as 'elderly', 'physically disabled', etc. Many Social Work departments and most health authorities had teams which specialised in these categories. The result was that services were developed for these particular categories, and when a social worker or district nurse went to assess an individual, they would have a package of services for the particular category of person. The assessment would consist of deciding which of these was most suitable in terms of its appropriateness and availability.

Under the new system, the person is to be treated as an individual (or as a consumer), and within the available resources will be asked what services they would like. On the basis of this, the social worker (or, in the case of health care, the district nurse or GP) will then try to provide the appropriate services.

Related to the ideas of the 'one door', and of treating the person as an individual, is that of the single contact person, to be known as the **care manager**, who will be responsible for organising the entire package of care for an individual client.

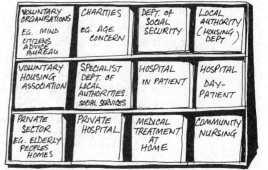

**Getting help in health and social services**

The easiest way of understanding the new approach to providing care is first to remember that Sir Roy Griffiths, author of the Griffiths Report, was managing director of the Sainsbury's supermarket chain. The traditional method of the Social Services department deciding what services they could fit people into seemed as absurd to him as the supermarket cashier deciding what food people ought to have.

### Enablers, not providers

The idea that welfare is the monopoly of the local authority Social Services departments has been abandoned. Instead, private, charitable and voluntary organisations are to be used wherever sensible. When the care manager examines the options available to a client, these will include private and voluntary alternatives to the State sector.

In certain situations, the legislation actually penalises local authorities if they wish to provide care themselves. An example of this occurs with the provision of places in homes for the elderly. If an elderly person is placed in a local authority EPH (elderly persons' home), then he/she is not eligible to receive Housing Benefit (see page 86). However, if the **care manager** (the social worker) places the elderly person in a private/charitable residential home, then full Housing Benefit is paid. This has led to the majority of local authority EPHs being made into 'trusts', with no involvement of the local authority representatives.

### Maintaining standards

The local authorities are to have the duty to maintain the quality of local provision. This is to be done through the regular inspection of all residential institutions in the area.

### Ethnic minorities

The legislation states that '... people from different cultural backgrounds may have particular care needs and problems.... Good community care will take account of the circumstances of minority communities and will be planned in consultation with them.'

This should mean that social workers will be able to look at the needs of somebody as a member of the ethnic minorities, rather than trying to fit them in to already existing provision, which is usually angled towards the servicing of the majority White population.

### ETHNICITY AND COMMUNITY CARE

A survey of social services departments conducted by the Commission for Racial Equality found that only a quarter had introduced ethnic record-keeping and monitoring procedures, and it expressed concern that race equality issues must not be downgraded by social services staff as new community care policies are devised and implemented. A comparison of the use of community services by whites and Gujurati Asians showed that the Asian households received fewer services.

Source: T. Chapman, S. Goodwin and R. Hennelly, 'A New Deal for the Mentally Ill: Progress or Propaganda?', *Critical Social Policy*, 1991

## Implications for social workers

Social workers will have a distinctly altered role. In the past, they organised services for clients on the basis of what was available from the State sector.

In future they will have the responsibility to obtain the best services for their clients no matter what the source. Whereas in the past, they had no control over financial matters, the community care legislation effectively means that they will be buying in services within a budget. Of course, the problem is the amount of money they will have to spend on their clients! In the areas where the new proposals have already been introduced (at the time of writing), the professional divisions between qualified social workers and others, such as home help organisers, have become blurred. People from both groups are being designated as **care managers**.

Other changes and implications for social workers are that there will need to be greater co-operation with workers in the voluntary and private services than in the past; social workers will be required to control standards of care in the community, through the new inspection role they have been required to perform by the legislation; and many residential social workers currently employed by local authorities will move to the new 'trusts' being set up to take over council EPHs.

## Implications for community nurses

Under the new proposals, the health authorities will only be required to provide the health component of care. Until very recently, because of the unclear boundary between social and health needs, health authorities have provided what many would regard as social care – in particular the provision of respite care and day centres. These facilities are often provided after assessment by community nurses. It is unclear whether this power of assessment will remain with them, or will be handed over to the social workers.

Community nurses will have to learn to disentangle health care and social care and know exactly what is expected of them. General practitioners have been given increased responsibilities under the new Act concerning the preventive health of their patients. It is quite likely that they will prefer to employ their own **practice nurses** to do this, rather than rely on health authority community nurses.

# Implementing community care

In April 1993, the new system of community care came fully into operation. We have looked at the general aims of the system and the reasons for its introduction. We now need to consider exactly how it is to function.

## Finance

The local authorities will receive all the funding which previously the Department of Social Security had given for paying for places in elderly persons' homes, for example. This amounts in 1993 to about three-quarters of the money available for community care. The government will also provide money directly to local authorities as part of the Spending Assessment Support that it gives to all local authorities to run all of their services.

Proposals in the Griffiths Report for government grant money to be 'ring-fenced' for community care (specific money given on the basis that it could only be spent on community care – see the extract on page 153) were rejected by the government.

Health Authorities have earmarked specific sums from their budgets to pay for their part of community care.

Once the local authorities receive the money, they will then work out their budgets for all community care activities.

Depending upon the organisational structure they use, the local authorities will then use this money to buy services from whatever organisation they choose to place contracts with. In the past, the local authorities provided a wide range of social services themselves, including elderly persons' homes, day centres, home helps, residential accommodation for the physically disabled, and many others. From April 1993, they have split their operation. Some of these activities have been handed over or sold to non-profit-making organisations (such as EPHs), and others have been made into self-contained operations, still owned by the local authorities but with significant independence.

On the other hand, Social Work departments have gradually moved to a role of assessing clients and then, using a budget, looking around for the best services available at the most reasonable costs and purchasing them from that particular provider. The provider may or may not be the 'independent' local authority provider.

The aim is to have a wide variety of competing providers who offer choice and high quality. Profit-making and charitable organisations have been encouraged to bid for contracts.

## THE PURCHASER/PROVIDER SPLIT IN COMMUNITY CARE

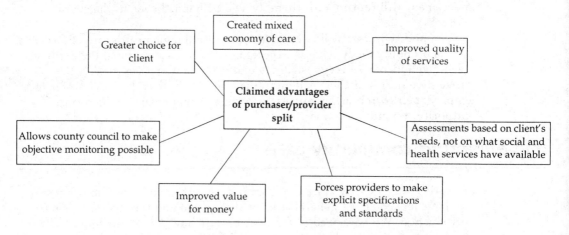

*Using the text and the diagram, copy and complete the table below.*

| Perceived advantages | Explanations and comments |
|---|---|
| Greater choice | |
| Value for money | |
| Improved quality | |
| Objective monitoring | |
| Client's needs as basis for assessment | |
| Specifications and standards | |
| Mixed economy | |

## The role of the professionals

As we have seen, the role of social workers in particular has changed, as they stop assessing individuals in terms of what services are available from the range provided by the local authority. They now assess the individual and then, within the very tight budget constraints imposed upon them, purchase the best quality care they can.

The second part of the job is then to monitor the quality of care being given and, if they are not satisfied, to buy services from elsewhere. In certain extreme situations in residential care, social workers have powers to stop the institution from continuing.

With the implementation of the 1990 Act, the role of the social workers (and to a lesser extent community nurses) within community care will be that of **care management**. The central elements of this are **assessment** and the implementation, monitoring and reviewing of a **care plan**.

## Assessment

The care manager will need to assess the needs of the client in a simple, quick and clear manner, which takes into account the wishes of the client, the level of funding available and the care manager's professional views of what is in the best interests of the client.

The assessment involves finding out the following information from the individual.

### Biographical details

Information concerning name, age, marital status, religion, and so on.

### Self-perceived needs

The assessment should always start with the views of the individual and his/her wishes.

### Self-care

What can the person do for him/herself – such as washing, cooking, dressing, etc.? An important point here is that the potential of the person should also be taken into account. For example, an elderly widower may have been used to being looked after by his wife. When assessed, he makes little effort to do anything for himself. The care manager must decide what the appropriate level of help for him is, given his own capacities and the resources available.

### Physical health

This is crucial, and a proper assessment of the person's health will be undertaken by a health professional, most probably the GP. Health problems often require both medical and social services, as ill health may prevent a person from performing self-care adequately.

### Mental health

Again, an assessment by an appropriate health professional is required – probably the community psychiatrist. The mental health of the individual may effect his/her perception of needs and the ability to perform a number of routine daily activities.

### Use of medicines

Many people need regular medication, and a common problem is the inability to self-administer this. Problems resulting from inadequate medication may affect the broader lifestyle of the person and their ability to achieve an adequate standard of self-care.

### Abilities, attitudes and lifestyle

Each person is unique in their views, abilities, lifestyle and personal range of family and friends upon whom they can rely. The assessment must take this into account and must not simply stereotype an individual, for example as an elderly person with arthritis living alone.

### Race and culture

The assessment must include an awareness of race and the cultural wishes that spring from this. The impact of racism on people's lives should also be considered.

### Personal history

Any relevant information that the individual provides which may help to understand their present needs – for example, the death of a partner, or past involvement with health or social services which they regard as unsatisfactory and which affects their attitude to the current assessment – should be taken into account.

### Needs of carers

Where there is currently someone providing care, their views also need taking into account. The individual being assessed, and the care manager, may make false assumptions about the wishes and attitudes of the carer. Regarding the carer, the following points should be covered in an assessment:

- relationship to the individual being assessed (wife/daughter);
- care provided;
- expressed needs for support;
- wishes and preferences;
- nature of the relationship (warm, distant).

## The care plan

There are three stages to the care plan, once assessment has taken place: implementing, monitoring and reviewing.

### Implementing

Implementing the plan consists of achieving the objectives of the care plan with the least intervention necessary. This means using the fewest services and personnel possible. This is to ensure that the individual understands the plan, and there is not a complexity of wasteful, overlapping providers.

---

#### Care plan checklist

- Has the user been involved to the limit of their capacity in the implementation process? ✓
- Have the inputs of the users and carers been maximised and have formal service inputs been geared to their support? ✓
- Has the pace of implementation been agreed with the user? ✓
- Has the budget for implementation been agreed with the user? ✓

- Has the budget for implementation been clearly defined, together with the responsibility for allocating that budget? √
- Have deficiencies in service availability been notified to service planning and quality assurance inspection respectively? √
- Have existing services been renegotiated to meet the care plan objectives more effectively? √
- Has the care plan been delivered to time and quality? √
- Have resources been co-ordinated in a cost-effective way? √
- Have reasons for any departure from the original plan been recorded? √
- Have arrangements been established to monitor the ongoing implementation? √

### Monitoring

The aim of monitoring within the care plan is to confirm the achievement of set objectives over a period of time, and to change the plan in line with the differing needs of the individual.

The extent of monitoring depends on how complex the community care provision is.

Monitoring specifically and formally checks that the implementation has been effective and as set down in the care plan. It records the reasons for objectives not being met, and leads to the final part of the care manager's role.

### Reviewing

This is the formal process which occurs at regular intervals, when, as a result of the monitoring, the care manager makes alterations to the care plan.

Do you know what the community care plans are for your local authority? Is the local authority fulfilling these plans?

Contact a local voluntary or private welfare organisation (such as Help the Aged). How departments for a copy of their community care plans. Compare their plans. What differences emerge?

Contact a local voluntary or private welfare organisation (such as Help the Aged). How involved have they been in the care plans? What are their views on the implementation of community care by the local authority?

Is your local authority doing what it says it is in the care plans? Ask your local Social Services department if you could interview some of their clients. Visit them, and ask their opinions on how the Social Services have behaved.

If the local Social Services are unable to help you in your research, then ask a client of a voluntary organisation.

# Carers

> When my wife was in hospital, it took four nurses to lift and turn her; now she's at home I have to do it all on my own. Is that what they call Community Care?
>
> **Source**: J. Pitkeathley, *It's my duty isn't it?* (Souvenir Press, 1989)

The health and social services only care for a tiny proportion of those in need of assistance – probably about 10 per cent at the very maximum.

## How many, how long?

In Britain today, approximately six million people are caring for sick, disabled or elderly persons on a regular basis. Over half of carers carry the entire burden of care alone, and about a quarter of them do so for at least 20 hours per week – there are approximately 1.5 million people in this category. Indeed, of this quarter, almost two-thirds of them (800 000 people) spend at least 50 hours each week caring. It has been estimated that if the State had to pay people to undertake these duties, then it would cost approximately £24 billion each year to the taxpayer.

There is going to be an increase in the numbers of carers in the next 20 years, as the elderly population (particularly those aged 85+) continues to grow, and as the effects of the switch towards community care begins to become apparent. There was no special provision in the 1990 Community Care legislation, however, for extra help for carers, and the success of the entire community care programme depends very much on the increasing efforts of carers.

## Who are the carers?

Of the six million carers, 3.5 million are female (and therefore 2.5 million are male), and over a quarter of all females aged 45–64 are carers, compared to 16 per cent of males. Apart from the differences in the proportion of males and females, carers are otherwise a typical cross-section of the community, reflecting the differences in class and education in the population at large.

When it comes to who looks after whom, and what the carers do, then the crucial importance of *the family* emerges.

In a recent study of elderly people, Evandrou found that nearly all the needs of the elderly respondents were met by spouses or other family members – for example, 91 per cent of those needing help to get in or out of bed, 84 per cent of those needing meals and 71 per cent requiring help with the laundry received it from their spouse or a member of the household. When it came to the other most common needs, help with shopping, walking outdoors and bathing, these were overwhelmingly provided by (adult) children, followed by other relatives. The activities performed by friends and neighbours ('the community'?) consisted of help with walking, unscrewing jars and bottle tops, and shopping – hardly a positive confirmation of the existence of *community* care!

There were only two areas of life in which the medical and social services made a significant contribution: 70 per cent of those receiving help with their toenails had them cut by one of these services(!), and 23 per cent of those receiving help with bathing were provided for by these services.

## What do carers need?

A recent study by the King's Fund ('Carer's Needs – a ten-point plan for carers') suggested the following needs (amongst others),

### Status

Carers in our society are invisible, because they are usually trapped at home, unable to go out, often unable to work, and, because of their commitments, they are unlikely to have friends or leisure activities. This may be the case even if the carer is a married woman with her own family.

Jill Pitkeathley of the National Council for Carers and Elderly Dependants states:

'... What carers need above all is recognition. They need to recognise themselves as doing a valuable job in society and be recognised by the Government.'

**Source**: The *Independent*, 1988

### Carers as individuals

It is important that when services are provided by local social services or community health agencies, they should be in response to the needs of the individual, and not come as a pre-determined package. The simple point here is that people need to be treated as individuals and that the social and health services need to recognise this. This point was made strongly by Sir Roy Griffiths in his report on community care.

### Cultural diversity

Services which are made available need to show a full awareness of race, culture and religion. Every effort should be made to provide services which recognise that people from different backgrounds may well have very different requirements. This ranges from the obvious, such as awareness of dietary differences, to more subtle requirements concerning issues of touch by members of the opposite sex.

### Leisure

Carers need time to have a break themselves, and to relax. Approximately 1.5 million people are caring for others for more than 20 hours each week, and the pressure of this can become unsupportable without some form of relaxation.

'Caring has made me a physical and mental wreck, totally unable to relax and without a clue how to even try to think of myself.'

**Source**: J. Pitkeathley, *It's my duty, isn't it?* (Souvenir Press, 1989)

### Support

Carers often want someone to talk to and someone with whom they can share their problems and frustrations. Related to this is the need to gain support from each other.

### Knowledge

There is a need for clear, detailed and accurate information about available services and benefits.

'I didn't know about the incontinence service until I went to the carers' group and someone there mentioned it. I suppose they worry that too many people will want it if they publicise it.'

**Source**: J. Pitkeathley, *It's my duty, isn't it?* (Souvenir Press, 1989)

## Benefits and services for carers

There is only one benefit specifically for carers – **Invalid Care Allowance**. This is available for people spending at least 35 hours a week looking after an ill or disabled person who is receiving Attendance Allowance or Constant Attendance Allowance (this latter is a benefit for those people who are seriously ill, or severely disabled, and need looking after day and night).

The conditions of eligibility for Invalid Care Allowance are that the person is of working age (16–60 or 65), and they must not be earning more than £35 a week 'after deductions for reasonable expenses' from other sources. Invalid Care Allowance was £32.55 a week in 1992.

# THE FORGOTTEN CARERS

At some point in our lives most of us will be either unpaid carers or cared for at home by relatives or friends. The General Household Survey's 'snapshot' of household circumstances suggests that at any one time six million people have caring responsibilities, of whom between 1.1 and 1.4 million regularly spend at least 20 hours a week on caring duties, with at least half a million people caring full-time....

Demographic change means an increasing proportion of older people in the country who are more likely to need care, and a decline in the number able to provide care. The NHS and Community Care Act has also highlighted the key role of carers. In evidence to the House of Commons' Social Services Committee the government acknowledged that: "Their total input was greater than the combined inputs financed from central and local government". Independent observers estimate that carers' work is equivalent to £24 billion a year which would otherwise be spent on paid workers.

But few carers expect to be paid a wage as such. Surveys of carers' needs usually reveal remarkably modest expectations. For instance, a recent survey showed that carers want more respite facilities (often just for an evening or a day); reliable and skilled help in an emergency; better information about welfare benefits and support services; a single 'key' professional with whom to keep in regular contact – not least to help with planning for when the carer can no longer continue.

Many full-time carers, however, are upset about the low level of benefit they can obtain – Invalid Care Allowance (available only to those regularly caring for at least 35 hours a week) is worth £32.55 a week. And the complex rules governing eligibility for Invalid Care Allowance means that only 10 per cent of carers receive it. Few full-time carers are able to cope with paid work as well, and they argue that at the least they should be able to claim the equivalent of Invalidity Benefit – the long term sickness payment for those unable to work – which starts at £54.15 a week.

## Financial consequences

Carers may also suffer from the financial consequences of giving up a paid job in order to look after a relative or friend, and this can include the loss of pension contributions, affecting their income in later life. Only a small proportion of carers have enough money to buy in much nursing or care assistant help. Research presented at Nottingham University shows that most carers have low personal incomes, of between £44 and £69 a week.

Carers and those for whom they care also have to meet the extra costs associated with chronic illness or disability. Several surveys show that carers' savings are often used up buying special equipment or just meeting everyday expenses like high laundry or heating bills.

It is no wonder that carers put help with benefits, and finances in general, at the top of their list of needs. Nor do financial problems stop when the person being cared for dies or leaves home. For example, women, who form the majority of carers, often have a very difficult time trying to get back into reasonably paid employment (and might have lost many years' seniority, pension rights and so on). Some carers are made homeless as they were living in the patient's home. Older women have found themselves worse off when their spouse goes into residential care, as his pension income might be used to pay the home's fees.

The stresses and consequent effects on health of living on a low income are widely recognised. But carers have the additional strains of the care task itself, and for some, like those looking after someone with advanced dementia, the 'job' is a 24-hour, 365-day-a-year commitment.

Fully 50 per cent of main carers are over pension age, and the strains of caring can become acute when, for example, lifting or bathing. This is particularly marked among those who have been caring for many years. The Spastics Society surveyed parents who have been caring for their children with cerebral palsy and found 78 per cent of them suffering from significant physical and emotional problems.

Fifty-five per cent of long-term carers exhibited significant emotional disturbance. This is not only attributable to the everyday strains reported by carers, but also to worries about what would happen to their spouse, son or daughter if they became ill or when they die. And not least, there is the stress of deep and often conflicting emotions about caring; anger and frustration about being in that position, guilt about not being able to do more, but also a remarkable and often self-sacrificing love.

**Source**: M. George, 'The Forgotten Carers', *Nursing Standard*, 30 September 1992

1 How many people have 'caring responsibilities', according to the extract?
2 How many spend at least 20 hours per week caring?
3 How many care full-time?
4 What is the proportion of carers in Britain? To work this out you will need to know how many people there are in Britain altogether – the information is not in the extract.
5 The general belief is that the State has taken over the bulk of caring from individuals. What comment is there in the extract about the worth of carers' work compared to the input of the State? How much do carers 'save' the State?
6 Make a list of what carers would like and explain what these are (you need to read the whole of the extract).
7 What benefits are available to carers? There is a leaflet (number FB31, 'Caring for Someone?') which you can obtain from your post office to help you with this.
8 What did the Nottingham University research show? What are the personal implications for carers (both in the short term and in the long term) and for the person they are caring for?
9 All carers face significant problems, but some face greater ones than others. Why do women have particular problems?
10 What percentage of carers are over retirement age? What particular problems do they have?
11 What effect does long-term caring have on the health of the carers?
12 Young carers have particular problems – what are they?
13 Having read the article, what comment could you make on the idea that carers are a homogeneous group (similar in their characteristics) and that we could devise simple strategies which would provide appropriate services for all carers?

Also available to carers are the range of benefits normally available to those who are unable to work or who have low incomes. These include Income Support, Housing Benefit, the Social Fund, Family Credit, assistance with NHS charges and exemption or assistance with the council tax.

There is also the **Crossroads Scheme**, which consists of volunteers who will 'sit' with the elderly/disabled person so that the carer can have a break, or can do shopping, etc.

There is no State assistance targeted specifically at carers who spend less than 35 hours a week caring.

---

The Co-operative Women's Guild have brought out a shocking report about the provisions for carers in England and Wales. A questionnaire sent to all local health authorities and social services departments showed more than a quarter of health authorities replying and more than one in seven social services departments made no provision at all for carers or their dependants.

What help is available is geographically quite unpredictable, so it is merely pot luck on where the carer lives as to the schemes provided.

**Source**: The *Independent*, 1988

# Criticisms of community care

## Ideal versus reality

The ideal of providing every person with all the services he/she requires, while allowing them to choose to live in their own home, is something that (virtually) everyone agrees with. However, the job of actually carrying this out is extremely complex and expensive. The gap between reality and ideals emerged when the government delayed the full introduction of the 1990

Community Care legislation from 1991, when it was originally scheduled to come into effect, until April 1993.

## Funding

The cost of providing adequate community care was originally believed to be less than the cost of running residential institutions. However, we now know that this is not the case. In fact, it may be more expensive to provide the required personal and health services in the community than it is to have them available in hospitals and social services institutions. Achieving increasing spending on the health and personal social services is very unlikely, given that the government would make no commitment during the phased implementation of the community care legislation to provide greater funds, believing as it did that savings could be made in the residential care budget of the Department of Social Security.

## Inequality of provision

Community care will be provided mainly by local authority Social Services departments, GP surgeries and by local community health units. There are going to be very great differences in the resources that these agencies will put towards community care.

The single biggest providers will be local authorities, yet the government does not say what they must spend on community care. This means that 'good' councils will provide greater funds, while 'bad' councils may prefer to spend their money on other activities. This is a particularly important point, because the elderly, the mentally ill and the disabled are very often the least powerful groups in society and have few means to persuade local authorities to devote greater resources to them.

With the fragmentation of services, there is greater difficulty in enforcing uniform standards of quality across the country.

## Co-ordination

Community care requires meticulous co-ordination between GPs, community health units and local authority Social Services departments. The evidence in the past shows that they were never able to achieve the necessary levels of co-ordination.

## The carers and the community

The basis of community care is that the social and health services support the existing (and increasing) networks of support for people in need of help. Yet all the evidence shows that the community simply does not exist. Help is overwhelmingly given by family members, usually the spouse or the daughter. The 'community' of friends and neighbours provides only a tiny proportion of assistance.

## Resistance

Some groups, such as the mentally ill, and even those with learning disabilities, produce feelings of fear and resentment amongst residents in areas where the health or social services wish to purchase group homes. The attitude of most people is to support the idea of community care as long as no 'abnormal' people live near them.

**'OUT IN THE WORLD'**

Margie was admitted to a hospital for the mentally handicapped when her mother died. Forty years later, with plans underway for the hospital to close, Margie, at 55, was considered a suitable candidate for community care....

Soon afterwards she was moved to a health training hostel near the city centre.

"I learned cooking, shopping, cleaning, money and how to take an interest in me clothes and hair. I also learned how to tell when I needed a bath—we were always told in the hospital."...

After 18 months of training she felt ready to make an informed decision about moving into her own home. She had no special friends at the hostel so it was decided that she should live with two women, Joan and Lucy, who had also completed their hostel training. Two years ago, a housing association offered them a three-bedroomed flat on a suburban estate. With money from the DHSS and the help of their support team, they chose their own furniture, clothes and personal possessions.

At first, social services staff supervised them 24 hours a day, but even so Margie found living outside quite a shock. "We were used to having everything done for us," she explains, "but suddenly it wasn't just training any more. These new staff made us do everything for ourselves. I had to walk to the shops by myself because I was terrified of getting on the bus in case a man sat next to me. At first I wished I'd never got out." But she soon gained confidence and now the home care aides just come in for the morning and a few hours in the evening to check that all is well for the night....

After the initial shock of independence, the three women had to learn how to get on together....

Then Joan's behaviour upset Lucy. "Lucy walked into some else's flat one day and blasted out all our troubles—we got a proper telling off for that." Alarm spread among the neighbours, mainly young families and single parents, who complained to social services about the noise. Rumours soon circulated that the three women were bullying children and feeling against them ran high. Negotiations between their support team and angry neighbours revealed that a few children were, in fact, taunting them. Now relations are cordial, but most people on the estate are busy with their own problems and pay them very little attention.

Apart from Joan and Lucy, Margie has made no real friends since she moved out—she regards the home care aides as her best friends....

Although Margie feels she had no part in the original decision that she should leave hospital, she now has no regrets. The privacy of her own room and possessions and the freedom to develop her own lifestyle have been worth the tremendous effort. "I never dreamt I could be free like this—I can fry onions every day if I want to," she says.

**Source**: M. Fullerton, 'Out in the World', *New Society*, 24 July 1987

**1** How was Margie trained to cope with living in the community?
**2** What level of supervision did she have? Could she have managed without this?
**3** What was the response of the neighbours to the three women?
**4** Is Margie 'part of the community'?
**5** What is her opinion overall? Better in or out?

## Potential danger

A few cases of crime and self-inflicted harm occurred in the first year of the process of discharge of mental patients from institutions, as a result of their failure to take the drugs that controlled their behaviour.

## Support

People who have spent a long time in institutions become 'institutionalised', and experience great difficulty coping with life 'outside'. Unless significant support is provided by the social services, the experience of living in the community can be too much and the person needs to return to the institution.

There is evidence that mentally ill people who have been discharged are likely to end up in prison, and it is believed that about 3 per cent of all prisoners are actually mentally ill.

# Assignment

You have been employed by a local newspaper to write a human interest story about the effects (or possibly potential effects) of community care on one person – it could be a disabled individual, someone with learning disabilities or an elderly person. You are to do an in-depth case study of this person and his/her situation, as well as his/her experiences of the social services in the past.

The editor has insisted that you should explain the background to community care, how it is functioning locally, and why it has been introduced. She also wants you to interview the care manager in the local Social Services department to find out their view on the effects of community care and whether the situation has improved or not for the client.

The final article must be supported by facts and statistics, and must relate these and their meaning to the life of the chosen individual.

# CHAPTER 8

# Residential Care

## Introduction

This chapter is closely related to chapters 7 and 15 on community care and mental illness and learning disabilities, and is also relevant to chapter 11 on the elderly. Here we explore the care provided for people in what Goffman once called 'total institutions'. By this he meant places in which people passed all their time and in which they develop particular patterns of living which differ from the normal lifestyle of people living 'outside'. Goffman points out that, for the majority of people, where they work and where they have their leisure and they sleep are usually different places. We could describe it as having different segments in our lives. However, for people in long-stay hospitals, nursing homes and elderly persons' homes, the segments are combined together – and, furthermore, these people have considerably less power over their choices than most people living in the community.

The first part of the chapter refers to the difficulty in defining exactly what we mean by residential care, and then goes on to explore the wide variety of groups that can be said to be living in some form of residential care.

Life inside a residential institution takes on a special quality of its own, and it is this pattern of life which we need to look at if we are to understand and improve the quality of life of clients. The key question concerns whether the residential institution aims to maximise the quality of life of the client or the ease of administration by the staff. The two can be very different indeed. The chapter explores this question by looking at concepts such as institutionalisation and normalisation.

Residential care has been the object of considerable criticism and has been compared unfavourably with community care. However, there are a number of advantages of residential care over community care which tend to be overlooked. We therefore look at the continuing need for residential care in certain circumstances.

## Defining residential care

In chapter 7 we discussed the problems of making clear distinctions between caring in the community and caring in institutions. However, for the purposes of this chapter, we will take residential care to mean care in any institution in which people live because they are *unable* (the very elderly infirm) or *unwilling* (private homes for the elderly), to live outside, or are simply *not allowed* (children and adolescents in care) to live outside.

There is a wide range of residential institutions, varying in size from enormous mental hospitals run by the health service, down to small privately run homes for the elderly (known as EPHs or elderly persons' homes).

## Functions of residential institutions

The Wagner Report (1988), which was an investigation into residential care, identified the following functions of residential institutions. Listing the functions also provides us with a way of distinguishing between the wide variety of institutions.

### Long-term care
Providing long-term care is the traditional role of the residential institution, and is still the most common role. This type of institution is gradually being closed down, and it is this type of institution about which most of the criticisms concerning 'institutionalisation' are made. Institutions providing long-term care include EPHs and children's homes.

### Respite care
Institutions providing respite care are those that take people being cared for at home for short periods so that the carer can have a rest. (Day centres provide the same service, except that the client only visits twice a week for the day.)

### Assessment
Institutions providing assessment are ones in which particular categories of clients, most often children and adolescents, will go while the social workers work out what is the best long-term plan for them.

### Rehabilitation
Institutions providing rehabilitation are, in a sense, the opposite of assessment units: they are usually at the end of the process of residential care and cater for people who are being taught to be self-sufficient. Examples of this type of residence are the rehabilitation units for the mentally ill prior to 'discharge'. There are also some residential drug dependency units, where drug addicts can go to overcome their dependency in a supportive atmosphere.

### Training
It is the function of some residential institutions to provide individuals with skills for use in the community. These sorts of institutions are particularly used for those with a learning disability and those with physical disabilities.

### Convalescence
Institutions providing convalescence offer care for those in need, but the length of time people can spend there is usually limited either because the patient/client gets well again or, as in the case of hospices, the patient/client dies.

### Flexible and emergency care
Institutions providing flexible care and emergency care are ones that do not provide permanent care, but are there as 'back-ups' to clients who can sometimes cope and sometimes not, in their own homes.

What is clear from this list of the functions of residential care is just how varied the tasks are. It also shows that residential care is not always an alternative, but is often complementary to community care.

*Are there any residential institutions in your area?*
*Find out how many there are, whom they cater for, and their functions.*
*You can find them by looking through Yellow Pages, contacting your local Social Services department, your NHS district or Trust, the educational authorities, the local NCVO, etc.*

## THE SPURIOUS ASSUMPTIONS OF COMMUNITY CARE

Both Labour and Conservative governments over the last 30 years have consistently argued the case for reducing the use of institutional-based services in the care and treatment of people experiencing mental health problems. Two main reasons have been advanced to support this position.

Firstly, it has been argued that with improved methods of treatment mental hospital throughput would increase, as people responded more rapidly to treatment. . . . This . . . has provided an important prop to the government's drive to close mental hospitals. . . . This position has been maintained despite the accumulation of evidence that modern forms of treatment . . . generally do not offer a cure. . . .

Secondly, the dangers of 'institutionalisation' have been highlighted, providing grounds for placing emphasis upon avoiding any further accumulation of long-stay patients. These views have been presented in numerous government documents over the last 30 years as almost self-evident truths, and are still maintained by the Department of Health.

One important problem with the rhetoric about the dangers of institutionalisation lies in the timing of events. It is often argued that the criticism of institutions that developed in the 1960s occurred *after* the decision by the Ministry of Health . . . to drastically reduce mental hospital accommodation, . . . and the supposed dangers of institutionalisation provided a convenient legitimating cover for this.

Over the last few years evidence has emerged to suggest that [the belief that] the dangers of institutionalisation far outweigh all other considerations is misplaced. Worryingly high proportions of the homeless and the prison population have been revealed to be people suffering from 'mental illness'. A recent study carried out in London estimated that a quarter of discharged psychiatric patients were without accommodation of any kind . . . a survey of Winchester prison . . . found that 40 per cent of inmates were deemed to be 'incapable of caring for themselves independently in the community at the time of arrest'.

Source: T. Chapman, S. Goodwin and R. Hennelly, 'A New Deal for the Mentally Ill: Progress or Propaganda?' *Critical Social Policy*, 1991

**1** Do the authors of this extract support community care?
**2** On what two grounds do they criticise it?
**3** What happens to a significant proportion of mentally ill people 'in the community'?

# Who provides residential care?

The four main providers of residential care are local authorities, voluntary organisations, the private sector and the National Health Service.

## Local authorities

The provision of residential care dates back to the setting up of workhouses in the nineteenth century, when those who were totally 'destitute' were forced to live in institutions where they had to work in extremely harsh conditions. The aim was to ensure that only those who were truly desperate would stay in. The workhouses took not only the poor, but the elderly and the ill as well.

Modern residential accommodation dates from 1948, when the National Assistance Act placed a duty on every local authority to 'provide residential accommodation for persons who by reason of age, infirmity or any other circumstance are in need of care and attention which is not otherwise available to them'.

In the Mental Health Act 1959, a further duty was placed upon local authorities to provide residential care for people with a 'mental handicap' or mental illness. By the late 1980s, there were approximately 16 000 places for those with learning disabilities, and 5000 places for the mentally ill.

## Voluntary organisations

These have been particularly interested in providing places for younger, physically disabled people. In 1987, approximately 7500 places were provided. A second role has been to provide accommodation for the elderly from specific religious or cultural backgrounds. More recently, there has been a substantial shift towards residential accommodation for those with mental or severe physical disabilities.

## Private organisations

This sector has grown enormously since the late 1970s, and with the government encouragement of the private sector in the 1990 Community Care legislation it is likely to become the largest provider of residential care. Its growth reflects the profits that can be achieved, the increasing numbers of the elderly, and the levels of financial support available from the government. In 1989, there were 155 600 places in private residential homes. In nursing homes, the figure was 112 600 – a rise of 25 per cent in just over a year. The estimated cost of meeting the bills for private (and to a lesser extent voluntary) institutions in 1993 is £2 billion.

## The National Health Service

This provides long-term care for the mentally ill and some geriatric patients. However, the government has tried to shift the responsibility for care for these groups towards local authorities, or towards care in the community under the supervision of health service staff.

# Groups in care

## The elderly

Women in particular are generally quite elderly when they enter residential care. They are therefore more likely to be confused, unable to walk and incontinent. The worse their condition, the more likely they are to be in local authority homes. However, the changes that have taken place as a result of the Community Care Act mean that there are far fewer places available in local authority homes. Traditionally, many private EPHs have been reluctant to take the more 'difficult' cases. It will be interesting to see what will happen over the 1990s as increasing numbers of incontinent and confused people are no longer able to turn to the public sector. A survey carried out by Warwickshire Social Services Department found that 40 per cent of the residents in its EPHs had no need to be there, as their needs could be met by home-based services.

A survey by Suffolk Social Services Department during 1985–6 showed that elderly people who had entered private residential care during the previous year had done so for a wide variety of reasons, mostly unconnected with their physical or mental conditions. Indeed, 37 per cent cited pressure from other people, and 24 per cent said their family could no longer cope.

## Those with learning disabilities

Increasingly, individuals with learning disabilities are being moved into the community as a response to the general move towards community care – a common pattern is for a group of three to four people to live together in a shared house or flat. Here they are visited daily by a social worker who ensures that they can cope.

However, those with particularly severe learning disabilities are more likely to live in residential institutions with social workers who form a permanent rota, thus ensuring that there is somebody available 24 hours a day.

There are also still large numbers of people with learning disabilities in long-stay hospitals.

## Those with physical disabilities

The voluntary sector looks after the majority of younger, severely physically disabled people. The elderly are more likely to be in private or NHS nursing homes. Unless individuals are severely disabled, they are likely to live in the community with a range of services provided by the NHS (such as community nurses) and by the Social Services (such as home helps).

Until the 1920s, residential care was often provided for orphans, those with learning disabilities and even 'unmarried mothers', as they were then called. Once in the system, it was extremely difficult to secure release. Here is just one story of a ruined life, amongst hundreds of others.

### WASTED LIVES?

John Sylvester remembers well what happened to him when he was six. He was sitting on the front step when a man rode up on a bicycle, handed his father a scrap of paper, lifted him up on to the handlebars, and pedalled off with him to the workhouse.

The lodgekeeper at the workhouse was called Charlie and kept a picture of the king on the wall. The king was George V, the year was 1916, and John was just starting a lifetime in institutional care.

It was not that he was mentally ill or disabled, nor that he had stolen an apple, an allegation he finds especially hurtful. It was simply that his mother had died and his father could not cope, and in the eyes of society at that time the workhouse was the only answer.

He never saw his father again, and his last contact with his family in Nantwich, Cheshire was a sister he saw 20 or 30 years ago. He does not know whether she is still alive.

Mr Sylvester spent 73 years in institutions. Today, at 81, with support from social services over the past two years, he shares a flat with two former mental patients in Stockport.

Alan Coates, a principal officer with Stockport social services, has known him for 12 years. "Having lived in his own home, he now realises that life cheated him," he said.

"The things he appreciates are being able to get up in the morning when you like, to have what you want to eat when you want to eat it, to watch the racing for an hour on TV in the afternoon, to chat to people, to have keys to your own front door— those basic things that are totally important."

Mr Sylvester has fond memories of some of the people he shared his life with in institutions, both residents and staff, and looks back on the times when he held positions of minor responsibility as high points of his life.

But he regrets the opportunities he never had—particularly for education, though he has taught himself to read and write. He also recalls staff who were unkind, the times he was moved on like a prisoner, without discussion, told simply to go and get his things, no time to say goodbye.

The idea of leaving hospital came as a result of the Government's care in the community programme. It took a year of pondering before Mr Sylvester agreed to have a try, and he spent about 18 months in a hospital before moving to his present address.

Mr Coates said: "If you don't manage it properly it is a disaster— that's why the transfer was so lengthy. If you just take someone out of a hospital and plonk them into the community, you deserve all the problems you get."

Mr Coates and his colleagues provide support for 800 mentally handicapped people in Stockport. "None of the people in hospital needs be there," he said. "Their needs can quite adequately and easily be met in the community."

Mourning a friend whose funeral took place yesterday, Mr Sylvester preferred not to speak for himself. "He is a wonderful man to know, so open, warm, and friendly," said Mr Coates. "I deeply regret it took us so long to give him this experience."

**Source**: The *Guardian*, 17 August 1991

**1** Could this happen now?

**2** On what grounds was Mr Sylvester put into the institution?

**3** What are his memories of life in the institution?

**4** Suggest ways in which people who are currently in institutions can ensure that their wishes are catered for, as far as possible. At the time of writing, the government is producing various 'Citizen's Charters'. See if they apply to those in institutions. (By the way, prisons are residential institutions – should prisoners have rights?)

Below are the brief biographical details of a selection of 'patients' who remain(ed) for most of their lives in a large hospital for those who were 'mentally deficient' (that is people with learning disabilities).

**David** Born 1912. Attended special school for six years until he was fifteen years old. Mother, a widow with five children, was unable to care for him. He was admitted in 1929. He worked in the hospital stores and pharmacy for many years until his retirement at the age of seventy-five. He was transferred to Abbey Grange in 1981. He is still awaiting sheltered accommodation.

**Doris** Born 1907. Attended a private school until the age of ten and then went to the local council school. She left at the age of fourteen. Is able to read and write but was said to be unable to do any housework, except under supervision. Father made application for admission following the death of her mother in 1936. Admitted at the age of twenty-eight. Little official information about her occupation in The Park. Did domestic work. Developed some long-standing friendships and moved with two of her friends to a residential home in 1988 at the age of eighty-one.

**Elizabeth** Born 1909. Admitted to The Orchards in 1927, three months after the birth of an illegitimate baby. Transferred to The Park in 1932. Worked as a domestic in a private house outside The Park in the 1950s. Afterwards attended the hospital industrial unit until her retirement at the age of seventy-five. Now attends on a voluntary basis, helping with tea breaks, washing up, etc. In 1984 she was transferred to a small flat in the hospital for rehabilitation. First attempt at living outside in a flat with three others after sixty-one years of institutional life was not successful because of the incompatibility of the group. Transferred to a residential home in 1989.

**Elsie** Born 1920. Suffers from spinal curvature. Attended special school but was discharged just before she was sixteen years old as being incapable of receiving further benefit from special school. Able to read fairly well. Was admitted in 1936 following parents' separation and mother's deteriorating mental health. On mother's admission to hospital, application was made for her detention. Transferred from The Park to Abbey Grange in 1973. Joined her friend Doris in residential home in 1989.

**Enid** Born 1913. Lived at home with her parents who did not wish her to go to an institution. No attempt made to educate her at all, possibly because of her physical handicaps. She was unable to walk and had a curved spine. She was admitted in 1963 following the death of her mother because there was no-one to care for her. Attended the hospital training departments until her retirement in 1977. She had some difficulty speaking but made great efforts to be understood. She died in 1988 in The Park, peacefully in her sleep.

**Ernest** Born in 1928. Suffered from spina bifida. Was admitted to the local general hospital in 1938 because of neglect. Transferred from general hospital to The Park in 1945. No record of any education. Largely self-taught. Worked in the hospital departments and on the villa where his academic skills were useful in organising the clothing store. Described as 'the most intelligent patient in the hospital', he was asked to speak on behalf of other residents on formal occasions such as moving a vote of thanks to the Lord Mayor. He wrote his own account of life in The Park in 1974 which is in the hospital library. His physical health was poor and he became increasingly physically disabled, relying on a wheelchair during his last years. He was sustained by a deep religious faith and his close relationship with a fellow resident which lasted from 1971 until his death in August 1989.

**Frank** born 1917. Attended a special school from age of eight to twelve years when he was discharged as ineducable. Afterwards attended a Junior Occupation Centre until 1932 when he was admitted following the death of his parents and the inability of his grandfather to care for him. He ran away a number of times. Developed arthritis in his late fifties and now has some difficulty in moving about. He became blind at the age of fifty-eight. He attended a centre for physically handicapped people outside the hospital for a few years before his retirement. He is very independently minded. He recently made his will and has expressed a strong desire to live outside The Park.

*Source*: M. Potts, *A Fit Person to be Removed* (Northcote House Publishers, 1991)

## Children and young people

Until the 1970s it was quite normal for children in need of care to be looked after by social workers in residential homes. Children moved in for long periods and could expect to stay there for their entire childhood. Since then, there has been a determined effort to place most children with foster parents on a short- or long-term basis. The argument is that children brought up in residential homes are unable to cope with life, as they have unusual childhoods which do not prepare them for self-sufficiency when they eventually leave the institution.

Children and young people in residential care today are often those with behavioural problems, who may have had considerable contact with the police and who find it very difficult to accept, or be accepted in, a foster home. Residential social workers who work in this area face particularly difficult problems controlling young people and helping them through their problems.

The periods spent in residential accommodation tend to be as short as possible, and the emphasis should be on rehabilitating the child and preparing him/her for life with a foster family or, for the older child, for self-sufficiency.

### Roles in residential work for young people

| Position | Qualified social workers? | Job |
|---|---|---|
| Officer in Charge | Yes | Runs institution. Very much determines nature of the place and attitudes towards residents |
| Deputy | Yes | Responsible for staff matters |
| 3rd in Charge | Sometimes | Ensures smooth running by having close contact with staff and some children. Specific responsibilities regarding such things as liaison with GPs, supervising cleaning and cooking, etc. |
| Residential Social Workers | Not in lower grades | Complete range of caring functions for children in their charge. They will be the **key worker** for a few named children, and will be expected to construct a special rapport with them |

### Roles in residential work for the elderly

| Position | Qualified social workers? | Job |
|---|---|---|
| Manager | Sometimes | Overall control; in the private sector, could be the owner |
| Deputy | Rarely | Specific tasks – in particular, finance and liaising with GPs. Ensures smooth running, organises social activities for residents |
| Care Assistants | No | Look after residents, both physically and at social level. Attempt to maintain quality of residents' lives |

# Models of residential care

We have seen the variety of types of residential care that exist, categorised by the functions they perform, but what actually happens inside these institutions? What forms of intervention are used?

Miller and Gwynne have suggested that there are three basic models which describe the approaches to caring within the institutions. These are **warehousing**, **horticulture** and **normalisation**.

## Warehousing

This is the type of institution in which people are simply dumped and left like furniture stored in a warehouse. Anyone who has visited the worst kind of elderly persons' home will have seen them inside sitting in rows, staring vacantly out of the window or at the television.

The object of the staff in institutions run along these lines is to contain the clients, feeding, washing and toileting them.

## 'TOTAL INSTITUTIONS'

First, there are the 'house rules', a relatively explicit and formal set of *prescriptions* and *proscriptions* that lays out the main requirements of inmate conduct. These rules spell out the austere round of life of the inmate. Admission procedures, which strip the recruit of his past supports, can be seen as the institution's way of getting him ready to start living by house rules.

Secondly, against this stark background, a small number of clearly defined rewards or privileges are held out in exchange for obedience to staff in action and spirit....

The third element in the privilege system is punishments; these are designated as the consequence of breaking the rules. One set of these punishments consists of the temporary or permanent withdrawal of privileges or the *abrogation* of the right to try to earn them. In general, the punishments meted out in total instutitions are more severe than anything encountered by the inmate in his home world. In any case, conditions in which a few easily controlled privileges are so important are the same conditions in which their withdrawal has a terrible significance....

The privilege system and the mortifying processes that have been discussed represent the conditions to which the inmate must adapt. These conditions allow for different individualistic ways of meeting them, apart from any effort at collective subversive action. The same inmate will employ different personal lines of adaptation at different phases in his moral career and may even alternate among different tacks at the same time.

First, there is the tack of 'situational withdrawal'. The inmate withdraws apparent attention from everything except events immediately around his body and sees these in a perspective not employed by others present. This drastic curtailment of involvement in interactional events is best known, of course, in mental hospitals, under the title of 'regression'....

Secondly, there is the 'intransigent line': the inmate intentionally challenges the institution by flagrantly refusing to cooperate with staff. The result is a constantly communicated intransigency and sometimes high individual morale. Many large mental hospitals, for example, have wards where this spirit prevails....

A third standard alignment in the institutional world is 'colonisation'; the sampling of the outside world provided by the establishment is taken by the inmate as the whole, and a stable relatively contented existence is built up out of the maximum satisfactions procurable within the institution. Experience of the outside world is used as a point of reference to demonstrate the desirability of life on the inside, and the usual tension between the two worlds is markedly reduced, thwarting the motivational scheme based upon this felt discrepancy which I described peculiar to total institutions....

A fourth mode of adaptation to the setting of a total institution is that of 'conversion': the inmate appears to take over the official or staff view of himself and tries to act out the role of the perfect inmate. While the colonised inmate builds as much of a free community for himself as possible by using the limited facilities available, the convert takes a more disciplined, moralistic, *monochromatic* line, presenting himself as someone whose institutional enthusiasm is always at the disposal of the staff....

Many total institutions, most of the time, seem to function merely as storage dumps for inmates....

**Source**: E. Goffman, *Asylums* (Penguin, 1968)

The sociologist, Erving Goffman, described in his book *Asylums* how many residential institutions which appear to have different functions for different groups of people, in fact all share certain common characteristics. He calls them 'total institutions', because the three elements of our lives which are usually kept separate – work, leisure and eating/sleeping – are all performed together in one place. Institutions as different as public schools, monasteries, long-stay hospitals and homes for the elderly all share the fact that there are rules laid down for the 'inmates' to follow, which appear to benefit the staff rather than the residents. Goffman also showed, as this extract indicates, that people tend to have a certain number of responses to their situation.

1 When a person enters an institution, what happens?

2 What happens to those who obey the staff?

3 What happens to those who annoy the staff, or break their rules? (Your answers to the questions above should include the terms 'privilege', 'system' and 'mortifying processes'. If not, please give a definition of each of these terms.)

4 Explain clearly, with examples, and in your own words, the adaptations to institutional life described by Goffman.

5 In Goffman's view, what is the main purpose of most institutions?

6 What is the official objective? Are Goffman's view and the official view the same? Please explain your answer.

7 Goffman, at the very end of the extract, suggests that the contradiction between actual and official aims forms the basis of the staff's activities. Could you explain this, or find examples of this in your own experience? (For example, in my experience, many teaching and administrative staff in educational institutions are rude to students as if the students are of no importance, yet the entire point of the institution is to serve them!)

## Horticulture

In this approach to the care of clients, there is the attitude that the full potential of clients has to be developed. This is obvious when applied to the physically disabled, for example, but less so with the elderly. However, in recent years approaches such as 'reality orientation theory' have stressed the need to work with confused patients, or those with learning difficulties, by encouraging them to engage in real-life situations and to provide them with stimuli to help them become more independent.

Most residents agreed that 'all their basic needs were taken care of', and the advantages of residential care, in terms of support with everyday tasks, are obvious enough. Residents are not concerned with looking after themselves, with cooking or with domestic tasks. However, the uncertainty of life in a community environment which makes excessive demands on an old person is exchanged for one which is routinised and predictable and denies a role to that old person – which may lead to general apathy. And the finding that physical settings are technically superior to life at home, with greater levels of care and comfort, is offset by the complexity and the lack of personalisation in the new environment. This creates a strangeness that cannot readily be overcome by the old person. The discovery that few residents could recall choice of discussion about their future before admission is testimony to the likelihood that 'institutionalisation' starts with an acquiescence which occurs well before an old person crosses the residential threshold. What about the limits of residential care? Staff at all levels in homes appear to conspire in the construction of a care package that is heavily weighted towards a range of domestic tasks. Indeed the priority given to the cleaning and tidying of physical spaces is also reflected in the urgency given to the cleaning and tidying of residents themselves.

**Source**: D. Willcocks, 'A Home from Home', *New Society*, 6 February 1987

1 What are the benefits of residential care?

2 To what extent is this offset by the disadvantages?

## Normalisation

This approach is the one that links most closely to community care. It is based on the belief that people should be integrated as much as possible into the wider society. In this model, the individual usually lives in some form of 'sheltered' or group home, where he/she can receive support, yet at the same time can lead a life which is as near normal as possible. It is because the aim is to provide a life as normal as possible for the client, that this form of social work intervention is called 'normalisation'. It is discussed in more detail in chapter 15, which looks at people with mental illness and learning difficulties.

# Criticisms of residential care

In her early thirties, Susan Baldwin was still living at home with her parents because she had never quite got around to moving out. Life was still inviting, with a busy social life and a job which she loved at a family centre dealing with young children.

When her father became ill she helped her mother to nurse him. He died. Weeks later her mother had a stroke which left her both physically and mentally disabled. Susan brought her home from the hospital to look after her. Three years later Susan is still caring for her. Her job is now part-time, and even keeping that is a struggle. The rest of her life is devoted to her mother, who has steadily deteriorated: she is incontinent, muddled, and unable to leave the house, get dressed or remember her tablets.

She is becoming increasingly dependent on Susan, jealous even of the few hours snatched for work.

Now, at the age of 39, Susan sees life closing in around her. She does not know how much longer she will be able to go on working, as it means leaving her mother alone for a few hours every afternoon. Going out in the evening is a rare occurrence as she has to find someone to sit for her. Her one regular break is every Thursday when a friend comes round so she can either pop out or just have someone to talk to.

Her mother is only 68; there could be many more years in front of her. Susan cannot wish it over when that would mean the death of her mother, whom she still loves. However, the relationship has changed: "It's as if she's my daughter and I'm her mother. Sometimes I feel I'm looking after a stranger."

1 After reading this account, do you think that residential care, for the mother, would have been better for (a) the mother and (b) Susan Baldwin?

2 What community services would have helped Susan to cope? Do you think the mother would have noticed if she had been in a nursing home?

3 Who should have the right to make decisions about community care – the individual in need, the carer or the professional? Explain your reasons.

In recent years, there has been a great shift away from providing residential care towards providing community care. Part of this shift has been driven by criticisms of the whole idea and the practice of residential care. The following criticisms have been made.

## Institutionalisation

Living within an institution is fundamentally different from normal life in the community. In normal life, individuals make decisions for themselves, wear the clothes they choose, eat at the times they want, and are usually living in their own home. The majority of people under retirement age also go out to work each day, meet people, commute and have a range of stimuli. In addition, most people can have leisure activities of their own choosing.

Living in an institution takes all these things away from individuals, and therefore deprives them of what most people would consider a decent life.

Perhaps even worse, is the fact that individuals in institutions have their daily lives controlled by others, such as staff members, who make decisions for them. For adults, and in certain circumstances young people, this can be a humiliating experience.

In my first job with mentally handicapped people I was part of a team of two providing house experience with a craft bias, for people living in a local hospital.

I'd thought of making patchwork cushions and had lots of different material cut up ready in squares. They filled a table. Ivan was the first to choose. All I'd asked was that each of them choose two pieces that they liked. Ivan was young, funny, extrovert.

He couldn't do it. He kept saying, 'No, you.' I kept explaining that, if I chose, it would be what I liked and not what he liked. He still couldn't do it. 'No, you.' I was worried that I had made the first task too difficult or that I hadn't managed to get across what I wanted. I tried to make it simpler by holding different pieces and saying 'Do you like this one?' and talking about the different colours. Eventually he did choose and carried on to make a patchwork cushion that incorporated many such choices. I thought of this again two years later when we were making something else. Curtains I think it must have been. Ivan was adamant that he chose the material. He insisted that we went to the local material shop so that his choice was larger than the pieces we already had. He chose and paid for the material by himself and carried it proudly back to the house. Ivan was the first person to teach me that living in an institution is about *not* making choices. I believe the initial choice was difficult for him because he feared he might get it wrong and be told off. He wasn't sure that it wasn't a trap of some sort. But if you are not actively encouraged to make choices it must be a fearsome thing to be faced with....

With the same class part of our weekly routine was to go shopping in the open market, usually for tea, coffee, biscuits, etc....At the same time as this, a day room had been completely kitted out with a new fitted carpet and a new velvet three-piece suite, with the result that for four months all outings of any sort were stopped for the residents because the funds were exhausted.

**Source:** 'Roles and relationships', in A Bredin and J. Walmsley (eds), *Making Connections* (Hodder & Stoughton, 1991)

1 What is one of the key things that an institution does for and to people?
2 Try a small experiment. Split into small groups of between three and five. For one day, or at least for one lunch-hour, one person makes all decisions about what to do – the rest of the group can only do something (this would include talking to people outside the group) with permission from their social worker. At the end of the allotted time, discuss your feelings.

## Maltreatment

Because of the imbalance of power in the institution, with residents being expected to do what they are told, and because of the lack of control over the activities of the staff, many examples of maltreatment of residents have been uncovered over the last 20 years.

## Poor condition of buildings

Many institutions are old and in poor condition, as public investment has not kept up with improvements in living standards in general.

## Cost

The costs associated with residential care have increased at a far greater rate than anyone would have predicted only 15 years ago. One example of this is that, in 1989, the DSS was paying approximately £1 billion towards the costs of maintaining elderly people in residential accommodation – and this excludes the costs to the NHS of long-stay patients in hospitals.

| Type of institution | Main features |
|---|---|
| Warehousing | |
| Horticulture | |
| Normalisation | |

Complete the table above using the information on pages 176–9. Which, if any, of the types of institution (or approaches to institutional care) would you describe as characterising each of the following cases?
(a)  Ivan (page 180)
(b)  Martin (page 182)
(c)  John Sylvester (pages 173–4)
(d)  Susan Baldwin's mother (page 179)

# Arguments in favour of residential care

However, the arguments for residential care are also quite strong. In certain cases there is little alternative to institutional care – for example, where a person is so enfeebled by age, or so seriously mentally ill, that the individual simply cannot continue to have an acceptable standard of life without constant care or supervision. Secondly, there is no reason why, *necessarily*, people's lives should come under the control of members of staff. It is quite possible to organise democratically run institutions, where, as far as possible, residents can enjoy significant power-sharing with staff. Thirdly, if the buildings are old and of poor quality, it is not residential care that is being criticised, but the lack of resources available for improving it.

### Client's needs in residential settings

**Source**: Derived from C. Towle, *Common Human Needs* (Allen & Unwin, 1973)

Residential care is something which is always seen as inferior to being with a family. However, there are often situations in which it is better, for both the carer and the person with disabilities, if the person goes into residential care. The following is part of an interview with a mother (aged 65) of a person with a learning disability.

### A POSITIVE VIEW OF AN INSTITUTION

I: And what, from Martin's point of view, are you happiest about?

M: He has a social life now, which he didn't have with me. He goes out, they go to the pub sometimes. And he goes down to his club... They'll go shopping, they'll go to the local town on the bus. They are giving an Easter party and they have meetings and they are consulted. And when Martin asked for a meeting – I mean, I can't believe it, my child, my son, saying 'Meeting, please'. Well, this is incredible, isn't it. I didn't ask him things. Martin is a more rounded person now. He is a personality now. He wasn't, he was my little boy here. [....]

I: How do you feel when you think about Martin now?

M: I'm happy for him. Except for the little hiccups, you know... And I like my relationship with the staff. I can go in there and say 'Is it all right to make a cup of coffee?' or they'll make me one. If a button's missing from Martin's shirt, I can get it, I know where things are. This is lovely. This is very important, that their parents should feel part of the child's life...

   And I feel I'm in Martin's *home*; they make me feel that. I feel I am going in my son's home. Another thing they do which I didn't do. I never knocked on Martin's bedroom door. They are giving him dignity. Even I didn't give him that dignity. Well, he was only my little boy, wasn't he? It's made me realise that I didn't really treat him as an adult. They are showing me...

**Source**: A. Richardson, 'If you love him, let him go,' in A. Bredin and J. Walmesley (eds.), *Making Connections* (Hodder & Stoughton, 1991)

# The Wagner Report

In 1988, the Wagner Report (*A Positive Choice*) was published. This highlighted the demoralised state of the residential social services, and uncovered what it called 'disturbing evidence of insensitivity . . . and examples of cruelty' in residential care establishments. The report itself was largely ignored, because the move towards community care was beginning in earnest and the Griffiths Report on this subject (see chapter 7) attracted much greater interest.

The Department of Health did, however, set up the 'Caring in Homes' initiative in order to build upon Wagner's recommendations. Finally, in 1992, 'Take the Initiative' was published. This showed the extent of the advances resulting from Wagner for all groups in residential accommodation, including elderly people, those with learning disabilities and those with physical disabilities.

Below are some of the findings and recommendations of the Wagner Report.

### Positive choice

The report said that people ought to want to enter residential homes, and not have it forced upon them. Homes therefore need to provide detailed information about themselves and the alternatives available.

### Monitoring

Staff need to carry out regular monitoring of the quality of life in the institutions, both as regards the individuals living there and the staff themselves. There should, as part of this, be a way for residents to express their discontent and feelings in an open way.

> 'We came across one woman who had been living in a home for 23 years and no one had discovered that she didn't like the food.'

### Part of the community

In the past, residential homes were cut off from the general community outside. There need to be as many useful links as possible between residential homes and the communities in which they are based.

### Co-operative planning

The aspirations of the individuals in the institutions, and of their carers/relatives, need to be part of the planning, delivery and monitoring of the services.

### Friendly environment

Residential homes often have a particular look and impersonal feel about them. This can be remedied by changing their appearance and the general environment.

*Institutions can be unwelcoming and unfriendly. They can give negative messages through their pictures, smell and general appearance. Is this true?*

*Ask to visit three local institutions. After your visit, write down your impressions. If your impressions were negative, what do you suggest could be done to change the environment? Why do you think the institutions are like they are?*

### Adequate training

Staff in residential establishments were traditionally poorly trained. The report recommended that specific training was needed. As a result, by 1992, a range of training needs had been identified.

# Assignment

Find the address of a local residential institution. If there are a group of you, choose different types of residential institutions, or ones dealing with different client groups. Arrange a visit, and while there find out about life in the institution for the clients and for the staff.

Would it be feasible for the clients to live in the community? Do they wish to do so? Devise a diagram which illustrates these points and which could be used to show to people and their relatives who are thinking of applying to move into residential care.

# CHAPTER 9

# The Voluntary Sector

## Introduction

In this chapter we explore the nature and role of the voluntary sector in providing welfare services. The idea of voluntary organisations to help those in need is very much a British tradition and the voluntary and charitable organisations have continued to play an important role, even with the existence of the Welfare State. In recent years the government has shown particular support for the voluntary sector, to the extent that it has insisted that the bulk of local authority spending on community care services must go to the voluntary (and private, profit-making) organisations. So 'voluntarism', rather than being a historical leftover of do-gooding from the nineteenth century, has taken the central place of the government as the way forward to provide care.

The chapter begins with a brief definition of the voluntary sector, and then continues to look at its history, with some comments on the reasons behind its rise and decline, before the present growth as a result of government policies. Following this is a brief section on fundraising and the various types of charitable and voluntary organisations that exist.

Many professionals are critical of voluntary organisations, as they claim that they get in the way of properly funded and organised State services. This is hotly disputed by the voluntary sector, and this debate is discussed here.

Whenever there is a large number of individuals or organisations working in the same area of welfare provision, there is always the possibility of confusion, overlap and a waste of resources. However, the voluntary organisations have developed a national council to co-ordinate their activities, and we examine the activities of this council.

Finally, we turn to look at the new role of voluntary organisations in government thinking and in particular their importance for community care. The government is particularly keen to encourage a mixture of welfare provision instead of having a monopoly provided solely by the local authorities, and so it is switching funding away from local authorities. The term used by social policy analysts to describe this move towards a mixture of central government, local authority, private and charitable welfare provision is the 'mixed economy of welfare'. We examine the reasons for this move and its perceived advantages and disadvantages.

# Voluntary or charity organisations

State and local government social services are only a part of the provision of organised help that people in difficulties receive. The other element of formal care is that of the voluntary or charity organisations. It is important to remember that the overwhelming bulk of the assistance that people receive in their everyday lives is, of course, that of informal care through family, friends and neighbours.

There are approximately 350000 voluntary organisations in Britain, of which about 40 per cent are officially defined as charities. This status allows them to gain exemption from some forms of taxation. The official definition of a charity is an organisation which 'benefits the community in some way, but does not engage in political activity'. Charitable organisations typically 'advance education, religion or relieve poverty'.

According to this definition of a charity, however, the organisation must not have any political or pressure group activity. A group such as the Child Poverty Action Group, which attempts to influence the public and the politicians to combat poverty more effectively, is therefore not a charity. If it confined itself to raising money for poor people, it would be. On the other hand, public schools (because they advance education) do have charitable status.

Some organisations which are charities spend large amounts of money on 'administrative costs'.

*What is your view? How would you define a charity? How would you control them? When you are asked to give money or help to a voluntary organisation, do you know what proportion of money is spent on the actual purposes of the organisation? Contact a cross-section of voluntary and charitable organisations. Devise a very short questionnaire which will cover the issues of (a) what percentage of money received is spent on administration, (b) whether the organisation is a charity, (c) what its purposes are and (d) what its achievements are.*

## PARTICIPATION IN VOLUNTARY WORK

1 *What information does the table give us?*
2 *Which social class is most likely to engage in voluntary work?*
3 *Which social class is least likely to engage in voluntary work?*
4 *Do males or females participate more in voluntary work?*
5 *Are there any reasons which you can suggest for the patterns that emerge?*
6 *Conduct a small survey of people in your local high street. Ask them their job and if they are regularly involved in charitable work. Ask them what the work is.*

**By sex and socio-economic group, Great Britain, 1987**

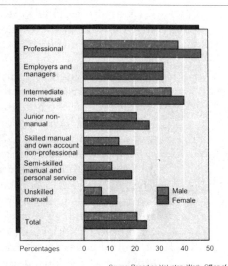

Professional
Employers and managers
Intermediate non-manual
Junior non-manual
Skilled manual and own account non-professional
Semi-skilled manual and personal service
Unskilled manual
Total

Male
Female

Percentages   0   10   20   30   40   50

*Source: Report on Voluntary Work, Office of Population Censuses and Surveys*

**Source:** *Social Trends* (HMSO, 1993)

## SELECTED VOLUNTARY ORGANISATIONS

| Great Britain | | | Thousands and numbers | |
|---|---|---|---|---|
| | Membership (thousands) | | Branches/ centres (numbers) | |
| | 1971 | 1991 | 1971 | 1991 |
| Age Concern England | — | 180 | — | 1,100 |
| British Red Cross Society[1] | 172 | 82 | 917 | 1,200 |
| Confederation of Indian Organisations | — | — | 52 | 82 |
| Disablement Income Group | — | 5 | — | — |
| Lions Club of the British Isles and Ireland[1] | 8 | 21 | 302 | 897 |
| National Association of League of Hospital Friends | 250 | 240 | 835 | 1,220 |
| National Association of Round Tables of Great Britain and Ireland | 29 | 23 | 1,072 | 1,220 |
| National Federation of Community Organisations | — | — | 564 | 921 |
| National Federation of Gateway Clubs | 8 | 77 | 200 | 723 |
| National Federation of Self-Help Organisations[1] | — | — | 400 | 2,500 |
| National Society for the Prevention of Cruelty to Children[1] | 20 | 21 | 217 | 220 |
| PHAB (Physically Handicapped and Able Bodied) | 2 | 50 | 50 | 500 |
| Retirement Pensions Association | 600 | 33 | 1,500 | 600 |
| Rotary International in Great Britain and Ireland | 50 | 65 | 1,125 | 1,760 |
| Royal British Legion | 750 | 655 | 4,135 | 3,268 |
| Royal Society for Mentally Handicapped Children and Adults | 40 | 55 | 400 | 550 |
| Royal Society for the Prevention of Cruelty to Animals | — | 21 | 207 | 207 |
| St John Ambulance Brigade[1] | — | 55 | — | 3,209 |
| Toc H | 15 | 5 | 1,046 | 412 |

[1] 1991 columns contain 1990 data.

**Source:** *Social Trends* (HMSO, 1993)

*This is a list of some of the largest voluntary organisations. Find out what they do.*

# History of the voluntary sector

There have always been various forms of charities and voluntary activities, especially those organised by religious groups. By 1869, the Charity Organisation Society (today the Family Welfare Organisation) had been founded with the aim of uniting the 640 charities that were operating in London. Some large organisations which influenced the structure of many modern forms of voluntary organisations emerged during the middle of the nineteenth century, examples being the founding of Dr Barnado's Children's Homes (1866) and the National Society for the Prevention of Cruelty to Children (1884).

There were various reasons for the emergence of such a large number of charitable organisations at this time. Some of the principal reasons are listed below.

## Awareness of problems

People had always been aware of poverty, but the sheer scale and extent of social problems were proved and publicised by a small number of academic researchers and political reformers, such as Mayhew, Booth and Rowntree.

## Ability to influence

The emerging democratic structure of British society meant that pressure groups were able to influence the politicians who were beginning to take into account the views of the voters. Remember, though, that the right to vote was limited throughout the nineteenth century to a minority of the adult population – for example, women did not fully attain the right to vote until 1928!

## Beliefs

The dominant ideology or belief system at the time was of *laissez-faire*, which meant that the government was not supposed to interfere in society, rather its role was to defend the country and to maintain law and order within it.

A second belief was that the financial position that people found themselves in was largely a result of their own hard work and good fortune. If people were poor, it was generally because they did not work hard enough, or they had personal failings.

## Organisations

Today, we accept the idea of organisations based on rules and bureaucratic procedures. If you are studying this book, you will probably be at a college or in employment where there is a complex organisation making specific demands. This way of undertaking tasks is a relatively new form of activity, however, and one which profoundly influenced industrialised societies – including the way of organising to combat social problems, as opposed to the unco-ordinated efforts of individuals.

## Rising power of the working class

The nineteenth century saw the organisation of the working class into unions and friendly societies (the influence of organisation again) to further their own interests. These organised charitable self-help groups.

## Social control

We noted earlier that the role of the government was to defend the country and to maintain law and order. Part of law and order involved ensuring that the demands of the working class and the poor were *not* met, as that would disturb the living standards and the political power of the rich. Charities formed a very useful way of doing this. Help to the poor was given, not as a right, but as an exercise in charity to which the poor had to be grateful. This strengthened the moral superiority and right to rule of the rich.

## The role of women

The nineteenth century saw a rise in the status of men and the imposition of their views as 'normal' in society. Undoubtedly women were repressed in a way that would shock most people today. Poor women were often forced into the roles of servants, and many were driven by desperation into prostitution. The wives of rich men were excluded from taking an active part in business affairs, no matter how capable they were. The only acceptable outlet for their drive, intelligence and energy was charitable work.

A subsidiary but important part of the drive towards statutory social services represented a deliberate move away from voluntary provision not least within the Labour Party. Faith was invested in statutory services as a way of guaranteeing provision that was comprehensive and universal, professional and impartial, and subject to democratic control. The immediate post-war implementation of social policies marked an attempt decisively to move away from social policies that were partial in scope, socially divisive in action, and socially controlling in intent. Voluntary organisations were regarded with not a little suspicion in the process.

While readily acknowledged for their pioneering contribution and their high-lighting of social problems, voluntary organisations were also seen as ill-organised, amateur and fragmented and unevenly distributed. With the rapid secularisation of British society between the wars, the voluntary organisations were no longer rooted in significant social groupings in a way that the mass of people could identify with. They were, in a society that continued to be riven with class divides, identified with middle-class patterns of patronage and charity.

In the construction of the new social service state we turned our backs on philanthropy and replaced the do-gooder by highly professional administrators and experts. From the 1920s on, the normal left-wing attitude has been opposed to middle-class philanthropy, charity and everything else connected with do-gooding. Those of us who became socialists grew up with the conviction that we must in this point ally ourselves with the professionals and trades unions and discourage voluntary effort particularly since it was bound to reduce the number of jobs available.

**Source**: M. Brenton, *The Voluntary Sector in British Social Services* (Longman, 1985)

**1** Why was it believed that statutory social services (established by legal right) were the way forward during the 1950s?

**2** What were the perceived disadvantages of the voluntary services?

Charitable and self-help organisations were in the forefront of providing help to the poor, those in ill-health, the disabled and the elderly until the introduction of the Welfare State in the 1940s, when it was believed that there would be no further need for voluntary groups.

# Charity begins at home

When the communist states of Eastern Europe collapsed in the early 1990s, Western experts were appalled at the conditions that orphans and the disabled lived in. Yet there seemed little concern by the local populations to try to improve the conditions of these people.

The main reason for the inactivity of the Eastern European populations was that they had no concept of voluntary work. The State had taken over all responsibility for individuals' lives, and people were simply unused to initiating help for those with needs.

'I hate them ... the way they treat me – as if I am some sort of beggar or something. Just because I'm here [in this state] ... it doesn't mean I'm ... worth less than them ... life's been unfair ... I mean I've been unlucky. As far as I am concerned they were born with money and I wasn't. It is the government which should help me, not these ... Lady Muck busybodies.'

**1** Is it true that voluntary workers act as superior to their clients? What are the motives of those who are volunteers – to help or to fill in their spare time?

**2** Would it be better if the State were to run all caring activities – as they effectively do with health care?

**3** Or would it be better to limit the role of the State to providing offices and some funding for charitable organisations?

# The variety of voluntary groups

The 1960s saw an increase in the numbers of voluntary organisations which had rather different methods and aims from the traditional ones. These organisations developed to fill the gaps in the Welfare State that had become apparent 20 years after it was set up.

The groups developed in different ways and for different purposes. These are listed below.

- **Political presure groups**   for example, the Child Poverty Action Group (poverty) or Shelter (housing).
- **Self-help groups**   for example, Alcoholics Anonymous, Gingerbread (for single-parent families).
- **Non-profit making providers**   for example, housing associations.
- **Educational purposes**   for example, AIDS charities such as the Terence Higgins Trust (although education is only part of its activities).
- **Direct Assistance**   for example, Help the Aged, Children in Need.
- **Advice and Counselling**   for example, Citizens' Advice Bureaux, Relate (marriage guidance).
- **Religious**   for example, the Salvation Army.

---

## WOMENS ROYAL VOLUNTARY SERVICE

## NEEDS YOUR HELP!

### ARE YOU AWARE THAT:

**MEALS ON WHEELS:** 650 meals are delivered daily from three centres covering Southend district.

➲ **DRIVERS AND ESCORTS ARE NEEDED**

**BOOKS ON WHEELS:** 250 needy persons receive Books in their own homes twice a month.

➲ **DRIVERS AND ESCORTS ARE NEEDED**

**SOUTHEND HOSPITAL** benefits by service given in the Shop and Tea Bar 6 days weekly and profits made pay for thousands of pounds worth of gifts for the hospital each year.

➲ **VOLUNTEERS NEEDED ON MORNING, AFTERNOON AND EVENING SHIFTS**

**THE HOSPITAL SHOP TROLLEY** volunteers serve the patients who are confined to their wards. Profits are used to provide special equipment as requested by the Trust.

➲ **2 VOLUNTEERS FOR EACH TROLLEY ARE NEEDED FOR AFTERNOONS**

All these services can only be maintained with your help. Two or three hours weekly or fortnightly would assist us to continue our long standing work in the hospital and the community.

1 What services does the WRVS provide?
2 How many women help them?
3 What is the age profile of the volunteers?
4 What problems do they find are most common in running a voluntary organisation?
5 In your opinion, are the services they provide useful/essential?
6 Do you think other organisations could or should do the work of the WRVS? Some critics of voluntary organisations argue that the volunteers are often acting for their own benefit as much as for the recipients of their activities. For example, the volunteers may be lonely or retired, with time on their hands. Furthermore, without training, they often act in a patronising way to the recipients of their activities. Ask your local WRVS, or any other voluntary organisation, for their views. What is your view?
7 How could you find out if any of these criticisms have any worth? (You could go into a selection of charity shops and ask for the attitudes of the staff. You could interview clients of a voluntary organisation. You could...?)
8 A famous social policy analyst, Titmuss, once described how, in simpler societies, the members of those societies were held togther by exchanging gifts and services. As a result of this, people became mutually indebted to each other, and so the society was underpinned by an interweaving web of favours, gifts, services and obligations. In modern society, where there is far less chance of informally performing services for those other than neighbours, family and friends, the role of the voluntary organisations is very important in creating a sense of belonging both for the givers and the receivers of assistance. How does the WRVS fulfil this role?

# The advantages of voluntary organisations

## Social integration

The giving and receiving of gifts (including our services) helps the integration of society by creating bonds between different groups of people, and entails them in mutual obligations. Those who give may lose their time or money, but they benefit from feeling they have been generous. Those who receive benefit directly through goods and services, but pay by demonstrating their gratefulness.

## Meeting of specific needs

Very often the specific needs of groups in society cannot be catered for by the huge and impersonal health and welfare services. Voluntary groups can fit into this gap in provision.

## Responsiveness

The voluntary sector can respond quickly to new needs that arise or new concerns of society. The growth in AIDS organisations occurred long before the government began to respond.

## Personal commitment

The health and caring services are staffed by professionals whose job it is to provide a good service, but who are trained to distance themselves from individual clients as a means of coping and treating all clients fairly. Voluntary organisations can often provide people who are personally committed to the particular group or charitable activity.

## Experience

Often, and especially in self-help groups, the carers are those who have themselves been through the particular problems and can therefore understand the issues and needs of the clients.

## Expertise

Often the real experts on a particular issue may not be the statutory services but the voluntary groups. For example, the problems of prisoners and their wives is better known by NACRO (the National Association for the Care and Resettlement of Offenders) than the authorities.

## Stigma

This is a particularly difficult issue. However, it is claimed that there is less chance of being 'labelled' when voluntary organisations, and particularly self-help groups, are involved.

# Disadvantages and criticism of voluntary organisations

## Welfare is the duty of the State

Many people are critical of the voluntary services because, they argue, it is the role of the government to ensure that all citizens have a decent standard of living. They claim that when charities and voluntary organisations provide welfare, the State steps back from providing these services. In some cases, the argument continues, the quality and coverage of the voluntary services are not as comprehensive as those of the State (or local authorities), and so overall the quality of services declines. The greater the intrusion of charities into health and welfare, the more the government retreats from its responsibilities.

The government is very much in favour of charities and voluntary organisations and, in the community care legislation of 1990, 75 per cent of the local authorities' spending will have to be with private and voluntary organisations.

## Patchwork

Voluntary services provide an uneven spread of services. The areas best covered are those which are attractive (looking after children), while others attract little interest (the elderly). The more effective an organisation is at gaining publicity and public sympathy, the more the resources are given to its particular client group. Also, geographical variations can occur, where one place has better provision, because there is a more enthusiastic group based there.

## Lack of skills and training

Professional social workers and health care employees are trained to undertake a particular task and have the relevant knowledge and skills. A misguided, enthusiastic amateur can actually do more damage than good.

## Inadequate funding

When a voluntary organisation has to rely on charity, then the flow of funds can be uneven or inadequate. This results in an insecure service, with inconsistent standards. Government funding ought to guarantee long-term planning.

## Duplication

The tasks which a voluntary organisation sets out to do may also be being performed by a statutory agency, and some confusion can result, unless close co-operation is undertaken. Agencies like the NSPCC (child protection) need to co-operate closely wherever possible with the Children and Young Persons team of social work departments.

## Putting people out of jobs

Social workers and health care professionals are trained for their work and undertake this as their employment. When volunteers perform these duties, they run the risk of taking jobs away from the professionals.

## Professional ethics

Part of the training that social workers undertake is in ethics and standards of behaviour. Those operating in the voluntary sector may also have this training, but if they are unqualified they may not operate to the same exacting standards of professional behaviour.

It is important to remember that voluntary organisations range from small groups of people who have no training at all to those which employ highly trained professionals. Therefore, the above criticisms regarding standards and training may well not apply. Indeed, it is argued by the bigger voluntary agencies that they do a better job than the local authority agencies.

### PROBLEMS FACED BY VOLUNTARY AGENCIES TODAY

Britain has always been a nation of volunteers.

Now, the theory goes, voluntary agencies are coming into their own. The NHS and Community Care Act has provided an opportunity for this ramshackle collection of enthusiasts to take their place alongside statutory bodies as service providers.

So why do they all seem so down in the mouth?

The National Council for Voluntary Organisations estimates agencies around the country have lost grants of up to £30m this year.

MIND policy director Liz Sayce says 40 per cent of MIND's 230 local associations have suffered funding cuts or a standstill budget. Charitable donations have fallen and there is a 'mismatch' between the amount of money available and the role expected of the voluntary sector.

Agencies are turning to charitable and corporate trusts to bail them out – and in the depths of a recession, companies say they have limited resources. Groups are reduced to combing the country to find obscure charitable trusts not yet tapped.

NCVO believes a £30m rescue package from the government is required this year, followed by a new ringfenced grant to enable local authorities to fund voluntary agencies.

The Department of Health says it is already doing its bit. It is giving NCVO £95,000 for the next three years to 'help the voluntary sector handle the contract culture'.

The community care act envisages a partnership between statutory authorities and the voluntary and private sectors. The concepts of the 'enabling authority' and the 'active citizen' are drawn together in a framework which, for the first time, is backed by cash.

'It's a fragmented system, and it's confusing for the voluntary sector,' he says, 'I think it purposely remains that way so they can't get ahead.'

But there remains a fear that contracting will change the nature of voluntary agencies beyond recognition.

Jo Woolf, policy development worker for London Voluntary Services Council, believes purchasers rather than users will become clients.

'The voluntary sector is moving from being a caring service to being a business service first,' she says.

Advocacy, advice giving and campaigning will take a back seat, she believes. Smaller, more independent agencies such as black and ethnic minority projects will lose out as larger organisations with more financial clout gain contracts – and contracts will go to agencies which become most like the authorities they are dealing with.

For a sector which has always relied on the enthusiasm of individuals, passionate about supporting people in need, the new professionalism could be a poisoned chalice. The men in grey suits seem to be taking over.

Source: *The Health Service Journal*, 4 July 1991

1 What does the term 'statutory bodies' mean?
2 Explain the term 'service providers'.
3 What is the aim of the organisation MIND?
4 Is there a balance in the funding and the expected role of the voluntary organisations? Explain.
5 What is the new role of the voluntary organisations meant to be, under the mixed economy of welfare?
6 What is your view of the adequacy of the funding by the Department of Health?
7 'Enabling authority' refers to the local authority or health services obtaining services from the best organisations – which would include both private and voluntary organisations. What does the term the 'active citizen' mean? (If you do not know, please turn to page 259.)
8 Is the system well co-ordinated, according to the article?
9 Some critics have argued that the new community care arrangements will change the very nature of voluntary organisations and move them away from their original purposes. Can you explain this?
10 Which groups are most likely to lose out?
11 Arrange to visit a local voluntary organisation. Gather information on their aims, organisation and finances. Ask their views on their role.

# Co-ordination of the voluntary organisations

Earlier we saw that the huge number of charities existing in London in the 1860s necessitated a new organisation to co-ordinate them. In 1869, there were 640 charities; in 1993, there were approximately 34 000!

In order to bring some order to this situation, there is a (voluntary) co-ordinating body which operates at both national and local levels to help prevent overlap and confusion. This is the National Council for Voluntary Organisations. It performs its task primarily through its network of (local) Councils for Voluntary Services. There are approximately 200 of these CVSs.

## CO-ORDINATION OF THE VOLUNTARY SECTOR

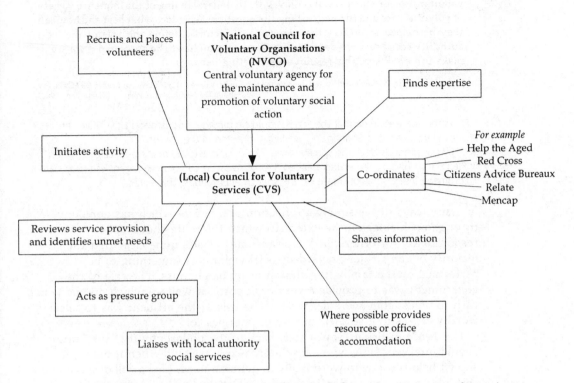

The chart shows the role of the NCVO and the CVSs in the co-ordination of the voluntary sector.

Arrange an interview with your local CVS (Council for Voluntary Services). Find examples of each of the functions shown above. Are there any other functions not on the diagram?

# The mixed economy of welfare

A serious concern of the Conservative governments of the 1980s and 1990s has been the way in which the State has taken over many of the caring responsibilities which politicians argued were the role of families, neighbours, friends and communities. The argument has been that when the government steps in and takes responsibility for the welfare of its citizens, then the social fabric of society – which consists of individuals giving and taking – is shredded. Gradually the attitude of dependency develops amongst those in difficulties – so the argument is that 'the government ought to do something'. On the other hand, those who are in a position to give through charity, or to help directly by shopping for a neighbour, no longer regard it as being their business.

### THE ROLE OF CHARITY

There are, then, many possible ways of providing support. Equally, there are many possible ways of financing it – whether from people's own resources, by social security payments, by charitable funds, by central and local government grants, or by explicit contracts of service between public service agencies and private or voluntary sector suppliers. It is only with an understanding of the immense variety of potential care and through asking the question 'Who does what best and how can they be helped to do it?', that we can satisfactorily define the role of the local authority social services department. The question has to be answered if we are to make use of all available resources in meeting need.

Source: Speech by N. Fowler MP, now Chairman of the Conservative Party, in 1984, quoted in M. McCarthy (ed.), *The New Politics of Welfare*, (Macmillan, 1989)

1 Does the speaker agree that the State should be provider and financer of welfare services?
2 List the various ways of financing welfare suggested in the speech.
3 On what grounds does the speaker argue for decisions to be made over care provision?
4 Please turn back to the extract headed 'Problems faced by voluntary agencies today'. What comment, if any, can you make on the speech after reading this extract?

In many ways this is simply a reflection of a debate which has gone on throughout history on the extent to which the State should take responsibility for others. In Victorian times, it was quite clear that the majority of the affluent regarded social welfare as something to be performed by the family, the church or by neighbours. The role of the government was to provide a very basic form of welfare which no one would turn to unless they were desperate. The role of the affluent was to select worthy causes to give their money or energies to.

The 1980s in Britain saw a shift back to the philosophy that the State should intervene only when absolutely necessary, and when it did so, it should help those who were really in genuine need. (For a full discussion on this, please see the section in chapter 2 'Debates in the provision of social security' which looks at universal versus targeted provision of welfare, pages 29–33).

The government has attempted to move away from a single provider – the State – towards a wide range of providers of welfare, drawn from the public, voluntary and private sectors. This system of mixed provision using volunteers, charitable organisations, professional agencies and profit-making hostels and hospitals is known as the **mixed economy of welfare**.

## Supporters of the mixed economy of welfare

Supporters of the mixed economy of welfare argue the following points in its favour.

### Sense of community
When the State takes over complete control of the provision of welfare, then the mutual obligations and sense of community of society weakens. By removing the dominant role of the State, more people will be drawn into welfare and there will be a regrowth of a sense of belonging and community.

### Higher quality of services
When the State is the monopoly provider of services, there is little incentive to provide high standards. By having a range of welfare agencies, there will be competition to provide better quality. Furthermore, a number of providers will create a range of types of welfare provision, and encourage new initiatives.

### Flexibility
The range of different welfare agencies will allow greater flexibility in that each welfare provider will offer different approaches to care and therefore there is greater likelihood of suitable provision for all needs.

### Choice
The greater the number and type of providers, the wider the choice for those in need – the consumers.

### Reduced costs
By using charities and voluntary organisations, the costs of providing services are lowered.

### Public preference for charities
The introduction of a mixed economy of welfare is linked to attempts to lower the costs of public services in general, and to cut taxes. With the extra money available to taxpayers, they can decide to give more money to the charity of their own choosing. This applies in particular to companies which can give to charity and improve their public image. This supporting of charities is often done through corporate trusts.

### More focused role of social services
The social services perform a very wide range of welfare functions. Some argue this range is simply too wide and complex for all the activities to be provided at a high standard and to be well co-ordinated. The Community Care changes, which came into effect in April 1993, begin to clarify the role of the social services as a purchaser of services for a number of its client groups such as those with disabilities and the elderly.

## DISTINCT ADVANTAGES IN HOMES TRANSFER

It is a pity that Geoffrey Heathcock (*Letters*, January 4) has taken a negative view about proposals to transfer the management of some of the county council's old people's homes to a not-for-profit trust.

He does not recognise that we are building on our successful arrangement with the Red Cross to run Brook House in Cambridge as well as on positive experience in other counties where groups of homes have been transferred to a trust.

It is important to emphasise, however, that we will continue to run a substantial number of homes ourselves.

Mr Heathcock seems to be implying that in order to ensure high standards the county council must run all services directly.

Does he really believe that organisations such as the Red Cross are not able to provide high quality care?

There are distinct advantages in transferring the management of some homes, particularly as a high proportion of the £5 million Community Care Special Transitional Grant has to be spent on buying services from voluntary and private organisations.

A trust can also attract capital from the private sector in order to improve the quality of buildings.

The county council still has some homes that are below the standards we set for other organisations providing care. In order to comply with legislation, work on sub-standard homes must be completed by 1995 at the latest.

An underlying principle of the community care legislation, which received all-party support in the House of Commons, was the need for a flourishing voluntary and private sector alongside good quality public services.

Conservatives on the county council remain firmly committed to this objective and will continue to promote policies that raise standards and widen choice.
ELAINE WHEATLEY
Social Services Committee chairman, Cambridgeshire County Council.

**Source**: The *Cambridge Evening News*, 14 January 1993

1 From which organisation are the elderly persons' homes being transferred?
2 Why are the homes being transferred to the not-for-profit trust? (You may need to look at chapter 7, 'Community care', pages 153–7).
3 What criticism(s) can you infer of the transfer, made by Elaine Wheatley in her reply to Geoffrey Heathcock's letter to the Guardian?
4 What advantages does she think will accrue to the homes by placing them under the care of the non-profit-making trusts?
5 The concept of a mixed economy of welfare is referred to in the letter in a different way. How does Ms Wheatley describe this concept?
6 What political party does she belong to?
7 What is your opinion of the final paragraph of the letter?

## Critics of the mixed economy of welfare

Critics of the mixed economy of welfare put forward the following objections.

### Dismantling of the Welfare State
The mixed economy of welfare is one way of bringing about the end of the Welfare State.

### Lower quality
The move away from public provision, with its moral basis of caring for people as citizens, to one based on charity or profit making (as in the private sector) would actually lower the standards of care.

### Lack of choice
The move towards the mixed economy of welfare will lead to a narrowing of choice as the public sector loses its (legal and financial) abilities to provide care. The only remaining providers of care will be the profit-making companies and a patchwork of charitable organisations.

### Increased costs
It will actually cost more money than at present, because the private homes and services (such as home helps) need to make a profit.

### Stigma
There will be a move back towards clients being seen as receiving charity or too poor to pay for their own welfare. This means a degree of stigma (see pages 291–3).

### Haphazard provision
As there will be no statutory body providing services in each local authority, the extent and the quality of services will vary from place to place.

# Assignment

The Department of Health has decided to fund a project to clarify the range and quality of services in your area. You have been commissioned to provide a detailed breakdown of the provision of private, State and voluntary social and health services in your area.

These should be grouped according to the type of service they provide, so you need to construct some form of categorisation. You need to describe what activities they engage in, how many clients they deal with, and the type of client they deal with.

Furthermore, you should provide the Department of Health with recommendations concerning how to improve the provision of voluntary and private services to groups in need.

# CHAPTER 10

# The European Community

## Introduction

The European Community is regarded by many people as some far-off bureaucratic organisation mainly concerned with paying money out to continental farmers and ensuring that large companies are able to export their goods across Europe without the problems of customs or trade barriers.

However, there is also an important and increasingly significant social side to the work of the European Community. Because of the political views of the British government, much of the developing social elements of the EC have been opposed by Britain. Nevertheless, employment regulations, hours of work, maternity pay, equal rights, and economic support for regions with particular social and economic problems, are all areas in which the EC is active. It is likely that as the economies of the European Community member states converge, and there is greater communication and co-ordination between the governments, then there will be a similar convergence in social affairs.

In this chapter, after looking briefly at the development of the EC, we examine the reasons why the EC felt it needed a social dimension, together with the aims of that dimension.

The next part of the chapter looks at the operation of the EC in the area of social activity. In particular we note its concern for equal rights, the position of the disabled and the elderly, public health, and the elimination of poverty in the member states of the EC.

Finally, the last section deals with the different approaches to welfare and the different sorts of welfare states which exist in the EC. These vary from the models which give a minimum of benefits and where the role of the State is relatively unimportant to ones where the State is the central agency in co-ordinating and providing welfare.

## History of the European Community

After the Second World War, a number of European countries decided that if they were to avoid the possibility of war for a third time in the twentieth century, then they should strive to integrate their economies and political programmes.

In 1951, the European Coal and Steel Community was founded. This co-ordinated the production of coal and steel across Germany, France, Italy, Belgium, Luxemburg and the Netherlands. It functioned so well that, in

1957, the Treaty of Rome was signed, which set up the European Economic Community. The aims of the EEC (now known as the European Community, or EC) were to strengthen peace, achieve economic integration and harmonious and balanced economic development and to work towards an 'ever closer union of the peoples of Europe'.

The UK had been suspicious of the EC, and did not join. However, the economic growth rates of the member states proved to be far faster than that of Britain and, after a number of failed attempts, Britain eventually joined the EC in 1973, along with Ireland and Denmark.

Greece joined in 1981, and Spain and Portugal in 1986, bringing the number of member states to 12.

## The Single European Act

In 1987, the Treaty of Rome was amended by the Single European Act. This was intended to create a Europe-wide free trade area by 1993, and give the European Commission an increased role. As part of this increased role, social policy began to be seen as an important element of the New Europe.

The 'single market' introduced the concept of freedom of movement for goods, capital, people and services. The one of particular interest to issues of health and welfare is that of freedom of movement of people.

## The Social Charter

The Social Charter was opposed by two countries: the UK, because it countries in December 1989. It formed the basis of the social chapter of the Maastricht agreement.

The key elements were:
- free circulation of workers;
- fair remuneration and a decent wage;
- minimum income and appropriate social assistance;
- freedom of association and collective negotiation;
- opportunities for professional training;
- equality of men and women;
- rights to information, consultation and participation for workers;
- minimum income for elderly people;
- protection of health and safety at work;
- protection of children, adolescents, elderly people and people with learning difficulties.

The Social Charter was opposed by two countries: the UK, because it would improve the powers, benefits and rights of workers by too much, and Denmark, because it would reduce the powers, benefits and rights of workers.

## The Maastricht Treaty (1992)

This treaty extended the aims of the Community members to include a commitment to economic union, and towards much greater political co-operation. Eleven of the 12 member states also agreed to move forward together to implement the measures of the Social Charter. In particular, social policy would be harmonised in areas such as health, employment and working conditions.

## THE BRITISH GOVERNMENT'S VIEW OF MAASTRICHT

Another issue discussed at Maastricht was whether the social provisions chapter of the Treaty of Rome should be changed, giving the Community more powers to establish laws in areas of employment and social policy such as working conditions. In the end, all members states agreed that the Community's social dimension would continue to be developed on the basis of the existing social provisions chapter in the Treaty of Rome.

Eleven member states had felt that the Community's powers should be increased to create more Community-wide standards of employment protection as the Single European Market develops. The United Kingdom, however, felt that the primary responsibility for employment and social policy should remain with national Governments, because of the risk that Community legislation would fail to take account of national differences in tradition and practice, increase the costs to employers of employing people and result in fewer jobs and higher unemployment. It was therefore agreed that eleven of the member states, not including the United Kingdom, might take additional common action in the employment and social area if they wished, beyond the action the Treaty of Rome allows the Community as a whole to take. Whatever the eleven member states decide under this agreement will have no effect on United Kingdom law.

1 How many countries out of the 12 wished to extend the remit of the EC to social policy?
2 Which country opposed it? List the reasons given.
3 The British government argues that higher wages, which would be the result of introducing a minimum wage, would increase unemployment. Turn to the extract on pages 213–14, where the extent of poverty is documented. Do you think a minimum wage would worsen the problem or improve it? (Further information can also be found in the extract on page 271, in chapter 13, 'Equal opportunities'.)
4 The 'social provisions chapter' of the Maastricht agreement is essentially the Social Charter. Look back at the summary mentioned earlier. Do you think these ideals should be introduced in Britain, as well as in the rest of Europe?
5 Go to your central college library and obtain copies of the newspapers for December 1991. Examine the various interpretations given by the press of the Maastricht agreement. You will find that the interpretation of events is very different from the one portrayed in the extract here. (If there are no actual copies of newspapers, you should be able to look up any quality newspaper on CD-ROM, or Microfiche.)

**Source**: *Europe Today* (London office of the Commission of the European Communities and the European Parliament in co-operation with the Department of Education, 1992)

# Decision making in the EC

The process of making Community decisions is a complicated one, with slightly different procedures for different subjects and different types of measure. However, the procedure is generally as shown in the chart on page 202.

## Types of EC legislation

EC legislation takes a number of forms including:
- treaties;
- regulations;
- directives;
- decisions;
- recommendations and opinions.

### Treaties
These are the major legislative forms which determine membership of the EC and major changes.

### Regulations
These must be enforced in the member states and have immediate effect. These regulations prevail over national law.

### Directives
These apply to some or all member states, but governments can decide how to put them into effect.

### Decisions
These apply to individual persons or member states and are binding on them.

### Recommendations and opinions
These have no binding force, but represent the view of the Commission.

# The need for a social dimension to the EC

## Industrial restructuring and unemployment

The European Community is striving to make itself the dominant economic force in the world, and the majority of member countries would like it to be one of the dominant political forces too. But the economic developments have *social* costs. In the drive to make European industry competitive with that of Japan or the USA, the various governments have agreed to rationalise and restructure some industries – making sure that there are not too many steel mills, for example, producing unwanted steel. In the long run this may be a good thing, but in the short term it means that there are large numbers of workers who are made unemployed. Something has to be done for the plight of the unemployed, to create more jobs and to retrain them.

## Regional disparities

The richest part of the EC is the London–Frankfurt–Milan triangle. This is the area at the centre of the EC, with good communications, large affluent populations and a host of industries and commercial institutions. There seems to be a tendency for companies to be drawn to this area because of the advantages. So the richer areas grow richer. On the other hand, areas which are on the fringes of the EC, such as parts of the Mediterranean countries (southern Italy, large parts of Greece, southern Spain) and the extreme North (Scotland, Eire), present few attractions for companies wishing to set up new industries or commercial ventures. The result is the possible widening of the gap between the richer and poorer parts of the EC.

## Training needs

We saw earlier that the process of industrial restructuring has been one of the priorities of the EC. This leads inevitably to unemployment. The only way out for the unemployed is to retrain in new skills. The pace of industrial change is increasing, and there is an ever-changing demand for skilled workers. What is necessary today, may be redundant tomorrow. Furthermore, the educational qualifications and the skills that people obtain should allow them to obtain jobs right across the Community.

## Social dumping

As there are no barriers to companies investing where they want in Europe, they will tend to be attracted to those places where the workforce is cheapest and where protection in terms of redundancy, health and safety and holiday entitlements is lowest. This means that a country which gives its workforce the least protection is likely to be the most attractive to employers. Consequently, the other countries of the EC, which strive to provide their workforces with good conditions and a high standard of rights, will be the least attractive.

The aim behind the social chapter at Maastricht was to ensure that there was a common standard of conditions for the workforces of all member states to make competition for employers equal.

Separately, there was the belief that the point of the EC was to improve the quality of life of the citizens of the EC countries by giving them rights and benefits. The British government rejects this, and prefers to minimise the rights of workers in order to make the British workforce cheap and responsive to employers' needs. It thereby hopes to attract employment. The point must be made that the quality of life and the standards of living of the British workforce are likely to be inferior to the rest of Europe, and the main benefits of a low paid, low skilled workforce, with few rights in the workplace and weak trade unions, are likely to go to employers.

## National and regional divisions

One of the problems of developing a united Europe has been the barriers, particularly of language and of misunderstanding between the different cultures, which exist. In the past these have led to wars – even now, outside the EC, there are conflicts based on nationalism and ethnicity.

## Social marginality

In most countries of the EC there are growing groups of marginal people, sometimes called an underclass, who are more likely than most to be excluded from the social and economic benefits of modern European society.

This situation of exclusion is known as social marginality. The people most likely to be marginalised are women (in particular low paid women and lone parents), certain ethnic and religious minorities, and those living in certain poorer or isolated regions of Europe.

# The aims of the social dimension

## Insertion

One aim of European social policy is to try to put the socially marginalised, which we mentioned above, back into the heart of European society. The ways in which the European Commission does this are discussed later. This attempt to 'insert' people who are living on the margins of society is not entirely without benefit to those who have been successful and are affluent, as we shall see below.

## Social cohesion

The argument continues that people who are marginalised are more likely than others to cause political and social unrest and to engage in crime. By offering training schemes, equal opportunity programmes and developing infrastructures to help create jobs, these marginalised people, and their children, are given the chance of employment and of having an interest in maintaining society as it is. The aim, then, is to have a cohesive society, in which people are pulled together by social bonds of mutual economic and welfare ties.

## Common social rights

Right across Europe there should be equal rights to social benefits, such as decent health care, pensions, unemployment benefits, maternity leave, equal pay and conditions, and the recognition of the rights of those with disabilities. Equal rights stems partially from the belief in a European citizenship, but is also a means of combating social dumping.

## Common identity

The EC is trying to create a sense of being European, so that we feel a sense of belonging to a transnational community. There ought to be easy communication between people with everyone being able to use a language other than their national one, and there ought to be understanding, and ideally sympathy, for the customs and beliefs of other groups.

# The activities of the social dimension

## The European Structural Fund

This is the general fund which comprises three elements which were previously known as the **Social Fund**, the **Regional Fund** and the **Agricultural Guidance and Guarantee Fund**. The funds were created in response to the Social Action Programme in 1972.

Overall, these funds support projects to improve the infrastructure of the poorer regions of the EC, to support rural development schemes, and training and employment initiatives.

There are five specific objectives:
- promoting the development and structural adjustment of the less developed regions: these are mainly regions in Greece, Spain, Portugal, southern Italy, Ireland, Northern Ireland and French overseas *départements* (colonies);
- converting regions seriously affected by industrial decline: this particularly affects Britain with over 30 regions receiving benefits;
- combating long-term unemployment by providing reskilling programmes;
- facilitating the integration of young people into employment, which usually means specialised training schemes;
- promoting the development of rural, agricultural areas: as agriculture declines in importance, the EC seeks to promote alternative means of earning a living.

Traditionally the structural funds were used by member governments as a means of subsidising existing projects, but the EC has begun to identify specific themes and programmes which it is interested in. For example, it has targeted declining steel areas in a programme called RESIDER, declining ship-building areas in RENEWAL, and declining coal mining areas with RECHAR.

In 1992, the structural funds amounted to 13 000 million ECUs. (You can find the current value of an ECU in £s in the currency rates of the quality national newspapers.)

## STRUCTURAL FUNDS

Taken overall, the countries of the EC are very rich compared with many other countries. But there are big variations within the EC. The richest country, i.e. the one with the highest income per head, is Luxembourg with £11,620. For Greece the figure is £4,420 (1990 figures). The differences between regions is even more marked. The income per head in the ten wealthiest regions is about five times greater than in the ten poorest ones. The poorest regions, and those facing particular problems such as industrial decline or high unemployment among young people, receive financial assistance from a number of Community funds. In 1992 spending from these 'structural funds' amounts to around £11.5 billion, a proportion of which benefits parts of the United Kingdom.

1 Are all the EC countries rich?
2 Give an example of the difference in income between two countries.
3 The extract mentions regions and gives examples of the differences in affluence between them. What are these differences?
4 What causes the differences in affluence between the regions?
5 What is the relationship between structural funds and the concept of social cohesion?
6 How much was spent by the EC on structural funds in 1992?

**Source**: *Europe Today* (London office of the Commission of the EC, 1992)

If you write to the European Commission Information Office in London (8, Storey's Gate, London SW1), they may send a speaker to talk about the EC. You should state in your letter your particular interest in social policy, so that you will feel free to ask detailed questions on this area.

## Equal opportunities

This has been one of the central social policy issues of the last 25 years in the EC. It refers not just to women, but also to migrants and people with disabilities. There are two main reasons for its importance, apart from the obvious one of social justice.

First, the more socially advanced countries in terms of equal rights, such as France, were concerned that their equal opportunity policies, which cost employers considerable amounts, would put them at a disadvantage compared to the countries with fewer rights.

Second, the Commission has also used the issue of equality as a battering ram to open up its competency to intervene in more general areas of social policy. This is because the various treaties are unclear as to the extent to which the Commission has the right to construct policies relating to health and welfare, for example.

The four areas of equal rights which have been targeted by the Commision are:
- equal pay;
- equal access to training and employment;
- equal treatment in social security matters;
- the provision of maternity rights and benefits, and child-care facilities.

An Equal Opportunities Office of the European Commission exists to ensure that equal opportunities are carried through. However, this is mainly concerned with opportunities for women.

### Women

It is estimated that women comprise one third of the working population of the EC, holding 23 per cent of industrial jobs, 35 per cent of agricultural jobs and 46 per cent of service sector jobs. Female unemployment on average is twice that of males. On average women are paid only 80 per cent of the wages of men.

### Legislation

The original treaty forming the EC included article 119 of the Treaty of Rome, which stated that 'men and women shall receive equal pay for equal work'.

- **1975 Directive on Equal Pay**: this is important because it extended and clarified the meaning of equal work. It stated that equal work meant work of equal value, so men and women did not have to be in the same job to get equal pay, but engaged in equally valuable work
- **1976 Directive on Equal Treatment**: this insisted on equal access to employment, training, promotion and working conditions
- **1979 Directive on Equal Treatment in Social Security**: this demanded equality of treatment from statutory social security schemes for those under retirement age. It covered equality for sick pay, accidents at work, unemployment, etc.

- **1986 Directive on Occupational Social Security Schemes**: demands equality of treatment for all non-State schemes provided by employers
- **1986 Self-employed Directive**: ensures equal treatment between self-employed men and women
- **1992**: most EC member states introduced equality of rights between full-time and part-time workers. This is particularly important to women, who form the bulk of part-time employees. This benefited women through an extension of sickness and redundancy rights and in many cases through pay levels. The UK has not introduced this legislation
- **1992 Directive on Maternity Rights**: this guarantees a minimum of rights to pregnant women of 14 weeks' maternity leave and pay at the minimum rate of statutory sick pay.

## A EUROPEAN DIRECTIVE IS BORN

British women will no longer have to work for two years full-time or five years part-time in one job to qualify for full maternity pay and job security, following the adoption of new EC laws this week.

Some 150,000 British women a year stand to benefit from the European Pregnancy Directive which is expected to be implemented in the UK by early 1994.

The new legislation guarantees working women across Europe, regardless of their hours or length of service, 14 weeks' maternity leave and pay at the minimum rate of their country's statutory sick pay. At current UK rates, this would mean £52.50 a week for those earning £190 or more a week and £45.30 for those on less.

It also protects women against losing their jobs because of their pregnancy and gives pregnant employees the right to paid time off to attend ante-natal examinations.

At present pregnant British women have to work full-time for the same employer for two years, or five years if part-time, to qualify for the minimum six weeks leave on 90 per cent of full pay plus 12 weeks on statutory maternity pay of £46.30 a week.

Joanna Foster, chair of both the Equal Opportunities Commission and the EC's Advisory Committee on Equal Opportunities said she was relieved that, "after three years' hard slog", the directive had got through despite last-minute fears that it would be vetoed by the Italians who were fighting for better minimum maternity benefits. "Of course, we'd have preferred original proposals for the right to 14 weeks maternity leave at full pay, which were blocked by the UK Government. Nevertheless, a lot of UK women will benefit and it is a step

towards a wider package recognising women's roles these days as mothers and paid workers."

... This means that only British women stand to benefit from the directive because other EC countries already offer better maternity rights.

Germany, Greece, Luxembourg, the Netherlands and Portugal offer between 12 and 16 weeks maternity leave on full pay while Belgium, France, Ireland, Italy and Spain offer between 16 and 20 weeks at 75 to 90 per cent of pay. Only the UK has a two-year qualifying period. Many also offer parental leave, sometimes paid, which mothers can tack on to the end of their maternity leave. Denmark, for example, offers 18 weeks maternity leave plus 10 weeks parental leave at 90 per cent of earnings.

**Source**: Adapted from the *Guardian*, 24 October 1992

1 What is the directive that is being introduced?
2 What is a directive?
3 How does the directive alter the situation in the UK?
4 If Britain does not want to implement the directive, can it refuse to do so?
5 Why did the Italians want to veto it?
6 What was the view of the Equal Opportunities Commission (EOC)?
7 Which country blocked better provision?
8 In how many countries in the EC will women benefit from this new directive?
9 Construct a simple chart to show the varying benefits across the EC.
10 Which country is the directive really aimed at?

Initiatives for women include:

- The Centre for Research on European Women (CREW): an EC-funded foundation to promote equal rights;
- NOW: an EC programme aimed directly at women. It is concerned to promote the access of women to employment programmes and links this to specific vocational training. It also supports the creation of small businesses and especially co-operatives which are to be formed by, and for the benefit of, women. It contains provisions for child-care funding;
- EUROFORM: a programme which aims to construct transnational partnerships to aid employment and training. It is not restricted to women, but includes other marginalised groups.

## CHILD CARE

### Places available in publicly-funded child care (for children aged 3 to compulsory school age) as a percentage of all children in that age group

Source: European Commission (1986-89 depending on country)

**Source**: The *Guardian*, 26 March 1991

### Different attitudes to child care in the UK and France

According to the Inland Revenue, no tax relief is available on child care costs that working parents pay themselves. However, parents who use a workplace nursery do not have to pay tax on the value of this benefit.... However, if employers provide any other form of assistance with child care such as cash allowances or child care vouchers, then these are fully taxed.

In France, working parents with children under the age of 7 can deduct the child care costs from their taxable wage, as long as the child is looked after by someone outside the family.

Furthermore, French working parents also get a grant from the government to pay for the social insurance contributions of any child-carer who looks after an under 3 years old, and who lives in. In contrast, the 'nanny' in Britain pays her own tax and National Insurance contributions.

1 What provision for child care exists in the UK to allow women to work?
2 Compare child care provision in the UK with that in France.
3 Why could the French system be seen as an example of insertion?
4 Are there any child-care facilities in your college? If so, are they adequate? Arrange to interview the parents of children in the crèche (if there is one). What limitations does child care impose on their careers?

5 Construct a questionnaire and ask a number of working parents, especially mothers, about their views on employment, marriage/partnership and child care. Also, ask them their views on the French system. (It is interesting to note, incidentally, that fewer French than British women are in employment.)

### The European Court of Justice and gender issues

The European Court of Justice was set up to make judgements on the interpretation, implementation and enforcement of Community law in member states. The role of the Court in the area of health, welfare and social rights has been quite considerable. In particular, it has consistently pushed forward equal rights for women, over issues of social security benefits and equal pay. It has done this, moreover, in cases where the British government has failed to implement Community law adequately.

One of the most interesting elements of the equal pay legislation has been the **Equal Pay Directive**, which states that there should be 'equal pay for work of equal value'. This can be interpreted to mean that where women do different work from men, but work of equal value, then they should be paid an equal wage. This is important for women, because they are often pushed into different forms of employment from men, with lower wages.

## THE EQUAL OPPORTUNITIES COMMISSION

The Equal Opportunities Commission failed yesterday in its High Court attempt to eliminate what it views as unlawful discrimination against part-time workers.

It accused the Government of failing to comply with European Community obligations to protect part-time workers from less favourable treatment than full-timers – particularly in relation to redundancy and unfair dismissal.

Lord Justice Nolan and Mr Justice Judge ruled that the UK was not in breech of provisions in the Treaty of Rome and EC directives.

The EOC said later it would consider appealing. "The judgment has serious implications for women who make up 90 per cent of part-time workers," a spokesman said.

The EOC had argued that the 1978 Employment Protection (Consolidation) Act indirectly discriminated against part-time employees because:
• An employee working less than eight hours a week cannot qualify for redundancy pay or unfair dismissal, regardless of the number of weeks worked.

• A full-time employee, working 16 or more hours a week, qualifies for redundancy pay and compensation for unfair dismissal after two years of continuous employment, while someone working between eight and 16 hours takes five years to qualify.

• Part-timers who have previously worked full-time are not given any credit for it when their payments are calculated.

**Source**: The *Guardian*, 11 October 1991

1 What was the point of the court action started by the Equal Opportunities Commission (EOC)?
2 Who would benefit most from the EC 'obligations?
3 What was the basis of the EOC's case of discrimination?

## SEXISM, SOCIAL SECURITY AND THE EC

The Beveridge Report and the post-war social security system were based on the assumption that the typical unit was a nuclear family with a male breadwinner. Married women were not expected to work outside the home and wives were treated as dependants of their husbands ... In 1978 the European Community issued a Directive on the equal treatment of men and women in social security, and the government took steps to comply with the directive in 1983 by giving men and women formal equality in the claiming of supplementary benefit [Income Support] and family income supplement [Family Credit] ...

Before 1986, the invalid care allowance, paid to those who are out of work and caring for a disabled person in receipt of attendance allowance, was not available to married or cohabiting women. There is no clearer indication of the assumption that women are the 'natural' carers. In 1985 this regulation was challenged in the European Court which found that the British government was in contravention of the Community Directive on equal social security treatment ... In July 1986 invalid care allowance became payable to married and cohabiting women.

... In a purely formal sense the social security system treats men and women equally, but indirect discrimination arising from factors outside the system is still a serious problem. For example, because women are often in low paid, part-time occupations with less continuous work records, their pension entitlements will be adversely affected. This will be true of all contributory benefits...

**Source**: 'Reconstructing the Welfare State' in *Social Security: Forwards or Backwards from Beveridge?*

1 What were the assumptions underlying social security at its introduction in 1948?
2 What was the role of the European Community in challenging this?
3 How has it the powers to do this?
4 What other factors exist which prevent women obtaining equality when it comes to contributory benefits?

## The EC and the disabled

Approximately 30 million people, or 9 per cent of the European population, are affected by a physical or mental disability.

The EC HELIOS programme has been funded to assist those with disabilities. It provides vocational training and rehabilitation, economic and social integration, and promotes an independent way of life for the elderly.

HORIZON was set up to provide funds for projects in underdeveloped regions of Europe to promote the 'social and professional integration of the handicapped and other disadvantaged people'.

A directive requiring a specific proportion of public and employer-provided transport to be able to accommodate disabled passengers should come into force in 1999.

## The EC and migration

The Commission has ensured that migrants from within the EC have the rights to obtain social security and health provision in exactly the same way as indigenous workers. The situation for immigrants from outside the EC is different, in that they do not have rights which run across the entire Community, but are subject to the rules of the particular countries in which they live.

Two European Parliamentary Commissions concerning racism have been set up. They have made recommendations concerning the rights of migrants from outside the Community. However, these were not accepted in the original form by the Council of Ministers.

Whereas there have been significant advances by the EC for women, this is not the case for migrants who live and work in the EC but are not EC nationals.

## The EC and the elderly

It is only recently that the full impact of the ageing of European society has come to be realised. On current forecasts, by 2025, 18.4 per cent of the European Community population, or 97 million people, will be over the age of 65. This compares with approximately 13 per cent in 1992. The ageing of the population is caused by an increase in life expectancy and by a fall in the birth rate. Major questions for the future centre on how it will be possible for Europe to provide and pay for pensions, health care and personal social services.

The EC funded an action programme for the elderly, between 1991 and 1993, which set out to improve the integration of the elderly into society and to recognise the positive contributions the elderly have to offer society. 1993 was designated 'The European Year of Older People and Solidarity between Generations'. During the period of the action programme the Commission initiated a number of research programmes and events which exchanged information between organisations concerned with the welfare of the elderly.

A pressure group known as EUROLINK, which is funded by the EC, has been raising the profile of the elderly in Europe. There is a limit on how much the Commission can do about the elderly, however, as there is no specific reference to them in any of the treaties, and so there is considerable dispute about the powers of the EC concerning this group of the population.

Nevertheless, there are currently discussions being carried out concerning EC directives on minimum incomes for the elderly across the whole of Europe. A section of the Social Charter concerns this.

## Health and protection in the workplace

Eight thousand workers die each year as a result of accidents in the workplace, and over ten million people are affected by incidents, accidents and illnesses related to their workplace. This costs approximately 20 billion ECUs per year, or about 7 per cent of all sickness insurance expenditure in the entire EC.

Since 1977, the EC has passed directives to protect employees at work, and this was enshrined in article 118A of the Single European Act, as well as being included in the Social Charter.

In 1988 the Commission proposed six new directives and, by December 1992, four of these had been enacted. The most important is the Framework Directive which provides the framework of rules for health and protection by specifying employers' duties and workers' rights. Employers must, for instance, assess and avoid risks, introduce preventive measures, use specialist health and safety advice, monitor potential hazards, and keep records on specified accidents and diseases. Employers also have to introduce safety training.

## Health initiatives

There has been very little work done on harmonising health care in the EC member states. However, it is argued that the concern over social dumping and the attempts to harmonise the conditions of work and quality of life in the EC will eventually impact on the health services of the EC.

Nevertheless, as well as the Health and Protection at Work Legislation, there have been some initiatives.

- In 1989, the EC adopted a directive on the labelling of tobacco products which provided for standardised warnings to be printed on cigarette packets from January 1992. (The UK government abstained in the vote).
- 1990: An action programme on nutrition and health began, which aimed to raise public awareness and stimulate research programmes. 1994 was designated

'The European Year of Nutrition'. There is currently a voluntary scheme for the labelling of the contents and nutritional value of foodstuffs.
- The EC has funded a number of Public Health Campaigns, such as the 1987 Europe Against Cancer campaign. The aim of this campaign is to reduce deaths from cancer by 15 per cent by the year 2000.
- There is a programme to combat AIDS.
- In 1992 the focus switched to combating heart disease.

The extension of the competence of the Commission in areas of public health is one of controversy. The British government in particular is concerned with limiting the powers of the Commission in this area. The Commission, on the other hand, is extremely keen to expand its powers and so attempts to set precedents by pushing its authority to the limits.

## The EC and professional workers in the area of health and welfare

The definition of a profession according to the EC is one which has at least three years' training, and is regulated. Nursing is therefore covered, while social work is not. Professionals (with three years' training) have the right to practise anywhere in Europe, provided that they have the necessary linguistic skills.

The most likely outcome of the directives on professionals' employment is that professionals from the EC will come to work in the UK, if they wish, while professionals in the UK will be prevented from employment in mainland Europe because of the length of professional training, and their lack of linguistic skills.

## Public health and the EC

Article 100 of the Single European Act states that when creating harmonisation of goods and services across Europe, member states should base regulations on a 'high level of public protection'. One example of the importance of this has been the introduction of the tobacco labelling directive. This directive insists that a prominent and strong warning is placed on the front and back of each pack of cigarettes sold in the EC. The member states wanted to harmonise the types of warnings on all packs across Europe, in the interests of free trade. (Strong warnings on the cigarette packets of one country, such as Ireland, could deter people from purchasing these cigarettes when they were exported to another country with very weak warnings, such as the UK.)

The result was that the toughest warnings of all European countries, those given in Ireland, were used as the model for all Europe. The basis for this was article 100A. It is worth noting that the UK government strenuously opposed the introduction of strong health warnings, and acted as the defenders of the tobacco companies rather than the champions of the good health of the public.

One of the main influences on health is the quality of food that people consume. 1994 was designated 'The European Year of Nutrition', in which healthy eating was promoted. The best known health promotion campaigns run by the EC are against the two biggest killers in the Community – cancer and heart disease. The two programmes are the Europe against Cancer campaign, and the Europe against Cardiovascular Disease campaign.

## The poverty programmes

The poverty programmes originated in the mid-1970s, but became more important in the 1980s when the poorer Mediterranean countries (Portugal, Spain, Greece) joined the Community.

In 1990 it was estimated that there were over 46 million poor people in the EC, representing about 14 per cent of the entire population. The Commission's definition of poverty is 'when the disposable income is smaller than half of the average personal income'.

There have been three poverty programmes so far. They have involved research and the setting up of specific projects to tackle poverty in areas with concentrations of poor people, encouraging people to set up co-operative and self-help groups. Broader initiatives have included tackling illiteracy, and encouraging more voluntary groups.

### POVERTY IN THE EC

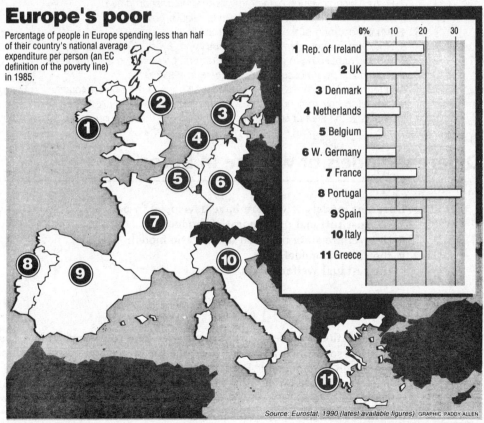

# Europe's poor

Percentage of people in Europe spending less than half of their country's national average expenditure per person (an EC definition of the poverty line) in 1985.

1 Rep. of Ireland
2 UK
3 Denmark
4 Netherlands
5 Belgium
6 W. Germany
7 France
8 Portugal
9 Spain
10 Italy
11 Greece

Source: Eurostat, 1990 (latest available figures) GRAPHIC PADDY ALLEN

**Source**: The *Guardian*, 2 July 1991

**Note**: These figures pre-date the re-unification of Germany.

According to the final commentary on the European Poverty Programme, published by the European Commission, more people are living in relative poverty in the UK than in any other European Community country.

One in five of all EC *residents* in poverty lives in the UK, while one in four of all poor EC *households* lives in the UK.

The pattern of poverty is also depressing reading for UK citizens. Between 1980 and 1985, the number of relatively poor people in the EC remained roughly stable, but in the UK, they grew by a quarter. The number of poor households actually increased by a third.

The information is drawn from comparing the Family Expenditure Survey in Britain, with comparable surveys in other EC countries. The definition of poverty is derived from spending patterns rather than income, and so the poverty in this study is defined as individuals or families spending less than 50 per cent of average national expenditure. Expenditure patterns were used, rather than income, as EC experts argued that income was not always fully disclosed in surveys.

The study found that 50 million EC residents lived in poverty in 1985, and that 10.3 million, or 18.2 per cent were in Britain. In terms of households, Britain had 3.8 million in poverty. The figures show that in 1980 Britain had the eighth highest number of households in poverty, and by 1985 it had the second highest number of poor households. Over the same period, poverty actually fell in Belgium, Greece, Spain and France, while remaining constant in Denmark and the former West Germany.

1 First of all, do the figures in the extract surprise you?
2 From which poverty programme was this information drawn?
3 Which country has the greatest level of relative poverty?
4 What proportion of the poor live in the UK?
5 How was poverty measured in the survey?
6 What is happening to poverty in the UK compared to the rest of Europe?
7 How many poor households were there in 1985?
8 In terms of households, where does the UK rank in the poorest countries in Europe?
9 The British government has consistently rejected moves to allow the Commission greater powers in the area of social policy. In the light of these figures, what is your opinion?

# Different models of welfare in Europe

Different models of welfare have developed in Europe. These include:
- the **institutional** or **corporatist model**;
- the **welfare state** or **social democratic model**;
- the **catholic model**;
- the **residual welfare state**.

## The institutional (or corporatist) model

The institutional model of welfare stresses generous employment-based rights and social insurance, but provides for fewer and weaker rights for those not in employment. Benefit rates are related to salaries.

This model is generally related to insurance-based health provision, in which money is deducted from salaries at source to pay for health insurance. The individual then pays a proportion of the final bill.

Examples of EC countries which operate this sort of system are Germany and Belgium.

### Characteristics of institutional-based systems
These systems have the following features:
- high levels of benefits for those who are insured;
- much poorer levels of benefits for those who are unable to insure themselves (these are provided by a State-organised health and welfare fall-back system);
- a distinction between an employee, who receives health and welfare benefits

as part of the benefits of employment, and a citizen of the country, who need not automatically have the right to health and welfare benefits;
- social security payments which are often very low and limited for those who are not insured, although they are very generous for a limited period of time (typically six months to a year) for employees who are made redundant or who are unable to work through illness;
- pension schemes are usually very good

### The advantage
Provision of services is very good for the insured.

### The disadvantages
- Coverage is poor for those who are not insured and who rely on charitable or State safety-net cover.
- A large amount of money is spent administering the system of collection, payment and reimbursement.

## The social democratic model

This model of welfare does not rely on a person being in employment, but gives a universal right to State benefits for those in need. The system is funded from general taxation, rather than insurance. Health services are based primarily on direct payment from the State, and the majority of hospital services are free to the client.

An example of an EC country with this system is Denmark. Until the 1980s the UK also had this model, but has since moved towards a residual system.

### Characteristics of the social democratic model
This model is characterised by:
- universal coverage of the population, with few distinctions between employed and non-employed;
- very high expense as a consequence of this;
- relatively low benefits because of the numbers in receipt of benefits and services;
- the system is run by the State and financed by it;
- relatively little choice as the State system provides virtually all the health, welfare and personal social services.

### The main advantages
- Everyone is covered by social security and health schemes.
- The cost of administering the service is very low indeed.

### The main disadvantage
- The wide coverage means high expense and correspondingly low levels of benefits paid out.

## The catholic model

This model stresses the role of the family and of voluntary and religious organisations in the provision of welfare. There is limited public provision, which exists only to fill the gaps left by the other organisations.

Examples of EC countries with the catholic model of welfare are Spain and Portugal.

### Characteristics of the catholic model

It is characterised by:
- wide range of provider agencies;
- geographical variations in provision;
- a strong belief in charity rather than rights of citizens to welfare.

### Advantages
- Underpins the family.
- Strengthens voluntary and charitable activities.

### Disadvantages
- Overall level of services is low and there are significant variations in quality.
- There are problems of access to services.
- It is poorly funded.

## The residual model

The State provision of welfare is dismantled and replaced by a mixture of private, charitable and State provision. Access is through a mixture of taxation and personal payments. The State becomes a safety net and people are actively encouraged to seek private and voluntary sources of help.

This is the system that the UK has recently moved towards.

### Characteristics of the residual model

It is characterised by:
- wide range of provider agencies
- State taking the role of controlling standards.

### Advantages
- It stresses the importance of the family.
- It gives choice.
- In certain cases it leads to a raising of standards.

### Disadvantages
- Means-testing usually results in low take-up.
- Quality varies, and there is a possibility of a two-tier system developing.
- There is stigma attached to requesting help.

# Assignment

You are a researcher for an MP and you have been asked to gather all the information you can on the activities of the EC in the areas of health, welfare, employment and education.

You will need to write to the Information Officer of the EC in Storey's Gate, London SW1, and you will need copies of Social Europe and the Eurostat publication Europe in Figures (available from your central or college libraries).

You must produce a 15-minute presentation under these headings:
- The decision-making structure of the EC
- The spending patterns of the EC
- Health
- Welfare
- Employment
- Education
- Prospects for the future

## CHAPTER 11

# The Elderly

## Introduction

In this chapter we examine the situation of the elderly in society and learn about the problems they face and the health and welfare services available to them. The chapter begins by looking at the increasing numbers of elderly people in society. As you will see, the most notable change in the nature of British and European society has been the increasing proportion of the population over retirement age.

But why should this matter? When we talk about the elderly, the image conjured up is that of weak, fragile people in need of help. This is true for some elderly people, but the majority lead active and contented lives. We therefore examine how images of the elderly have been created and how they can distort the attitudes of younger people and thereby influence patterns of social care provision.

We then move on to look at the situation of the elderly in society discussing issues of health, dependency, employment and poverty. Finally, we take a detailed look at the range of health, welfare and financial services available to the elderly in contemporary Britain.

*Write down five to ten adjectives or phrases which you would associate with the term 'the elderly'. Retain these for use later.*

---

**Growing old – and invisible**

Amazing isn't it? You spend the best part of a lifetime doing your best to be a good citizen. Paying income tax, rates or poll or council [tax], retirement and other state contributions.

You even join the civilians or armed forces in keeping the Nazi hordes from our land, whilst millions of others die in the process.

At the end of this longest day, what have you got? A pension that is nowhere near commensurate with your efforts nor compatible with the rest of Europe.

But worse, you are reminded how lucky you are to have paid your mortgage and have wage and salary earners contribute towards your pension!

But perhaps we should be grateful if some do remember us occasionally if only to point out what a drag on the economy we are. Because thousands of pensioners will testify that when you become old you are apparently invisible.

Invisible to those idiots – adult as well as kids – who threaten our weary bodies with their bikes on pavements and pedestrian precincts. And to those who never think of holding a door for us, or offering a touch of Christian priority.

Carry on smoking! Carry on boozing! Carry on thrombosing! There is certainly no incentive to getting old!

**Source**: Letter to the *Southend Standard Recorder*, 1 October 1992

# Demographic changes

Today, there are over 8.5 million people over 65 living in Britain, and the figure is rapidly increasing. There are actually four million people over the age of 75, and 180 000 over the age of 90. The growth of the elderly in society is significant in that these numbers of elderly people have never occurred before in history.

## POPULATION OF PENSIONABLE AGE[1]

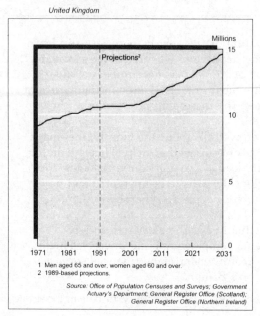

*United Kingdom*

1 Men aged 65 and over, women aged 60 and over.
2 1989-based projections.

*Source: Office of Population Censuses and Surveys; Government Actuary's Department; General Register Office (Scotland); General Register Office (Northern Ireland)*

**Source:** *Social Trends* (HMSO, 1993)

1 What was the approximate number of people of pensionable age in 1991?
2 Is the number of elderly decreasing after this? What happens in about 2008?
3 What will the numbers of people of pensionable age be in 2031?

## The burden of dependency

The 'burden of dependency' is the term used to describe the proportion of people working and paying taxes in proportion to those who are not in employment or not producing wealth for the economy.

The term is usually used to illustrate the proportion of people of working age (16–60/65) compared to the numbers of people in full-time education (too young) and in retirement (too old). The larger the number of people who are not in the workforce, the greater the 'burden' of taxation on the working population. The term can also be used to include the numbers of unemployed.

## EXPECTATION OF LIFE

### Expectation of life[1]: by sex and age

| United Kingdom | 1901 | 1931 | 1961 | 1991 | 1996 | Years 2001 |
|---|---|---|---|---|---|---|
| **Males** | | | | | | |
| At birth | 45.5 | 58.4 | 67.9 | 73.2 | 74.0 | 74.5 |
| At age: | | | | | | |
| 1 year | 53.6 | 62.1 | 68.6 | 72.8 | 73.5 | 74.0 |
| 10 years | 50.4 | 55.6 | 60.0 | 64.0 | 64.7 | 65.2 |
| 20 years | 41.7 | 46.7 | 50.4 | 54.3 | 54.9 | 55.4 |
| 40 years | 26.1 | 29.5 | 31.5 | 35.2 | 35.8 | 36.2 |
| 60 years | 13.3 | 14.4 | 15.0 | 17.8 | 18.2 | 18.7 |
| 80 years | 4.9 | 4.9 | 5.2 | 6.5 | 6.7 | 7.0 |
| **Females** | | | | | | |
| At birth | 49.0 | 62.4 | 73.8 | 78.6 | 79.5 | 79.9 |
| At age: | | | | | | |
| 1 year | 55.8 | 65.1 | 74.2 | 78.1 | 78.9 | 79.3 |
| 10 years | 52.7 | 58.6 | 65.6 | 69.3 | 70.1 | 70.5 |
| 20 years | 44.1 | 49.6 | 55.7 | 59.4 | 60.2 | 60.6 |
| 40 years | 28.3 | 32.4 | 36.5 | 39.9 | 40.6 | 41.0 |
| 60 years | 14.6 | 16.4 | 19.0 | 21.8 | 22.4 | 22.7 |
| 80 years | 5.3 | 5.4 | 6.3 | 8.1 | 8.6 | 8.8 |

1 Further number of years which a person might expect to live. See
Appendix, Part 7: Expectation of life.

*Source: Government Actuary's Department*

**Source**: *Social Trends* (HMSO, 1993)

1 Overall, what has happened to the expectation of life for people in the twentieth century?
2 What implications does this have for health and social services provision? (Look at the table on page 227).
3 Which sex is likely to live longer?
4 For those women who reach 80 today, what expectation of life remains in 2001? Compare this to 1901. What are the implications for health and welfare?

# The social construction of old age

Being physically old does not mean anything in itself, much more important is the way that we interpret age in our society. Older people are often viewed as useless, and a burden to the rest of us. The young and middle-aged look to the future with dread at the idea of being 'old'. However, this view of age is socially constructed. In other societies in history and even in present day China, for example, old age is seen as a period of physical decline but also as a time when an individual has gained wisdom from a lifetime of experiences.

In fact, the majority of retired people are physically fit and mentally alert until their death or a short time prior to this. It is only a minority who become seriously disabled, and this increases with age. In any form of definition of disabled, about 30 per cent of the over 75s can be classified as such. Only about 5 per cent of all retired people suffer from forms of confusion.

About 330 000 people live in some form of residential home, nursing home or sheltered housing. These account for approximately 60 per cent of those over the age of 60. However, the proportion of each age group within residential care increases quite significantly amongst the older groups in society. For every one thousand aged 65 to 74, six people will be in residential care, and by the age of 75 the figure has risen to 49.

Approximately 80 per cent of all residents in elderly persons' homes (EPHs) or similar establishments will be over 75.

Of course, there is another way to look at these statistics, which is that 951 people out of every 1000 over the age of 75 are living at home!

## VARIATIONS AMONG THE ELDERLY

The underlying assumption is that the elderly are a problem for society. The growing proportion of the population who are elderly is emphasised, and particularly the burden of the 'old' elderly (i.e. over seventy-five years old) and the 'very old' elderly (over eighty-five). These two groups are [seen] as a burden on the State because they are high users of health and welfare services. They are also seen as a burden on women because policies of community care mean that most...care of the elderly is done by women.

The elderly are primarily seen as a homogeneous [single group with similar characteristics] group and attention is given to age relations, rather than class or gender differences among the elderly.

...[They are also seen]...as of low moral worth—evident from the 'social problem' focus and from the more general image of the elderly as poor, disabled, dependent and passive.

But how does social class influence these age relations? We have only to consider the Queen Mother, the House of Lords and many elderly judges and politicians to realise the sharp contrast they provide to the more general image of the elderly.

**Source**: S. Arber, 'Class and the Elderly', *Social Studies Review*, 1989

**1** What is the assumption when talking about the elderly?
**2** What two groups of the elderly are seen as particularly burdensome?
**3** Why is it incorrect to talk about the elderly as a homogeneous group?
**4** Is it true, as the writer argues, that we hold the elderly in 'low moral worth'? Why do you think we hold some elderly in respect, as indicated in the extract, and the majority of the elderly as of 'low moral worth'?
**5** At present, in your family, are the oldest generation contributing positively to the quality of life of the younger members of the family or you personally?
**6** Make a list of the costs and benefits of the elderly in your family and your community.
**7** Within your group or class, how many of you would be prepared (or are doing so now) to look after your parents should they become unable to look after themselves?
**8** Whose responsibility are the elderly?

# Health and dependency

By dependency, we mean the extent to which people need assistance to carry out what most of us would consider normal, everyday tasks necessary for an adequate quality of living. For example, dressing oneself, cooking a simple meal or being able to wash and, in the case of men, to shave.

One measurement of dependency is arrived at by assessing the extent to which you are able to look after yourself, are continent and are mentally alert. According to this measurement, out of every 100 people in residential accommodation, 17 are severely dependent, 42 moderately so and 41 reasonably independent. But what does dependent mean? Someone, for example, may be able to look after themselves but are incontinent, another person may be mentally confused but perfectly fit and strong; and even those people who are unable to move and who may be incontinent are often fiercely independent in their own way. Therefore, dependency is a difficult concept to define. In dealing with the elderly, professionals cannot categorise but need to respond to elderly people in terms of their specific needs, just as with any other age group.

The vast majority of the elderly are capable of a range of normal living activities and the stereotype of the elderly as being incapable (as opposed to having constraints placed on them by the infirmity associated with age) is wrong. Of every 100 individuals over 75:

- asked if they had suffered from any 'restricted activity over the last 14 days', 75 replied No;
- asked if they were 'housebound or restricted to bed', 90 said No.

We also know that eight out of ten of the over 80s suffer from no confusion or dementia whatsoever.

However, although the majority of the elderly are independent, they are on average less likely to be healthy than younger members of society. A person over the age of 75 costs the NHS over six times more than a person of working age. The majority of the disabled are formed from the elderly, as are those suffering from some form of mental confusion.

The problem of **dependency** is particularly acute in EPHs and nursing homes. Those who live in these institutions are generally considered to be unable to live in any other environment – that is they are categorised as dependent. Yet many are physically dependent, but mentally independent, others may be confused and therefore dependent, and others may simply have been in a social situation where there was no alternative but residential accommodation. The question, therefore, is what is the aim of residential accommodation for the elderly?

## DENIED A VOICE

Many elderly people living in homes are denied privacy, control over money and choices in other areas of their life, a report published today says.

The charity Counsel and Care says that residents of homes are often afraid to criticise because they are in a powerless position. Its report adds: "To criticise a home from within may carry real risks. Usually the responsibility for investigating a complaint lies with the organisation criticised which has many subtle but powerful possibilities for exacting retribution."

The charity interviewed 200 people aged between 60 and 99 who were living in their own homes about what they would want from residential care if they ever needed it. These views were compared with those of 100 residents in 39 private homes in London and 15 run by voluntary agencies.

"Homes may claim to be all providing but nothing can compensate for the loss of the capacity to buy small goods and services, or even, as one resident pointed out, the stamp for a letter of complaint," says the report.

Most people wanted to be able to choose what time they got up, but only 52 per cent were given a choice. "There could be no more damning statistics of the inhumanity of institutionalisation."

**Source**: The *Guardian*, 5 October 1992

1 List some of the normal rights which 'many elderly people' are denied, according to the extract.
2 Why are they afraid to criticise?
3 Which style of residential accommodation does this reflect (see pages 176–9)?
4 What do elderly people seem to miss, according to the research?

**5** Ask three residential homes near you if you could question residents about their views on residential care and what their preferences are. Do be careful not to ask provocative questions and discuss your questions with the owners/managers of the residential home. Of course, any replies from residents should be confidential. If a residential home is unwilling to let you talk to their residents, then you ought to ask them why. After all, a good residential home should be pleased to show you examples of good practice. Discuss your conclusions. What recommendations would you make concerning the provision of services, etc., in residential accommodation? Write up a report on your research.

## Styles of residential accommodation

Various models which we discussed on pages 176–9, have been suggested. These include the following:

- **Warehousing**   This is when the elderly simply have their medical, physical and accommodation needs met.
- **Horticulture**   An alternative model is that of 'horticulture', in which there is an attempt to develop the skills and abilities of the elderly.
- **Normalisation**   This model is discussed further in chapter 14 on people with disabilities, but the aim here is to make life as normal as possible for the elderly.

## Assessing dependency

When it comes to deciding whether someone ought to have a home help or some other form of social support, there is always the problem of measuring the degree of dependency.

Sainsbury has suggested the following activities as ones which elderly or disabled people may have difficulty with, and which they are likely to need to perform regularly in their daily lives.

### Measuring dependency

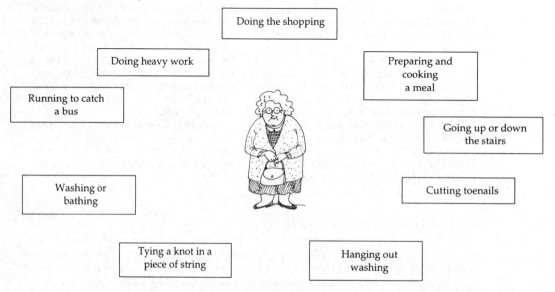

| | |
|---|---|
| Doing the shopping | |
| Doing heavy work | Preparing and cooking a meal |
| Running to catch a bus | Going up or down the stairs |
| Washing or bathing | Cutting toenails |
| Tying a knot in a piece of string | Hanging out washing |

**Source**: Adapted from S. Sainsbury, *Measuring Disability* (G. Bell, 1973)

These measure such things as the ability to undertake sustained effort, mobility, reach, concentration, co-ordination and sudden effort.

The individual is measured on a scale of 0 to 2, where 0 = no or little difficulty, 1 = difficulty and 2 = unable to perform the task.

By doing this, Sainsbury suggested that the assessor was measuring the reality of a person's experience in everyday situations, as opposed to accepting a medical diagnosis which tells us about physical ability as opposed to functional ability (in other words, what functions the person can achieve).

## Retirement

Between 1931 and 1971 the proportion of men aged 65 and over who were retired increased from under half to 78 per cent and by 1984 the figure was around 94 per cent. Thus in a relatively short space of time 'old age' has come to be socially defined as beginning at retirement age.

> Like experience of work the experience of retirement and attitudes towards it are socially divided. There are those, mainly salaried workers in a career structure, who are able to choose whether or not to leave work at the retirement age or to leave prematurely or perhaps to work on. Then there are those, predominantly manual workers, who are effectively coerced into retirement and sometimes early retirement by poor working conditions, ill health, redundancy and unemployment. Thus in industries which have arduous working conditions or boring and repetitive work workers are likely to welcome retirement at the earliest opportunity.
>
> **Source**: A. Walker, 'The Social Construction of Dependency in Old Age' in M. Loney (ed.), *The State or the Market* (Sage, 1987)

**1** In the extract on page 220, 'Variations among the elderly', we looked at differing views on the elderly. What does the extract quoted here tell us about the elderly in terms of their attitude towards retirement and how this relates to their working lives?

**2** What possible implications does this have for developing policies towards the elderly? (It may help you if you think of old age as being simply one part of a lifetime of experience, along with employment, income, etc.)

### Leisure

If a person reaches 60 years of age, they can anticipate (depending on whether they are male or female) another 15 or 19 years of active life.

The involvement of the elderly in 'constructive' pastimes (such as sport, education, etc.) is quite low, so that only two out of 100 use parks regularly and only one in 100 attend the cinema, although the retired do watch more television than most other groups.

Their relationships, too, are rather limited:
- one in ten never visit friends or relatives, and one third receive no visits from friends;
- one in five are visited by relatives less than once a month;
- one in 20 never receive visits from relatives.

# The elderly and employment

The idea that the old are useless is closely linked to the fact that they are not in employment and so have very limited power and very limited incomes. Yet there is no natural reason why people should retire at 60 or 65, indeed in the

1960s over a quarter of all people continued in employment beyond retirement. Rather it is a combination of pressures from employers to slim down their workforces, from the government to decrease unemployment, and from people themselves who wish to have some time without working, before they die.

There are a number of consequences of the elderly being removed from the labour market.

- Work provides the majority of people with social contacts. Removal from work means loss of friendships.
- Status derives from employment – the terms 'retired' or 'pensioner' are ones which almost always carry a stigma. Many people will therefore refer to themselves in a way which refers to their previous occupation (for example, retired teacher). Therefore the elderly feel stigmatised.
- A job means a salary, and the extremely low pension that most UK pensioners receive means that retirement for many involves a life of poverty – and the implications of poverty include poor health, poor housing and less leisure.

The idea that the elderly are a *problem* as such is incorrect. It is true to say, however, that the elderly are more likely to encounter problems of health and poverty than other groups in society.

# The elderly and poverty

The elderly form one of the single largest groups in poverty (see chapter 3). There are a number of reasons for this.

- Most elderly people rely on a private or State pension (or a combination of both). The State pension is relatively low and according to many commentators it does not enable a pensioner to reach an acceptable standard of living.
- For those pensioners who have savings, the pace of inflation in Britain since the 1960s means that the true value of these savings is eroded. The value of the savings declines over time.
- Many pensioners have particular costs associated with age – for example, they may have limited mobility and if they wish to go out public transport is inappropriate. The costs of taxis may therefore limit their activities.
- They have higher fuel bills, as they are at home all day and often need higher levels of heat than younger, more active people.
- They may only be able to keep in contact by telephone and are constrained from doing so by the costs of calls.
- They are less able to do household repairs and tasks, and so require the services of professionals for which they must pay.

## Pensions

The main income for elderly people, as we said earlier, is their pension. Almost 9.5 million people receive pensions. Approximately 20 per cent of pensioners claim extra help through Income Support (see 'The benefit jigsaw', below); however, it is estimated that as many as a further 9 per cent are eligible, but either through ignorance (did you know about the benefits available through supplementary benefit?) or through the desire not to accept charity and to remain independent, they have not submitted a claim.

Pensions were the first thing to be introduced this century when the State became involved in 'welfare provision', as we understand the meaning of the term. They were introduced by a Liberal government in 1908, and were free for all retired people over 70.

1 At what age are people eligible for retirement benefit today?
2 What happens to men who are unemployed over the age of 60?
3 Find out how many people over 70 there were in 1908, and over retirement age?
4 What implications are there for the provision of pensions?

In 1925, a contributory pension scheme was introduced for those aged over 70, for widows and orphans.

The Beveridge Report (1942) recommended a pension scheme in which people paid the same amount irrespective of income. This would be invested for 20 years, and then the proceeds would be paid out on a flat-rate basis (that is the same for everyone) with a 50 per cent contribution from the government.

However, in 1946, the government introduced the National Insurance Act, which included a pension scheme based on the idea of 'pay as you go' – meaning that people paid contributions but there was no fund that was invested. The contributions people make today pay for the pensions of the retired today. The assumption was that there would always be enough people in employment paying their National Insurance to fund the numbers of elderly in retirement at that particular time. In the 1990s, this has been found to be a doubtful assumption.

In 1975, the pension system was reformed to bring in a relatively generous earnings related pension system known as SERPS (State Earnings Related Pensions Scheme). However, the sheer costs of providing a reasonable pension scheme for the whole of the population proved too much, in the eyes of the government, and so, in 1986, the Social Security Act limited the amount of the government's contribution and consequently the value of the benefits for most employees. It also encouraged people to switch to private pension schemes, which are based on a 'funding' principle. This means that the money is invested in stocks and shares and then the money earned is distributed, after the fees of the insurance company have been deducted, to the pensioners.

The value of pensions can still be considered too low, but the effect of the gradual intervention of the government in forcing people to have private or State pension schemes has been to lessen the extent of poverty for the elderly.

1 Pay-as-you-earn pension systems involve using the money taken in contributions from the younger age group today to pay for the pensioners today. There is no investment.
   (a) There is a growing population, and plenty of work available – is this good or bad for pay-as-you earn pension schemes?
   (b) There is a declining or static population with an increase in the numbers of the elderly – is this good or bad for pay-as-you-earn pension schemes?
   Explain your answers.
2 The proportion of people receiving pensions will increase relative to the employed population by the end of the century to 2·3:1·6. What does this mean, and what are the possible implications?

Frank Field, a Labour MP, and a well-known campaigner against poverty has argued in a recent speech that in future increases in the state pensions should be limited to only the poorest pensioners.

Mr Field argued that there was no question of taking the right to pensions away, but that if private sector pension reform was achieved then it may not be necessary for all people to have their state pensions uprated each year.

This argument is a move away from the 'universalist' principle of paying equal benefits to everyone, which was established under the Beveridge Report of 50 years ago, which ushered in the Welfare State. Mr Field pointed out that the richest 10 per cent of pensioners have an income which is six times higher than that of the poorest, and that the £1 billion pounds spent on uprating pensions for all, might have been better spent on the poorest pensioners only.

1 What does Mr Field mean when he argues that we should move away from the 'universal' principle? (You may need to look at pages 29–31.)
2 What is the alternative to the universal model? What are the advantages and the disadvantages of the universal model and its alternative?
3 Give one example of the universal model and one of the alternative model.
4 Why does Mr Field think that we should move away from the universal model for pensions? What is your opinion? Give reasons to support it.
5 Find out the current level of State pension for (a) a single person and (b) a married couple. Interview a small sample of retired people (possibly relatives) and ask them about their budgets. (Your relatives may have a private pension, so try to see how they would manage if they had only a State pension. This will involve some detective work, as you will have to take into account the rules for eligibility for exemption from payment of such things as the council tax, home helps, and any other means-tested benefits). Could you manage on a State pension? What level would be appropriate in your opinion? If there are approximately 11 million (and 13 million by the year 2000) retired people, what would be the cost of your plan? How would you fund this?

## The benefit jigsaw

Writing in July 1992, the following are the benefits for a couple aged 68–75, in relatively good health, who have less than £3000 in savings and who own their own house.

As they have less than £3000, they are able to apply for Income Support. They are entitled to £66.00 normal Income Support benefit plus £25.00 enhanced premium (see leaflet IS1). This totals £91.60.

But their pension is only £86.74 per week, so they are able to claim the difference of £4.90. Therefore they will have a benefit of £91.60.

The couple will be eligible for exemption from the local authority council tax.

Pension £86.70.

They will also be eligible for a range of free health service benefits (for example, free eye tests, no prescription charges, etc.).

Construct a very simple questionnaire. Ask a sample of approximately ten younger people (16–25) what they associate with the term 'old people'. Ask them how they would define (in age terms) 'the elderly'. Tape-record their replies and then try to pick out any words, phrases and attitudes which you feel are significant.

Next, ask a sample of people over retirement age what they associate with the terms 'old people' or 'the elderly'. Ask them also how they would define (in terms of age) 'the elderly'.

Compare the replies, and also include your own views expressed at the beginning of this chapter. Are there any differences? If there are differences, how would you account for these?

# Services and benefits for the elderly

## EXPENDITURE ON HEALTH AND PERSONAL SOCIAL SERVICES

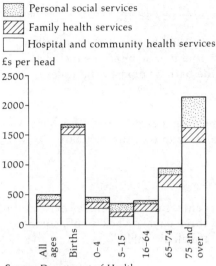

Personal social services

Family health services

Hospital and community health services

£s per head

Source: Department of Health

The following is a graph showing the breakdown of expenditure on various elements of the Welfare State. The statistics given are per head, by age, 1990–1.

1 Overall, which service of the Welfare State shown in this diagram has most money spent on it?
2 Which has the least?
3 Which age group has most money spent on it overall?
4 Looking at the diagram service by service, is there any noticeable change in the amount of money spent from one age group to another on each of the following?
   ● Personal social services
   ● Family health services
   ● Hospital and community health services.

**Source**: *Social Trends* (HMSO, 1993)

## State benefits

The State benefits available specifically for the elderly are pensions and Income Support premiums.

**Pensions** are available to all women over 60 and all men over 65.

**Income Support** is based on the principle of providing a minimum income for all members of society. Certain 'targeted' groups, which include the elderly, are eligible to receive **premiums** above Income Support level. For example, at the time of writing, the premium categories relevant to the retired are 60–74, 75–79 and 80+. The amount paid increases with each age group. One other premium category relevant to the elderly is if one or both partners of a couple are receiving Attendance Allowance, Disability Living Allowance, Invalidity Benefit, Severe Disablement Allowance or are registered as blind.

As the disabled and their carers are most likely to be found amongst the elderly, the benefits mentioned above are also most likely to be applied for by those over 70.

## Services for the elderly

The services available for the elderly include the following.

### Home helps

There are approximately 130 000 home helps, employed by the Social Services departments of local authorities. Their job is to visit elderly people who need light housework done, or shopping or perhaps cooking. Until recently, most councils provided these free of charge, but since 1990 the majority of councils have introduced charges.

### Meals on wheels

These are provided directly by local authorities or by contract mainly with the WRVS (Women's Royal Voluntary Service). Only a very small proportion of the elderly receive meals – about 3 per cent. However, these account for 20 million meals delivered to people's homes each year.

### Aids and adaptations to the home

Local authorities can pay for alterations to people's homes if this will allow them to lead more independent lives. Most common adaptations include handrails for climbing stairs and grips on the bath or next to the toilet.

### Lunch clubs

These are for the active elderly who can meet on a regular basis for both food and company. These clubs are most often run by churches, but sometimes by local authorities.

### Day centres

Usually provided by Social Services departments, some day centres exist in the NHS. Here elderly people attend for up to three days a week. Food, some entertainment, bathing, hairdressing, etc., are all available.

### Medical services

The normal range of medical services are available for the elderly. The most important people are the GPs, and the community nurses who visit and maintain the health of elderly people.

### Social workers

Social worker teams for the elderly deal with the most vulnerable people.

### Voluntary services

Groups such as Help the Aged provide a very wide range of services from selling cheap insurance, acting as a pressure group, through to organising day centres.

### Elderly persons' homes

Residential homes for the elderly have been the 'growth industry' of the 1980/90s. These are mainly private establishments since the National Health Service and Community Care Act 1990 placed various barriers in the way of local authorities who wish to run their own residential homes.

### Nursing homes

There are relatively few NHS nursing homes, the majority are now private.

### Hospitals

The provision of long-stay accommodation and treatment for the elderly with chronic conditions is now not seen as the role of the NHS. However, certain hospital services continue, especially for the psychiatrically disturbed or confused elderly in the form of long-stay wards (geriatric wards) and psycho-geriatric wards.

### Sheltered accommodation

Sheltered accommodation consists of housing or flatlets in which elderly people live, with some communal lounges and a resident warden. They may be provided by the private sector, by housing associations, or by local authorities.

### Informal services

Overwhelmingly the most important services are still provided informally through families, usually the partner or daughters and, to a lesser extent, neighbours and friends. (See the section on carers in chapter 7.)

## ELDERLY PEOPLE IN RESIDENTIAL ACCOMMODATION[1]

United Kingdom

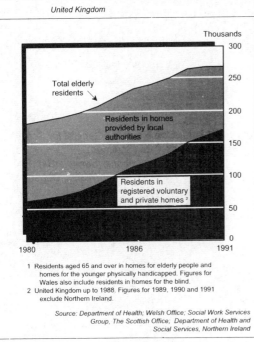

1 Residents aged 65 and over in homes for elderly people and homes for the younger physically handicapped. Figures for Wales also include residents in homes for the blind.
2 United Kingdom up to 1988. Figures for 1989, 1990 and 1991 exclude Northern Ireland.

Source: Department of Health; Welsh Office; Social Work Services Group, The Scottish Office; Department of Health and Social Services, Northern Ireland

1 What was the total number of residents in residential accommodation in 1991?

2 How many were in private and voluntary homes compared to local authority homes?

3 How has the situation changed since 1980?

4 What effect will the NHS and Community Care Act 1990 have in the future? (See pages 153–61 for further information.)

5 What are the advantages of private and voluntary homes compared to local authority ones, and what are the disadvantages?

**Source**: *Social Trends* (HMSO, 1993)

# Assignment

You are engaging in research for a local church organisation which is trying to find out the extent to which family ties are still important for the elderly people, and which hopes to use your information to provide more effective help for elderly people. In particular it does not want to infringe on the services most commonly provided by family members but instead wishes to know how it can complement them.

It has been suggested that you obtain permission to interview a range of elderly people from local authority day centres, elderly persons' homes, lunch clubs and church and other voluntary organisations.

You should draw up a very clear and simple questionnaire to find out the following information:
- what family connections the person has;
- how often the person sees members of the family;
- how services are provided by those family members.

You must then draw up a clear report and present the conclusions and recommendations.

# Chapter 12

# Families and Children

## Introduction

This chapter explores the importance of the family for the health and welfare of individuals. The family, it is often claimed, is the basic unit of our society and its activities in the area of economic, health, housing and welfare provision for its members cannot be replaced as effectively by any other agency. Much of the government's spending on welfare goes on supporting families, and where the family does not perform its functions to a level which is regarded as adequate by society, then social workers intervene.

The chapter begins by discussing the importance of the family for the health and welfare of its members, and then moves on to look at how the family has changed over time, both in terms of structure (in particular the growth of single-parent families) and in terms of relationships between family members. A picture emerges of a growth in inequality in the family, where the woman still has clear caring roles. Increasingly, through divorce and single parenthood, the British family with only a mother as family head is being seen as 'normal'. The next part of the chapter examines how the Welfare State is responding to these changes, by providing financial and social services.

So far a fairly rosy picture of the family has been painted. However, there is a dark side too – such as the problem of domestic violence, in which men routinely use violence against their wives or partners. We look at this phenomenon, and what steps have been taken to combat it. A further dark element of family life is that of widespread physical and sexual abuse of children, usually by fathers. The issue of child abuse has become very prominent in the media; we examine it using some disturbing examples. We also look at the ways in which the social services intervene. This part of the chapter concludes with an examination of fostering and adoption services.

The final part of the chapter looks more at the position of children in social policy, and at the development of legislation to protect children. At the time of writing one of the most important pieces of legislation coming into effect is the Children Act 1989 which seeks to give children a much greater say in their lives and to strike a balance between the views of children, the social services and the parents. We discuss this and look at some of the implications.

## The importance of the family for health and welfare

The family forms the foundation for the provision of health and welfare services. Most social policy in Britain is based on the principle of the 'normal' family, which looks after its members in childhood and in old age. The State and its welfare services only step in when there is a breakdown in this 'normal' pattern.

The importance of the family in matters of health and welfare can be seen in all the following areas.

- **Health**  The physical health of individuals, particularly children, is often related to the family and its economic situation, eating habits and type of housing.
- **Mental health**  A person's mental health is often related to the way in which other family members treat them and respond to them. This is closely linked to socialisation.
- **Socialisation**  The way people think and behave is very often related to the way in which they have been brought up by their parents. Attitudes towards health, welfare, employment, gender and race are all elements of the socialisation process.
- **Maltreatment**  It is often within the family that children are physically and sexually abused.
- **Education**  Success in education is closely related to parents' interest and support.
- **Caring**  It is within the family that most people receive care and support in periods of illness, old age and childhood. This will sometimes continue for an entire lifetime if, for example, a person is born with disabilities. The family, or more exactly the women within the family, are the ones most likely to provide this care. As a result, their lives are marked by patterns of caring within the family.
- **Sense of belonging**  In most people's lives a sense of being important and of belonging is necessary for their general well-being. The family provides this, or fails to.
- **Administrative unit**  The State uses the family as its 'administrative unit' for providing care, social security benefits and the whole range of services.
- **Housing**  The quality of family housing influences the health, education and general quality of life of its members.
- **Income**  Possibly this is the most important factor in the lives of people. The family serves as an income and expenditure unit. The wages of the adults provide the quality of life for the family, and influence choices of housing, health care, nutrition and education amongst other things.

# The changing family

The family in Britain has been changing considerably over the last 25 years. The changes are twofold: changes in the structure of the family, and changes in the relationships of family members.

## Family structure

By the structure of the family we mean first the type of bonds between people – whether individuals live in couples or alone; in large families of three generations, or simply as couples with their children; the numbers of people who divorce, and possibly remarry; the numbers who live alone, particularly if they have children. We need to know these things, as the provision of services to people will vary depending on the structure of the family. For example, the more elderly people who live alone, and relatively isolated from their families, the more the State may need to provide community care services. If there are more single-parent families, there may be greater need for Income Support or Family Credit, given that it is difficult for a lone parent to support a family without State aid.

### Definitions of family types
- **Lone- (or single-) parent family** – only one parent, usually the mother. This reflects the rise in the divorce rate and the growth of childbirth outside marriage.
- **Nuclear family** – mother, father and their children. Relatively isolated from the wider family.
- **Extended family** – usually consists of three generations living close together.
- **Reconstituted family** – where the parents have previously been married (or in in a long-term partnership), and join together with some or all of their children from the previous marriages.

What implications for health and welfare are there for each of the following family types? You may find it useful to list the advantages and disadvantages of each type.
- Lone-parent family
- Nuclear family
- Extended family
- Reconstituted family

Issues you might want to think about include poverty, stress, isolation, violence, support, abuse, freedom, constraints, caring and appropriate housing.

## DIVORCE RATES

**Divorces in Europe per 1000 marriages, 1989**

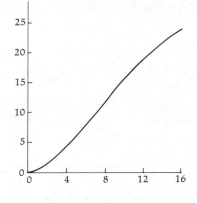

**Children/family in divorce, % cumulative, by age, UK**

**Source:** *Population Trends* (HMSO, 1990)

1 Which country has the highest divorce rate in Europe?
2 Where is Britain in the league of divorce rates?
3 What implications do you think there might be for the provision of health and welfare services in countries with high divorce rates, compared to those with low divorce rates?
4 In the UK, what proportion of children are in divorced families by the age of 16?

## HOUSEHOLD STRUCTURE

### People in households: by type of household and family in which they live

| Great Britain | Percentages and thousands | | | |
|---|---|---|---|---|
| | 1961 | 1971 | 1981 | 1991 |
| **Type of household** | | | | |
| Living alone | 3.9 | 6.3 | 8.0 | 10.7 |
| Married couple, no children | 17.8 | 19.3 | 19.5 | 23.0 |
| Married couple with dependent children[2] | 52.2 | 51.7 | 47.4 | 41.1 |
| Married couple with non-dependent children only | 11.6 | 10.0 | 10.3 | 10.8 |
| Lone parent with dependent children[2] | 2.5 | 3.5 | 5.8 | 10.0 |
| Other households | 12.0 | 9.2 | 9.0 | 4.3 |
| **All people in private households[3] (= 100%) (thousands)** | 49,545 | 52,347 | 52,760 | 24,607 |

2 These family types may also include non-dependent children.
3 1961, 1971, 1981 Census data. 1991 General Household Survey. 1991 column contains sample size.

*Source: Office of Population Censuses and Surveys*

**Source**: *Social Trends* (HMSO, 1993)

*The table indicates how people are divided into households in the UK. Look at the figures for 1991.*

1 In what type of household/family type did people live?
2 What proportion of the population is this?
3 What proportion of the population lived in households categorised as one parent with dependent children? How has this changed over time?
4 What was the second most likely household in which people lived in 1991? What is the percentage?

## BIRTHS OUTSIDE MARRIAGE

### A  Live births outside marriage as a percentage of all births (UK)

*Source*: OPCS, General Register Office (Scotland), 1991

### B  Live births outside marriage as a percentage of all births: by registration

*England & Wales*

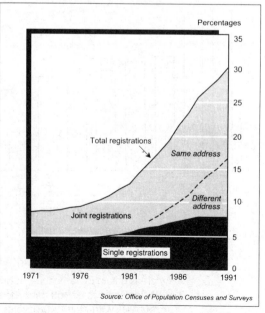

*Source: Office of Population Censuses and Surveys*

**Source**: *Social Trends* (HMSO, 1993)

1 Overall, how would you summarise the information given in graph A?
2 Look at graph B. What percentage of all births are registered as joint births, that is both parents register the birth of the child as parents? How does this compare to the total number of births outside marriage?
3 What is the main implication of joint registrations for the relationship between the parents?

## MARRIAGE, DIVORCE AND CHILDREN

More than one in six families are now headed by lone mothers. The typical lone mother is divorced or separated, aged 35–40 with two children.

The number of never-married lone mothers has risen sharply – in 1971 they represented 1.2 per cent of all families, today the figure is 6.4 per cent.

**Marriage UK (thousands)**

|                                        | 1971 | 1981 | 1985 | 1989 |
| -------------------------------------- | ---- | ---- | ---- | ---- |
| Total Marriages (1st Marriages 243,000) | 447  | 398  | 393  | 382  |

Source: *Social Trends* (HMSO, 1992)

**Divorce and children UK (thousands)**

**England and Wales**

|      | Total no. of divorces | % of divorcing couples with children under 16 | Number of children under 16 of divorcing couples | Average no. of children per family |
| ---- | --------------------- | --------------------------------------------- | ------------------------------------------------ | ---------------------------------- |
| 1978 | 143.7                 | 60%                                           | 162.6                                            | 1.13                               |
| 1986 | 153.9                 | 56%                                           | 152                                              | 0.99                               |
| 1988 | 152.6                 | 55%                                           | 150                                              | 0.98                               |

Source: OPCS Marriage & Divorce Statistics England and Wales 1990

1 What changes have taken place in the number of marriages between 1971 and 1989?
2 What proportion of these, in 1989, were second or subsequent marriages?
3 In 1988, what was the total number of children aged 16 whose parents were divorcing?
4 In 1988, what percentage of divorcing couples had children under the age of 16?
5 List some of the implications for this for (a) parents, (b) children and (c) social/health services.

# Lone-parent families

In England and Wales, over 10 per cent of all households are headed by lone parents. However, they form more than 19 per cent of all families with dependent children. Lone-parent families are usually headed by a woman (17.5 per cent of all families, lone fathers comprise 1.4 per cent). These families are more likely than families with two parents to have substandard housing, to be poor, to have poor health and to be clients of Social Services departments.

### Low pay and lone-parent families

Lone-parent families are most likely to be low income families, or ones claiming Family Credit or Income Support. This is due to two main reasons.

● The majority of people who head lone-parent households are women. In Britain women are more likely than men to be employed in low paid work.

- Women with families to support are unable to move to find work, and when they do find employment they have to make arrangements for child care. Often this means that the women can only work restricted hours.

## FAMILY INCOME

### Gross Weekly Household Income levels of Family Types (1990)

| Family Type | Level of Income | | | | | | |
|---|---|---|---|---|---|---|---|
| | Under £60 % | £60– £100 % | £100– £225 % | £225– £325 % | £325– £425 % | Over £425 | No of families sampled |
| One adult, 1 child | 15.68 | 36.75 | 29.73 | 10.27 | 4.86 | 2.71 | 185 |
| One adult, 2 or more children | 2.54 | 41.42 | 39.89 | 9.59 | 4.02 | 2.54 | 198 |
| One man, one woman, 1 child | 0.36 | 4.62 | 13.09 | 24.53 | 17.74 | 39.66 | 542 |
| One man, one woman, 2 children | 0.02 | 2.20 | 12.77 | 21.47 | 24.56 | 38.99 | 759 |
| One man, one woman, 3 children | 1.13 | 3.77 | 16.60 | 25.28 | 23.04 | 30.18 | 265 |
| Two adults, 4 or more children | 1.03 | 2.06 | 31.95 | 17.54 | 13.40 | 34.02 | 97 |
| All families with children under 18 | 1.75 | 8.67 | 17.24 | 19.33 | 17.95 | 35.06 | 2390 |

Source: OPCS. Family Expenditure Survey 1990

*Compare the percentage of families within each gross income band (a) with one adult and one child, against those with one man, one woman and one child and (b) with one adult and two or more children, against those with one man, one woman and two children. What statement can you make about family income and lone-parent families?*

However, it is not correct to see single-parent families only in terms of problems. There are also benefits – for instance where the mother and children have escaped from a violent or abusive father. The quality of life for the children and mother in these cases can improve quite significantly once they become a 'lone-parent family'.

## Family relationships

Traditionally, the wife stayed at home and looked after the children and the husband went out to paid employment. The male was regarded as head of the household, and the tax, social security and pension systems were all based on these assumptions. However, as we have already seen, the structure of the family has changed, with an increase in the number of single-parent families, a growth of serial monogamy (that is people remarrying after divorce), and an increasingly popular preference for cohabitation (that is couples living together without being formally married).

Changes within the home have taken place too, which affect the way children are treated. These changes reflect the changing role of women in the wider society. There has been a move to greater equality between husbands and wives. In particular, there is a much greater acceptance by males of their responsibilities as fathers and partners. Men are now far more likely than they were 20 years ago to engage in household tasks such as shopping or housework.

Some commentators have gone so far as to suggest that the relationship between husband and wife is now one of 'symmetry', indicating that they both share domestic tasks equally. However, this is probably an exaggeration. Piachaud conducted a small-scale survey to find out what 'basic' tasks fathers/husbands do in the home. He suggested that, by isolating certain unavoidable and possibly less pleasant child-care tasks, we could find out how much the male contributes to the household.

Piachaud tested the basic tasks as follows:

- getting children up and dressed;
- toileting and changing nappies;
- taking children to their school, childminder or nursery and collecting them again;
- finding extra time for shopping;
- giving extra time for meals;
- washing and bathing children;
- putting children to bed;
- finding extra time for washing and ironing;
- clearing up and cleaning after children.

He concluded that 'By far the greater part of the time spent on child-care tasks was spent by the mother – overall, 89 per cent of the total time.'

One important factor influencing the amount of time the husband contributed was whether the wife was in full-time employment.

*Using the list of domestic tasks given above, conduct a small survey of young couples to see who regularly performs which tasks. You may wish to compare the results with the habits of some older couples. If you can, compare couples who cohabit with those who are married – are there any differences? What happens when the children are ill?*

*Surveys tend to indicate that husbands and wives have different views on who performs the majority of household tasks – you may wish to consider interviewing spouses separately.*

The importance of this for social policy is that the traditional role of the wife/mother/daughter as carer continues. Women are expected to shoulder much higher proportions of child-care and domestic responsibilities, even where both partners have full-time employment. When it comes to caring for elderly relatives or chronically ill children or husbands, it is regarded as the duty of a woman to do this. Without the taken-for-granted work of women in families, the State would have to step in to look after the very young, the very old, the sick or the disabled, or they would be left to fend for themselves. The next chapter, on equal opportunities, discusses the position of women in more detail.

# Child-care services

The increase in the numbers of women working has altered the extent to which they can carry out their traditional role of staying at home and caring for children. The issue is of particular importance for the under fives. The majority of women with young children either work part-time or wait until their children start school before they return to work. However, approximately 5 per cent of all working mothers use some form of formal child-care arrangements.

The Children Act 1989 requires local authorities to review the provision of day care and other services for children to the age of eight. It also requires authorities to provide a range of services for children 'in need', including day care for the under fives and appropriate care and supervised activities for children in need outside school hours. The Children Act also requires local authorities to take into account racial and religious factors.

The following services currently exist.

## Service for young children

**Day nurseries**
Where children are looked after during the parents' hours of work. These can be private, run by the local authority or attached to a workplace or educational institution.

**Childminders**
These are usually women who provide an infant care service from their own homes. They will usually only take a few children. Childminders are required by the Children Act 1989 to be registered with local authorities and to meet certain minimum standards. There are places for 5 per cent of all under fives in Britain.

**Playgroups**
These are privately or local authority run, and they usually use a local hall for morning sessions. Playgroups have to be led by individuals who hold a recognised Pre-school Playgroup Association (PPA) qualification. There are places for 35 per cent of all children aged three and four. Average attendance is two to three sessions per week.

**Nursery schools and classes**
These are privately run, or may be part of a Social Services family centre.

**Provision for under fives in primary, special and independent schools**
There are places for approximately 2 per cent of all under fives, with fewer than 100 000 places for the 3.8 million under fives in the UK.

In total, 25 per cent of the UK's three- and four-year-olds are now in some form of nursery education.

> Our view is that it is for parents who go out to work to decide how best to care for their children. If they want or need help in this task, they should make the appropriate arrangements and meet the costs.

> **Source**: E. Currie (then Junior Health Minister), *Hansard*, 12 July 1988

**1** Does the quote above indicate that the government was in favour of providing government funded child care provision?

**2** What is your view of the matter? Is it up to the individual or is it a right that women (and of course men) should demand to have?

# Families and the Welfare State

There is a range of benefits and services to which families are entitled.

## One Parent Benefit

This is a tax-free weekly cash payment on top of Child Benefit for any lone parent (whether man or woman, divorced, separated or unmarried). It is paid for the first child only and is paid regardless of income or National Insurance contributions. However, it is not paid (or it is taken into account) if the person is on Income Support.

## Child Support Maintenance

In 1991, the Child Support Act was passed, and the legislation came into effect from April 1993. The Act requires lone parents who obtain Income Support, Family Credit or Disability Working Allowance to answer questions about the absent parent.

A new agency, the Child Support Agency, will question all single parents in receipt of any of the benefits mentioned above and will require them to name the absent parent. The agency will then attempt to find the missing parent and require them to pay a contribution to the costs of caring for the child. The amount varies with the income and the outgoings of the absent parent.

Single parents receiving benefits who refuse to name the absent parent may face a reduction in their personal allowances.

Under the system which operated before April 1993, those parents left caring for the chldren could go to court to obtain a maintenance order. Under the new legislation, however, they must now apply instead to the Child Support Agency for an assessment of the appropriate child support maintenance.

## Income Support

A single parent who is not working is entitled to Income Support, plus a lone parent premium.

### MINIMUM COSTS OF A CHILD

The table below contrasts the allowances given by local authorities for fostering, the minimum cost of keeping a child as calculated by the Child Poverty Action Group, and the Income Support allowance.

**Minimum cost of child compared to Income Support level (UK)**

| Age | Fostering allowances (outside London) £ | Minimum cost £ | Income Support Allowance (As of Oct 1991) £ | % I.S. as a proportion of cost of a child |
|-----|-----|-----|-----|-----|
| 2 | 47.46 | 14.94 | 13.60 | 91 |
| 5 | 55.44 | 16.97 | 13.60 | 80 |
| 8 | 60.69 | 20.64 | 13.60 | 66 |
| 11 | 66.01 | 21.82 | 20.00 | 92 |

Source: CPAG 1990, National Foster Care Association 1992

1 What is the minimum cost of keeping an eight-year-old child?
2 How much was the foster allowance?
3 How much was the Income Support payment?
4 What was the percentage actually provided by Income Support of that which was considered necessary by the Child Poverty Action Group?
5 Overall, what was the relationship between Income Support levels and the costs of keeping a child?

## Tax allowances

For individuals bringing up a child alone, there are tax allowances available.

## Widow's allowances

A widow can claim Widowed Mother's Allowance, which is a taxable weekly benefit for widows of any age who have at least one child receiving Child Benefit. The more children, the higher the rate.

## Family Credit

This is paid to individuals or couples with at least one child under the age of 16. One of the partners must be working for at least 16 hours each week. You must not have savings of more than £8000, and savings over £3000 affect how much is paid. Family Credit is calculated on 26-week cycles, and even if the circumstances of the claimants change during that period, the payments remain the same. (This six-month cycle of calculations can either hinder or benefit a low income family quite significantly.)

**1** Family Credit is calculated every six months, and payments do not change within that period. What are the implications for the family receiving Family Credit? If you cannot decide, then contact your local Social Security office and enquire, or use one of the Social Security freephone enquiry lines (0800 666 555).

Obtain a copy of leaflet FC2 from your local Social Security office, and answer the following questions:

**2** You are a single mother working for 40 hours each week. You have two children, a girl aged six and a boy aged 11. You earn £150 each week and you receive £25 (in total) each week in maintenance from their father, who you have no other contact with.
Are you eligible to apply for Family Credit?

**3** Your cousin is married with three boys aged 14, 16 and 19. He takes home £192 per week. He claims and receives Housing Benefit, but you are not sure how much as he is rather secretive. Would you advise him to apply for Family Credit?

### FAMILIES IN RECEIPT OF BENEFITS

**Great Britain (thousands)**

| Benefit | Total | No. of families | | Date of information |
|---------|-------|-----------------|---------|---------------------|
| | | Single parent | 2 parent | |
| Income Support | 1110 | 812 | 298 | 31/5/91 |
| Family Credit | 341 | 131 | 210 | 30/4/91 |
| One Parent Benefit | 773 | 773 | — | |

**Source**: Department of Social Security, 1991

**1** How many families were receiving Income Support in 1991?
**2** How many families were receiving Family Credit?
**3** How many families were receiving One Parent Benefit?
**4** Were there any differences between the benefits received by single-parent families and those received by two-parent families? Could you offer any explanations?

## The Social Fund

This is a system by which the poorest families can borrow money from the Department of Social Security, without paying interest. The borrowing facility replaced the old system of discretionary payments (pre-1988), where the local office of the DSS could give people money for the purchase of essential items if they were satisfied that the individual or family were truly in need. The Social Fund has been severely criticised for the fact that the individuals who borrow only do so because their benefits are inadequate to meet basic needs. By having to borrow, and then pay back the loan, they simply become even more desperate.

### THE EFFECT OF THE SOCIAL FUND

More than four in 10 of the poorest families are having their social security cut to repay loans from the social fund, a survey shows today.

Taking account also of deductions for poll tax and fuel debts, more than half of all families dependent on social security are having their benefit cut before they receive it, says the survey by the National Children's Home charity.

Fewer than one in three of the poor families surveyed said they were managing on their income without being in debt.

Fewer than one in 10 said they were not worried by money.

Tom White, NCH chief executive, said the findings painted a shocking picture of family life for tens of thousands of households struggling to survive.

"The survey shows that whilst families were spending their inadequate budgets sensibly, current benefit levels simply do not match their basic needs....

*Deep in Debt; Information Department, NCH, 85 Highbury Park, London N5 1UD; £5.*

**Source**: Adapted from the *Guardian*, 27 October 1992

1 Who are the people most likely to be borrowing from the Social Fund?
2 Why were they borrowing?

## The National Health Service

People under 16 are eligible for free NHS prescriptions, dental treatment, sight tests and vouchers for spectacles. These benefits continue to age 19 for those in full-time education. Free dental treatment continues to age 18 for those who are in employment.

Other services available to families under the NHS include ante- and post-natal health services, family planning and vaccinations.

## Education

For young people staying at school beyond 16, there are grants available and assistance with the purchase of clothing. For full-time higher education there is a means-related grant.

The majority of 16–17-year-olds cannot claim Income Support, but are required to attend Youth Training – which is skill-based education. While on this training programme, run by Training Education Councils (or TECs) in collaboration with employers, the trainees can claim an allowance.

## Housing

Single parents, and families with young children, are able to gain extra points on local authority waiting lists for housing. They are also likely to be looked upon more favourably by housing associations. Single young people, however, have virtually no chance of being housed in local authority stock, as the result of the 'right to buy' legislation (see page 71) has been the disappearance of new local authority housing development.

## Child Benefit

This was introduced in 1977/78, and replaced family allowances and income tax allowances. It is a non-contributory benefit paid to all children. It represents one of the few universal payments in the British welfare system. This means that it is paid to all mothers (or fathers) on behalf of their children, irrespective of family income. It is payable for each child under 16, and continues up to age 18 for those in full-time education. It is paid monthly.

### One Parent Benefit
This is an additional benefit for the first child, payable to single parents.

## The controversy surrounding Child Benefit

Child Benefit has been the centre of great and continuing controversy, as it is virtually the only remaining universal State benefit, paid to all parents regardless of their income. The controversy is less about paying benefits to parents to help them defray the costs of caring for children, it is more an argument over paying *all* parents Child Benefit regardless of income. A person earning £100 000 per year receives the same benefit per child as a family with an income of £10 000.

### Arguments in favour of universal Child Benefit
- Although husbands/fathers may earn a high wage, there is considerable evidence to show that they do not always spend it on their family.
- Child Benefit is the income brought in by the child and therefore the child clearly has the right to have the money spent on her/him.
- Universal Child Benefit ensures that every child in Britain has the opportunity to receive the cash. If it was means-tested, then it is likely that there would be parents who would fail to claim and, as a result, children would suffer.

### Arguments against universal Child Benefit
- It is a waste of resources paying Child Benefit to families who are not in need.
- If the benefit was targeted on fewer 'need' families, then it would allow the government to pay a higher benefit to the children in these families.
- If husbands/fathers do not give adequate amounts of their earnings to the family, then that is regrettable but a private matter within the family as long as the children are not in need.

Ronald didn't like me buying anything for the children. If I went out and bought them a pair of shoes and he wasn't with me, there was hell to pay when I got home. He just didn't like me spending money without his consent. If he wanted to go out and buy things that was different. He was very keen on photography and he bought a lot of photographic equipment. What things he wanted to buy was OK, but the basics and things I needed to get for the children, he thought were unreasonable.

Source: H. Graham, 'Being Poor: Perceptions and Coping Strategies of Lone Mothers', in J. Brannen and G. Wilson (eds), *Give and Take in Families* (Allen and Unwin, 1987)

A survey by CPAG...documented the importance of Child Benefit both to middle-class and working-class mothers – Child Benefit was often crucial in 'making ends meet', and generally in providing for the day-to-day needs of children which typically fell to the mother.

**Source**: M. Henwood, L. Rimmer and M. Wicks, *Inside the Family* (Family Policy Study Centre, 1987)

At bottom, most of the women with the housekeeping allowance (where the husband allocates the wife a set amount for housekeeping per week), together with some of the others, regarded the husband's income as his to dispose of as he saw fit, on the grounds that he earned it, rather than as a genuinely joint resource.

**Source**: A. Walsh and R. Lister, 'Mother's Life Line: A Survey of How Much Women Use and Value Child Benefit' (CPAG, 1985) quoted in M. Henwood *et al.*, *Inside the Family* (Family Policy Study Centre, 1987)

# Domestic violence

No one knows just how much violence goes on in families. Women are usually reluctant to report their husbands/partners to the police for a number of reasons. These include a fear of further violence, a view that violence is a personal matter between spouses, the fact that women often blame themselves for the violence and a belief that the police are not interested.

Once I made an appointment to see the doctor but I never kept it. I felt too embarrassed and ashamed to go really. I was badly bruised and had a cut underneath the eye. My legs were aching quite a bit – he's got a truncheon.

**Source**: M. Borkowski, M. Murch and V. Walker, *Marital Violence: The Community Response* Tavistock, 1983)

A man on the run from police stabbed his common law wife's mother to death as she celebrated her 50th birthday, a court was told yesterday....

She told a jury at Leeds crown court of their 11 years of "ups and downs" during which Mr Moffatt tried to chop off her fingers with a knife, poured bleach over her while she was in the bath and dowsed her with petrol threatening to light it. The court heard that Mr Moffatt resolved to kill her mother, Mary Appleyard, because he was fed up with her interfering in rows with her daughter.

Mr Moffatt has pleaded not guilty to murdering Mrs Appleyard, two counts of assaulting his wife causing actual bodily harm and threatening to kill. Louise Godfrey, QC, prosecuting, said Mr Moffatt demanded a sandwich after the couple had been out celebrating Christmas.

His wife told Mr Moffatt that the turkey was not cooked and he flew into a rage.

Miss Godfrey alleged: "He seized the meat from her, threw the hot juices at her and then threw the dish out of the door. As she cleaned up on the floor, he put a poker into the fire and attacked her with the hot poker and then hit her over the head with a piece of wood."

She suffered burns to her face, head, neck and hands.

Mr Moffatt then "laid low" until Boxing Day, knowing that the police were looking for him.

Mr Moffatt stole a kitchen knife from a friend's house.

Mrs Appleyard died from a single 3½-inch knife wound between the shoulder blades. After police arrested him at a friend's house, the blood-stained kitchen knife was found inside a newspaper.

The trial was adjourned.

**Source**: Adapted from the *Guardian*, 10 November 1992

*Do a content analysis of newspapers in your local library. Ideally this should be over a period of one year. Choose two examples of daily papers for each week of the year. (Some libraries only keep newspapers for three months, but they are also available on microfiche or CD ROM). Look through all the articles on murders. What is the relationship of the accused and the victim in the majority of cases?*

## Explanations for domestic violence

Explanations for the causes of domestic violence vary, and are to some extent contradictory. The main ones, grouped in two categories, are given below.

### Individual explanations

- **Alcohol** seems to precipitate violence, but is not a *cause*.
- **Violence in childhood home** – evidence links violence at home to late adult use of violence.
- **Deviant marital relations** – male feels he is not in control of marriage or partnership and turns to violence to maintain that control.

### Structural explanations

- **Culture of male violence** – men are encouraged to express themselves through violence and are brought up to be 'tough'. Therefore, use of violence against a partner is not abnormal.
- **Fiction** – images of macho men in books and stories.
- **Advertising** contains images similar to those in fiction.
- **Childhood socialisation** includes the influence of and attitudes to gender relations.
- **Belief in male dominance** pervades our society.

## Responses to domestic violence

Help and support are offered to the victims of domestic violence in a number of ways.

### Women's refuges

These provide short-term accommodation and exist specifically for women and their children who are at risk of violence. The refuges are run by charitable groups and are often partially funded by local authorities. They were first set up in the early 1970s to enable women who were the victims of male violence to escape and live in a place of safety. There is at least one refuge in most larger towns in Britain. This is perhaps the best proof of the very widespread existence of male violence towards women.

### Changing attitudes of the police and judiciary

Historically, the attitude of the police and the judiciary towards male violence to women was that of the 'threshold approach'. By this, police officers and magistrates operated on the principle that if there was no significant hurt done to a woman then the issue was relatively trivial and not worth instigating criminal proceedings. Today, the police are more likely to take complaints seriously, although women's groups argue that they still do not intervene as often as they should. The police, however, are far more likely to intervene if a child appears to be at risk.

There is considerable evidence to show that women are reluctant to press ahead with charges against violent partners, or even to report an incident to the police. Explanations which have been suggested include the following.

- Many women are afraid of further violence.

- Many women regard the violence against them as a personal matter between themselves and their partner.
- They may find admitting that violence occurs against them too embarrassing.
- Women often blame themselves for the violence, believing that they are partly to blame for the situation.
- It is a widely held belief that the police are indifferent to this type of violence and regard it as a private matter.

### Intake teams

Intake teams often have to deal with instances of domestic violence. The intake team consists of social workers who first deal with enquiries from the public. They will advise the client of her rights and liaise with the police. If necessary, they will contact the women's refuge.

### Family centres

These are usually run by the local authority Social Services departments, or by a voluntary organisation such as the NCH (National Children's Homes). The aim of the family centres is to teach parenting and relationship skills. Very often domestic violence is coupled with violence by the parent(s) towards the children (though it is almost always the male in the family). The main work of family centres, however, is to teach parenting skills, and usually to the mother.

### Relate

This is the organisation that counsels people with marital or partnership difficulties. Couples can arrange to meet a counsellor on a regular basis to overcome their problems if possible, or if this is not possible at least to terminate the relationship in a way that minimises bitterness between the ex-partners. An incomplete or bitter ending to a relationship can often lead to further violence by the male.

> Jenny...married her husband when she became pregnant, hoping that family responsibilities would stop him from drinking, which often made him violent and abusive.... Her husband's continuing violence towards herself and occasionally the children led her to tell the health visitor how trapped and angry she felt and she was put in touch with the nearest NCH family centre.... after a particularly violent episode, the Family Centre workers helped her to get an injunction to have him evicted and the family eventually rehoused.
>
> **Source**: *The NCH Fact File – Children in Britain 1992* (NCH, 1992)

**1** How many agencies were involved in helping Jenny?
**2** What were they?
**3** In this particular case what was the apparent cause of the violence?
**4** Was it only the woman who was the subject of violence?

# Child abuse

Child abuse refers to the sexual or physical maltreatment of children. It is one of the most emotive issues dealt with by the welfare services, and sexual abuse intervention is certainly the most controversial of all social work activities. The Children Act 1989 (which we describe on pages 253–6) was introduced largely as a result of very strong concerns about the lack of clear legal safeguards that children and parents appeared to have.

## CHILDREN AT RISK

A force equivalent to a road traffic accident fractured two ribs of a baby girl, the Old Bailey was told yesterday.

"Baby Y" was taken to hospital by her parents on Christmas Day 1989, after her father said that she had gone "floppy" during her morning feed. An examination by doctors of the seven-week-old girl revealed bruises to the face, chest and legs, as well as bleeding around the brain.

The parents, Robert Rouse, 22, and Lyndsay Morris, 19, both from Croydon, south London, deny cruelty to the baby. They also deny murdering her six-week-old sister Sudio nearly a year later by smashing her head against a wall, and then filling the dent before taking the body to a hospital.

Dr Susanna Hart, a consultant paediatrician who examined Baby Y at Mayday Hospital, near the couple's home, told the court: "If those injuries were caused by Y's parents at the time, then the blow must have been extremely forceful.... It needed a force equal to a road traffic accident, which was why fractures in babies were typical of non-accidental injuries.

The court was also told how the baby began to have convulsions 36 hours after being admitted. A scan showed bleeding around the brain, which could have been caused by the baby being held upside down and slapped on the back. Babies' necks were weak, Dr Hart said. In those circumstances the head would shake "like a heavy ball on a string".

Both parents told doctors,

including Dr Hart, that they might have accidentally injured the child by holding her too hard when they tried to give her gripe water. Mr Rouse is alleged to have clasped her face with his hand, causing severe bruising. Later, because she was choking, they said they banged her hard on the back and held her upside down to wind her.

The court was told that after an investigation by social workers, Baby Y was put on an "at risk" register and entrusted to foster parents in January 1990. She was returned to her parents five months later, but last November her sister died, and Baby Y was readmitted to Mayday Hospital with horrific injuries.

The trial continues today.

**Source:** The *Independent,* 4 October 1991

A mother who turned a blind eye while her brutal husband battered their newborn daughter to death was jailed for two years yesterday.

Little Melanie Pinhorn died aged just 26 days after her father Andrew smashed her head against a wall.

In earlier attacks he had broken 16 of her ribs, and every breath Melanie took during the last 10 days of her short life at the family's flat in Hersham, Surrey, would

have been agony, the Old Bailey heard. Her mother Trudy, 26, who was suffering from post-natal depression, was sent to prison for cruelty on the grounds of neglect.

Her husband was jailed for life earlier this month for murdering his daughter on October 26 last year.

Judge James Rant demanded an inquiry after hearing a health visitor and midwife had seen bruises but accepted excuses they were accidental.

**Source:** *Today,* 23 July 1991

1 What is the 'at risk' register (see the pie chart on page 247 and the table on page 248)?

2 What was the role of the social and health services in these two cases?

3 The health and social services have often been criticised for not intervening in cases such as these. Look at the figures on pages 247 and 248 and note the numbers of children on the register. Does this provide any defence for health and social workers?

4 The extracts may upset you, or even make you angry. However, some people argue that this sort of violence is simply an extreme version of smacking a child, and that smacking should also be a criminal act. Allowing any form of violence against children, whether smacking or any other form of physical discipline, is wrong as it culturally 'legitimates' violence against children. What is your view on this argument? Should children be smacked? What is the permissible limit? Why don't we smack adults?

**5** *Violence within certain limits within the family is generally regarded as acceptable, but not violence against individuals outside the family. For example, to smack someone else's child is regarded as completely unacceptable behaviour. Why?*

No one knows the extent of child abuse in Britain, but the National Society for the Prevention of Cruelty to Children has suggested that as many as 1.5 million children suffer some form of cruelty. Four categories of abuse have been used.

- **Neglect** – any behaviour which results in the serious impairment of a child's health or development.
- **Physical abuse** – physical injury to a child which was caused deliberately or was knowingly not prevented.
- **Sexual abuse** – the involvement of dependent, developmentally immature children and adolescents in sexual activities that they do not fully understand, to which they are unable to give informed consent, or that violate social rules regarding family roles.
- **Emotional abuse** – the severe effect on the behaviour and emotional development of the child caused by persistent emotional ill treatment.

## TYPES OF ABUSE

### Children on child protection registers: by reason, 1991[1]

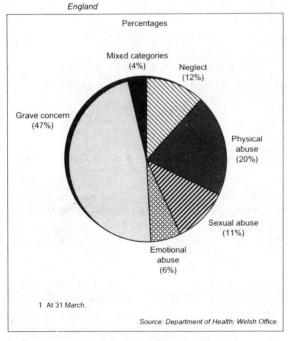

*England*

Percentages

Mixed categories (4%)

Neglect (12%)

Grave concern (47%)

Physical abuse (20%)

Sexual abuse (11%)

Emotional abuse (6%)

1 At 31 March.

*Source: Department of Health; Welsh Office*

**Source**: *Social Trends* (HMSO, 1993)

**1** Which is the most common form of abuse?

**2** What proportion of children on registers are at risk because of sexual abuse?

**3** Why do you think the largest single category on the chart is 'grave concern'? What does it mean?

## A brief review of the law and child abuse

- The neglect of children first became an offence in 1868, when the Poor Law Amendment Act made it illegal not to provide food, housing, medical aid, etc., for one's child. However, the main aim was to save the ratepayers money by not having these children looked after by the local authorities.

- Violence and poor treatment of children led to the founding of the National Society for the Prevention of Cruelty to Children (NSPCC) in 1884. An Act was passed in 1889 providing legal protection for children.
- In 1908, a Children's Act marked the first time when children were treated differently from adults.
- In 1933, ill treatment and neglect became criminal offences.
- In 1948, the local authority was given the duty to receive a child into care when the child was orphaned, or the parent was unable to look after the child, or ill treated him/her.
- By 1952, the Children's departments of local authorities were required by law to investigate cases of cruelty or neglect.
- In 1963, the departments were to work with families to prevent possible abuse or neglect.
- In 1969, a major Act gave yet more powers to the local authorities, particularly in their legal rights to take children into care.
- In 1989, a major piece of legislation (the Children Act) defined the rights of children, parents and the social services. This is the basis of current practice towards children and their treatment.

## THE EXTENT OF ABUSE

Child protection registers were established by local authorities in 1974, to act as a record of information for social workers.

**Number of children (under 18) on Child Protection Register and number of registrations**

| England (thousands) | 1988 | 1989 | 1990 | 1991[1] |
|---|---|---|---|---|
| Number on Register at 31 March | 39.3 | 40.7 | 43.9 | 45.2 |
| Rate per 1000 under 18 | 3.5 | 3.7 | 4.0 | 4.17 |
| Number of Registrations during year ending 31 March | 21.3 | 22.0 | 26.8 | 28.2 |
| Rate per 1000 under 18 | 1.9 | 2.01 | 2.5 | 2.6 |

1. 1991 figures include estimates for authorities unable to submit returns in the requested format or in sufficient detail. Comparative figures between 1988 and 1990 are thus not straightforward.

**Source**: DoH Children and Young Persons on Child Protection Registers, year ending 31 March 1991 (England), quoted in NCH report, 1992

The most reliable UK findings suggest that between 12 per cent and 59 per cent of all women (and [between] 8 per cent and 27 per cent of all men) have experienced some form of sexual abuse before the age of 18.

**Source**: National Children's Homes, 1992

**1** What was the number of children on the Child Protection Register in 1991?
**2** How does this compare to 1988?
**3** Does this necessarily mean what the official figures show? Explain your answer.
**4** What is happening overall to both the rate and the number of registrations?

# The role of the Social Services departments

Social Services departments have a statutory duty (one based in law) to look after children and protect them if they are suffering harm. In the majority of cases the Social Services intervene when abuse is reported to them, and deal with it in a number of ways. These include the following.

- **Family centres**   These are centres where parents can go to learn parenting skills and be counselled.
- **Monitoring**   This can take the form of social workers informally visiting possible problem families and keeping an eye on the situation. However, parents have the legal right to refuse entry to their home. An alternative form of monitoring is to have the parents see the social worker at the local Social Services department on a regular basis.
- **'At risk' register**   Where the social workers are very concerned about the possibilities of abuse, they will put the child on the 'at risk' register. This is a list of all children/families where the local Social Services department feel there is sufficient evidence for close scrutiny of the family, and so a formal record is kept of the condition of the children.
- **In care**   Children at risk will be taken into care, either with a foster family or in a residential children's home.

### Criticisms of Social Services departments

Social Services departments have been severely criticised both for their lack of response to physical abuse, and for their over-eagerness to intervene when they perceive sexual abuse.

Factors affecting their inefficiency in protecting children have been noted in a range of reports. One of these is the Department of Health's *Child Abuse: A Study of Inquiry Reports 1980–1989* (HMSO, 1991). This report suggested that factors influencing the poor performance of social work departments in protecting children were:

- lack of experience and naivity of social workers;
- poor training of social workers in this area;
- poor performance of their duty by social workers and other professionals such as health visitors;
- poor management of Social Services departments;
- poor communications between social workers and between social workers and other agencies (such as the health service);
- ignorance of legal powers.

On the other hand, in the case of child sexual abuse, social workers were criticised more for their over-activity. This was shown by the Cleveland Child Sexual Abuse case. In 1987, in Cleveland, 121 cases of abuse were diagnosed by doctors over a period of five months. As a result of the diagnoses, these children were removed from their homes by social workers. After considerable political and legal wrangling between the parents and the Social Services department, the majority of the children were eventually returned home. An official inquiry by Judge Butler-Sloss concluded that the social workers had acted with excessive zeal and over-confidence. In the cases she examined, Lord Justice Butler-Sloss stated that the rights of the parents had been ignored. She also commented critically about poor management and lack of communication.

## A POSITIVE VIEW OF PARENTS

> Parents Against Injustice (PAIN) said only one family in three is being given verbal information about child protection conferences, at which decisions may be made to take their children into care. Only one in five is being given information in writing.
>
> Fewer than half the families involved are being invited to attend all or part of such conferences....
>
> PAIN's data relate to 164 families ... 60 per cent of them caught up in cases of alleged sexual abuse of their children. Of all the cases, only 19 per cent were said to be based on the children's allegations.

1 What criticisms are being made of Social Services?
2 Should the parents' view be given greater importance?
3 Should children always be believed, according to the extract?
4 Where there is the possibility of abuse in a family, it is often said that it is better to be safe than sorry and to take the child into care. What is your view?

## Who abuses?

It is generally the case that sexual abuse of children is the result of the activities of the father/stepfather or another male close to the child. However, the statistics of abuse are notoriously unreliable, as there appears to be widespread abuse of children by other males outside the family. The explanation appears to be that when children are asked about an act of abuse they indicate a wide range of activities which occur in public, such as indecent exposure; however, when it comes to sexual interference, then it is far more likely to be a close male relative.

Approximately 30 per cent of cases of sexual abuse are committed by young people under the age of 21. In a study by Horne in Liverpool, 34 per cent of allegations concerning sexual abuse of young children consisted of young persons abusing another child.

## Reasons for abuse

Three main reasons which have been put forward to explain why children are abused are as follows. Firstly, the abuser is seen as psychologically disturbed, possibly as a result of poor socialisation. Secondly, the abuser may himself have been abused in childhood – research has shown that this is often the case. The third reason is the 'domination theory' – feminist writers have pointed out that the male and female roles in our society are ones of domination and submission. It has been suggested, as explanations for rape (of a woman) as well as for sexual abuse of children, that the abusers are trying to maintain the role of the dominator.

## How is abuse spotted?

It is unlikely that a parent would voluntarily report the abuse of a child. Incidences of child abuse generally come to light in one or more of the following ways.

- **Visit to the doctor** – doctors and nurses are trained to spot signs of possible abuse. These can include physical signs in girls and boys, and behavioural signs.
- **NAI** – each hospital Accident and Emergency Unit keeps a Non-Accidental Injuries (NAI) register, which they pass to the social services. The medical staff will judge the type and extent of injury against the explanation offered by the parent. Most Accident and Emergency Units also keep a check on the frequency of visits of children for treatment.
- **Neighbours and relatives** – people close to the family concerned may contact the social services to voice their concerns.
- **Childline** – this is a free, direct and confidential telephone service which children can use to inform others of abuse against them.
- **Schools and educational welfare officers** – abuse is often seen by teachers in school, either through physical signs or through disruptive behaviour. In particular, Educational Welfare Officers may be called in to discuss the issue with the child, and to liaise with the social services.
- **The role of the NSPCC** – the National Society for the Prevention of Cruelty to Children is an independent, charitable organisation which is recognised as having great expertise in the area of child abuse. The NSPCC is given specific independent powers to investigate child abuse, and works in harmony with the social services, whilst maintaining its independence.

*Contact your local branch of the NSPCC. Ask a representative to visit your institution (perhaps you could offer some fundraising activity in return). Use the opportunity to devise a list of questions about the work of the NSPCC, and about the causes of child abuse and the best way to combat it.*

# Fostering and adoption

As we have seen elsewhere in this book, the numbers of children going into residential care has dropped quite significantly over the last 15 years. Consequently, there has been a corresponding development of fostering and adoption services.

## Fostering

In certain extreme circumstances, Personal Social Services departments may have to take the responsibility for the care of children. This can occur because:
- the parents (or more commonly the remaining parent) are unable to look after the child;
- there is evidence of abuse; or
- there is evidence of neglect.

Traditionally, the children were placed in childrens' homes and were likely to stay there until adolescence. However, there has been a significant movement away from this. Now it is normal for these children to be looked after by foster parents on a short-term or long-term basis.

The essence of foster care (sometimes the term 'boarding out' is used) is that children are placed with families who try to treat them as part of the family, giving them stability and affection. Foster parents receive an allowance or wage from the Social Services department, which covers their expenses and a relatively small amount for their caring activities.

Fostering is considered superior to residential care in a number of respects.

- It does not institutionalise the child.
- It is more like a normal family situation.
- There is greater opportunity for the child to develop a personal relationship with the foster parents than with a worker in the children's home.
- The foster family is more flexible and is there all the time, as opposed to the work patterns of employees in residential accommodation, who will work in shifts.
- Foster families are considerably cheaper for Social Services departments.

### Types of fostering

Fostering may be on either a long- or short-term basis.

- **Long-term fostering** – as implied by the name, the child lives in the foster family as if it were her/his own family. However, the child remains under the authority of the Social Services department, and the foster parents have no legal rights unless they adopt the child.
- **Short-term fostering** – this is an increasingly common activity. Where social workers decide to intervene in a family and take the child out of the situation, the foster parents may be asked to care for the child temporarily while the social workers attempt to sort out the family problems.

Short-term fostering includes:

- **emergency fostering** – where foster parents are able to take on children in an emergency for a short period; and
- **relief fostering** – where the foster parents take children in order to give the natural parents a respite from caring. This occurs in situations where the behaviour or the health of the child places particularly great demands on the parents. It does not mean that the natural parents are unable to cope, merely that they receive a break.

## Adopting children

Adoption means to become the legal parents of a child, as if that child was born to the adults. The process of adopting is a complex business and usually involves fostering on a long-term basis and then, if the social services agree, they will support the legal moves to adopt.

Traditionally, couples adopted newly born or very young babies. However, with the increase in birth control and abortion, the numbers of young babies available for adoption has shrunk dramatically.

Today, children available for adoption are likely to be older (the advertisement below is typical) and, quite possibly, to have some degree of behavioural problems. There has been a wide-ranging debate about the children of Afro-Caribbean origin available for adoption, as it is the policy to place these children with people of the same ethnic origin. However, because of a shortage of Afro-Caribbean foster parents and couples looking to adopt children, there is a higher proportion of Black children unable to be placed in what are considered to be suitable homes.

## JANUARY'S CHILDREN

**JANUARY'S CHILDREN**

Ten year old twins, RUSSELL and OLIVER, need a new home where they can grow up together.

The boys have lived with foster carers since February 1991, following the death of their mother; unfortunately no other family member could care for them. They are very well liked by their foster parents, who feel that they will give a great deal of pleasure and fulfilment to an adoptive family.

**RUSSELL** is a friendly, likeable and usually happy boy, who is described as living much of his time in a fantasy world. Sometimes he can be disruptive; of the two, Russell has had the most difficulty adjusting to the loss of his mother, and is benefitting from counselling. He attends a mainstream school, where he needs a lot of individual attention.

**OLIVER** is a bright boy who enjoys routine. He is good at games and swimming, and is doing well at school where he has produced some excellent artwork and models. Although he is very sociable and has lots of friends, there are times when he will spend long periods in his bedroom, building with Lego.

The twins are of white English descent and need a white adoptive family who can show them attention and love and allow them occasional contact with their extended family. They should be the only or youngest children.

**RUSSELL and OLIVER** are among 120 children featured in Be My Parent, a family-finding newspaper published six times a year by British Agencies for Adoption and Fostering. If you would like some more information about them, a free copy of the newspaper or general information on adoption and fostering, please phone 071-407 9763.

**Source**: Advertisement in the *Guardian*, 23 January 1993

1 How old are the boys?
2 Why are they to be adopted?
3 Why are they to be the only or youngest children?
4 What is the ethnic origin of the foster parents to be?
5 How are the personalities of the boys described?

Find out how you become a foster parent or how you adopt children. (You can contact your local Social Services department or use the phone number in the advertisement.)

With the information you obtain, construct a diagram or flow chart which shows the various stages that have to be gone through before a person can foster or adopt.

If possible, either through personal contacts or through your local Social Services, see if you can interview a couple who foster children. Perhaps you could invite them to your college to give a brief talk and to answer questions. If the adopted/fostered children are older, they may be prepared to talk about their own experiences.

# The Children Act 1989

The Children Act of 1989 is one of a long line of Acts which have redefined the position of children in our society. The changing nature of legislation concerning children has reflected the changing views towards children over time. In the nineteenth century, the idea gradually developed that children were not simply little adults, but were vulnerable members of society who needed care and protection. This concept of the child as vulnerable dominates twentieth-century thinking.

## A brief history of provision for children

- Legislation regarding young people developed piecemeal over the centuries, reflecting very different concerns. For example, the Factory Act of 1833 began the process of limiting the exploitation of young people in British industry.
- Education for all children was introduced in 1870.
- The plight of orphans and abandoned children – a common problem in Victorian England – was tackled by Dr Barnado in 1870.
- Concerns over children's health surfaced in the Education Act 1906 which permitted the introduction of school dinners.
- After the Children Act 1908, the criminal justice system began to treat children differently in that they no longer saw them as culpable as adults. Rather, children were to be tried in different courts and to be punished or

rehabilitated in a different way from adults.

- One of the primary reasons for setting up Social Work departments came from the requirements of the Children Act 1948, which required local authorities to set up Children's departments with responsibility for the care of children deprived of a normal home life.
- In 1952, local authorities were given the duty to investigate cases of neglect or cruelty.
- By 1963, the Children Act conferred a duty on local authorities to perform preventive work with potential and actual problem families. This was the result of the findings of the Ingelby Committee.
- In 1970, the re-organisation of social work merged the old Children's departments into the new 'generic' (covering all areas of work) local authority Social Services.

## Principles and substance of the Children Act 1989

The Children Act 1989 came into force in October 1991. It was a major piece of legislation which defined the rights of parents, local authorities and children themselves. Underlying the Act are a series of principles, which include the following.

- The upbringing of children is primarily the responsibility of parents, but in cases of need the local authority should be ready to help.
- The relationship between the local authority and the parents should normally be a voluntary and supportive one.
- The legal powers of parents should only be transferred to a local authority if it could be clearly proved in a full court hearing that there was evidence of significant harm to the child.
- In any court cases parents should have full legal representation.
- In the event of emergency powers being granted to local authorities to remove a child from his/her home, it should be for a very short duration and it should be possible for the parents to challenge the situation.

The Act has 12 parts, of which the following are most important.

### Part One

The interests of the child are predominant, and if an order of any kind is made concerning a child it should be clear that it would definitely benefit the child. In order to see that the child would benefit from any intervention by the State, a 'checklist' was provided which guides the court. The court should consider:

---

- the ascertainable wishes and feelings of the child concerned (considered in light of his age and understanding);
- his physical, emotional and educational needs;
- the likely effect on him of any change in his circumstances;
- his age, sex, background and any characteristics of his which the court considers relevant;
- any harm he has suffered or is at risk of suffering;
- how capable each of his parents, and any other person in relation to whom the the court considers the question to be relevant, is of meeting his needs;
- the range of powers available to the court under this Act in the proceedings in question.

## Part Two

This has a number of sections. Of particular interest are the section 8 orders, which are a series of legal orders specifying the relationship between parents and children in cases of dispute with Social Services departments. There are four section 8 orders – residence, contact, prohibited steps and specific issues.

- **Residence order** – states with whom a child should live.
- **Contact order** – states who has the right to visit and contact the child through letter and telephone.
- **Prohibited steps order** – limits the power and responsibility of the parent to take certain actions regarding the child without the permission of the court.
- **Specific issues order** – is a court decision about a particular matter where there is dispute about the correct course of action. For example, over medical treatment, the decisions of the parent could be over-ruled by the court.

## Part Three

This part sets out the principal responsibilities of local authorities regarding children in need. It draws together the scattered pieces legislation which previously applied to local authorities and children in need.

## Part Four

This sets out the grounds under which courts may make an order (whether under Part Two section 8 or under Part Five). For a court to make an order, there would have to be evidence of significant harm, or likelihood of this in the future. Harm is defined as ill treatment (which could be physical abuse, sexual abuse or emotional abuse) and the impairment of health or development.

A girl of 11 has won a court order allowing her to leave her mother's home and move back with the couple who fostered her as a baby. The girl, from Leeds, is believed to be the youngest to invoke rights given a year ago under the Children Act for youngsters to apply for their own court rulings on where they should live and other issues affecting their upbringing.

Within 48 hours of consulting a solicitor, she was granted an interim residence order allowing her to move to the home of the Leeds couple who fostered her for more than two years from the age of three months....

The case follows two similar cases involving teenagers. Courts have sanctioned moves by a 14-year-old girl from Ilford, Essex, who left her mother to stay with her boyfriend's family in Surrey, and a 15-year-old Birmingham girl who moved out of her wealthy father's home to live with her grandparents....

The girl, who has an older brother and three younger sisters, consulted Mr Babbington, a solicitor, on the advice of a social worker and her head teacher after a social services case conference concluded that her home circumstances revealed insufficient grounds to apply for an emergency protection order or care order.

Mr Babbington obtained emergency legal aid and the next day a district judge made the interim order, giving the mother 24 hours to comply. The judge did not see the girl but read extracts from her diary and a long letter.

Leeds social serices department has since removed her brother and sisters from home under emergency protection orders, after discovering that her mother's current boyfriend has a conviction for an offence against children.

The girl went into care at three months because of physical abuse by her father. She was returned to her mother at the age of 2½ after her parents separated, but kept in contact with her former foster parents, whose own children are grown up.

**Source**: Adapted from the *Guardian*, 5 November 1992

**1** Who did the girl win the right to live with?
**2** Why did she do this?
**3** Under what powers did she do so?
**4** Is this an isolated case?

5 What does this tell us about the attitude of the law (and perhaps society) to young people?
6 Did the Social Services department make the legal moves on behalf of the girl? What was their attitude?
7 Why do you think they took this viewpoint?
8 What happened subsequently to the children in the family?
9 In general, do you think that children at any age should have the right to opt out of a family?

## Part Five

Part Five of the Children Act relates to emergency protection for the child. Under the Act, an **emergency protection order** was introduced, which was limited to a maximum of eight days, and extendable only once up to a limit of seven days. If the parents were not present at the original court hearing, then after 72 hours they can apply for the order to be discharged.

The person applying for the emergency protection order need not be the local authority, but could be grandparents or others interested in the welfare of the child. Police officers have particular powers to enforce emergency orders.

## Parts Six to Twelve

These consist of a revision of various issues regarding residential accommodation for children in local authority and private (institutional) homes; fostering; standards concerning nursery and child-care arrangements for under fives; and court arrangements for dealing with children.

# Assignment

You are a journalist working for a local newspaper and the editor has passed you the table shown below. She says that she wants you to investigate the truth of the matter and to write a hard-hitting story. The table shows the absolute minimum costs of keeping a child in January 1992.

Go to your local supermarket – work out how much food, and what type of food, you could obtain for the money in the table.

Add up the cost of clothing for one year and see what you could purchase new. Do not forget the different seasons of the year, the need for underwear, pyjamas, etc.

### Minimum Weekly Cost of a Child by Item of Expenditure (UK)

| Item | Age of Child | | | |
|---|---|---|---|---|
| | 2 years £ | 5 years £ | 8 years £ | 11 years £ |
| Food | 8.64 | 9.77 | 12.88 | 13.33 |
| Clothing, footwear | 2.48 | 2.84 | 2.87 | 3.16 |
| Household provisions | 0.69 | 0.69 | 0.69 | 0.69 |
| Heating, lighting | 1.35 | 1.35 | 1.35 | 1.35 |
| Toys, presents | 0.09 | 0.14 | 0.17 | 0.27 |
| Pocket money | — | 0.29 | 0.67 | 0.95 |
| Schooling | — | 0.20 | 0.29 | 0.38 |
| Entertainments | 0.43 | 0.43 | 0.43 | 0.43 |
| Holiday | 1.26 | 1.26 | 1.26 | 1.26 |
| Total | 14.94 | 16.97 | 20.64 | 21.82 |

Source: CPAG, 1990. (Figures uprated for inflation as of January 1992)

Multiply the amount calculated for toys per week by 52, and then see what could be bought.

Compare this with the amount given for children in Income Support or Family Credit payments.

What are your conclusions? (Do remember that the figures are for January 1992, and you may need to adjust the figures to allow for inflation.)

If possible, through friends, family or contacts at college, try to interview an individual or couple with children who are living on Income Support. Get their views on how they manage and their feelings about family life in these circumstances.

# CHAPTER 13

# Equal Opportunities: Women and Ethnic Minorities

## Introduction

The concept of equal opportunities refers to the fact that certain groups are less able than others to obtain a fair share of the benefits available in society. In an unequal society, in which people compete for privilege, status and financial benefits, some groups tend to lose out more than others. These groups include most of those discussed in this book, the elderly, the disabled, the mentally ill, the poor. In this chapter we focus on two groups which are not specifically covered elsewhere in this book – the ethnic minorities and women.

Inequalities tend to cluster together around certain groups. We know, for example, that the overwhelming majority of the poor are women and that the overwhelming majority of the disabled are women, that women form the majority of the very elderly and that women are more likely to be suffering from forms of mental illness. So, if we talk about the poor or the disabled, we are also talking about women. Similarly, when we look at the situation regarding ethnic minorities in Britain, we see that they are over-represented amongst the poor and the poorly housed, yet they seem to receive fewer benefits and social services provision than the majority of the population.

This chapter examines the situation of these two underprivileged groups in society. We start by examining the concept of citizenship – the term used to describe the starting point for any discussion on why anybody should have rights to a decent standard of living or to reasonable health care. What does it mean to be a member (or citizen) of any society? Are there any grounds for women or ethnic minorities reasonably to complain that they suffer more disadvantages than many other groups in society?

We then look specifically at the problems of the ethnic minorities and examine the evidence that they really do suffer greater disadvantage than the majority of the population. The evidence is quite conclusive: ethnic minorities are more likely to be poor, in worse employment, to have specific health and social services needs and to have worse housing conditions. We therefore turn our attention to why this is so, and examine the concepts of racism and discrimination. Finally, we note the legislation that has been introduced to try to combat racism and discrimination.

The chapter then turns to the situation of women in our society, and you may well see the parallels with the situation of ethnic minorities. There are some differences, however. In particular, there is the role of women in our society by which they are expected to be the carers. This profoundly influences their experience of life and limits them in terms of employment opportunities. It is usually women who disrupt their careers to care for children or for aged parents. The section on gender therefore starts with a discussion of the caring role of women and its implications. We then look at the relationship of women to employment, poverty, health and housing, amongst other things, and our conclusions are that they still suffer significant discrimination. The chapter then looks at what has been done to help women and examines certain social security benefits which have been designed to support them. Finally, there is a brief examination of the legislation which has been passed to outlaw discrimination against women.

# Citizenship

Most people using the term 'citizen' do so with some vague idea that it is linked to the fact of being born in a particular country and having voting rights. But the question asked by social policy analysts is just what does it mean to be the citizen of a country? Is the provision of health and welfare services something that a good government provides when it can, or is that provision somehow a fundamental right of each person in the same way that voting rights and the right to a fair trial are seen as absolutely central to a democracy?

If a government were to say that it had decided that only the people who paid a certain amount of money could vote in local elections in future, then there would be a national outcry as to the unfairness of it. (Indeed, when the Conservative government introduced the so-called poll tax, the situation was not very different from this.) However, if the government says that in future free health care will be restricted to certain groups – to what extent do people regard this as an attack on their fundamental rights as citizens?

R. Titmuss has suggested three elements to citizenship: legal, political and social.

## The legal element of citizenship

In Britain today, everyone should have the same rights and obligations under the law. If any person is accused of an offence, the chances of a fair trial should be equal for all. Although there often appears to be a gap between practice and theory, everyone agrees that this is what should happen.

Laws apply equally to all members of society. Legal rights developed over hundreds of years. Although Magna Carta is supposed to have enshrined the equal legal rights of people for the first time, it seems more accurate to describe the nineteenth century as the period which moved the legal element of citizenship forward most significantly. At this time there were numerous reforms of the law in an attempt to bring greater justice.

## The political element of citizenship

This refers to the democratic rights of voting and free speech. The majority of people over 18 can choose politicians to represent them. People are free to express opinions, within certain limits, and to put themselves forward for election on the basis of those opinions if they should so wish. Political rights of citizenship developed through the latter part of the nineteenth and the early parts of the twentieth centuries.

## The social element of citizenship

This is a far more contentious issue, and one which is at the heart of health and welfare provision. To what extent do people have rights as citizens to decent health services, to social security provision and to the support of the personal social services? For many commentators, particularly those from the right of the Conservative Party, people do not necessarily have rights to health and welfare in the same way that they have rights to political and legal equality. The current policy towards the Welfare State in the UK is based less on the idea that people have rights to these services as citizens and more on a belief that they should instead rely wherever possible on charity or on means testing.

### The three elements of citizenship

In our discussion of the position of ethnic minority groups and women, we review some of the evidence concerning their treatment. The question is to what extent do they enjoy full citizenship of Britain, if we use the criteria provided by Titmuss?

**1** What do you think – do people have a right to free health care and to welfare benefits?
**2** If you think so, then why should they have rights to health care, but not to free transport (or free cars), and to free food, entertainment, etc.?
**3** Should only some people – perhaps the poorest – have health and welfare rights?

One point needs to be made when reading the following sections. We are not saying that *all* people who belong to ethnic minority groups and *all* women are disadvantaged in society (although they may face discrimination and racism). What the evidence suggests is that women and members of the ethnic minority groups are *more likely* to be disadvantaged in society.

# Ethnic minority groups

## Race and health

The poorer health of ethnic minority groups in Britain appears to be closely related to their higher levels of poverty and poorer standards of housing. In a study of over 500 children in inner London suffering from respiratory tract infections and gastro-enteritis, over 48 per cent were from Asian, African or Caribbean families, although these represented only 18 per cent of the population of the area.

Specific health problems of ethnic minority groups include:

- sickle cell disease, a form of anaemia which mainly affects Afro-Caribbeans;
- rickets, which are more likely amongst Asians;
- tuberculosis, particularly amongst those with the worst housing conditions.

Ethnic minority groups also have a very low take-up of ante-natal and post-natal services.

## Race and mental health

There is clear evidence to show that rates of mental illness are significantly higher for Afro-Caribbean-born males than for the British-born population. Rates are higher for Indian, African, Pakistani and Afro-Caribbean females than for British-born females.

Of those attending hospitals as in-patients, Indian males were found to be three times more likely than British-born people to be diagnosed as schizophrenic, and Afro-Caribbean males and females five times more likely.

Comparing British-born Blacks against British-born Whites aged 16–19, Harrison found that the Blacks were 16 times more likely to be diagnosed as schizophrenic. It is thought that this may be partly explained by misdiagnosis due to lack of understanding of cultural behaviour.

## Inequalities in the NHS

### Doctors

A Commission for Racial Equality study in 1987 concluded that doctors from ethnic minority groups suffered from poorer training, lower promotion prospects and lower pay than Whites. They were also more likely to be found in the lower prestige areas of mental health and geriatrics.

In 1988, St George's Hospital Medical School in London was found to discriminate in a way contrary to the Race Relations Act 1976 in its selection procedures.

### Nurses

Afro-Caribbean and Asian nurses form approximately 10–15 per cent of nurses in the UK, yet there were less than half this figure in more senior positions. Like the doctors, the nurses are more likely to be working in mental health and geriatrics.

Reporting in 1991, the Equal Opportunities Task Force...found that while most health authorities had set up equal opportunity policies, few had translated their policies into a timetabled programme for action, or had allocated responsibilities or sufficient resources. Most had failed to produce data about the ethnic composition of the workforce or monitored the outcome of selection decisions especially in regard to promotion procedures and outcomes. Few health authorities complied with the recommendations of the CRE [Commission for Racial Equality] code of practice, while equal opportunities had not yet become part of the formal and routine duties of health service managers.

Source: R. Skellington and P. Morris, *Race in Britain Today* (Sage, 1992)

## Race and social services

Under section 71 of the Race Relations Act 1976, local authorities were required to take steps to tackle racial discrimination and promote equality of opportunity. Yet a study by the Commission for Racial Equality in 1989 concluded that only very limited progress had been made. In a survey of 116 of the 208 Social Services departments in the UK, only 33 per cent had a written equal opportunities policy, and only about 50 per cent translated information about the availability of services into minority languages.

Black and Asian groups appear to be significantly under-represented as clients of welfare agencies. In Birmingham, for example, a survey showed that, while the Asian population comprise approximately 30 per cent of the population, they form only 8 per cent of referrals.

### Children in care

Yet very high proportions of Britain's Afro-Caribbean children are taken into care. The CRE found in one study of a northern city that the figures in the mid-1980s were 20 per 1000 for White children, 24 per 1000 for Afro-Caribbean and a staggering 142 per 1000 for mixed-race children. Studies of London boroughs have indicated that over half the children in care are Black.

The reasons for entering care appear to be closely related to race. More Black children were referred to the child-care procedures of local authorities because of family relationships, marital difficulties, financial and material problems; while more White children were referred for delinquent behaviour and sexual abuse.

## Race and benefits

Under 1971 and 1988 legislation, immigrants must be able to prove that they have relatives already settled in the UK, they must have proof of accommodation and they must have sufficient finance for maintenance without 'recourse to public funds', if they wish to settle in the UK. One of the questions on the Income Support claim form asks for the date of arrival in the UK.

Under the Social Security Act 1986, the lower rate of benefit for single, childless people under 25 applies to groups who are particularly susceptible to youth unemployment. Although it is not discriminatory in intent, the effect of the legislation is to hit Afro-Caribbean and Asian youths disproportionately – they have much higher rates of unemployment.

The National Association of Citizens' Advice Bureaux pointed out in a study in 1991, that certain minority groups whose first language is not English may lose benefits. This is because some forms are printed only in English and often there is no one able to speak the appropriate language in social security offices.

## LANGUAGE AND THE ETHNIC MINORITIES

Three people were sitting in a room when another walked in and handed them each a form, which was written in a script they did not understand. A woman started speaking to them very loudly and repetitively in a language they didn't know. She was obviously asking them questions and telling them to fill in the answers on the form, but the three, helpless to reply, eventually started giggling and making embarrassed remarks to each other.

Section 20 of the Race Relations Act imposes a legal duty on all authorities to ensure that services are delivered without discrimination, and to promote equality of opportunity between different racial groups. Section 13 of the 1983 Mental Health Act states that people have to be interviewed "in an appropriate manner".

Marsha Sanders of the London Interpreting Project (LIP), which campaigns for good community interpreting services, explains: "People's access to services depends on their ability to communicate with the people working in them. Research has shown that linguistic minorities are greatly disadvantaged in terms of health care, social services, housing and education. Without an interpreter, workers often have to use relatives to translate. Children have been asked to translate in child abuse investigations or husbands in mental health cases where they may be part of the problem."

Being an effective public sector interpreter involves much more than being bilingual, Sanders stresses. "You have to have an understanding of statutory structures, a sensitivity and commitment to confidentiality and a high degree of accuracy."

**Source**: *Social Work Today*, 7 January 1993

1 Why is it important to have a person to interpret?
2 What problems are there with using unofficial interpreters?
3 What qualities are required to be an effective public sector interpreter?
4 What languages are available in your local Social Services department and your hospital?
5 Try this exercise. Two people from your group agree on a problematic situation of some kind. These two play the clients. One other person from the group, who does not know what the problem is, acts as a social worker.
   The clients must explain their problems to the social worker, who in turn must offer some advice. The only problem is that the clients are not to speak to the social worker but must communicate in gestures or in any way that does not involve using a mutual language.

Fear of creating problems, concern that any fuss might affect residence, the lack of translated information, and no recognition by the DSS of any responsibility to provide interpreters, have all created a climate in which black citizens are less likely to assert their rights, doubting their entitlement benefits.

**Source**: C. Oppenheim, *Poverty: The Facts* (Child Poverty Action Group, 1990)

1 Why are ethnic minority groups less likely to claim benefits?
2 How could these problems be solved?
3 Are these completely accurate criticisms? Look in the back pages of DSS leaflets concerning benefits – you can find these in any main post office.

## HOUSEHOLD STRUCTURES AND ETHNIC MINORITY GROUPS

### Households[1] with dependent children: by ethnic group of head, 1989 and 1991 average

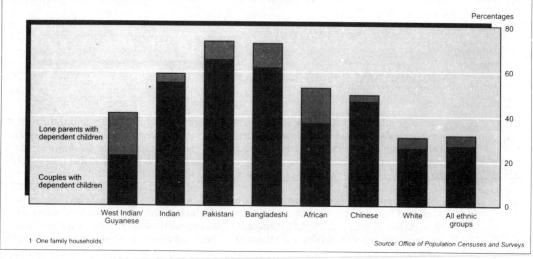

Great Britain

Source: Office of Population Censuses and Surveys

1 One family households.

**Source**: *Social Trends* (HMSO, 1993)

Lone-parent families are particularly vulnerable to poverty, low pay for women and expensive childcare provision, tending to keep lone parents on benefit.

**Source**: C. Oppenheim, *Poverty: The Facts* (Child Poverty Action Group, 1990)

**1** Summarise the differences in household composition between the various ethnic groups.
**2** Which group has the highest number of lone parents with dependent children?
**3** What is the significance of this for income and poverty?
**4** Which groups have the highest levels of dependent children? What implications are there for standards of living and housing?.

## Race and poverty

Poverty is indirectly related to race, in that members of the ethnic minority groups are more likely to be found in low paying occupations, to have higher levels of unemployment and, amongst Afro-Caribbeans, to have higher rates of lone-parent families, whilst Bangladeshi and Pakistani families tend to have higher than average numbers of children.

The low paid, large families, lone-parent households and the unemployed form virtually all the groups living in poverty. The only significant group in poverty amongst which ethnic minorities do not figure disproportionately is the elderly. This is because of the age structure of the ethnic minorities, which has relatively few elderly compared to the general population of the UK. This relative 'youth' is caused by the fact that only now are the first post-war immigrants moving into the elderly age bracket.

It is generally agreed that one of the major contributing factors to the high numbers of ethnic minorities in low paid occupations, or who are unemployed, is that of racism.

Every indicator of poverty shows that black people and other ethnic minority groups are more at risk of high unemployment, low pay, shift work and poor social security rights. Their poverty is caused by immigration policies which have often excluded people from abroad from access to welfare, employment patterns which have marginalised black people and other ethnic groups into low paid manual work, direct and indirect discrimination in social security and the broader experience of racism in society as a whole.

**Source**: C. Oppenheim, *Poverty: The Facts* (Child Poverty Action Group, 1990)

## The language of prejudice

### Racism
Racism is the belief that there are distinctive races, and that some of these races are superior to others.

### Racial prejudice
This is when people are liked or disliked solely because they belong to a particular ethnic group.

### Racialism or racial discrimination
Treating people unequally simply on the grounds of the perceived ethnic group to which they belong is racialism or racial discrimination.

### Discrimination
Treating people unequally on the basis of their inclusion in, or exclusion from, a particular category of people – such as religion, gender, race or physical and mental abilities – is discrimination.

### Explanations for racial prejudice
- **Stereotyping**  This occurs because many White people perceive Afro-Caribbeans and Asians, for example, as having negative characteristics – noisy, lazy, mean, etc. All the people sharing a similar skin, culture or religion are portrayed this way. Stereotyping allows people to treat the stereotyped group in a worse way without feeling guilty about it: 'Why should I give him the job? Everyone knows those people are lazy.' Stereotyped views amongst British people derive from our colonial past, when all non-Whites were regarded as inferior. Today, such views are usually based on ignorance, but stereotyping continues in jokes and in media images of ethnic minorities.
- **Scapegoating**  During periods of economic decline or social tension, people search for simple, clear answers to the problems facing them. Blaming an easily identifiable group, especially if it is powerless and can do little to challenge the way in which blame is placed upon them, is a common occurrence. When there is great prosperity, the powerless group may still be regarded as inferior, but social tensions are less. Scapegoating occurs particularly over scarce resources such as jobs, housing and education.

## Race and violence

One example of racism is the number of violent attacks on Afro-Caribbeans and Asians (with significantly more on Asians). In 1990, for example, there were 6359 recorded attacks in England and Wales.

There is concern that no one has yet been convicted for the murder of Panchadcharan Sahitharan, aged 28, a Tamil refugee.

"He was doing nothing more than making his way home, minding his own business," said the Crown counsel in the trial of the man who was cleared of murdering him last week. "The tragedy is he was in the wrong place at the wrong time."

Mr Sahitharan was one of a number of black people to suffer similar unprovoked assaults in the area, and his friends are bewildered that no one has been successfully prosecuted for the death.

Among other recent killings, that of Ruhullah Aramesh, aged 24, an Afghani refugee, occurred in July in Croydon, south

London, in circumstances described at the time as racial murder.

Richard Adams, whose son, Rolan, was killed in Thamesmead in 1991 after being attacked by a group of white youths, said: "A bill and a national mobilisation against racist attacks is urgently needed. It has to come mainly from black people. We need to be pro-active rather than reactive."

**Source**: The *Guardian*, 9 November 1992

## Race and housing

Throughout the 1980s, the CRE undertook a lengthy series of studies on race and housing, and found significant differences in the quality of housing tenure across ethnic groups.

West Indians and Asians are more likely to live in pre-1945 dwellings (60 per cent and 74 per cent respectively) than the white population (50 per cent). They are also twice as likely to live in the terraced property so commonly associated with inner city residence. Overcrowding remains housing provision.

In the 1980s then, the NCWP minorities still live in significantly worse quality housing and in poorer, less popular areas than the white British population. This holds both across and within tenures. Indeed, the high level of owner occupation amongst Asians (72 per cent as against 59 per cent of the general population) provides no guarantee of good housing . . . the

a particular problem amongst Asians (35 per cent live in overcrowded conditions compared to 3 per cent of whites) and, in recent years, homelessness has increased greatly . . . Black people may now have a bath and W.C., but they are also likely to be the casualties of other inequalities in prevailing trend in many cities over the last two decades has been one of growing residential segregation between NCWP minorities and whites, with the former becoming increasingly over-represented in the poorest areas. This is particularly true of the Asian population, whose potential for residential mixing has been reduced by their relative absence from council housing.

**Source**: D. Phillips, 'Searching for a decent home – ethnic minority progress in the post-war housing market', *New Community*, 14, 1987

1 Which group is most likely to live in pre-1945 dwellings?
2 How do we know from the housing type that this group is more likely to live in inner cities?
3 What are the relative rates of overcrowding for Whites and Asians?
4 Which group has the highest level of owner occupation?
5 Is it true to say that different ethnic groups are mixed, and live in the same residential areas?
6 Is your town mixed, in terms of the way different ethnic groups live together, or segregated? Most local authorities have some information on the ethnic mix of the various neighbourhoods. Approach your local authority, and explain clearly what you are doing. Ask them if they have the information and whether they would provide you with it.

Get a map of your town and mark the different groups and the areas they live in.

Approach representatives of the various local ethnic groups in your town. Interview them about their views on social services provision, health service provision and, if racial segregation in housing does exist, ask them for reasons as to why they think this is.

## Race, housing and local authorities

Traditionally, local authority housing stock has been the means by which the lowest paid could obtain accommodation. However, the 'right to buy' legislation (see page 71) has led to the sale of over one and a half million council houses. This has taken away the opportunity for the poorest in society to obtain housing, and as ethnic minority groups are over-represented amongst the poorest, they have been particularly hard hit. We should note especially the over-representation of Afro-Caribbeans amongst those in, or seeking, local authority accommodation.

In investigations by the CRE into the treatment of ethnic minorities, a wide number of councils were criticised. For example, in 1990, the London borough of Southwark was found to have given a disproportionate number of new properties, after an improvement scheme, to White tenants.

In 1988, the CRE found that the London borough of Tower Hamlets allocated poor accommodation (both housing and bed-and-breakfast accommodation) to Bangladeshis, and that Bangladeshis waited longer than other groups to be housed.

In a study of the two 'worst' estates in terms of the quality of housing, Asians were found to be over-represented by five times more than would be expected.

In Liverpool, the CRE found that Whites were twice as likely to get a house, four times more likely to get a new house, twice as likely to get a centrally-heated home, and four times as likely to get a garden.

### Race and housing associations

In order to combat the perceived problems faced by ethnic minority groups, the Federation of Black Housing Organisations was set up. This promotes the interests of Black and Asian communities to housing organisations and monitors the extent to which housing associations cater for Black and Asian tenants.

In the late 1980s, of 2600 housing associations, only 12 were controlled by ethnic minority groups. To promote greater participation of Black and Asian groups in the housing association movement, the Housing Corporation gives £100 000 per year. Equal opportunity policies are now required to be built in to all housing associations' activities.

In the Liverpool study mentioned earlier, which was undertaken in 1989, of 2000 nominations made by housing associations for local authority places, those nominations from Black housing associations were routinely given the poorest quality homes.

In the mid-1980s, of almost 1300 sheltered accommodation places for the elderly, only two were given to Afro-Caribbean or Asian households.

### Race and homelessness

Ethnic minority groups are four times more likely than White households to become homeless. Of the young homeless, a study of a number of London boroughs found that young Blacks were disproportionately represented. For example, in Newham (east London) over 50 per cent of referrals to hostels for the homeless were for Black single people.

---

### RACIAL HARASSMENT – THE REALITY

Mrs A is an Asian single parent with four children aged 11 months (twins), five years and eight years. She lived with her disabled uncle in a two storey council flat which she had moved into in 1983.

Mrs A and her family began to experience extreme racial harassment three months after moving into the flat. She had no friends or relatives in the borough and hers was the only black family in the block. The neighbours were openly hostile to her, slamming doors in her face, for example, and when the children went out to play they were verbally abused and physically assaulted. Sometimes they were tied to railings and left there. They even had their hands tied behind their backs and were put in the large communal dustbins and left there, their clothes having been removed first. The whole family were continually abused and chased on their way to shopping, etc. The children sometimes had their heads banged against walls by 10–14-year-old white youths. Mrs A and her twin babies were spat on when she asked them to stop.

During 1985 the harassment became very frequent. Mrs A's milk bottles were smashed and pushed through her letter box almost daily, her door was urinated on regularly, lighted material was put through the letter box on five occasions and eggs were frequently broken through the letter box. All the tyres of her car were slashed on one occasion and her windscreen wipers were broken. Eggs were also frequently broken over the car.

A group of white adult men, after drinking in a nearby pub, would abuse the family verbally and throw stones, bottles, etc at Mrs A's bedroom windows, sometimes until 1 am. They would also bang on her front door at these times and shout racist abuse.

Eventually, Mrs A's family were moved in February 1986 and experienced racial harassment in their new flat. Mrs A's condition deteriorated and she then applied for a mutual exchange and moved to another London borough.

Invite representatives of the local Asian or Afro-Caribbean community in to your college and find out if racial harassment is going on in your area. What can local housing authorities do about racial harassment? What can the police do about it? What can the local Asian/Afro-Caribbean communities do about it? Is there any role for Whites in combating racism in housing?

## Race and employment

Members of the ethnic minority groups are more likely to be unemployed and to be in lower paid occupations.

### UNEMPLOYMENT RATES

**Unemployment rates: by sex and ethnic origin, 1990 (Great Britain)**

|  | Percentages |
| --- | --- |
| **Males** | |
| White | 7 |
| West Indian or Guyanese | 13 |
| Indian | 8 |
| Pakistani/Bangladeshi | 15 |
| Other[1] | 12 |
| All males[2] | 7 |
| **Females** | |
| White | 6 |
| West Indian or Guyanese[3] | 14 |
| Indian | 11 |
| Pakistani/Bangladeshi | |
| Other[1] | 9 |
| All females[2] | 7 |

1 Which group of males has the highest unemployment rate?
2 Which group has the lowest?
3 Which group of females has the highest unemployment rate?
4 Which group has the lowest?
5 What clear statement can you make about race and unemployment?

[1] Includes those of mixed origins.
[2] Includes those who did not state their ethnic origin.
[3] 1989 figures.

**Source:** *Social Trends* (HMSO, 1992)

# Race relations legislation

### Race Relations Act 1976

This Act made it illegal to discriminate directly or indirectly in the provision of goods or services to the public or in the areas of employment and housing. It also became illegal to incite racial hatred.

The Community Relations Commission (CRC) was established to promote inter-racial harmony. The Race Relations Board (RRB) was formed to investigate complaints of racial discrimination.

### 1976

The Commission for Racial Equality (CRE) was set up to replace the CRC and the RRB, as it was felt they had been ineffective. The CRE was granted greater powers than the RRB.

The CRE can bring people to court for cases of both

- **direct discrimination** (for example, when a person is denied employment because she is Black); and
- **indirect discrimination** (where, for example, an organisation creates rules which apply to everyone, but the result of the rules is that certain ethnic groups are particularly disadvantaged).

### THE ROLE OF THE CRE

The CRE is funded by the Home Office. The Home Secretary appoints its commissioners from a wide range of ethnic groups and backgrounds. The CRE's job is to advise people who believe they have suffered racial discrimination. It also provides legal representation for them in a court or an industrial tribunal.

The CRE can take action on its own (against discriminatory advertisements, for example). It can investigate organisations where racial bias might have been acted upon. It can also advise employers, trade unions, health and local authorities about how to eliminate racial discrimination.

The CRE issues codes of practice on how to promote equality of opportunity and eliminate discrimination. Codes in employment and rented housing have received Parliamentary approval. They are not legally binding, but anyone who breaks them could be found liable in an industrial tribunal or court. The Commission for Racial Equality, with local authorities, also funds a network of Racial Equality Councils.

**Source**: CRE

1 Is the Commission for Racial Equality an official government organisation?
2 What activities does the CRE undertake?
3 Are all its activities legally enforceable? Please explain your answer.

# Gender

## Caring

Throughout this book we have seen the way in which the woman's role in the family is often that of carer. It is usually women who take on the role of looking after children, the elderly, the sick and the disabled. This is largely an unpaid role, but an essential one for the family members and for the wider society. If women did not do this caring, then the State would be forced into finding an alternative and expensive way of doing it.

However, in taking on the role of carer, women generally have to give up full-time employment during the period of their lives when they are bringing up children, for example. Women therefore become dependent on their husbands, their partners or the State.

**A**

Thus women continue to care for the young, the old and the dependent, mainly exempting men and state services from these tasks.... The price of such caring work is economic dependence. Looking after people is either done for no pay, within the family, or for low pay in the public sector.

**B**

> Where institutional or residential care is available, it is regarded as inferior precisely because it differs in conception so markedly from the family model of care. As a result, it is undervalued and often of low quality, and the staff who provide the care within it are badly paid, of low status, often unqualified – and usually women.

**C**

If the dependency of women cannot be wished away, neither can the dependency of most who are cared for. The dependency of elderly and handicapped people is more a traditional theme of social policy writing than the dependency of women. However, analysis which fails to recognize the connections between the two kinds of dependency is often less than illuminating. The care of most dependants has been the province of women, has belonged to the domestic arena, and has been unpaid. It thus made women dependent.

**Sources**: Extracts A and C from G. Pascall, *Social Policy: A Feminist Analysis* (Tavistock, 1986); extract B from G Daley, *New Society*, 28 August 1987.

## Income

Women form the single largest group of people in poverty. This is often hidden in the way the figures are presented, by dividing the poor into categories such as pensioners, those in full-time employment, single parents and the sick and disabled. However, all these categories are dominated by women. The only significant group in poverty which is not dominated by women is that of the unemployed. It is important to note, however, that the classification 'the unemployed' refers largely to males (and less often females) who are heads of households, and that the Income Support they receive is meant to support a family – which is highly likely to include a non-working woman. Once again, therefore, women are drawn into poverty.

### POVERTY

Graph A below shows the breakdown of the poor into the various categories, in proportion to their size. We therefore know from the graph who comprise the poor, and in what proportion.
   Graph B shows the proportion within each of the categories identified in graph A of people who live in poverty. Clearly, not every unemployed person is poor, nor is every sick or disabled person – so we need to know how many people within these groups actually are poor.

**A**

### Percentage of the population of Great Britain in poverty by vulnerable group, 1987

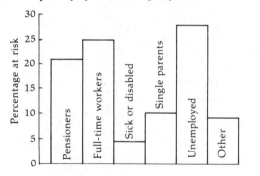

**B**

### Risk of poverty in Great Britain by economic status, 1987

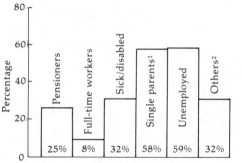

Proportion living in poverty
(below 50 per cent average income after housing costs)

**Notes**: ¹Single parents who are not in full-time work.
²Men aged 60–64, widows, students, people
temporarily away from work, carers, people
who are unemployed but not available for work.

Source: C. Oppenheim, *Poverty: The Facts* (Child Poverty Action Group, 1990)

Look at Graph A.
1 Which group comprises the single largest number of people in poverty?
2 Rank the groups in poverty in order of size, stating what percentage of the poor they form.
3 Explain why pensioners, people in full-time employment, the sick or disabled, and single parents are all likely to have particularly high proportions of women among them.
Look at Graph B.
4 What proportion of single parents are likely to be in poverty?
5 What proportion of the sick and disabled are likely to be in poverty?
6 What proportion of full-time workers are likely to be in poverty?
Both graphs.
7 Look back at the section on race and poverty. What relationship, if any, can you see between the groups in that category and the figures presented here.

## EARNINGS

### Gross weekly earnings of full-time employees: by sex and type of employment, 1990

| | Males | Females |
|---|---|---|
| **Manual employees** | | |
| Mean (£) | 237.2 | 148.0 |
| Median (£) | 221.3 | 137.3 |
| **Non-manual employees** | | |
| Mean (£) | 354.9 | 215.5 |
| Median (£) | 312.1 | 191.8 |

Source: *Social Trends* (HMSO, 1992)

1 What do we mean by the mean and the median?
2 What is the relationship between male and female wages?
3 Approximately what is the relative percentage wage of women compared to that of men for (a) manual and (b) non-manual employees?
4 If you were asked to suggest just two measures to lessen poverty in the UK, decide, as a group, what they would be. Could these realistically be achieved?
5 Look in Social Trends (HMSO) for the current differences. What are they?

## Women and employment

Women are less likely than men to be in full-time employment, and are more likely to have lower-paid, less secure positions. They are also less likely to be found in the senior positions in employment. This is just as true for areas of employment which are traditionally associated with women, such as nursing or social work.

## Reasons for taking a part-time[1] job: by sex and marital status, Spring 1992

| United Kingdom | | Percentages and thousands | | |
| --- | --- | --- | --- | --- |
| | | Females | | |
| | Males | Married | Non-married | All females |
| **Reasons for taking part-time job** | | | | |
| *(percentages)* | | | | |
| *Student/still* | | | | |
| *at school* | 32.8 | 0.4 | 31.1 | 7.1 |
| *Ill or disabled* | 3.4 | 1.2 | 1.7 | 1.3 |
| *Could not find a* | | | | |
| *full-time job* | 22.4 | 6.5 | 17.0 | 8.8 |
| *Did not want a* | | | | |
| *full-time job* | 40.7 | 91.7 | 50.0 | 82.6 |
| | | | | |
| **Part-time workers[2]** | | | | |
| **(=100%) (thousands)** | 885 | 3,972 | 1,109 | 5,081 |

1 Part-time is based on respondent's self assessment.
2 Includes those who did not state the reason for taking a part-time job.

*Source: Labour Force Survey, Employment Department*
**Source**: *Social Trends* (HMSO, 1993)

## Economic inactivity: by sex and reason for inactivity, Great Britain, 1990

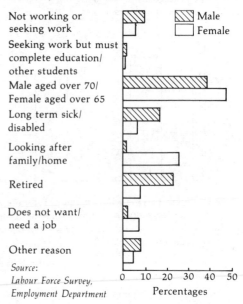

*Source:*
*Labour Force Survey,*
*Employment Department*

**Source**: *Social Trends* (HMSO, 1992)

**1** Why do women take part-time employment, according to the table? Could you give reasons for this?
**2** Why are women more likely to be economically inactive, according to the bar graph?
**3** What are the likely implications for women's lives of the information given here?

## WOMEN IN THE NHS

The commission found that although women make up nearly 80 per cent of the NHS workforce, they make up just 17 per cent of unit general managers, 4 per cent of district and regional general managers and just 1 per cent of consultant general surgeons.

Thirty-seven per cent of women work part time in the NHS compared to 2.3 per cent of men, and part-time opportunities are concentrated in both the low paid jobs and lower graded posts.

Female dominated professions within the NHS are lower paid than the male dominated groups, and women from black and ethnic minority groups, or women who are disabled, are further disadvantaged.

**Source**: 'Putting Gender on the Management Executive', *The Health Service Journal*, 15 August 1991

The NHS may be wasting more than £1bn worth of talent each year because it largely fails to cater for women employees that wish to combine work with parenthood, the Equal Opportunities Commission said yesterday.

Although the health service, with a million female staff, is the largest employer of women in Western Europe, it pays only lip service to equal opportunity ideals, the commission said in the first comprehensive nation-wide survey of women's employment in the NHS.

Some 93 per cent of health authorities said they had equal opportunity policies, but one-third had not communicated them to staff and three-quarters did not monitor the impact of the policies.

The Commission ... discovered that one-fifth of authorities included potentially unlawful questions on job application forms.

Many asked for detailed information about family responsibilities and about any children the applicant had.

> Only 50 per cent of authorities offered training opportunities to those in part-time work, with the result that most women remained at or near the bottom rung of the career ladder.

**Source**: The *Guardian*, 2 August 1992

1 What proportion of those employed by the NHS are women?
2 What proportions of senior positions do they hold?
3 Are there any other groups which are similarly disadvantaged?
4 What is the estimated cost to the NHS of the waste of female talent?
5 Do the extracts suggest that equal opportunities policies actually work?
6 What suggestions could you make for ensuring equality of women in the NHS?

## Women and housing

The single biggest obstacle for women to overcome in obtaining decent housing, if they are single or separated, is that of income. Access to a mortgage relies on an adequate income to repay the loan. As we have just seen, women are far more likely than men to be living in poverty, or to have a low wage.

Single women are often, therefore, priced out of the private housing market and are not a priority in the local authority sector. Only 11 per cent of households headed by a woman can afford to purchase a house through a mortgage, compared to 43 per cent of male-headed households; and 42 per cent of female-headed households are local authority tenants, compared to 25 per cent of those headed by a man.

According to a number of reports, both on housing and the state of lone-parent families, the main problem, after finance, was that of poor standards of housing. Although single parents are a priority group for housing by local authorities, the reality is that shortage of funds for building new homes means that single mothers are likely to be placed in Bed-and-Breakfast accommodation (see page 83).

Housing has further significance for women. As it is often so difficult for women to obtain housing, they can be forced into a dependence on men in situations which are physically or emotionally difficult. One study showed that the main reason why women delayed leaving violent partners was fear of homelessness. At present, over 45 per cent of women whose marriages break up have their housing needs met through the public sector or through housing associations.

## Women and social security

Critics of the social security system have constantly claimed that it fails to meet the needs of women. The system was originally designed in the 1940s on the assumption that women would marry, have children and stay at home to care for them, while the male was the breadwinner. Pensions, unemployment benefit, Income Support (as it is now called) and disability benefits were all based on this pattern. However, the changing nature of society, of the family and, in particular, of the role of women has left this model outdated, and discriminatory against women.

During the 1980s, strong attacks on the system of benefits led to some changes, but the system still fails to recognise adequately the situation of women.

### Failures of the system

The following are just some examples of how the social security system today can disadvantage women.

- Women in part-time employment are not entitled to benefits to cover loss of earnings through sickness or unemployment. Yet it is because of domestic commitments that many women are forced into part-time work.
- Maternity benefits are minimal, paid only at the level of sickness benefit. This fails to recognise the economic and social costs to mothers.
- Women who are unable to provide evidence that they are *immediately* available for work are at risk of losing their Unemployment Benefit. This ignores the fact that women may not be immediately available because of having to make child-care arrangements.
- As we have seen earlier, women are more likely to be in part-time employment because of family responsibilities, even if they would prefer full-time employment. This can mean that women fall between two types of benefit – the one designed for those out of work, the other designed for those in low paid employment.
- **Income Support** assumes that claimants are not working, and any earnings above a certain minimal level are deducted from the benefit. This penalises women who wish to work part-time.
- **Family Credit** is designed to boost the income of people in low paid employment who are working more than 16 hours each week. Yet for many women this threshold of hours of work is too high, so that they are ineligible to claim this benefit. Therefore, a woman working 12 hours a week would find it better to give up work and rely solely on Income Support. (If she claimed Income Support, whilst continuing to work, she would lose benefit for the hours worked, and she would not be able to claim Family Credit as she would be below the minimum hours threshold.)

## FAMILY CREDIT

 **WHAT IS FAMILY CREDIT?**

Family Credit is a regular tax-free cash payment for working people with children.

The amount that you can get depends on the number of children you have, how old they are and how much money is coming into your home at the time you claim.

 **WHO IS IT FOR?**

Family Credit is for people who are working for 16 hours or more a week and who have at least one child.

It's for self-employed people as well as people who have an employer.

It's for lone parents as well as couples.

**Some more facts about Family Credit**

- It's not a loan - you don't have to pay it back.

- It lasts for 26 weeks at a time - so it can add up to a worthwhile sum. And the payments stay the same even if earnings go up during that time.

- You can choose how the money is paid

  - into your bank or building society account

  - with a book that you cash at the post office.

While you get Family Credit you and your family can also get free NHS prescriptions, dental treatment and sight tests, and help with the cost of glasses.

Sixteen per cent of female employees work for 15 hours per week or less, compared to 2.7 per cent of male employees, and 21 per cent of self-employed women work for 15 hours per week or less, compared to 3 per cent of self-employed men.

The extract (left) is a copy of some of the information given in the Family Credit Claim Pack. It accompanies the Claim Form which needs to be completed to obtain Family Credit.

What implications are there regarding women?

# Women and the health services

Women's experiences of health and health care are related to their positions in society. The main influences on women's health include:
- poverty and deprivation;
- wider material conditions, such as urban deprivation and poor housing;
- their greater length of life, which means that they are more likely to suffer from chronic illness and disability;
- their role as carers, in both paid and unpaid capacities.

## WOMEN AND HEALTH

...While women live longer, they report more illness, acute and chronic than men....The rate of long-standing illness reported by women in the lowest socio-economic group is more than twice that of women in the highest group. Among women in households at the bottom of the social scale, nearly half are suffering from a long-standing illness. It is estimated that two-thirds of the 4 million disabled people in the UK are women.

More women than men are admitted each year to mental hospitals...women predominate among those...suffering from neurotic and depressive disorders.

...Women, and working-class women in particular, tend to normalise and accommodate symptoms, stressing the importance of keeping going and coping with suffering.

Because of the greater time that women spend in the home, housing conditions have been found to be a more important influence on women's than on men's health. Overcrowding, dampness, and high rise housing have all been linked to health problems in women and the children they care for.

**Source**: H. Graham, 'Women, Health and Illness', *Social Studies Review*, September 1987

## WOMEN AND CARING

While the exact numbers are unknown, the composition of this vast army of carers is easy to gauge. We know that 'care by/in the community' almost always means care by/in the family, with little support from outside. We also know that family care is a myth: one person tends to be identified as the main carer and, once identified, other relatives withdraw. In the vast majority of cases, the principal carer is a woman and a relative of the dependent person. Thus it is wives, daughters and daughters-in-law who are in the main carers for adults with physical disabilities and illnesses and for the dependent elderly. (Estimates suggest that 75 per cent of these carers are women.) It is mothers who should bear the burden of responsibility for caring for children with disabilities or chronic illnesses. (Surveys put the figure at nearly 100 per cent.) Similarly, mothers are the principal carers to mentally handicapped adults living at home: surveys suggest a figure of 80 per cent.

**Source**: H. Graham, 'Women, Health and Illness', *Social Studies Review*, September 1987

1 Who are the carers in society?
2 What are the implications for their lives?
3 Through a voluntary organisation (such as Crossroads or the Alzheimer's Society) or your local Social Services department, arrange an interview with some carers. Try to gain a picture of their lives. What services would they like? What services are provided?

## Legislation regarding equal pay and equal rights

### The Equal Pay Act 1970

This came into effect in 1975, and stated that where women and men are doing the same or broadly similar work, they have to be paid the same.

### The Sex Discrimination Act 1975

This made it unlawful to treat anyone less favourably on the grounds of sex. This included advertising for the vacant posts.

Secondly, it set up the Equal Opportunities Commission (EOC), which has a variety of tasks. These include:

- investigating cases of apparent or alleged violation of equal opportunities;
- issuing non-discrimination notices which request employers or organisations to stop certain discriminatory practices. If these are not complied with, the EOC may take the employers or organisations to court;
- reviewing the workings of the Sex Discrimination Act itself.

### The Legal Aid Act 1974

This provided small amounts of legal aid to assist women in their preparations and representations before an industrial tribunal.

# Assignment

You have been the victim of what you consider to be discrimination on the grounds of gender, but you did not know where to turn, at the time, for help. You have decided that you would not want anyone else to be in a similar situation. You therefore decide to find out exactly what the official process is when a person suspects they are being discriminated against.

You decide to construct a clear, step-by-step guide for women explaining the procedure they must follow when they make their complaint. The idea is that the guide will be given to all female employees by their employers.

The guide should also explain the law and the growing importance of Europe. Just to underline your point, you also wish to include in your guide some evidence of the way in which women are disadvantaged in British society.

(If you wish, you can do this assignment using the issue of racial discrimination.)

# CHAPTER 14

# People with Physical Disabilities

## Introduction

This chapter explores social and welfare issues relating to people with physical disabilities. We begin the chapter by examining the numbers of people in Britain with some form of disability – most people are surprised at the huge numbers. We then move on to examine definitions of disability and handicap, as many find these terms confusing.

Having clarified these issues, we need to examine the various changes in legislation that have been passed and which are intended to benefit those with disabilities. Considering the numbers of people concerned, the legislation is surprisingly small and limited.

The following section examines the range of services available for the disabled, both those provided by voluntary organisations and by the State. This is followed by a look at two particular facets of disability which are often overlooked – first that the majority of those with disability are elderly (and, incidentally, female) and secondly that disability and poverty are inseparable. Following this is a detailed examination of the social security benefits available for people with disabilities.

The chapter finishes with an examination of the problem that faces all people with disabilities, physical or mental – that of stigma. A person with a disability is rarely treated as an *individual* who has a disability, usually they are treated as a disabled person, with the overriding stress on their disability.

**1** Can you guess what disability the young man in the photo has? (Turn to page 293 for the answer.)

**Source**: RNID
'My disability is easy to overlook.'

2 What image is conjured up in your mind when you think of the term 'people with disabilities'?

3 Does the young man in the photo conform to the stereotype?

4 Do you think that the name and the image have any importance at all for the way we treat people with disabilities?

# The extent of disability in Britain

In 1988, six million adults experienced some form of disability. The figure is not entirely accurate, because it is difficult to define exactly what 'disability' means.

**The percentage of men and women who are disabled at different ages according to the severity of their disabilities**

| Sex and age | Low severity | Medium severity | High severity | Number |
|---|---|---|---|---|
| Men | | | | |
| 16–59 | 63 | 19 | 18 | 905 000 |
| 60–74 | 69 | 15 | 16 | 1 014 000 |
| 75+ | 53 | 19 | 28 | 627 000 |
| Women | | | | |
| 16–59 | 57 | 23 | 20 | 1 024 000 |
| 60–74 | 60 | 21 | 19 | 1 141 000 |
| 75+ | 41 | 23 | 36 | 1 492 000 |
| *n* = | 3 490 000 | 1 255 000 | 1 458 000 | 6 203 000 |

**Source**: J. Martin, H. Meltzer and D. Elliot, *The Prevalence of Disability Amongst Adults* (HMSO, 1988)

1 Which sex has the greater number of disabled?

2 What age group has the highest percentage of people with high severity level of disability? What are the appropriate figures for each sex?

3 Which age group has the lowest levels of people with high severity disabilities? Have you any explanation for this?

4 Bearing in mind the different ranges of ages combined together to form the three age groups used in the table (16–59, 60–74 and 75+), which age group do you think has the highest proportion of disabled people in proportion to the total number in that age group in Britain?

# Defining disability

In defining disability, we need to be familiar with certain frequently used terms.

- **Impairment** means 'lacking all or part of a limb, or having a defective limb, organ or mechanism of the body'. This term is used to describe the physical state of a person.
- **Disablement** means 'the loss or reduction of functional ability'. This term is used to describe the lack or loss of ability to perform actions.
- **Handicap** means 'the disadvantage or restriction of activity considered normal, for a particular age, and in a particular culture, caused by the disablement'. This refers to the *result* of the disablement for a person's life.

Explain in your own words the meaning of the terms impairment, disablement and handicap, and give examples of each.

'Deviancy is always in the eye of the beholder. What is normal or acceptable in one context or for one group of people is abnormal or wrong in another context. Sitting at a table having a meal or a drink with someone in a wheelchair is OK, but what about getting up to dance with them? You dancing normally, while they are enjoying expressing themselves by moving themselves around in their wheelchairs?'

*This quotation helps us to understand the difference between disability and handicap. How does it do so?*

A major issue in the delivery of services to the disabled is the exact definition of when a person can be considered disabled. For most people, disability is associated with a wheelchair, yet only 200 000 of the six million disabled use a wheelchair. The government tends to use a medical definition based on the extent to which a person can use their limbs or organs, but this is only one of a number of possible definitions. Townsend, for example, has grouped definitions into five categories.

1 Anatomical, physiological or psychological abnormality or loss (for example, the loss of a limb).

2 A clinical condition – disease or illness which interrupts physical or psychological processes (for example, arthritis or schizophrenia).

3 Functional limitations on everyday living – this definition relates the meaning of disability to such factors as age. For example, it is quite normal for elderly people to be unable to perform a number of activities which are normal for younger people, so is this disability or the normal results of ageing?

4 Disability behaviour – this refers to the fact that the physical aspect of disability is only part of the definition. People with similar disabilities may respond (and be responded to) in very different ways. The physical disability interacts with a person's motivation to produce the behaviour of being 'disabled' or not.

5 Social definition – here Townsend says that what most disabled people have in common is that they are poor, as they are excluded from the better paid jobs and even from employment. To this, we could add that disabled people suffer from discrimination and stigma.

## DISABLED MYTHS

PHYSICAL DISABILITY is not one problem, but a wide range of problems of different kinds. It includes people who have lost limbs, who are blind or deaf, who have difficulty moving or walking, who are unable to sustain physical effort for any length of time, and so on. . . .

The treatment of disability as if it was a single problem may mean that disabled people receive insufficient or inappropriate assistance. One of the first things to appreciate is that *most disabled people in Britain are old*. Not only are elderly people overall in the majority, with more than a third of people over 75 suffering from some kind of impairment, but they are vastly in the majority when the most serious disabilities are focused on. Relatively few chronically sick or disabled people are under 50. Despite this, provision for the disabled is often concentrated on *young* disabled people, or at least people of working age.

Sheltered workshops and employment quotas have little relevance to most disabled people, as do special schools. . . .

A second myth is that disabled people are likely to be in wheelchairs – an image encouraged by the symbol used on 'disabled' stickers. But there are probably less than 200,000 wheelchair users in the country, out of some 3 to 7 million disabled people, depending which estimate you use. And measures which are suitable for some disabled people are not necessarily appropriate for others. A public building with a large, flat floor (like Euston station) is fine for people in wheelchairs, but a nightmare for blind people, who often prefer stairs or solid physical obstacles which make it easier for them to orient themselves. A kitchen with a low sink and cupboard is useful for some wheelchair users but may be a nuisance for anyone who has problems bending – a common complaint in 'mobility' housing. The most common cause of disability is probably arthritis, which usually limits mobility in a different way to a wheelchair.

Thirdly, there is a tendency to rely on medical evidence of

disability. But functional problems are often more important than medical ones. The assessment of a social worker or occupational therapist may be far more relevant than a doctor's.

Another common misconception is that, because the cause of disability is physical, so is the solution. The problems that disabled people have in common are not so much their physical capacities, which are often very different, but limitations on their life style. Income tends to be low –

partly because many disabled people are old and female, partly because they may have special income needs, and because long-term sickness late in someone's working life undermines financial security as they grow older. Socially, disabled people may become isolated, as their health declines, they struggle to manage on the resources they have, they have difficulties in visiting people, and other people find it difficult to come to terms with the disability.

**Source**: P. Spicker, 'Disabled Myths', *Housing*, March 1986

1 Are we accurate in our use of the term 'the disabled'?

2 In what ways does this term cause difficulties in the provision of services for those with disabilities?

3 Which group accounts for the majority of disabled people? On which group, according to Spicker, is most provision centred? Do you agree with this focusing of provision? Explain why you agree or disagree.

4 What proportion of disabled people are wheelchair users?

5 Dr Spicker refers to medical and functional issues regarding disability. Explain what is meant by these two terms and the importance of the differences between them.

6 Disability has other social effects on people – what are these and what role can the State or the voluntary/social services play?

7 Ask a sample of 20 people to define what is meant by a 'disabled person' and ask them to give one example of such a person. The majority will probably talk about people in wheelchairs or with mobility problems. Ask them to name two other groups of 'disabled people' – the majority may well have difficulty thinking of any other group.

What are the implications for people with disabilities of the fact that most people think 'disability equals wheelchair'? Make a list of issues.

How could the stereotype be changed? What good, if any, would it achieve?

# Legislation

### The Disabled Persons (Employment) Act 1944

This requires employers of certain sized companies to employ a 'quota' of disabled employees. For companies employing more than 20 people, the quota is 3 per cent. The Act also requires the Secretary of State for Employment to:

- reserve certain kinds of work for those with a disability – this has resulted in the work of car park attendants and lift attendants being reserved for those registered as disabled!
- provide sheltered employment to severely disabled people – the best known company of this type is Remploy;

- provide vocational training – this is usually provided by the local authorities Personal Social Services departments or through the Department of Employment's Employment Rehabilitation Centres.

### The National Assistance Act 1948

This Act obliged local authorities to provide suitable accommodation for all those people who had need of shelter because of age or infirmity. Social Services departments were not obliged to provide the accommodation themselves, although they generally did; they also supervised private and voluntary homes.

### The Chronically Sick and Disabled Persons Act 1970

This was the Act that created a range of responsibilities for local authorities, at the time of their reorganisation following the Seebohm Report (see page 127). The new departments were required to keep a register of the disabled in each area, and had a legal duty to provide a range of services for those who were defined as in need (not everyone on the register falls into this category). These services include:

- adaptations to property to enable people to be mobile in the home, or at least to be able to undertake a range of normal household activities. Adaptations could include such things as chair lifts to enable the disabled to go up and down the stairs. Assessing and arranging for 'aids' is undertaken by occupational therapists employed by the local authorities;
- recreational and certain educational facilities. This includes a wide range of activities and services, including holidays, provision of radio and TV facilities, recreation in day centres, etc.;
- provision of meals.

### The Disabled Persons (Services, Consultation and Representation) Act 1986

This Act was designed to give people with disabilities a greater say in the decisions taken regarding them. The Act provided those with disabilities with four basic rights – to assessment, to information, to consultation and to representation. The Act gives a person with disabilities the right to have an 'advocate' (a social worker, for example) to be present at all meetings and in all procedures where their needs are being assessed. Furthermore, the Act requires that authorities must consult with organisations representing disabled people in policy decisions.

### The National Health Service and Community Care Act 1990

This Act placed the requirement on local authorities to appoint a care manager to draw up individual care plans for disabled people in the community and to ensure that the plans were carried out. Funding for this was to come from the government through grants and from local authority funding; where appropriate, additional funding would be provided by the NHS.

# Services for the disabled

There are a large number of services provided for those with disabilities. The main problem is one of fragmentation and lack of co-ordination.

## Educational services

Whenever possible children with disabilities are taught in ordinary schools and are fully integrated. If this is regarded as inappropriate for the individual because of severe physical or mental disability, then special schools, hospital teaching or even home visits by trained teachers are provided. During the school-age period of their lives, those with disabilities are the responsibility of the Department of Education; after they leave school, the responsibility for their further training (if not in higher education) returns to the local authority.

## Medical services

Medical treatment is free under the NHS, and there is a wide range of specialist services provided for particular disabilities – for example, physiotherapists, occupational therapists and speech therapists. People with severe disability may also receive visits from community nurses and/or practice nurses (who work directly for GPs).

1 What do the following people do:
- Physiotherapists?
- Occupational therapists?
- Speech therapists?
2 What different functions do they provide? Find out, by contacting your social services and your local health services, how a person goes about obtaining these services.

## Mobility schemes

- For those without certain limbs, there is the Disablement Services Authority which provides artificial legs and arms.
- For those who need transport, the Department of Health provides wheelchairs.
- For those who wish to travel longer distances, the Mobility part of the Disability Living Allowance enables some of those with disabilities to put additional State benefit towards the purchase of a car.
- The government also helps to organise, in conjunction with the motor car manufacturers, a charity known as Motability, which provides discounts for those with disabilities on leasing or credit purchase of cars.

### Orange badges
Local authorities also issue orange disabled stickers for cars to enable those with disabilities to park in certain restricted areas. About 5 per cent of cars carry these badges.

## Employment

The relevant elements of the 1944 Act described above apply here. Basically, certain jobs are reserved for people with disabilities and employers are required to employ a small number of disabled people.

## Lobbying

Social services and voluntary organisations for particular disabled groups provide a wide range of specialist services. However, more importantly, the various specialist organisations 'lobby' the decision-makers at both local and central government and in the media to achieve benefits for their members. (For more details on lobbying and pressure group activity, please see pages 11–12.) One of the most influential and active pressure groups is the Independent Living Movement, which derived from the example set by the USA.

## MOTABILITY

## MOTABILITY

IF YOU ARE IN RECEIPT OF A DISABILITY LIVING ALLOWANCE OR MOBILITY ALLOWANCE, THEN CALL IN AND SEE US ABOUT A NEW VAUXHALL CAR NOW

We can give friendly, helpful advice and help select the best scheme for you.

HOME VISITS AT YOUR CONVENIENCE

We are the Vauxhall registered dealer for the area

### Jessops
**Moulton Road, Eastcliff-on-Sea**
**Tel: Westend (0712) 343344**

Source: Adapted from advertisement by Jessups, Westcliff-on-Sea, Essex

Go to local car showrooms and ask them about the Motability scheme. Get as much information as you can.

Prepare a clear brochure for local people with disabilities explaining the scheme and listing its advantages and defects. Include in your brochure examples of prices. Do not forget to include running costs, including insurance (do people with disabilities obtain a discount for their insurance?), tax, etc.

What services do the AA and RAC offer to those with disabilities? Why is this especially important? What discounts do they offer?

Given the financial position of the majority of people with disabilities, do you think the Motability scheme is of great use? Ask a local dealer just how many people with disabilities use the scheme.

The dealer may be unwilling, but ask if he/she would contact someone who has used the scheme in order for you to interview them to examine how the scheme could be improved. If the dealer agrees, arrange to interview the person.

## DISABILITY IN THE USA – DIRECT ACTION

**Disabled people abandoned their wheelchairs at the foot of the steps, hauling themselves up to the Capitol in a powerful symbol of exclusion**

As Britain toys with the idea of outlawing discrimination against disabled people, many eyes are turning to the USA, where anti-discrimination legislation is already on the statute books. . . .

The Americans with Disabilities Act 1990 marked a watershed in the treatment of disabled people in America. . . .

The Act made good economic sense: 'Not a hand out but a hand up'; an incentive to self-help, in the best interests of the American ideal and the best traditions of the USA.

'There is not one nickel of a handout . . . not one dollar of a giveaway'. . . .

Why? Because the Act is about civil rights, and enabling disabled people to compete with able-bodied people in getting access to education and jobs, so they are able to pay their own way in society, no longer

dependent on benefits, or housed unhappily and at great cost in inappropriate institutions. Disabled people will be one step closer to living in their own homes, paying taxes and contributing to the community to which they belong.

These are salutary thoughts for policy-makers in the UK as anxiety grows about a shrinking adult workforce in the future. Anti-discrimination legislation breaks down barriers and lowers 'the ramp of opportunity' for all.

There was plenty to excite and inspire at the TASH conference, a huge annual get-together of families, practitioners, and people with severe disabilities united by a determination to create a society of integration, not exclusion, and to inform and educate.

Hank Bersani, in his workshop on empowerment, showered the participants with a confetti of tips on how to use the political system and the media to gain a better deal for disabled people and their families, based on his own experiences in

Oregon.... For instance,... people with learning difficulties using communication boards, or making simple but powerful statements to their elected representatives about threatened cuts in supported employment. 'I put clothes on clothes hangers in the department store. Nobody puts clothes on clothes hangers better than me. I don't want to lose my job. What are you going to do about it?' ... They handed out school photographs of children with disabilities, with names and phone numbers on the back: 'Here's my son Bret. Make sure you think of him in the debate on the budget.'

A retired father and his disabled son fighting for a better deal visited 88 of their 90 legislators and then got the local press to do a story on their case and the two who had not bothered to meet them....

**Source**: L. Ward, 'Opportunity Knocks', *Community Care*, 18 June 1992

1 What is the title of the Act referred to in the text?
2 Why do you think it has that particular title?
3 What are the aims of the Act?
4 Why is it 'not a hand out, but a hand up'? How does this differ from many British approaches to disability?
5 The article refers to activities by pressure groups to gain or retain rights for people with disabilities – is this done in Britain?
6 In the late 1980s, some people who had mobility problems tried direct action against London buses, arguing that they had rights to public transport like anyone else. Try some detective work – can you track down information about the protests, and even find some of the campaigners?
7 What facilities for disabled people are available from your local transport organisations, including railways?
8 How do groups which represent people with disabilities campaign in Britain?

## Residential services

Both the NHS and local authorities provide residential accommodation for the disabled. In the last ten years there has been a strong movement towards community care, but for those with disabilities which prevent them from living in the community there is still a continuing need for the provision of residential accommodation. Most people accept this continuing need, but a debate exists over the best and most appropriate type of provision. For example, more than half the physically disabled adults between the ages of 16 and 65 live in geriatric wards of hospitals or in community homes for the elderly. This is despite the fact that the Chronically Sick and Disabled Persons Act 1970 ruled that those in hospitals for long-term care should not be placed in wards or units with those who were elderly or 'prematurely aged' (that is they had dementia of some kind).

Since the 1960s, there has been a development in the provision of special young disabled units (YDUs), which provide accommodation for disabled people of working age.

## Local authority and voluntary organisations services

Services under this heading include Meals on Wheels, home helps, social work advice and counselling, telephones, recreation, day centres, holidays, occupational therapy, etc.

# Age and disability

Although we mentioned earlier that too many young people with disabilities are placed in homes for the elderly, the fact remains that the overwhelming majority of the disabled are, in fact, elderly. Of the estimated six million disabled, approximately four million are over retirement age. The most seriously disabled are also predominantly drawn from the elderly.

However, the fact that the majority of the disabled are elderly does not seem to have been a major factor in determining benefits and services. The social security benefits available are generally targeted at the younger disabled (for example, Disability Living Allowance, Severe Disablement Allowance and Invalidity Benefit). Employment programmes and training schemes have no relevance for the elderly. Instead, the elderly disabled are seen simply as part of the elderly population and receive the same services – home helps, day centres – that the 'normal' elderly receive.

# Poverty and disability

Earlier we gave different definitions of disability, but concluded that the majority of the disabled could be categorised in one group in the sense that they all share one quality – they are poor. A study by Layard of poverty and disability found that over half of all families in which the male partner was disabled were living in poverty. Why is this so?

- The elderly disabled are likely to be receiving old age pensions, and the extra State benefit they are eligible to receive (Attendance Allowance) does not cover the extra costs of disability.
- Disabled people of working age are more likely than the able-bodied to be unemployed. An OPCS (Office of Population Censuses and Surveys) study in 1988 found that people of working age with disabilities are half as likely to be working as able-bodied people.
- Disabled people who are in employment are likely to be in low paid work. On average, the earnings of males with disabilities are slightly less than 80 per cent of the average male wage in Britain. The situation for disabled women is even worse, given the differences in earnings between males and females in employment in Britain. Certain jobs are reserved for the disabled under the 1944 Act, but, as we saw earlier, car park and lift attendants cannot be considered as high-paying, career-oriented jobs!

Christine Saltmarshe saves the state several hundred pounds a week by choosing to look after her severely disabled daughter at home, rather than put her into residential care. In return, the state has cut the value of the family's social security payments by freezing the weekly income support to Annabel, her 20-year-old daughter, for the last four years.

"It seems so unfair," said Mrs Saltmarshe, who lives with her family in Huntingdon, Cambridgeshire, and is herself on income support. "It's hard to make ends meet, let alone see that Annabel gets some pleasure out of life."

Annabel has a weekly benefit income of £136. Of this, £70.43 comes from mobility allowance and disability premium, and these are uprated annually in line with inflation. But the remainder, £65.57 in income support and transitional addition, is the same as the supplementary benefit that preceded the 1988 legislation. [That £65.57 would have risen to £83.15 in 1992 if it had not been frozen]...

Annabel was brain-damaged at birth and is wheelchair-bound and totally dependent on others to meet her needs. She requires a special diet to control her epilepsy so as to lessen her dependence on drugs. "It's a high-protein diet that was prepared for Annabel by the Great Ormond Street hospital [in London]," her mother said. "Her food alone adds up to about £45 a week.

"Then, because Annabel is incontinent, that generates quite a lot of extra washing and drying. The lack of money means all sorts of things don't get done. My house is worth £10,000 less than my neighbour's because I can't afford to keep up with repairs."

Among Annabel's few enjoyments are her Riding for the Disabled sessions, and listening to music....

The government's position, meanwhile, remains as it was set out by John Major, her MP, in a letter to the family last December. The Prime Minister, who was the social security minister responsible for steering the 1988 legislation through the Commons, wrote to Mrs Saltmarshe, regretting that he could offer no solution to the "real difficulties" she faced.

He went on: "It has not been possible to identify a means whereby Annabel and other severely disabled people, with large dietary costs, can be given further help without at the same time providing an uncovenanted benefit, at very large cost, to people whose financial circumstances would not warrant it."

Source: The *Independent*, 28 August 1992

1 How does Christine Saltmarshe help the State to save money?
2 What is the total amount of the benefits that her daughter receives?
3 What difference would it have made if her benefits had not been frozen at the 1988 rates?
4 Some people argue that those with disabilities need higher than average incomes to pay for problems associated with their disabilities. How does this extract illustrate the point?
5 Can you explain in ordinary English what the Prime Minister's letter to Christine Saltmarshe means?

# Benefits and disability

## A brief history of benefits

### Poor Law Act 1601
This was the very first Act concerning those with disabilities, and it required the local authorities of the time (the parishes) to provide support for the elderly, the poor and the sick.

### Workman's Compensation Act 1897
Under this Act, payments were introduced for certain categories of workers injured at work.

### National Insurance Act 1911
Once again, this Act covered for sickness or for injuries resulting from employment. It did not cover those born with disability, nor those who had not subscribed to the National Insurance scheme as a result of unemployment.

### National Health Service Act 1946
This provided for free treatment and, where possible, rehabilitation.

### National Insurance Act 1946
This provided weekly benefits for the disabled.

### National Insurance (Industrial Injuries) Act 1946
This marked a further development in compensation for those injured at work, providing both benefits and pensions.

Many of these Acts were intended to compensate those disabled through industrial or commercial injuries. They were, however, irrelevant to the vast majority of people with disabilities, who were either elderly or unable to gain employment precisely because of their disability.

## Contemporary benefits for the disabled

### Attendance Allowance
This benefit is paid to those people who become disabled at or after the age of 65 and who can prove that they need to be looked after. It is payable at two rates. The lower rate is paid for those who need attendance during the day (or night) only, and the higher rate is paid for those who need help both day and night. You have to have needed help for at least six months to be eligible. Attendance Allowance is tax free and is paid on top of other benefits.

### Invalidity Benefit
This is tax free and consists of three components – invalidity pension, invalidity allowance and additional pension.
- **Invalidity pension** is paid if someone is incapable of work after 28 weeks, which is when sickness benefit ends.
- **Invalidity allowance** is paid on top of invalidity pension, if the disability or illness began before the age of 55 for women or 60 for men.
- **Additional pension** is an earnings-related amount starting from 1978.

You can work and earn a limited amount (£39 in 1992) and still be eligible for Invalidity Benefit.

### Severe Disablement Allowance
This is payable to people who cannot claim Invalidity Benefit because they have not paid enough National Insurance contributions. SDA is payable to those under retirement age. However, if you become disabled after your twentieth birthday, you can only get a maximum of 80 per cent of SDA.

If the person with disability is under 19 and in 'normal' education, then they may claim SDA, but not if they are in some form of special education.

### Disability Living Allowance
This is a tax-free benefit split in two parts – a care component and a mobility component.
- **Care** for people under 65 (but over 16) and needing help with personal care (such as washing, dressing or using the toilet) and/or cooking a meal.
- **Mobility** is available for people over five (and up to 65) if they have difficulty getting around.

Assessment of eligibility for this benefit, and the different payment scales (three different levels for the care component and two different levels for the mobility part), make this a very complicated system to administer.

### Disability Working Allowance

This is a tax-free but income-related benefit for people aged 16 and over who are working for a minimum of 16 hours each week, but who have some form of disability that limits their capacity to earn.

Eligibility depends on getting Disability Living Allowance or on having an invalid three-wheeler from the DSS.

Savings of £3000 and more affect the levels of payment.

*There appear to be many exclusions and regulations concerning age in the eligibility for benefit if you are disabled. Devise a simple table or chart to illustrate which age groups can obtain which benefits.*

*Why do you think the government has introduced this complex system related to age?*

### Invalid Care Allowance

This is available for carers rather than for the person with disability. If the carer spends more than 35 hours each week looking after someone who receives Attendance Allowance, then they can claim Invalid Care Allowance. The carer cannot earn more than £30 a week from other sources.

### Income Support

Income Support is the general benefit for those with incomes below set levels. It can only be claimed by those without work or those working for fewer than 16 hours per week. People of working age with disabilities are normally eligible, as they have higher unemployment rates than those without disabilities and, if employed, are likely to be in low pay employment.

### Industrial Injuries Disablement Benefit

For people ill as a result of industrial diseases known to be linked to certain kinds of employment, this benefit is paid on top of Invalidity Benefit. You need to be 14 per cent disabled to qualify. Related to this benefit are two other allowances – Constant Attendance Allowance and Exceptionally Severe Disablement Allowance.

## DISABILITY LIVING ALLOWANCE

*The extract below, from a magazine for professional social workers, explains the Disability Living Allowance. It is fairly complex. To help you make sense of it, it is worthwhile getting a Disability Living Allowance Claim Pack, available from DLA, Warbreck House, Warbreck Hill, Blackpool FY2 0YJ.*

The disability living allowance (DLA) was introduced in April 1992 to cover some of the extra costs of disability. It replaced mobility allowance and attendance allowance for people who become disabled before the age of 65, and hence includes both mobility and care components. (Attendance allowance still exists for people who make a first claim after age 65)....

There were significant numbers of people who never claimed disability benefits to which they were entitled before April, and now even more clients of social services departments will be entitled to DLA....

Not only are the rates significant in themselves, but DLA is payable on top of income support and can increase weekly income support by giving entitlement to disability premiums....

Unmitigated chaos has occurred since the Benefits Agency started accepting DLA claims in February and the House of Commons Social Security Committee has announced an inquiry into its introduction.

There have been extensive delays not only with new DLA claims, but also in the conversion of old mobility and attendance allowance awards, renewals, outstanding reviews and appeals. The chief executive of the Benefits Agency has recently announced that the aim is to be up-to-date with all new claims of DLA and attendance allowance by the end of October....

Communication between Benefits Agency sections is poor and tracking claims down is difficult. Social workers wanting a progress report on a claim can ring 0000 XXXXXX (now operating between 8 am and 5 pm).

Assessment for DLA does not require a medical examination. The move towards "self-assessment" was welcomed. However, during the first four months of the scheme, only half of the claim forms contained enough information for a decision to be made.

Despite consultation and a pilot scheme, problems have also been caused, for both claimants and advisers, by the sheer bulk of the claim pack and the length of time it takes to complete. It is difficult to know how this can be avoided but some questions could certainly be re-worded. The claim packs are currently being reviewed and, if you have any comments, do let CPAG know.

The form includes pages for two statements: one to be completed by someone who is aware of the effects of the claimant's disability and the other by a doctor or other professional who is more involved in the case. Social workers should attach as much information as they think relevant. The form is in two parts and problems have resulted when the two portions have not been sent together.

Initially there were difficulties getting hold of claim forms. This should now have eased. The Benefit Enquiry Line (BEL) – 0800 882200 – will answer general enquiries and send claim forms dated from the time of the telephone calls.

If the claimant wants help completing the form, BEL will arrange for the regional centre to telephone at a set time to go through the form. Although there are limited visiting officers, the Benefits Agency has made a commitment to visit those who request such help with DLA applications.

**Source**: E. Knights, 'Slow Claim Coming', *Social Work Today*, 20 August 1992

1 When was the Disability Living Allowance introduced?
2 What is the Disability Living Allowance?
3 What is the Benefits Agency?
4 Why has there been 'unmitigated chaos'?
5 If you were a social worker trying to find out about your clients' claims, what would you do?
6 How do you obtain claim forms if they are not available in post offices, etc.?
7 The Mobility Allowance, which was paid before DLA replaced it, required a doctor to assess mobility. Does the DLA? Is this better or worse in your opinion, and what problems have resulted?
8 Obtain a copy of the DLA claim pack. Work your way through it. Do you agree or disagree with the criticisms in the text? How could it be improved?

## Claiming benefit

During the 1980s, it was estimated that possibly a third of those eligible for Attendance Allowance were *failing to claim*; and amongst the elderly the figure was as high as 60 per cent. Failure to claim benefits is caused by:

- lack of knowledge – before individuals can claim for Attendance or Mobility allowances, they must be aware of the existence of these benefits;
- the complexity of the claim system and the rules determining who is and who is not eligible – government publications explaining the types and availability of benefits are complex, even though the writers of the publications have tried to make them as simple and as clear as possible. This is because the actual claim system and the rules governing eligibility are, in reality, very complex;
- the complexity of the forms – the complexity can confuse people and persuade them that it is not worth the effort to complete the forms;

- the stigma attached to the term 'disabled' – this is discussed later, but many people do not wish to be labelled as handicapped or unable to look after themselves;
- the strict tests of disability – the Department of Social Security apply strict tests to determine the eligibility of people to disability benefits.

*Go to your local post office and obtain a copy of the current guide to benefits for the disabled. At the time of writing (April 1992), the pamphlet was entitled 'Sick or Disabled?' and its number was FB28. Read the document.*
- *Write down any criticism you have of the pamphlet.*
- *Write down any positive points you have for the pamphlet.*
- *What improvements, if any, could you suggest?*

*Now consider the case of Mrs D, a woman aged 50 who has been in part-time employment for most of her working life, while she has brought up three children. She was diagnosed ten years ago as having multiple sclerosis, and this has only recently resulted in her losing her ability to walk. She also has some recurring, but not permanent, difficulty with her eyesight. Her three children are aged 11 to 17. She is divorced, and her ex-husband sends £100 per month for the family. She owns her own home.*
   *Mrs D wants to find out what benefits she is entitled to as a result of her disability, and to claim what she is eligible for. (Please add to or amend this general scenario in any way you want.)*
   *Start by finding out how much Income Support Mrs D is getting. Then:*
*1 Go about the process of finding out about and obtaining the correct forms.*
*2 Complete the forms.*
*3 According to the information you have been given, are you able to work out Mrs D's entitlement?*
*4 Contact the local DSS, or the local authority Welfare Rights Adviser, or your local Citizen's Advice Bureau, or any local charity which looks after the rights of the disabled (I will leave you to find out about this as part of the exercise). You should be able to arrange for one of these to come to see you and work out the benefits Mrs D is eligible for and the amount she is entitled to. Incidentally, it would probably help to persuade them if you said you would undertake some activity on behalf of, or with, people with disabilities.*

# Measuring disability

Earlier, when we looked at the figures showing the extent of disability, we noted that the numbers given were only approximate – because there is considerable argument over what we mean by 'disability'. We then looked at a variety of definitions which are used, and we saw that people with similar levels of physical problems may be able to approach and cope with these in very different ways. However, when it comes to providing financial support and social services, these academic issues do not help the professionals working with people with disabilities to make decisions about who should receive services and who should not.

   To help professionals, therefore, a number of scales have been devised which provide a guide to the extent of disability. Based on this, the professionals can allocate an appropriate level of services or, in the case of State benefits, the person can be judged 'disabled' enough to receive the benefits.

# Stigma and disability

The term 'stigma' is used when people with certain characteristics are regarded as inferior or deviant by many members of the normal society. A person with physical or mental disabilities is often not seen as a person but as a disabled person. It is often assumed that such a person does not have normal feelings, that he or she cannot or should not attempt the things that 'normal' people do. Furthermore, disabled people are often viewed with a mixture of pity and fear.

## DIFFERENT!

*The following is an extract from* My Left Foot, *an autobiography (also made into a film) of the childhood of a boy with disabilities.*

> Before I knew it my fifteenth birthday had come around. Mother managed to give a party. It was a gay turn-out and some of my old pals came along. Unknown to me my sister Mona had invited Jenny to it, and she came. But she was not the small, freckled-faced Jenny that I had known in our back-yard romance, but a lovely sweet sixteen, a smiling young girl in a grey satin frock, her nails polished and her dark hair scented. I looked at her across the table and our eyes met. But whatever little resemblance she had to the old Jenny vanished the next moment when she came over to me and took my hand without the least sign of hesitation or shyness.
>
> "How are you, Christy—well?" she asked me in a half-frolicsome, half-placating way. "Yes, yes, that's good, don't excite yourself," she said soothingly as I strove to say something. I almost hated her for that.
>
> After the little party was over and they had all gone, mother asked me if I had enjoyed it. I told her I had. It was a lie, for my head was aching painfully. But worse than the headache, worse than anything else, was the terrible heart-ache I felt as I lay down to sleep that night.
>
> I knew I was a child no longer, but neither was I 'grown-up'. I was poised between the blissful ignorance of childhood and the awakening pain and frustration of adolescence. I longed to be ignorant and happy as before. But I knew childhood had gone. I had seen the hopelessness and futility of my future that day in the back yard when a child gazed on me with a look of pity in her eyes.
>
> **Source**: Christy Brown, *My Left Foot* (Minerva)

*The concept of stigma is one which describes the situation where someone is treated differently because they are not regarded as being normal. In what way does the extract illustrate this?*

## STIGMA AND THE SOCIAL WORKER

Mr Miller, a young man with a progressive disabling disease, went to seek the advice of a social worker about his problems. In particular, he wanted a confused social security position clarified. He returned a little bewildered:

> 'I don't really know what was going on. I just wanted these forms filled in. She kept going on talking about the disease – what I felt about it – what my wife felt about it. Coming to terms with it. All I want to come to terms with is these forms!'

> **Source**: M. Oliver, *Social Work with Disabled People* (Macmillan, 1983)

*1 What view did the social worker have of Mr Miller?*
*2 In your opinion, could this be described as a form of stigma?*

**3** Do you think that this is the best way for the social worker to deal with the problems of Mr Miller?

**4** What do you think the social worker was trying to achieve?

**5** How would you have dealt with the problems raised by Mr Miller?

In a well-known study on the relationship between people with disabilities and others, F. Davis examined the way in which disabled and non-disabled people 'interacted' with each other in social situations. His principal findings were as follows.

- **Domination by disability**   The study showed, as we noted earlier, that perceptions of disabled people by the non-disabled were dominated by the disability. When the disabled individuals were interviewed, they said they were aware of the others' discomfort and 'the confused and halting speech, the fixed stare elsewhere, the artificial levity [humour]' amongst other things.

- **Stigma**   A second response was to express openly feelings and emotions that would normally be considered inappropriate in casual meetings. Those without disability would display horror, disgust, pity and fear quite readily.

- **Contradiction**   The third response by others to a disabled person who is acting normally is to point out the apparent (to them) contradiction – such as a disabled social worker actually helping others! (See also the case of Mr Miller, on page 291.)

## Stigma and the professions

When teaching a group of social workers recently, one student, who as a result of a car crash has difficulty walking, told me of a visit to a new client. He got out of his car, opened the front gate, walked with the aid of two crutches to the front door and knocked. When the potential client opened the door, the student said, 'Hello, my name is John Smith from Shire Social Services,' and showed the client his identity. With a look of absolute horror, she burst out, 'Oh, my God, I didn't think they were going to send a cripple to help me!'

**1** Explain clearly and in detail how the true story above illustrates the issue of stigma.

**2** If you were the student social worker, how would you have responded?

**3** What would have been different if the client had been the person with mobility problems? Is there an issue of stigma here?

**4** An interesting experiment is for one or more of your colleagues to pretend to have an obvious disability (blind with a stick, using a wheelchair, etc.), and then to wait in a public place, observing the responses of others. This must be done with discretion and sensitivity, however. At the end of the experiment, each person pretending to have had mobility problems or to have been visually impaired should explain their feelings.

When we did this experiment, the person in the wheelchair was a particularly attractive and vivacious student of 19. She was used to being looked at and admired, but in the wheelchair, when people made comments, it was in terms of 'What a shame – if she could walk she would be really attractive!'

## Coping with stigma

People with disabilities must learn to cope with the stigma placed upon them by others. They cannot be sure, for example, if assistance they are given is offered through courtesy or pity. If they are invited to a social occasion, are they really wanted or are they there because the host feels sorry for them? This makes people with disabilities face additional handicaps beyond those caused directly by the physical impairment itself. In face-to-face situations, Davis suggests that people with disability must 'manage' the interaction in some way as a means of trying to cope.

One way of coping is to set up situations in which everyone, both with and without disabilities, pretends that all is normal. The disability is not referred to, but there is an awareness by both parties of the disability and that mention of it is deliberately being avoided.

An approach commonly used by those with disabilities is to project a particular image of themselves which stresses how 'normal' they are and how others should respond to them. The disability itself is shrugged off.

A third stage, which usually occurs once people know each other well, but not before, is when the relationship between disabled and non-disabled comes to depend on the people as individuals. Each person responds to the other genuinely and naturally, and brings in the issue of disability only where it is relevant.

# Assignment

A widow of a successful local businessman has recently died. In her later years she suffered from quite severe disabilities, and had previously cared for her husband who had been disabled after a road accident. In her will, there is a bequest for a charity to be set up for the benefit of local people with disabilities and a sum of £0.75 million is provided. Before this can be done, the following tasks have to be carried out.

- Find the extent of disability in the area.
- Break down the total into specific groups, such as problems with mobility, visual impairment, etc.
- Interview a representative sample of people from each group, asking them what services they would most want.
- Use the money to try to provide these services.

You have been employed by the trustees to undertake the first four of these tasks, and to write a report with a series of recommendations as to how the money should best be used.

*Answer to question 1 on page 277*
He is deaf.

# CHAPTER 15

# People with Mental Illness and Learning Disability

## Introduction

In this chapter we deal with two quite distinct areas of work in the health and caring professions – mental illness and learning disabilities. They are included in the same chapter only because government policies and the development of the appropriate services have tended to link the two quite distinct groups of people. When you read this chapter, therefore, be careful in your own mind to distinguish between the two groups of people, while at the same time appreciating that the policies proposed to support the two groups often overlap.

To underline the importance of the distinction, we begin the chapter with a discussion of the meanings of mental illness and learning disabilities. This is followed by examining the causes and treatment available.

Of course, we cannot understand the treatment of the mentally ill or of those with learning disabilities until we have examined the various government Acts that have created the framework for policy. The chapter therefore turns to these next.

Traditionally, both groups have been housed in institutions isolated from the world outside, and this has had a profound effect on their lives. We look at the problems associated with institutions and at the lives of people who have lived in them. Today, the method of working with both mentally ill people and those with learning disabilities is to provide community care or small group living wherever possible. This is not examined here in detail as chapter 7, 'Community care', deals with most of the issues relating to contemporary problems.

One approach which has come to dominate the treatment of those with learning disabilities, and to some extent those with mental illness, is that of 'normalisation'. This is a process in which the client is encouraged to live as 'normal' a life as possible, and those who encounter the client with the particular learning disability are asked to treat them in a non-patronising way. We end this chapter with a review of this process.

## Mental illness (or challenging behaviour)

Mental illness is the term used to describe behaviour which is generally regarded as abnormal and inexplicable within the expected patterns of behaviour associated with particular roles in society. An exact definition is difficult to give, as what is described as 'mad' in one society, or in one period of history, or at one stage in a person's life, may be acceptable in other circumstances. This is very much more than an academic point as, in extreme cases, the result of being considered mentally ill can be that a person is placed in an institution or administered drugs against their wishes.

## Types of mental illness

Mental illnesses are generally categorised into two types, **neuroses** and **psychoses**, although a third group of less common ones are grouped under the term **behavioural disorders**.

### Neuroses

These usually involve an extreme exaggeration of relatively normal concerns. For example, one of the most common neuroses is depression. For most people, depression is a matter of a degree of sadness. Depression as a neurosis, however, actually prevents a person from undertaking any normal activity whatsoever.

Other common neuroses are:

- **phobias**, which involve great fear of a relatively normal situation, (for example, agoraphobia or fear of open spaces); and
- **obsessions**, the symbolic repetition of certain actions or speech.

### SCHIZOPHRENIA: TWO STORIES

#### A

For 10 years, Eve Thompson has struggled to find treatment for her 28-year-old schizophrenic son. Now, chair of the National Schizophrenic Fellowship (NSF), she says changes in mental health law are a red herring. What is needed is high levels of care for the mentally ill who need round-the-clock help and supervision.

After her seriously disturbed son had been diagnosed as a schizophrenic, the hospital sent him home. After a spell in a therapeutic project which led to a very bad breakdown, he was home again.

"We felt guilty but we just couldn't cope with looking after him full-time. He wasn't well enough to go into a group home or a flat. He is intelligent but his living skills are nil and he is absolutely incapable of living alone. For six years he was in hospital during the week and came home to us for the weekends," she said.

For the last year, he has been living in an eight-bed hostel run by the NSF and the local authority – one of the few in the country which offers round-the-clock care and is at last getting the care he needs.

"Because there is so little reasonable support accommodation, the buck stops with parents. Mentally ill people who are living alone get priority for daytime care and the homeless mentally ill get priority for any accommodation, so parents get stuck with their child," says Mrs Thompson.

*The National Schizophrenia Fellowship: 081 547 3937.*

*SANE-LINE helpline is open every night on 071 724 8000.*

Look at extract A.
1 what does 'therapeutic project' mean?
2 Can you find an example of one?
3 Find out the meaning of the term 'schizophrenia'.
4 In what way has it affected Mrs Thompson's son? (You will need to discuss the term 'living skills'.)
5 What criticisms does Mrs Thompson have of provision for schizophrenics?
6 According to her who suffers most?
7 What has helped her son and her most of all?

B

"My son is dirty, smelly. He looks like a dosser. People shrink from him in the street," says Elizabeth Isles, mother of a 25-year-old who has suffered from schizophrenia for five years.

After Luc Isles spent a year and a half in hospital his condition seemed to have stabilised. But the hospital refused to hold him against his will. He left and reneged on promises to take his medications. His condition deteriorated rapidly.

"We had to look after him 12 hours a day. It was like having a six foot, 12 stone baby," says Mrs Isles. He became so aggressive that she, her foster son and partner fled the family home.

Luc refuses to return to hospital. Unless he hurts himself or someone else, no magistrate will agree to have him "sectioned" – "This is not care in the community," says his mother. "This isn't freedom. You can't give schizophrenics choices about whether to be treated. There must be compulsory treatment in the community orders. Schizophrenics don't think they're ill. Luc thinks he's got the best brains in the world apart from four New Zealanders."

**Source**: The *Guardian*, 5 January 1993

Look at extract B

8  How long has Luc Isles suffered from schizophrenia? What has been the result of his condition?
9  What were the affects on Mrs Isles?
10  Explain the meaning of the term 'sectioned' (see also page 301).
11  What dangers are there in compulsory treatment?
12  In your view, should people with mental illness be forced to take medication or be treated in institutions if it is the view of the doctors – even if they are apparently no risk to others or themselves?

## Psychoses

This category of illnesses affect people in their clarity of thought, their ability to act rationally and their grasp of what most people consider to be reality. An example of schizophrenia, wherein the individual exhibits all or some of a wide variety of symptoms such as hallucinations, extreme variations in mood, and a sense of being disconnected from the world outside.

Other psychoses are:

- **manic depression**, an extreme form of depression in which violent swings of mood occur; and
- **senile dementia**, the state in which an elderly person becomes vague and confused.

## Behavioural disorders

These consist of a group of disorders which are generally characterised by a lack of interest or sense of conscience towards others. The best known and most extreme case is that of psychopaths, who are regarded as people without any interest in the effects of their actions on others.

## MENTAL ILLNESS IS COMMONPLACE

...about 250 people per 1000 of the population are likely to experience...a degree of mental disorder or symptoms of psychological distress. Of these 230 will consult their GP about their symptons,...and 140 will be diagnosed by the GP as suffering from psychiatric disorder...most will be treated by the GP him/herself. Only 17 will be referred to the specialist psychiatric services and of these only 6 will be admitted to hospital.

**Source**: R. Smith, *Mental Health: the Social Worker's Role* Bristol Papers, School of Applied Social Studies Univ. of Bristol

1 What proportion of the population will seek help from their GP for some mental or psychological disorder? Does this surprise you?

2 If you went to your GP for mental health problems, would you tell other people? Give reasons for your answer.

3 What is stigma? How does this relate to mental illness?

4 If you were an employer and you found during an interview that a person had in the past suffered from mental illness, would this affect your views on employing them?

5 You are a parent with two children aged 8 and 11. The babysitter discloses to you that she saw her GP two years ago for mental problems (unspecified). Would you still employ her?

## Causes of mental illness

The causes of mental illness are very diffuse and there is great debate regarding the real cause or causes. Explanations vary from **physiological** ones, based on physical disorders of the brain or drug imbalance, through arguments concerning **incorrect socialisation** by parents, to explanations which argue that 'mad' people respond as they do in order to cope with **extreme situations**. In a sense the latter are not mad but are simply coping with an apparently unresolvable problem.

## Treatment of mental illness

As might be expected by the great differences in explanations for the causes of mental illness, the various treatments are quite remarkably different.

- Behaviour-altering **drugs** are commonly used in physiological cases.
- A second approach, related to the socialisation model, is to engage in **therapy** in which the person labelled as mad discusses events which may have caused them to behave in the way they do.
- A third approach is to examine the social context of the individual (such as the family) and to see what particular **pressures** he/she is reacting to.

# Learning disability (or mental handicap)

Until relatively recently people with learning disabilities were often put away in long-stay hospitals, where they lived in what are now recognised as very poor conditions. Below are a few memories of the older residents of one such hospital.

Ernest recalls:

Patients had to be careful how they behaved in their work and on the villa or wherever they were 'cos there was strict staff in those days and any offence, they used to be up before one of the senior doctors. In the case of first offences, they were warned of the serious nature of the offence and what would happen if that or anything like it was repeated. Then they were placed before the doctor and they lost all their privileges for a certain length of time. As far as privileges were concerned, (they) used to be going to films and concerts and in the hospital grounds, recreation hall and money included.

Staff had their own way of dealing with minor problems. Problems such as incontinence created extra work and could lead to punishment even when a person's physical handicaps prevented them from having control of their bladder and bowels.

Margaret remembers:

If you were bursting to go somewhere and you wet yourself, you know like with me, you got punished. Say you were in a wheelchair and you couldn't talk to tell them, you still got punished – couldn't go out, couldn't see your visitors.

Shall I tell you sometime else – if you leave your food, you know what they used to do? If you didn't eat your dinner – leave it for your tea. And if you didn't eat it for your tea, you had it for your supper and if you didn't eat it for your supper you had it for your next meal. It's true!

**Source**: M. Potts, *A Fit Person to be Removed* (Northcote House Publishers, 1991)

Learning disability covers a wide range of conditions. They have in common the fact that the intellectual development of the individual does not follow a normal pace, and therefore the individual finds coping with the daily problems and issues that most people regard as simple and taken-for-granted relatively difficult. The degree of disability varies from the severe, where the person requires help in almost everything, to a situation where the person may simply be regarded as dull-witted.

An OPCS survey in 1988 concluded that there were approximately 1.4 million adults with some form of learning disability (the term the report uses is 'intellectual functioning'). In 1989, in a similar study they found 97 000 children (under 16 years of age) with learning difficulties.

## A STORY OF A FAMILY

Bob and Jane Armitage live in a small, two-bedroomed council house with their 23-year-old daughter, and a pet poodle. They have two married sons and two grandchildren, and have recently celebrated 33 years of marriage. An ordinary family – except that Jane Armitage has severe learning difficulties....

Jane and Bob Armitage's courtship met with opposition from the beginning. Jane's parents did not approve of Bob and Bob's mother offered him 'three suits a year not to get married'. After Jane discovered she was pregnant they decided the best thing they could do was to get married.

There were no congratulations when they broke their news. Three doctors called on Bob at work to try to persuade him not to go through with the marriage. They warned him that once Jane had given birth they would remove the child. Bob recalls the incident bitterly. 'I said "what are you trying to make out she is?" I said "even animals have their own young".'

As soon as their son was born Jane's parents intervened. Jane's mother collected her from the hospital without telling Bob and took both mother and baby home....

The grandparents would let neither of them have anything to do with their baby.... In a desperate bid to ease her anguish, Bob contacted Jane's social worker and asked her 'to take the child in care...'.

Bob reasoned that once the baby was in a children's home they would be able to visit 'and have the advantage of picking the child up, and letting my wife have a chance of picking the child up so she feels like a mother and I'll feel like a father'. Tony was a month old when he was taken into care.

It was seven years before they had their second child. Jane spent the greater part of this time in a psychiatric hospital where she was sent following a domestic dispute. She and Bob were having an argument one day when a friend tried to come between them. He grabbed Jane by the arm and she picked up a bicycle lamp and hit him over the head causing a gash which needed 12 stitches. It was four and a half years before she was released....

They had two children in fairly quick succession. Soon after the birth of their third child Jane was sterilised....

Two children brought new responsibilities and new pressures. Jane was frightened in case she dropped or injured the babies.

Bob gave up his job and became a full-time father....

As soon as the children were a little older, Bob took a job doing a 12-hour night shift. This allowed him to be at home when the children needed personal care....

But the physical strain of working nights and caring by day eventually took its toll on Bob's health. He began suffering recurring migraines and dizziness. Following a brain scan, a specialist told him to stop working. He now acknowledges that he could have done with 'a bit of help', but at the time 'I were too independent to ask for owt'. He felt he had something to prove to all those who had been against them marrying and having children.

### DIFFICULT YEARS

Bob and Jane saw the children through the difficult early years on their own, and take pride in the fact that they managed against all opposition. They moved house a lot in order to escape the constant harassment Jane met from local youngsters. But slowly life became easier as the children grew more able to take care of themselves, even though money was always short.

When the children were nine- and ten-years-old, the family life the Armitages had worked so hard to create was shattered. Forced to seek emergency help with a broken gas cooker from the social services, the social worker they saw asked to have a word with the children on their own. When she returned she said their son had told her that his father had been hitting him across the legs with a dog chain. They were not to take them home.

Bob and Jane were devastated. Bob admits that he used to 'tap' them on the knees with a puppy lead if they were talking when he and Jane were watching television, but still denies vigorously that he ever hit them....

PUZZLED

Their son and daughter were put into a children's home, and Jane and Bob were allowed to visit once a week....

Bob and Jane appealed against the care orders four times, but it was only after they changed their solicitor that they finally won their case for custody. Their children were 14 and 15 before they came home....

Today, their first son has two children of his own, although he is now separated from his wife....

Their second son has recently married, has a good job, his own house and is extremely attentive to his parents. Jane goes to see him and his wife every Saturday, and she will often go shopping with her daughter-in-law's mother.

Their daughter still lives at home, and has a full-time job. She does most of the shopping for the family, and all of the ironing....

Like other marriages, the Armitages' has had its ups and downs. There have been problems with the children but the children have also often brought them back together again in times of trouble. It has been a source of comfort and support during ill-health, and a bulwark against the outside world. It has lasted for 33 years.

Bob and Jane have made their marriage work where many others might have broken down under the pressure. Bob acknowledges that for the 'biggest part of my life I've had to fight for Jane, and I've also had to fight for the children. I've never had a smooth-run sort of thing'....

ORDINARY FAMILIES

First, parents with learning difficulties do not form a pathological group. Their experiences of parenthood and child-rearing show more similarities than differences with ordinary families.

Second, having learning difficulties is not a disqualification from enjoying a lasting marriage, bringing up children or leading an ordinary family life, any more than not having learning difficulties is a guarantee of success.

Third, many of the problems experienced by parents with learning difficulties derive more from poverty, poor housing, harassment, victimisation and lack of support, than from their own deficiencies in parental competence.

And last, professionals are a major cause of upset and trouble in the lives of parents with learning difficulties. When Jane says, 'They're to help you, not to shout at you', she echoes the sentiments of many other mothers in her position. For Bob and Jane Armitage the biggest battles have been against the ingrained attitudes of people who 'didn't think Jane was marriageable, that she wasn't fit to get married'.

Bob knows better. 'No one can tell me that a person like Jane isn't the marrying type. You've to live with a person before you can experience it. She's a lovable woman, she's a person you could love. Well, I have done up to 30-odd years. The point is with Jane, you've got to show her the respect.'

**Source:** *Community Care*, 23 April 1992

1 Do you have sympathy with Bob and Jane, or with the social workers and medical staff dealing with them?

2 Given the information you have, how would you have dealt with the family?

3 What does the extract tell us about the following?
- Stereotyping
- Learning disabilities
- Stigma
- The relationship between social problems and poverty
- The role of professionals

## Causes and treatment of mental handicap

The vast majority of people with learning disabilities are born with the disability or it occurs through a problem at birth. In other cases it is the result of an accident. There is no treatment, but special forms of education and training help individuals to attain a greater capacity to cope.

Several decades after eugenics sank into disrepute in the West, it has re-emerged in China with programmes to sterilise mentally retarded people who wish to marry.

Since Gansu province in north-western China adopted a eugenics law in 1988, leading to the sterilisation of more than 5,000 mentally retarded people, several other regions have adopted similar laws. The Prime Minister, Li Peng, has backed the measures and a national eugenics law is being drafted.

The measures have aroused a ripple of protest abroad, but virtually no opposition in China. "Mentally retarded people give birth to idiots," Mr Li told a committee last year. "They can't take care of themselves, they and their parents will suffer, and they'll be detrimental to our aim of raising the quality of the people."

Peasants Daily put it more concisely: "Idiots produce idiots."

Source: The *Guardian*, 17 August 1991

1 What does 'eugenics' mean? (If you do not know, look it up in a dictionary.)
2 According to the eugenics programme, what happens to people with learning disabilities?
3 What is your view?
4 What are the dangers of eugenics?

# Legislation

The ways in which mental illness and learning disability have been confused is very much reflected in the various policy options followed by governments. Below we take a brief look at the development of policies for the mentally ill and for those with learning disabilities and outline the basis of current practice.

## Mental Deficiency Act 1913

This Act was based on the belief that the mentally ill and those with learning disabilities were more or less the same group of people. They were believed to be socially and morally 'degenerate', and through their irrational and immoral behaviour they were seen as dangerous threats to society. The moral element was very important indeed, and anything that was then defined as immoral, such as becoming pregnant outside marriage, was regarded as proof of mental handicap!

## Mental Health Act 1959

In 1957, a Commission on the Law Relating to Mental Illness and Mental Handicap reported to Parliament, and this resulted in the Mental Health Act 1959. In revulsion at the way in which people had been forced to enter institutions, the Act placed fairly strong safeguards on the extent to which people could be placed in institutions against their will. Treatment was to be based on the same principles as for physical illness. Where there was compulsion, it was on the basis of a medical decision, and even then, tribunals sat to review the medical decision. The Act also advocated an expansion of community care services.

## Mental Health Act 1982 and Mental Health Act 1983

In 1982 and 1983, two more Mental Health Acts were passed. These form the basis of current practice.

### Section 1

This defines mental disorder as 'mental illness, arrested or incomplete development of mind, psychopathic disorder or disability of mind'. This clearly links learning disability and mental illness.

The (1982) Act emphasises the rights of individuals to be treated voluntarily, but says that a doctor can hold a patient for 72 hours, and a nurse for six hours, if there is no doctor available.

### Section 2

This covers compulsory admission to mental institutions of those people considered to be a danger to others or to themselves. Doctors and social work professionals have the powers under section 2 of the Act to admit people against their wishes within the following limits. A maximum of 28 days' admission can be enforced by two doctors, one of whom must hold approval from the Secretary of State for Social Services as having special expertise in the area of mental disorder, and be in possession of a form 'requesting admission' from the person's 'nearest relative' or a suitably qualified social worker. This process is known as **sectioning**.

To ensure the rights of the people labelled as mentally ill, there are Mental Health Review Tribunals, consisting of three persons (lawyer, doctor, lay person), which consider the cases of patients challenging the decisions of the medical profession.

### Section 3

This allows the compulsory treatment of a person to be extended to six months.

### Section 4

Section 4 allows 48 hours' compulsory admissions in emergency situations on the written recommendation of one doctor, and the person's social worker.

The role of the social worker in each of these situations is central, in that it is the social worker who generally initiates the process of sectioning, and who must also co-ordinate the actual admission. In addition, the social worker must be attentive to the legal and social rights of the person.

# National Health Service and Community Care Act 1990

This placed a duty on local authorities in collaboration with the health service to provide appropriate community care for those with learning disabilities.

## Discharges from mental illness and learning disability hospitals and units: stays of five or more years

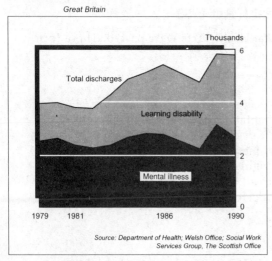

Great Britain

Source: Department of Health; Welsh Office; Social Work Services Group, The Scottish Office

**Source**: *Social Trends* (HMSO, 1993)

1 Which two groups of people are examined in the graph? What was the total number of discharges for those staying in institutions for five years or more in 1990?
2 What was the total in 1979?
3 Overall, what has happened to the number of discharges? Explain the pattern by referring to the figures given for 1979, 1981, 1986 and 1990.

## PRISONS AND THE MENTALLY ILL

Attempts to divert mentally disturbed offenders from prisons – where they constitute an estimated fifth of the population – are "un-coordinated and slow", according to a group of health care and prison reform bodies.

Stephen Shaw, director of the Prison Reform Trust, said prisons were used as a "dumping ground" for the mentally ill. "The prison service has neither the skills nor the facilities to provide proper psychiatric care. The way people with psychiatric problems are treated in prison is utterly at variance with good practice in the NHS."

Research for the Home Office by Professor John Gunn of the Institute of Psychiatry, suggests that up to one-fifth of the sentenced prison population have mental health problems and that 3 per cent of prisoners – about 1,300 – require immediate hospital treatment. The letter says there is an even higher proportion of remand prisoners with mental health problems; many of whom were in custody because of homelessness or for psychiatric assessment.

The number of mentally disordered offenders, like the homeless, is believed to have risen since the Government adopted the policy of closing down residential hospitals for the mentally ill.

Often arrested for minor offences, such as drunkenness or disorderly behaviour, they are usually remanded in custody because they have no address to which they can be bailed.

**Source**: The *Independent*, 22 July 1991

1 What proportion of people in prison are mentally disturbed, according to the extract?
2 How many need immediate hospital treatment?
3 What reasons are given for the rise in the numbers of mentally disturbed people in prison?
4 What solutions could you suggest?

# Appendix

## Voluntary organisations concerned with issues relevant to health and welfare

Please note, if you do write to any of these organisations, you should always enclose a stamped, addressed envelope.

**Age Concern England**: Astral House, 1268 London Road, London SW16 4EJ
Represents the views of elderly people.

**Alcohol Concern**: 305 Gray's Inn Road, London WC1X 8QF
Raises the level of public awareness of the risks of alcohol abuse.

**Association for Residential Care**: The Old Rectory, Old Whittlington, Chesterfield, Derbyshire S41 9QY
Concerned with residential care for people with a learning disability.

**Barnados**: Tanners Lane, Barkingside, Ilford, Essex IG6 1QG
Works with children, young people and their families who face disability or disadvantage.

**British Agencies for Adoption and Fostering**: 11 Southwark Street, London SE1 1RQ
Promotes good standards of practice in adoption and fostering.

**British Institute of Mental Handicap**: Wolverhampton Road, Kidderminster, Worcs DY10 3PP
Aims to raise standards of treatment, care and management of mentally handicapped people.

**Campaign for People with Mental Handicaps**: 12a Maddox Street, London W1R 9PL
Advocates a radical programme, including complete community care for all mentally handicapped people.

**Cancer Relief Macmillan Fund**:
Anchor House, 15–19 Britten Street, London SW3 3TZ
Provides nurses specially trained to look after cancer patients.

**Centre for Policy on Ageing**:
25–31 Ironmonger Row, London EC1V 3QP
Research on ageing policy.

**Child Poverty Action Group (CPAG)**:
4th floor, 1–5 Bath Street, London EC1V 9PY
Works for children and low income families; provides advice, publications and training.

**Disability Alliance**: Universal House, 88–94 Wentworth Street, London E1 7SA
Pressure group to improve welfare rights provision and information for disabled people.

**Disabled Living Foundation**:
380–384 Harrow Road, London W9 2HU
Identifies daily problems faced by disabled people of all ages and seeking solutions.

**Family Policies Studies Centre** (successor to the Study Commission on the Family):
231 Baker Street, London NW1 6XE
Research on the family.

**Family Service Units**: 207 Old Marylebone Road, London NW1 5QP
For disadvantaged families and communities unable to achieve their full potential.

**Family Welfare Association**:
501–505 Kingsland Road, Dalston, London E8 4AU
Offers centres for families, children and people with disabilities. It also runs community mental health projects and homes for independent living.

**Gingerbread (association for one-parent families)**: 35 Wellington Street, London WC2 7BN
Self-help association for one-parent families.

**Help the Aged**: St James's Walk, London EC1R 0BE
Campaigns to improve the quality of life for elderly people.

**Hospice Information**: St Christopher's Hospice, 51–59 Lawrie Park Road, Sydenham, London SE26 6DZ
Resource and link for members of the public and health care professionals.

**Institute of Race Relations**: 2–6 Leek Street, King's Cross Road, London WC1
Promotes the study of relations between racially defined groups; provides information on race relations.

**Mental Health Foundation**: 8 Hallam Street, London W1N 6DH
Grant-making charity; research and community care projects in the field of mental health and disorder.

**National Association of Councils for Voluntary Service**: 3rd floor, Arundel Court, 177 Arundel Street, Sheffield S1 2NU
Provides information and advice service to new and existing CVSs and other similar bodies.

**National Association for Mental Health (MIND)**: 22 Harley Street, London W1

**National Childbirth Trust**: Alexandra House, Oldham Terrace, Acton, London W3 6NH
Information and support in pregnancy, childbirth and early parenthood.

**National Children's Bureau**: 8 Wakley Street, London EC1V 7QE
Concerned with the care of children.

**National Children's Home**: 85 Highbury Park, London N5 1UD
Provides services to support family life and children.

**National Council for One-Parent Families**: 255 Kentish Town Road, London NW5 2LX
A national organisation offering support, information and advice for lone parents on issues such as welfare benefits, housing, divorce, maintenance, legal matters and bereavement.

**National Council for Voluntary Organisations (NCVO)**: Regents Wharf, 8 All Saints Street, London N1 9RL
Promotes interests of voluntary organisations.

**National Society for the Prevention of Cruelty to Children (NSPCC)**: 67 Saffron Hill, London EC1N 8RS
Protects children from abuse.

**Parents Against Injustice (PAIN)**: 11 Riverside Business Park, Stansted, Essex CM24 8PL
Offers support and advice to family members and others when a child is mistakenly thought to be at risk or to have been abused.

**Physically Handicapped and Able Bodied (PHAB)**: PHAB UK Ltd, 12/14 London Road, Croydon CR0 2TA
Furthers the integration of people with disabilities in the community.

**Pre-School Playgroups Association (PPA)**: 61/63 King's Cross Road, London WC1X 9LL
Supports and trains people for children's playgroups.

**Relate (marriage guidance)**: Herbert Gray College, Little Church Street, Rugby CV21 3AP
Counsels those with problems of personal relationships.

**Release (national drugs and legal helpline)**: 169 Commercial Street, London E1 6BW
Provides advice, counselling and referral on drugs, both illegal and prescribed.

**Richmond Fellowship for Community Mental Health**: 8 Addison Road, Kensington, London W14 8DL
Provides facilities for people who are recovering from emotional disturbance.

**Royal Association in Aid of Deaf People**:
27 Old Oak Road, Acton, London W3 7HN
Employs interpreters, community workers,
social workers and welfare rights workers
for the deaf.

**Royal National Institute for the Blind
(RNIB)**: 224 Great Portland Street,
London W1N 6AA
Provides services for the blind and visually
impaired.

**Royal National Institute for the Deaf**:
105 Gower Street, London WC1E 6AH
Represents the interests of deaf, deaf/blind
and hard of hearing people.

**Royal Society for Mentally Handicapped
Children and Adults (MENCAP)**: MENCAP
National Centre, 123 Golden Lane,
London EC1Y 0RT
Concerned with people with learning
disability and their families.

**Royal Society of Health**: RSH House,
38a St George's Drive, London SW1V 4BH
The advancement of health.

**Salvation Army**: 101 Queen Victoria Street,
London EC4P 4EP
Responsible for various homes, hostels and
centres, and other work with the homeless.

**SHAC (The London Housing Aid Centre)**:
189a Old Brompton Road, London SW5 0AR
Gives advice, information and help on
housing issues.

**Shaftesbury Society**: Shaftesbury House,
2a Amity Grove, London SW20 0LH
Cares for people who are physically or
mentally handicapped or socially deprived.

**Sickle Cell Society**: 54 Station Road,
London NW10 4UA
Gives support and welfare to sufferers and
their families.

**Simon Community**: St Joseph's House,
129 Malden Road, London NW5 4HS
Work with homeless where there is usually
no other provision.

**Spastics Society**: 12 Park Crescent,
London W1N 4EQ
Provides services for people with cerebral
palsy and their families.

**Terrence Higgins Trust**: 52–54 Gray's Inn
Road, London WC1X 8JU
Informs, advises and helps on AIDS and
AIDS-related issues.

**Women Against Rape, London**: King's Cross
Women's Centre, 71 Tonbridge Street,
London WC1H 9DZ
Provides support to women with all aspects
of rape and other violence.

**Women Against Sexual Harassment**:
242 Pentonville Road, London N1 9VN
Legal, counselling, employment and
women's rights.

**Women's Aid Federation England (WAFE)**:
PO Box 391, Bristol BS99 7WS
Contact point for Women's Aid refuges in
England.

**Women's Health**: 52 Featherstone Street,
London EC1Y 8RT
Information and resource centre for
women's health.

**Women's Royal Voluntary Service (WRVS)**:
234–244 Stockwell Road, London SW9 9SP
Variety of welfare work; trains members to
help in emergencies.

# Index

## COMMUNITY CARE

A recent report by the National Schizophrenic Fellowship has been published which records more than 100 cases of people who have died or have killed in tragic circumstances.

The report examines two initiatives which were introduced as part of the new Community Care provisions which followed the 1990 Act: the Care Programme Approach which gives a key worker and a care plan to each person discharged from mental institutions; and the Mental Illness Specific Grant, which consists of £30 million given to local authorities to spend on the mentally ill.

According to the Report, no additional funds were provided for the Care Programme Approach, instead funds were diverted from other areas of treatment of the mentally ill.

A key part of the Mental Illness Specific Grant was that local authorities had to contribute 30 per cent of the funding before they could apply for the remaining 70 per cent from central government. Yet the Report states that some local authorities could not raise their 30 per cent.

The Chief Executive of the Fellowship is reported as saying that 'there are increasing numbers of people discharged from mental hospitals who are lacking real community care, and exist in conditions of loneliness, poverty and neglect, mostly ignored by health and social services...'

During 1978 and 1990, according to the chairman, mental health beds were reduced by 33,000, yet fewer than 11,000 community places have been provided.

The Health Minister, stated in reply to the publication of the report that £155 million was being spent on mental illness between 1992 and 1995. She was quoted as saying 'Hospital beds must not be shut unless there is an alternative for that person in the community, and the mentally sick person has someone to give them support. I am with the NSF and we have helped to fund them substantially'.

1 What two initiatives were introduced in 1991 to help mentally ill people discharged from hospital?
2 Have these been effective, according to the article?
3 What financial problems were faced by local authorities? Who suffered as a result?
4 How does the report by the National Schizophrenia Fellowship describe the conditions of some of the discharged ex-mental patients?
5 How many patients were discharged between 1978 and 1990? How many have been found community care places?
6 What has happened to the rest?

# The problems of institutions

Critics of the way institutions are organised have pointed out that mental hospitals seem more concerned to deal with the perceived physical needs of the patients in so far as they do not clash with the comfort of the staff. One writer, Wolfensberger, has even gone so far as to compare the care for mental patients to the caring of animals. He suggests that institutions will have the following characteristics.

• Because behaviour is sometimes poor, the institutions are designed to be as 'abuse-resistant' as possible – the emphasis is not on the comfort of the people who live there.

• Because residents are assumed to be destructive and possibly violent to each other, the emphasis is on control and order.

• There is the assumption that the residents are incapable of choice and therefore lights, temperature gauges, etc., are kept out of their control.

- Because animals have to be 'kept', residents too have to be looked after but in a routine way that offers them no choices – so they are fed at the time the institution wants, and made to get out of bed at fixed times.

## ADMISSIONS FOR TREATMENT

**Percentage of admissions for men and women by age group for mental illness**

| | Age | | |
|---|---|---|---|
| | 55–64 | 65–74 | 75+ |
| Male | 38 | 36 | 30 |
| Female | 62 | 64 | 70 |
| | 100 | 100 | 100 |

Women = 66 per cent of dementia patients
67 per cent of depression

1 Which sex is more likely to enter a mental institution?
2 What percentage of patients aged 75+ are female? Why are there so many women patients compared to men, at this age? Can the same explanation be true for the other age groups?

## Mistreatment in institutions

Although Wolfenberger's description of the way people are treated in institutions seems extreme, there is considerable evidence to show that this has in fact been the means of treatment in the past (and possibly still in the present).

In 1967, an inquiry into the treatment of patients at Ely Hospital, Cardiff found that there was definite evidence of unduly rough treatment and of undesirably low standards of nursing care; accusations of cruelty were made.

In 1971, prison sentences were imposed on staff at Farleigh hospital.

In 1974, South Ockenden in Essex was criticised for violence and for the cruelty of its staff, and for such things as patients having to queue naked for their baths.

After an inquiry in 1978 into practices at Normandsfield Hospital, which concluded its investigation with descriptions such as 'appalling standards of hygiene' and 'degrading' forms of dress for patients, the Jay Committee was set up to review what could be done about the situation. This recommended the replacement of nursing staff with specialists holding a social work qualification, an increase in staff numbers and the replacement of hospitals by homes and hostels. Due in part to the opposition of the Royal College of Nursing, the reforms were not implemented.

Maltreatment is not a thing of the past – throughout the 1980s and early 1990s allegations were made against prison officers in a number of secure psychiatric institutions in the UK.

## Normalisation

In 1972, Wolfensberger first proposed a new philosophy of 'normalisation', which as the name implies argues that people with any form of disability should be encouraged to live as normal a life as possible. The idea of putting people away in institutions and segregating them from the wider society, for their own protection, was, Wolfensberger argued, harmful and simply led to them being stigmatised and stereotyped. Furthermore, they never had a chance to taste 'normal' life and as a consequence their behaviour became more and more institutionalised. This made them even more different from the bulk of the population.

Normalisation derives from the belief that people reject others because of their differences. Putting them in institutions and trying to 'help' them could do nothing about society's attitudes. The other underlying belief is that individuals have the right to be valued for themselves (as opposed to being valued as handicapped or disabled people) and, furthermore, have the right to participate in and experience all the normal activities which 'normal' people engage in.

The implications of this approach for all those with disabilities is enormous – as it emphasises that the role of the social services and the health services is to help people to live absolutely normal lives with the same range of choices as those without disabilities.

In later writing, Wolfensberger saw the task of normalisation (or social role valorisation, as he later called it) firstly as the creation of valued roles for people who were in some way regarded as deviant – being proud of themselves; and secondly, as helping people with disabilities to develop their own skills and capabilities to the full.

The implications of this for professionals was that they should:

- ensure that individuals with learning disabilities should be seen to be present in the community and not hidden away;
- encourage those with learning disabilities to make their own choices and to understand their situation;
- encourage and develop the competences of individuals, so they can have confidence in their ability to function in normal situations;
- enhance the respect for people with learning disabilities, so that the terms used and the status accorded them was not as second-class citizens but as valued members of society;
- ensure that individuals play a full role in society, by participating and having a wide network of relationships.

The philosophy of normalisation has been very influential in policy making since the 1970s, and in particular in the attempts to develop community services for those with learning disabilities and for those with mental illness. One can immediately see, for example, that the underlying ideas for community care spring from this philosophy.

In 1975, the White Paper, *Better Services for the Mentally Ill*, provided the policy framework for all later developments. It advocated the expansion of local authority personal social services to provide a range of support for the mentally ill – including residential, domiciliary, day care and social work support and the provision by the NHS of specialist services in the local community.

These psychiatric services are provided in district general hospitals (or Trusts), which have units for both inpatients and outpatients. There will also be clinics provided in the community. The teams of workers comprise psychiatrists, nurses, social workers, therapists and psychologists, and they are encouraged to work together in a co-ordinated way. By April 1991, each district had to have a fully organised care programme to provide co-ordinated care for people disabled by mental illness and living in the community.

The result of the build up of community care has been the rapid run-down of the long-term residential institutions. However, critics have pointed out that large numbers of those being sent out from residential institutions do not appear to be receiving help from community teams.

1 In what way does normalisation differ from the traditional methods of looking after those with learning disabilities?
2 Why, according to this approach, does putting people in institutions actually make the problems faced by those with learning disabilities worse?
3 Explain the two main tasks of normalisation according to Wolfensberger.
4 There are five objectives which professionals should attempt to achieve with their clients or 'service users'. Explain, in your own words, what these are.
5 Earier, we saw that the idea of normalisation underlay community care. In what ways can this be true?

# Assignment

You are working for a charitable organisation which wishes to set up a drop-in centre to provide for the non-medical needs of the mentally ill. The local authority and the NHS Trust have suggested that they would consider providing some funding for this. The charity wants you to write a report on the need for and use of such a centre in an inner city area.

You need to provide the background information on the extent of mental illness and the most common kinds of illness. You also need to find out just what the main needs of the bulk of the mentally ill are.

● Where should the centre be sited?
● What activities should be undertaken?
● What groups should be encouraged to use the centre – including families and carers?

A useful starting point would be to contact your local NHS Mental Health Community Services and arrange an interview with a manager or a mental health community nurse.

# Index

**Royal Association in Aid of Deaf People**:
27 Old Oak Road, Acton, London W3 7HN
Employs interpreters, community workers,
social workers and welfare rights workers
for the deaf.

**Royal National Institute for the Blind
(RNIB)**: 224 Great Portland Street,
London W1N 6AA
Provides services for the blind and visually
impaired.

**Royal National Institute for the Deaf**:
105 Gower Street, London WC1E 6AH
Represents the interests of deaf, deaf/blind
and hard of hearing people.

**Royal Society for Mentally Handicapped
Children and Adults (MENCAP)**: MENCAP
National Centre, 123 Golden Lane,
London EC1Y 0RT
Concerned with people with learning
disability and their families.

**Royal Society of Health**: RSH House,
38a St George's Drive, London SW1V 4BH
The advancement of health.

**Salvation Army**: 101 Queen Victoria Street,
London EC4P 4EP
Responsible for various homes, hostels and
centres, and other work with the homeless.

**SHAC (The London Housing Aid Centre)**:
189a Old Brompton Road, London SW5 0AR
Gives advice, information and help on
housing issues.

**Shaftesbury Society**: Shaftesbury House,
2a Amity Grove, London SW20 0LH
Cares for people who are physically or
mentally handicapped or socially deprived.

**Sickle Cell Society**: 54 Station Road,
London NW10 4UA
Gives support and welfare to sufferers and
their families.

**Simon Community**: St Joseph's House,
129 Malden Road, London NW5 4HS
Work with homeless where there is usually
no other provision.

**Spastics Society**: 12 Park Crescent,
London W1N 4EQ
Provides services for people with cerebral
palsy and their families.

**Terrence Higgins Trust**: 52–54 Gray's Inn
Road, London WC1X 8JU
Informs, advises and helps on AIDS and
AIDS-related issues.

**Women Against Rape, London**: King's Cross
Women's Centre, 71 Tonbridge Street,
London WC1H 9DZ
Provides support to women with all aspects
of rape and other violence.

**Women Against Sexual Harassment**:
242 Pentonville Road, London N1 9VN
Legal, counselling, employment and
women's rights.

**Women's Aid Federation England (WAFE)**:
PO Box 391, Bristol BS99 7WS
Contact point for Women's Aid refuges in
England.

**Women's Health**: 52 Featherstone Street,
London EC1Y 8RT
Information and resource centre for
women's health.

**Women's Royal Voluntary Service (WRVS)**:
234–244 Stockwell Road, London SW9 9SP
Variety of welfare work; trains members to
help in emergencies.